Inheritance Tax Planning Handbook

Other titles available from Law Society Publishing:

Contentious Trusts Handbook
Carl Islam

Varying the Disposition of an Estate after Death
Lesley King

Lasting Powers of Attorney, 4th edition
Craig Ward

Elderly Client Handbook, 6th edition
General Editor: Caroline Bielanska

Will Draftsman's Handbook, 10th edition
Julie Bell

Inheritance Act Claims, 2nd edition
Miranda Allardice, Tracey Angus, Paul Hewitt and Penelope Reed

Titles from Law Society Publishing can be ordered from all good bookshops or direct (telephone 0370 850 1422, or visit our online shop at **www.lawsociety.org.uk/bookshop**).

INHERITANCE TAX PLANNING HANDBOOK

General Editors: John Bunker and Anthony Nixon

IM irwinmitchell

The Law Society

ISBN-13: 978-1-78446-147-8

Published in 2021 by the Law Society
113 Chancery Lane, London WC2A 1PL

Reprinted in 2022

Typeset by Columns Design XML Ltd, Reading
Printed by Hobbs the Printers Ltd, Totton, Hants

The paper used for the text pages of this book is FSC® certified. FSC (the Forest Stewardship Council®) is an international network to promote responsible management of the world's forests.

FSC
www.fsc.org
MIX
Paper from responsible sources
FSC® C020438

Contents

PART III ESTATE PLANNING, WILLS AND VARIATIONS

Preface

Inheritance tax (IHT) is often described as the most hated tax, but it is also true that it combines Benjamin Franklin's two certainties: death and taxes. To help clients mitigate IHT, there are no easy answers but we hope to show you a range of ideas that we believe are workable in practice. This is a working handbook, which we hope practitioners will find a valuable resource to dip into for guidance when advising clients on new issues, or old ones that need some new ideas, to help you to come up with good solutions for your clients. If you happen to be reading this in a personal capacity, please excuse the references to clients as it is primarily for solicitors and other professionals to use, but we hope it will prove useful.

While it is not meant to be a textbook, we start in **Part I** with some of the basics, to put IHT planning into the context of the main rules for estates and trusts. This includes some key elements of the taxation of trusts which are such a vital element of IHT planning. We hope that, if some of the main planning chapters in **Part III** raise questions on the basics you can find some help back in **Part I**, or **Part II** on practical probate and trusts. **Part IV** then addresses some more specialist areas that may arise less often.

As well as addressing specific needs for planning advice, one aim of the book (as in **Chapter 9** and then throughout **Part III**) is to encourage thinking about ways to proactively offer clients opportunities to mitigate tax in the course of e.g. writing a will or administering an estate. This is particularly relevant to the residence nil rate band (RNRB) where the law is very complex and still quite new, and a really good example of where clients don't know what they don't know! The comments in **17.2** on RNRB planning practice are perhaps of wider relevance and worth reading for all practitioners approaching this subject.

In **Chapter 4** we describe the main anti-avoidance measures, through which any planning needs to navigate. The context for these measures and the Professional Conduct in Relation to Taxation (PCRT) rules to which we refer, see **4.2**, is a growing pressure from HMRC to limit the scope of 'tax planning' and to seek to outlaw increasing amounts of planning as morally reprehensible 'tax avoidance'.

Care must be taken with the PCRT rules, as to breach them could be disastrous for professional reputations, and of course it is necessary to help clients avoid ever engaging in 'tax evasion', which is illegal. However, it is important to uphold genuine tax planning, which we try to outline in this handbook, and enable our clients to plan appropriately. The PCRT rules say that practitioners covered:

> must not create, encourage or promote tax planning arrangements or structures that i) set out to achieve results that are contrary to the clear intention of Parliament in enacting relevant legislation and/or ii) are highly artificial or highly contrived and seek to exploit shortcomings within the relevant legislation.

Our clear aim, and our considered view, is that nothing in this book is 'highly artificial or highly contrived'. We aim to help you make the most of the legitimate planning opportunities that IHT legislation and practice allow, without straying into dangerous territory which might be considered tax avoidance.

The law is stated as at October 2020.

John D. Bunker and Anthony A. Nixon
October 2020

Acknowledgements

When I was invited by the Law Society to edit this new book, I put together a team of colleagues with the right expertise to share in the writing, starting with my co-editor Anthony Nixon who is a true inheritance tax (IHT) 'guru' and expert in the taxation of trusts, which are such an important part of IHT planning and this book. Anthony has played a major part particularly in the text of the first 10 chapters.

I have learned a great deal about editing over the last 18 months, and have developed great respect for the whole role of editors, way beyond any understanding from my work on articles and publications for my firm, and writing training notes. In the course of this process, I have been enormously grateful to a number of colleagues who have helped in ways beyond the writing of the chapters.

I am indebted to my colleagues Gillian Coverley, Kelly Greig and Vicky Day who helped with editing, especially on my personal chapters. Vicky especially also helped in various ways, over many months, both a great sub-editor and a really good encourager! I also wish to thank my colleague Joanne Wade who has been a wonderful help to me throughout the project with the 'form' editing, to go with my attention to 'substance', for which I am eternally grateful.

Finally, I thank my wife, Elspeth, who has lived with this book (as well as me) for a long time now, and I deeply appreciate her forbearance and encouragement. I hope you, as a reader, feel our efforts were worthwhile.

John D. Bunker
October 2020

Notes on contributors

GENERAL EDITORS

John Bunker LLB CTA TEP is a Solicitor, Chartered Tax Adviser and freelance lecturer on inheritance tax, wills, trusts and estate planning. He supports technical and training work in Irwin Mitchell's Tax, Trusts and Estates (TTE) practice, a role he started in 2012 after 23 years as a partner with Thomas Eggar. Chair of the Chartered Institute of Taxation's Private Client (UK) Tax Committee, he has over 30 years' experience as a solicitor specialising in this field and serves on HMRC's Capital Taxes Liaison Group, the HMCTS Probate Advisory Group (representing STEP) and TACT's Private Trusts Committee. He seeks to illuminate technical details with practical insight, in his writing and training for MBL, CLT, Professional Conferences, individual firms, the Law Society, local law societies and branches of STEP, SFE and CIOT.

Anthony Nixon MA CTA ATT (Fellow) TEP is a Solicitor and Chartered Tax Adviser, partner in Irwin Mitchell PLC, member of STEP Council and regular lecturer on IHT and trusts to other professionals. Anthony advises on all aspects of succession and property law and the associated taxes. He advised the taxpayers, pro bono, on their successful tribunal appeal (obtaining IHT business relief) in *Personal Representatives of Graham (deceased)* v. *Revenue and Customs Commissioners* [2018] UKFTT 306 (TC) and led the team advising the executors in their successful Supreme Court appeal (obtaining IHT charity relief) in *Routier and another* v. *Revenue and Customs Commissioners* [2019] UKSC 43. He is a regular contributor to *Taxation Practitioner* and other journals.

CONTRIBUTORS

Liz Beadsley CTA is the Chartered Tax Adviser, tax manager and Partner of Irwin Mitchell who runs the Chichester Tax Compliance team.

Eleanor Black CTA is a Solicitor and Chartered Tax Adviser, Practice Development Lawyer in Irwin Mitchell's national TTE team.

Sarah Cardew is a Solicitor and Partner in Irwin Mitchell, who heads the corporate and property tax team in Irwin Mitchell's Business Legal Services, based in the London office, working closely with the firm's TTE team.

Helen Clarke TEP is a Solicitor, Partner of Irwin Mitchell's London office specialising in estate planning for high net worth clients, especially with business assets and the structuring of businesses. Helen has the STEP Advanced Certificate in Family Business Advising.

Vicky Day TEP is a Solicitor, Senior Associate and head of the Estate Planning and Administration team at Irwin Mitchell's Chichester office.

David Gooding FPFS is a Chartered Financial Planner and Senior Wealth Manager for Irwin Mitchell Wealth Management.

Kelly Greig TEP is the Solicitor and Partner of Irwin Mitchell who heads the firm's Later Life sector.

Ashley Hill CTA is the Chartered Tax Adviser and Partner in the Irwin Mitchell London TTE International team.

Hollie Marcham TEP is the Solicitor Associate in the Irwin Mitchell Leeds TTE team.

Emma McCann TEP is a Solicitor and Partner at Irwin Mitchell, head of the Estate Planning team at the Sheffield office and secretary on the STEP Yorkshire committee.

Alex Ruffel is a Solicitor and Partner in the Irwin Mitchell London office specialising in tax planning, cross-border personal tax and international wealth structuring.

Tanya Wadeson ATT AAT TEP is a Senior Associate, Trust Manager responsible for trust tax and accounting at Irwin Mitchell, and Member of ATT National Council.

Kirstie Williamson MA ATT (Fellow) TEP is an Associate and head of the Tax & Trust compliance team at Irwin Mitchell's Sheffield office.

Table of cases

Table of statutes

Table of statutory instruments

Table of EU and international legislation

Abbreviations

5MLD	Fifth Money Laundering Directive
A&M	accumulation and maintenance
AHA 1986	Agricultural Holdings Act 1986
AIM	Alternative Investment Market
APPG	All Party Parliamentary Group
APR	agricultural property relief
APS	additional permitted subscription
ATT	Association of Taxation Technicians
BADR	business asset disposal relief
BD	business development
BMT	bereaved minor's trust
BPR	business property relief
CGT	capital gains tax
CIOT	Chartered Institute of Taxation
CLT	chargeable lifetime transfer
COP	Court of Protection
CTA	chartered tax adviser
CTA 2009	Corporation Tax Act 2009
CTA 2010	Corporation Tax Act 2010
CTLG	Capital Taxes Liaison Group
D/T	discretionary trust
DEFRA	Department for Environment, Food and Rural Affairs
DFM	discretionary fund manager
DIM	discretionary investment manager
DOTAS	disclosure of tax avoidance schemes
DOV	deed of variation
DPT	disabled person's trust
EEA	European Economic Area
EMI	Enterprise Management Initiative
EOT	employee ownership trust
ER	entrepreneurs' relief
EU	European Union
FA	Finance Act
FAD	flexi-access drawdown

FBT	farm business tenancy
FDR	formerly domiciled resident
FIC	family investment company
FLP	family limited partnership
FP	financial planner
FTBR	first time buyers' relief
GAAR	general anti-abuse rule
GROB	gift with reservation of benefit
HMCTS	Her Majesty's Courts and Tribunals Service
HMRC	Her Majesty's Revenue and Customs
HMT	Her Majesty's Treasury
HRAD	higher rate for additional dwellings
IFA	independent financial adviser
IHT	inheritance tax
IHTA 1984	Inheritance Tax Act 1984
IHTM	Inheritance Tax Manual
IIP	interest in possession
IPDI	immediate post-death interest
IR	investors' relief
ISA	individual savings account
ITA 2007	Income Tax Act 2007
ITTOIA 2005	Income Tax (Trading and Other Income) Act 2005
L/T	life tenant
LBTT	land and buildings transaction tax
LOW	letter of wishes
LPA	lasting power of attorney
LTR	long-term resident
LTT	land transaction tax
MCA 2005	Mental Capacity Act 2005
NICs	national insurance contributions
NRB	nil rate band
OECD	Organisation for Economic Co-operation and Development
OEIC	open-ended investment company
OMB	owner managed business
OPG	Office of the Public Guardian
OTS	Office of Tax Simplification
PAYE	pay as you earn
PCRT	Professional Conduct in Relation to Taxation
PET	potentially exempt transfer
POAT	pre-owned assets tax
PPR	principal private residence
QIIP	qualifying interest in possession
QRI	qualifying residential interest
QSR	quick succession relief

RDR	Retail Distribution Review
RNRB	residence nil rate band
RPI	retail price index
RPT	relevant property trust
SDAs	same day additions
SDLT	stamp duty land tax
SDRT	stamp duty reserve tax
SRA	Solicitors Regulation Authority
STEP	Society of Trusts and Estates Practitioners
TAAR	targeted anti-avoidance rule
TCGA 1992	Taxation of Chargeable Gains Act 1992
TEP	trusts and estates practitioner
TNRB	transferable nil rate band
TRNRB	transferable residence nil rate band
TRS	Trust Registration Service
TSEM	Trusts, Settlements and Estates Manual
TSI	transitional serial interest
TYA	10-year anniversary
UKRPI	UK residential property interest
USP	unique selling point
UTR	unique taxpayer reference
WIQS	Wills and Inheritance Quality Scheme

PART I

Estate and trust essentials

CHAPTER 1

Inheritance tax principles

Vicky Day

1.1 KEY POINTS

This chapter sets out some of the basic principles of and terminology used when describing inheritance tax (IHT):

- What is IHT and when is it payable?
- The key concepts of 'transfers of value', 'chargeable transfers' and 'potentially exempt transfers' (PETs).
- The meaning of 'estate' and the relevance of domicile and worldwide assets.
- The differences between lifetime charges to IHT and charges on death.
- Rates of tax; the key concept of 'open market value' for valuation; and liabilities.

1.2 WHAT IS INHERITANCE TAX AND WHEN IS IT PAYABLE?

IHT is primarily a tax on the value of a person's estate on their death. It replaced the old capital transfer tax, which was designed as a tax on lifetime gifts as well as on death. Only a few lifetime gifts now attract inheritance tax. IHT is also charged on the value of assets in some types of trust. With judicious planning, a taxpayer may arrange their affairs to take advantage of the generous reliefs and exemptions from IHT to reduce their tax liability.

Inheritance tax was introduced by changes to what was originally the Capital Transfer Tax Act 1984. The renamed Inheritance Tax Act (IHTA) 1984 came into effect in 1986.

Although the wording of the legislation is complex, its principles are simple:

- When someone dies, the value of their estate is taxed so that part of inherited wealth is redistributed.
- There are generous tax reliefs for some assets like businesses, farms and those held in the national interest, for the greater good of the economy and the nation.

- There are tax exemptions for gifts to some beneficiaries like married couples and civil partners (generally together referred to as 'spouses' in this book), charities and political parties to aid social cohesion and encourage philanthropy.
- There are generous reliefs and exemptions on lifetime gifts to encourage redistribution of wealth by individuals.
- There are limits on the value that can be given tax-free into long-term trusts in lifetime.
- Where assets have been given into trust, so do not form part of anybody's estate, a separate IHT regime applies to ensure that some part of that wealth is redistributed.

1.3 TRANSFERS OF VALUE, CHARGEABLE TRANSFERS AND POTENTIALLY EXEMPT TRANSFERS

IHT is a tax on a 'chargeable transfer'. A chargeable transfer is a 'transfer of value' that is not exempt.

Transfers of value are dispositions by which the value of the transferor's total assets (the transferor's estate) is reduced, so this covers most lifetime gifts. In addition:

- **Death** – There is a transfer of value on death, when the deceased is deemed to have given away all their assets.
- **Trust-related** – As well as on lifetime gifts to most trusts, there are also deemed transfers of value on every 10th anniversary of trusts, on the value of assets distributed out of trusts and on the value of trusts on their termination. (See **Chapters 5** and **7**.)

A gift is only liable to IHT if it is a chargeable transfer or becomes a chargeable transfer. The IHT is levied not on the value of what is given, but on the value by which the transferor's estate is reduced (the loss to the donor). The amount of the reduction is the amount of the 'transfer of value'.

Example 1.1

John owns a pair of boxing gloves signed by the champion who wore them in his winning fight. Each glove individually is worth £10,000 but the pair of gloves is worth £25,000. If John gives one of the gloves away, his remaining glove is worth only £10,000 so the 'transfer of value' he has made is £15,000.

A gift by an individual to another individual is a 'potentially exempt transfer' (PET). There is no IHT payable at the point the gift is made. If the transferor dies within seven years of the date of the gift, the value of the gift is brought back into account when calculating the IHT payable on their death.

1.4 MEANING OF ESTATE (IHTA 1984, S.5)

For IHT purposes, a person's 'estate' includes:

1. The value of assets in the person's outright ownership.
2. The value of the person's half share of any assets jointly owned as joint tenants.
3. The value of the person's percentage share of any assets jointly owned as tenants in common.
4. The capital value of any trust in which that person has a qualifying interest in possession (QIIP) – see **5.5**.
5. The value of any assets given away in the person's lifetime which are still subject to a gift with reservation of benefit – see **4.5**.
6. The value of assets given away in the seven years preceding death; while not part of the deceased's estate, this is brought into account in calculating IHT on death.

1.5 WORLDWIDE ASSETS

A person who is domiciled or deemed domiciled in the UK is liable to IHT on their worldwide estate.

A person who is not domiciled in the UK is liable to IHT on only their UK assets.

'Domicile' is a UK principle under general law and is not directly related to residence or nationality. Broadly speaking, a person's domicile is either a domicile of origin or a domicile of choice. (Minors have a domicile of dependence.) A domicile of origin is established on birth. A person will inherit the domicile of their father, if their parents were married, but otherwise of their mother. For example, a person born in England to an English father who has always lived in England, and whose parents have always lived in England, will have a UK domicile. A domicile of choice is established by moving to another country/jurisdiction and choosing to make a permanent home there. A domicile of origin is always only suspended and will be resumed if a person leaves the country/jurisdiction of choice. In some circumstances, IHT will be payable by a person with deemed domicile in the UK.

Domicile is a complex subject and is set out in more detail in **Chapter 27**.

1.6 LIFETIME CHARGES

Lifetime gifts are subject to IHT unless they fall within one of the exemptions or reliefs (see **Chapter 2**). IHT on any lifetime gift is charged at half the rate chargeable on death.

1.6.1 Gifts to individuals

An outright gift from one individual to another is a PET. At the point the gift is made, there is no IHT payable, whatever the value of the gift. If the donor survives seven years, the gift becomes a fully exempt transfer and no IHT is payable. If the donor does not survive the seven years, then the gift becomes a chargeable transfer and its value is aggregated with the value of the donor's estate on death for the purposes of calculating IHT.

1.6.2 Gifts into trust – bare trust

A gift into a bare trust is also a PET. This is because it is equivalent to an outright gift to an individual. The beneficiary of a bare trust is treated for all tax purposes as the beneficial owner of the trust assets. Care is needed to ensure it is genuinely a bare trust with no contingencies, i.e. that the only reason the beneficiary cannot call for the assets is because they are a minor or lack mental capacity.

1.6.3 Gifts into trust – qualifying interest in possession trusts

A lifetime gift into a QIIP trust is also a PET. Since 22 March 2006, the only QIIP that can be created in lifetime is a disabled person's trust (DPT) (see **Chapter 5**). Any other lifetime trust created is a relevant property trust (RPT) (see **Chapter 5**).

1.6.4 Gifts into trust – relevant property trust

A gift into a discretionary trust or a life interest trust (which is not a disabled person's interest) is a gift into an RPT. Such gifts are 'chargeable lifetime transfers' and liable to IHT. To the extent that the gift is covered by the donor's available nil rate band (NRB) (see **1.6.5**), IHT is charged at 0 per cent. To the extent that the value exceeds the available NRB, IHT is 20 per cent of the loss to the donor.

1.6.5 Available nil rate band/seven-year cumulation

The value on which a taxpayer pays IHT at 0 per cent is set out in IHTA 1984, Sched.1. This is currently £325,000. This is known as the NRB. When a taxpayer makes a chargeable gift, to assess the IHT payable, they must look to see how much of their NRB is available. If they have made no chargeable gifts in the preceding seven years, their whole NRB is available. If they have made chargeable transfers, then that part of the current gift that falls within their available NRB is tax-free (charged at 0 per cent) but any part that exceeds the NRB is charged to tax.

Example 1.2

Joan created a trust for her grandchildren in 2007 (when the NRB was £300,000). She gave £100,000 to the trust. She had not made any gifts into trust in the previous seven years. The gift was within her NRB and no IHT was payable. Joan made a further gift of £200,000 into the trust in 2015 (when the NRB was £325,000). More than seven years had elapsed since the previous gift, and the new gift of £200,000 was within her new NRB of £325,000, so no IHT was payable. Joan made a further gift of £250,000 into a new trust for her nieces and nephews in 2018 (when the NRB was still £325,000).

Because less than seven years had passed since her previous gift into trust, the gift she made in 2015 was aggregated with the gift she made in 2018, i.e. £200,000 + £250,000 = £450,000. Only £325,000 was taxable at 0% so the balance of £125,000 was taxable at 20% resulting in a tax liability of £25,000 on the 2018 gift.

1.7 CHARGES ON DEATH

1.7.1 IHT is charged on the value of an estate on death

This includes the assets held in the deceased's name, their share of jointly held assets, any gifts subject to a reservation (see **Chapter 4**) and the value of any gifts made within the preceding seven years.

1.7.2 Reliefs and exemptions

The value of that part of the estate passing to exempt beneficiaries and/or the value of certain assets which attract relief (see **Chapter 2**) is not included in the valuation of the taxable estate.

1.7.3 Rates

The rest of the estate is charged to IHT at two rates (see **1.8**).

1.7.4 Lifetime transfers which become chargeable on death

Where a PET or a lifetime chargeable transfer was made within the seven years preceding the death, their values are brought back into account and added to the value of the estate for the purposes of calculating IHT.

1.7.5 Lifetime transfers do not exceed the nil rate band

There is no additional tax payable on the transfer, but the tax in the estate will increase.

Example 1.3

Tricia gives £200,000 into a discretionary trust in 2015 and dies in 2017 with an estate comprising investments of £800,000. The total gifts within the preceding seven years do not exceed Tricia's available NRB so there is no further tax payable on the 2015 gift. However, only the balance of the NRB, i.e. £125,000 is available to the executors, making a taxable estate of £675,000.

1.7.6 Where potentially exempt transfers exceed the nil rate band

Where PETs exceed the NRB, they will become chargeable and liable to IHT.

Example 1.4

Tania gives £500,000 cash to her daughter in 2016 and dies in 2018 with an estate comprising investments of £700,000. The 2016 gift will use up the NRB of £325,000, and so £175,000 of the gift will become taxable at 40%. The entire estate of £700,000 will be taxable at 40% because there will be no NRB to allocate to it.

1.7.7 Taper relief

Where PETs become chargeable on death, the tax is tapered depending on how much time has elapsed since the date of the gift. There is no relief for gifts made up to three years before death. This relief is much misunderstood, as it does not reduce the taxable amount of the gift. If the gift is within the NRB, there is no tax to reduce and thus no taper.

The following table shows how the relief is applied:

Years before death	Tax payable
0–3	100%
3–4	80%
4–5	60%
5–6	40%
6–7	20%
7 +	0%

Example 1.5

Tina gives £500,000 cash to her daughter on 1 October 2010 and dies on 11 November 2015. The gift uses the whole of the NRB of £325,000, so £175,000 of the gift becomes taxable. Because more than five years have elapsed, 40% of the 40% IHT is payable, or £28,000.

Compare this with **1.7.5** where there is no taper relief because the lifetime gift does not exceed the NRB.

1.7.8 14-year trap

In some circumstances, gifts made more than seven years ago (up to 14 years before the date of death) affect IHT on death. This occurs where a chargeable lifetime transfer (CLT) has been made more than seven years before the death but a PET has been made within the seven-year period before death. On first glance, it would appear that the CLT can be ignored. However, the effect of death within seven years is to make the PET a CLT. When calculating the tax payable on the newly converted CLT, the executor must look back seven years from the date of the gift and bring the value of previous CLTs into account.

Example 1.6

Thelma gives £200,000 to a discretionary trust in 2010. This is a CLT but Thelma has the whole of her NRB available so the tax is payable at 0%. Thelma gives £300,000 to her daughter in 2016. This is a PET so no IHT is payable. Thelma dies in 2018. The 2016 PET becomes chargeable. The executor must look back to the seven years preceding 2016 and take into account any previous CLTs. The 2010 CLT therefore uses up £200,000 of the NRB and the 2016 gift becomes taxable, i.e. only £125,000 of the NRB is available for the 2016 gift, and so £175,000 is taxable on death.

1.8 RATES OF TAX

1.8.1 On death

The rates of IHT on death are set out in IHTA 1984, Sched.1:

- The value within the NRB (currently, in 2020/21, £325,000) is charged at 0 per cent.
- The value in excess of the NRB is charged at 40 per cent. In theory, the NRB increases in line with inflation each year but it has been frozen at the current value since 2009, by successive governments.

1.8.2 During lifetime

The rates of IHT payable on CLTs are half of the death rates. Any value transferred falling within the NRB is charged at 0 per cent. Any value in excess is charged at 20 per cent.

1.8.3 CLTs within seven years of death

Any tax chargeable is payable at the death rate of 40 per cent, subject to tapering after three years as outlined at **1.7.7**. Credit is given for the 20 per cent lifetime tax already paid.

1.9 VALUATION

The basic principle when valuing assets for IHT is that the value is the open market value – i.e. 'the price which the property might reasonably be expected to fetch if sold in the open market at that time' (IHTA 1984, s.160).

Property held in T's estate is 'related property' (s.161) to any property held in the estate of T's spouse or civil partner. Where the value of T's property would be less than the proportion it bears to any related property, it is nevertheless valued at that proportion.

Example 1.7

Tania and Tania's civil partner each own half a set of 19th-century Jane Austen books. The whole set of six books is valued at £13,000. Three books together are valued at £4,500. Because Tania's three books and her partner's three books are related property, each of their half sets is valued at half of the value of the whole, i.e. £6,500.

The related property rule applies to a valuation on death, but not after one spouse has died. This will be seen later in planning around the NRB discretionary trust – see **Chapters 13** and **14**.

Where land or buildings are owned jointly, and are not related property, it is usual to discount the value of each proportion by 15 per cent where another joint owner is in occupation (see *Wight* v. *Commissioners of Inland Revenue* [1982] 2 EGLR 236) and 10 per cent where no owner is in occupation (see *Palliser* v. *Revenue and Customs Commissioners* [2018] UKUT 0071 (LC) at para.48, which records that there was no dispute that a 10 per cent discount should be applied to an 88.4 per cent share).

1.10 LIABILITIES

The value of an estate is reduced by the value of any liabilities payable from the estate. Where the liability is not to be paid at the date it is taken into account, it is still valued at the date it is taken into account.

A liability that is an encumbrance on a particular asset, such as a mortgage loan charged on a property, is taken to reduce the value of that particular asset (IHTA 1984, s.162(4)).

A non-UK liability to a person resident outside the UK reduces the value of non-UK property first (s.162(5)).

Any liability which is a result of borrowing against excluded property (see **Chapter 28**) or against an asset which attracts an IHT relief is not deductible from the value of the estate for the purposes of calculating IHT.

For the liability to be deducted from the value of the deceased's estate on death when calculating IHT, the liability must be discharged or repaid either from the deceased's estate or from the deceased's assets which are excluded property (s.175A).

CHAPTER 2

Exemptions, reliefs and allowances

Vicky Day

There are a number of occasions when property is transferred and no inheritance tax (IHT) is payable. This may be because the transfer of value is exempt, because there is a relief according to the type of property being transferred or because of an allowance.

2.1 KEY POINTS

This chapter will cover:

- the main exemptions and gifts between spouses and civil partners (Inheritance Tax Act (IHTA) 1984, s.18);
- annual exemption (s.19) and other exemptions; and
- allowances; reliefs; and events that are not transfers of value.

2.2 EXEMPTIONS

Some transfers of value are exempt from inheritance tax (IHTA1984, ss.18–28).

The most commonly used exemptions are:

- transfers between spouses or civil partners;
- transfers within the annual exemption;
- small gifts;
- regular gifts out of excess income which are part of the taxpayer's normal expenditure;
- gifts on marriage/civil partnership;
- gifts to charities.

Other less common exempt transfers are:

- gifts to housing associations;
- gifts for national purposes;
- gifts for public benefit;
- maintenance funds;
- employee benefit;

- employee ownership trusts;
- loans;
- abatement.

2.3 GIFTS BETWEEN SPOUSES AND CIVIL PARTNERS (IHTA 1984, S.18)

A gift from the taxpayer to their spouse is exempt. So both on lifetime gifts and on death, there is no IHT payable (but see below). As in other legislation, the relief is specifically extended to civil partners and all that is said in this section with reference to 'spouses' applies to married couples and civil partners in the same way.

Where the taxpayer is UK domiciled but their spouse is non-UK domiciled, there is a cap on the value that is exempt, currently (2020/21) £325,000. Any gift in excess of the cap is charged at the usual rates of IHT. If there is an unused nil rate band (NRB), then in practice a total of £650,000 can normally be gifted, using the combination of the limited spouse exemption and the NRB. If the NRB is used in part, then the balance would be usable in this way. See **27.4** on the ways in which non-UK domiciled spouses can elect into UK domicile either while both spouses are still alive or within the two years after the UK domiciled spouse's death.

Where both the taxpayer and the spouse are non-UK domiciled, there is no limit on the spouse exemption on property in the UK passing between them.

Where the gift is into a qualifying interest in possession (QIIP) trust for the spouse, the spouse exemption also applies. However, the only two occasions where this can now happen are on a lifetime gift into trust for a disabled spouse which qualifies under IHTA 1984, s.89 or a gift into an immediate post-death interest (IPDI) trust or disabled person's trust (DPT) on death. Any lifetime trust with a life interest for a spouse would now normally be a relevant property trust (RPT).

2.4 ANNUAL EXEMPTION (IHTA 1984, S.19)

A taxpayer has an annual exemption of £3,000 in each tax year (6 April to 5 April the following year). They may give one person £3,000 or a number of people smaller sums which add up to £3,000 (but see **Example 2.2**).

To the extent that the taxpayer does not use the exemption in a tax year, it can be carried forward one year only. Any gift made will use up the exemption of the current year before using up the brought-forward exemption.

Example 2.1

A taxpayer gives £1,500 in 2017/18 and gives £2,000 in 2018/19. Both gifts are within the annual exemption so free of IHT, but the taxpayer can only carry forward to 2019/20 the unused £1,000 of exemption from 2018/19, and the brought-forward amount of £1,500 from 2017/18 is lost.

Where IHT is or becomes payable on gifts in excess of the £3,000 in any tax year, the exemption applies to the earlier gifts rather than the later.

Example 2.2

A taxpayer gives £3,000 to their daughter in June and £3,000 to their son in December of the same year. The gift to the daughter is exempt, the gift to the son is a potentially exempt transfer (PET).

Where the gifts are made on the same day, the exemption is apportioned between the gifts according to the value they bear to each other.

Example 2.3

A taxpayer gives £200,000 to their daughter and £400,000 to their son on the same day. These are the only gifts they make in this and the previous tax year (so that annual exemptions of £6,000 can be set against the taxable values). The taxpayer dies two years later. They made no other gifts in the seven years preceding their death.

So, £2,000 of the combined exemption is set against the daughter's gift and £4,000 against the son's gift. The tax they each have to pay is apportioned in the same way.

2.5 OTHER EXEMPTIONS

2.5.1 Small gifts (IHTA 1984, s.20)

A taxpayer can make any number of gifts to individuals in any tax year providing those gifts do not exceed £250 each. To take an extreme example, a taxpayer could give away £250,000 exempt of tax by giving 1,000 people £250 each. However, they cannot claim both the annual and small gift exemption on giving £3,250 to one person. This would not qualify as a small gift and so only the £3,000 would be exempt.

2.5.2 Gifts out of normal expenditure (IHTA 1984, s.21)

A gift is exempt if it is made as part of the taxpayer's normal expenditure and is made out of excess income, i.e. when taking one year with another, after allowing for the other usual expenditure of the taxpayer, they have more income than they spent and the gift was made out of the excess. A pattern of giving must be established. This exemption is discussed in more detail in **Chapter 12**.

2.5.3 Gifts in consideration of marriage or civil partnership (IHTA 1984, s.22)

Gifts by a taxpayer to a person in consideration of their marriage or civil partnership are exempt up to a certain value. As with the relief on gifts between spouses, this extends to civil partnership in exactly the same way. The gift must be made to a party to the marriage. Up to £5,000 can be given outright (or in trust) to a child; up to £2,500 can be given outright (or in trust) to a grandchild or remoter descendant; and up to £1,000 can be given outright to any other individual. A child can be illegitimate, adopted or a stepchild, as can remoter descendants.

The exemption also applies on gifts up to £2,500 where one party to the marriage makes an outright gift or gift into trust for the other (before the ceremony).

The exemption only applies to a gift into trust if the only other people who can benefit/potentially benefit from the trust are the children and remoter descendants of either or both parties to the marriage, their spouses or future spouses of the parties.

2.5.4 Gifts to charities (IHTA 1984, s.23)

A gift is exempt if it is made outright to a charity or registered club, or is made into a trust for charitable purposes only. The gift is not exempt if it is subject to an earlier interest or is deferred. Gifts of land or buildings where the taxpayer tries to retain some benefit from the gift – for example, a right to occupy the land rent free for life before it passes to the charity – are not exempt.

In the past, HM Revenue and Customs (HMRC) argued that the exemption was limited to charities in the UK, but this was extended, from 27 January 2009, to include equivalent organisations in EU countries, Iceland and Norway. In 2019, the Supreme Court ruled (see *Routier* [2019] UKSC 43) that a 2007 gift on trust for charitable purposes in Jersey (and so outside the EU) was IHT exempt because the only restriction was in a 1950s case that must be disapplied because of the right under EU law to the free movement of capital. It is not altogether clear how this would be applied to the current rules on what is charitable for tax purposes.

There is no problem obtaining the exemption for a UK charity, such as Oxfam or Save the Children, most of whose work is done overseas.

In addition, a gift on death of at least 10 per cent of a taxable estate to charity triggers a reduction in the rate of IHT on the taxable estate from 40 per cent down to 36 per cent. See **14.6** for more details.

2.5.5 Gifts to political parties (IHTA 1984, s.24)

A gift to a political party is exempt. To qualify as a political party for the purposes of this exemption the party must, in the last general election before the gift was made, have had two members elected to parliament or received at least 150,000 votes.

2.5.6 Other exempt gifts

Gifts are also exempt if they are made:

- to housing associations (IHTA 1984, s.24A);
- for national purposes (s.25);
- into trust for the maintenance of historic buildings (s.27);
- into employee trusts (s.28).

2.6 ALLOWANCES

2.6.1 Rates of tax (IHTA 1984, s.7)

There are two rates of IHT on death. The value of the part of the estate falling within the available NRB is taxed at 0 per cent; the value of the part of the estate that is in excess of the NRB is taxed at 40 per cent.

Where tax is chargeable on an individual during their lifetime, it is taxed at half the death rate. So the value within the NRB is still taxed at 0 per cent; the value in excess of the NRB is taxed at 20 per cent.

Different rates apply to IHT within RPTs (see **Chapter 7**).

2.6.2 Chargeable lifetime transfers (CLTs)

A gift by a living taxpayer into a trust (other than a disabled person's trust) is chargeable to inheritance tax.

2.6.3 Potentially exempt transfers (IHTA 1984, s.3A)

A gift by a living taxpayer to an individual (which does not fall into any exemption set out above) is a PET. If the taxpayer survives seven years from the date of the gift, the gift becomes a fully exempt transfer. If the donor does not survive the seven years, then the gift becomes a chargeable transfer and its value is aggregated with the value of the donor's estate on death for the purposes of calculating IHT.

A gift by a living taxpayer into a disabled person's trust (under IHTA 1984, ss.89–89C) is a PET.

2.7 RELIEFS

2.7.1 Death on active service/emergency service personnel (IHTA 1984, ss.153A–155A)

A special relief applies to the estates of members of the armed forces (including civilians subject to service discipline) who die from a wound or accident or disease originating when on active duty (IHTA 1984, s.154). The relief applies to deaths triggered by events not only when a person was on active service but also when a person was on services of a warlike nature with comparable risks and when responding to emergency circumstances as a member of the armed forces. The relief also applies where the member dies from the aggravation of a pre-existing condition when on active service. In these circumstances there is no IHT payable on the estate (including on failed PETs which have become chargeable).

A similar relief applies to emergency service personnel who die from an injury or accident or disease originating when responding to emergency circumstances in their capacity as an emergency responder or who die from a pre-existing condition which is aggravated when responding to emergency circumstances. In these circumstances there is no IHT payable on the estate (including failed PETs which have become chargeable).

There is a similar relief (IHTA 1984, s.155A) where members of the police and of the armed forces are targeted because of their status. Where such a person dies from an injury or disease because they were targeted for being a police constable or member of the armed forces, their estate is not subject to IHT. Where the injury aggravated an existing illness hastening death by that illness, the relief still applies. The constable/member of the armed forces does not have to be acting in the course of their duties at the time of the targeting and can be a former member. The relief still applies.

2.7.2 Business property relief (IHTA 1984, ss.103–114)

There are generous reliefs on the transfer of a business or business assets. Where the value transferred relates to 'relevant business property', there is IHT relief of either 100 per cent or 50 per cent. 'Relevant business property' is defined in IHTA 1984, s.105 and includes an interest in a business, unquoted company shares or a controlling interest in a company (whether the shares are quoted or unquoted). In certain circumstances it includes land, buildings, plant and machinery used by the business, partnership or company in which the transferor has the interest.

To attract business property relief (BPR), the business property must have been owned continuously for two years before the transfer.

Businesses which are mainly investment businesses do not qualify for BPR.

Parts of the business property which have not been used mainly for the business in the last two years or are not specifically required in the business in the future are 'excepted assets' and excluded from BPR. The most common example of this is cash accumulated in the business which is not designated for a specific future purpose in the business. For more detail see **Chapter 15**.

2.7.3 Agricultural property relief (IHTA 1984, ss.115–124C)

Where a transfer relates to agricultural land or buildings, there are also generous reliefs, but only on 'agricultural value'. No relief is given on any value attributable to potential development, or a possible use other than agriculture.

'Agricultural property' is defined in IHTA 1984, s.115 and includes farmland and farm buildings (including cottages and farmhouses where appropriate) and specifically includes stud farms and associated grazing land.

As with BPR, there are certain conditions for agricultural property relief (APR) to apply. The transferor must have owned the property for at least two years before the transfer. Where the transferor does not farm the land themselves, they must have owned it for seven years before the transfer and the land must have been farmed continuously throughout that period.

The relief is generally 100 per cent of the agricultural value but only 50 per cent on some tenanted land.

APR is discussed in more detail in **Chapter 15**.

2.7.4 Woodlands relief (IHTA 1984, ss.125–130)

Where woodlands do not qualify for BPR or APR, there is a specific relief on their value on death (not on a lifetime transfer).

The woodlands must have been owned for five years before death, or must have been given/inherited, i.e. not bought. The personal representative has two years from the date of death to claim the relief, and the relief extends only to the value of the trees or underwood on the land, not the land itself. Woodlands relief is a deferral of tax only. If the trees/timber are subsequently sold, IHT is payable on the proceeds of sale.

In practice it may cost more to claim woodland relief than not. This is because the deferred IHT has to be paid when the timber is sold, and is then assessed on its actual sale value. This is likely to mean a larger tax bill.

2.7.5 Heritage reliefs (IHTA 1984, ss.77–79A)

Land or buildings or works of art or artefacts which are of particular national, historic, artistic or scientific interest may be designated 'national heritage property'. A gift of national heritage property is a conditionally exempt transfer. No IHT is payable at the point of transfer provided that certain conditions are met. The relief is only available on lifetime transfers if the property has been owned for six years before the transfer, or was inherited as conditionally exempt property. The donee must also undertake not to let the property leave the UK; to keep it maintained; and to allow reasonable public access to the property. If, on the death of the owner, the property is given or sold to a national museum or organisation (listed in IHTA 1984, Sched.3) the conditional exemption becomes fully exempt.

As with woodlands relief, claiming a heritage relief may ultimately be expensive. If the undertakings are breached – for example, if the conditionally exempt property is sold – the deferred IHT has to be paid on the value at that time, for example the actual sale value.

2.7.6 Taper relief

Taper relief is a relief on the rate of IHT payable on a failed PET or CLT made more than three but less than seven years before death. This relief is much misunderstood, as it does not reduce the taxable amount of the gift. If the gift is within the NRB, there is no tax to reduce and thus no taper.

Taper relief reduces the rate of tax, as set out in the following table:

Years between gift and death	Tax rate charged
Less than 3	40%
3–4	32%
4–5	24%
5–6	16%
6–7	8%
7 +	0%

Credit is given for the 20 per cent lifetime tax already paid on a CLT, so there is no additional IHT to pay on a CLT made more than five years before death.

2.7.7 Fall in value reliefs (IHTA 1984, ss.178–189 and 190–198; and ss.131–140)

The reliefs in IHTA 1984, ss.178–189 and 190–198 apply where qualifying investments (usually shares) are sold for less than probate value within the year after death or land or buildings are sold for less than probate value within four years after death. The IHT on the difference in value can be reclaimed.

The claim must be made by the appropriate person, i.e. the person liable to pay the IHT (in most cases the personal representative) and, in either case, the claim must be made within the four years following death.

Qualifying investments mean quoted shares, authorised unit trusts and shares in open-ended investment companies (OEICs). The investments must be sold within 12 months of death for the relief to apply. It is the aggregate value of all the investments sold in that period which is deducted from the probate value for the purposes of calculating the repayment of IHT.

Example 2.4

Jack dies leaving some Barclays shares valued at £150,000 and some Lloyds shares valued at £200,000 on the date of his death. Jack's estate is taxable. His executors sell the Lloyds shares for £180,000 six months later, and the Barclays shares for £160,000 two months after that. His executors cannot claim relief just on the £20,000 loss on the Barclays shares. They must deduct the aggregate sale proceeds (£340,000) from the aggregate probate value

(£350,000) which gives a £10,000 loss on which 40% or £4,000 IHT can be reclaimed. See **9.5** on planning for losses and gains.

For the relief relating to land and buildings which is sold within four years of the date of death at a lower value than probate value, again, the appropriate person must make the sale and the claim. There is a de minimis exception where the change in value is less than £1,000 or five per cent of the value, whichever is the lower. There are anti-avoidance provisions where the relief cannot be claimed if the sale is to connected parties. Again, it is the aggregate of values of land sold within the four years that is substituted for the probate values.

A similar relief in IHTA 1984, ss.131–140 can reduce the additional tax payable on death within seven years of a PET or CLT. If the asset given is still owned by the donee when the donor dies, but is worth less than it was at the time of the gift, the additional tax is assessed by reference to the lower date of death value.

2.7.8 Quick succession relief (IHTA 1984, s.141)

Where a person (A) dies leaving assets to another person (B) on which IHT is paid, and B dies within five years of A, quick succession relief can be claimed on any IHT due on B's estate relating to those assets. The relief is 100 per cent of the tax on those assets if less than a year has elapsed reducing by 20 per cent for each additional year to 20 per cent if more than four years has elapsed.

2.7.9 Estate duty transitional relief (IHTA 1984, Sched.6)

There is a transitional relief when a very old interest in possession trust for a surviving spouse comes to an end. Usually there would be a charge to tax on the ending of a QIIP trust. Prior to 1974, where one spouse created an interest in possession trust by will for another, estate duty was paid at that time. So where there is a QIIP created by a spouse who died before 13 November 1974, there is no IHT charged on the underlying capital value of the trust and no aggregation with the free estate.

2.8 EVENTS THAT ARE NOT TRANSFERS OF VALUE

There are some occasions where assets are transferred between parties (or where rights to receive an asset are not exercised) which are not 'transfers of value' for inheritance tax purposes (IHTA 1984, ss.10–17). These are specifically excluded by the legislation.

These include provisions relating to pensions, not withdrawing benefits from pension schemes after retirement age, employee benefit schemes and waiver of remuneration and dividends which are not within the scope of this handbook. The most common for private client practitioners (and even these are not that common) are usually referred to using the designation of the relevant section number of IHTA 1984 – these are s.10 (dispositions not intended to confer gratuitous benefit) and s.11 (dispositions for maintenance of family).

2.8.1 IHTA 1984, s.10 transfers: dispositions not intended to confer gratuitous benefit

IHTA 1984, s.10 transfers are dispositions made in arm's length transactions where the parties are not connected and the disposition was not intended to confer any gratuitous benefit on any person. Section 10 is most often seen to apply in commercial transactions. HMRC applies the test stringently and it is for the taxpayer to prove that there is no intention to confer a gratuitous benefit.

Example 2.5

The three directors and shareholders of Company X want to ensure the continuity of the company in the event that one of them dies, by retaining control with the remaining shareholders. They each take out a life assurance policy which they transfer into a trust for the benefit of the others. (If one of them dies, the trustees of the trust will pay the policy proceeds to the survivors to enable them to buy the shares of the deceased shareholder, thus ensuring the business is protected for the future.) As each transaction is part of a commercial agreement and not intended to confer any gratuitous benefit on the other shareholders, IHTA 1984, s.10 applies to the transfer of the policy into trust and it is not a transfer of value for IHT purposes.

2.8.2 IHTA 1984, s.11: dispositions for maintenance of family

IHTA 1984, s.11 protects expenditure on some family members or dependent relatives from being taxable. Like main residence relief in the capital gains tax (CGT) legislation, the effects of this provision are so commonly taken for granted, many people do not question whether the IHT legislation applies at all.

There is no transfer of value (and so no occasion of potential tax) when:

- a spouse/civil partner provides for the other spouse's maintenance;
- parents provide for the maintenance or education (or training) of their minor children or stepchildren (including when they are in full-time education unless the providing parent has not had the care of the child for substantial periods of time);
- a former party to a marriage or civil partnership transfers assets to the other party on the dissolution of the marriage or civil partnership (or on a variation of that disposition in a financial settlement);
- a taxpayer makes reasonable provision for the care or maintenance of a dependent relative, e.g. parents or parents-in-law, or a more remote relative, who is too old or too ill to look after themselves.

'Maintenance' is not defined in IHTA 1984, but HMRC considers it to mean 'the supply of necessaries, such as food or clothing, so as to maintain a qualifying beneficiary in the condition of life which is appropriate to a dependant of the transferor' (*Inheritance Tax Manual*, HMRC, 20 March 2016, updated 28 August 2020, IHTM04172). This is a subjective test and what is considered excessive in one family may be considered as maintenance in another.

In practice, s.11 is unlikely to be used where spouses make provision for each other because of the more generous spouse relief under s.18. Where it may be relevant is where a UK domiciled spouse wants to make provision for a non-UK domiciled spouse in excess of the current relief available (s.18 relief is currently (2020/21) limited to £325,000 where the receiving spouse is non-UK domiciled.)

It is also unlikely to be used in the context of the dissolution of a marriage or civil partnership where the court has ordered the terms of the financial settlement or the parties have agreed a settlement then embodied in a consent order. In *Haines* v. *Hill and another* (2007) the court has held that the applicant's right to have provision made for them is consideration of the equivalent value to the assets or property then transferred to them. Therefore, there is no transfer of value because of the consideration.

Where a taxpayer is making provision for a dependent relative, under s.11(3) the care or maintenance must be reasonable (compare provision for a spouse or child). Again there is no definition of 'care' or 'reasonable' in IHTA 1984. HMRC's interpretation is that 'care' suggests the provision of services, whether privately or in an institution; and that 'reasonable' would suggest such amount as is reasonably necessary for the purpose of providing care and maintenance (but no more), having regard to the financial and other circumstances of the transferor and the relative and the degree of incapacity or infirmity of the latter.

Any planning to utilise this provision must be made carefully. A capital sum made outright or (more commonly) into a trust for the relative's care/maintenance must be carefully calculated. See the case of *McKelvey* [2008] STC (SCD) 944 for an illustration of a terminally ill daughter making lifetime provision for her widowed mother, with the transfer to her of income-providing assets. This was held to be reasonable provision in part and that part was not a transfer of value thanks to IHTA 1984, s.11; the remainder was a PET which came into charge on the daughter's death a few months after the gift.

CHAPTER 3

Further nil rate bands (NRBs)

Hollie Marcham

NB: In this chapter, for simplicity we will use the term 'spouse' to also denote a civil partner.

3.1 KEY POINTS

- Transferable nil rate band (TNRB) – the basics of how it works.
- Residence nil rate band (RNRB) – a very basic introduction, as this is covered more fully in **Chapters 16** and **17**. The legislation (all 15 new clauses in the Inheritance Tax Act (IHTA) 1984) is outlined in **16.2**.

3.2 TRANSFERABLE NIL RATE BAND

3.2.1 Background

Inheritance tax (IHT) is charged on death at 40 per cent. The 40 per cent rate is only charged on the value of the deceased's assets that exceed the nil rate band (NRB). The NRB is currently (2020/21) £325,000 per individual, and has been unchanged since 6 April 2009.

If a spouse has previously died and did not use all of their NRB, because the value of the estate was under the threshold or because some or all of their estate passed to an exempt beneficiary, then the unused NRB can be claimed on the widow's or widower's death as TNRB. Most commonly this is because much or all of the first spouse's estate has passed to the widow/er and been exempt thanks to the spouse exemption.

Before 9 October 2007, gifts between spouses on the first death often resulted in an IHT charge on the death of the survivor. Their joint estates all ended in the estate of the survivor, with only a single NRB to set against the total value. The NRB of the first to die would be wasted.

TNRB allows any unused NRB of the first spouse to die to be carried forward and added to the NRB available on the survivor's death.

TNRB applies to civil partners in exactly the same way as to married couples. However, it cannot be claimed by unmarried and cohabiting couples or by other family members who may co-own property.

3.2.2 The legislation

The rules on TNRB are contained in IHTA 1984, ss.8A–8C.

3.2.3 The rules

To claim TNRB:

(a) the survivor must have been the spouse of the first to die at the time of death;
(b) some or all of the NRB of the first to die must have been unused; and
(c) the survivor's death must have occurred on or after 9 October 2007.

The NRB of the first spouse to die might have been used either by gifts within the seven years before death, or by gifts on death that were not exempt or fully relieved.

A gift to a spouse, during lifetime and on death, will have been an exempt transfer and does not affect the amount of TNRB available. There is an exception to this rule where the recipient spouse is domiciled outside the UK where, since 6 April 2013, the exemption has been limited to £325,000; until 5 April 2013 the limit was £55,000.

Example 3.1

Mr Chapman died in October 2009 leaving all of his estate to his wife. In December 2018, Mrs Chapman gives her son a house as a gift worth £600,000. This is a PET so no inheritance tax is payable at the date of the gift. Mrs Chapman has a fatal accident soon afterwards in January 2019. The NRB is £325,000 and Mrs Chapman's estate is worth £3,000,000, including the PET.

Mrs Chapman's personal representatives make a claim for TNRB from her late husband's estate. Since none of Mr Chapman's NRB was used on his death, this increases Mrs Chapman's NRB to £650,000. The PET uses up £600,000 of this, leaving £50,000 NRB for the remainder of the estate.

The rules do not allow a claim for TNRB if both spouses died before 9 October 2007.

If the predeceased spouse died before 18 March 1986 and so before the introduction of IHT, the treatment of transfers and gifts between spouses was different. TNRB may still be available, but the position must be checked very carefully.

It does not matter if the value of the estate of the first to die was less or more than the NRB and this value is not considered in the calculation. The only value taken into account is the fraction of the NRB available on the first death that was unused. If the whole NRB was used then there is no TNRB to transfer.

A surviving spouse may have been married more than once and there may be parts or all of more than one unused NRB. The surviving spouse's estate can claim unused parts from both previous spouses, but TNRB cannot increase the NRB of the survivor to more than double the NRB in effect on the survivor's death.

Example 3.2: Remarriage

Mrs Smith was married to Mr Smith for 20 years and he died in July 2008. Mr Smith left his whole estate to Mrs Smith except for a gift of £100,000 among his children from a previous relationship. The NRB at the time was £312,000, so £212,000 of Mr Smith's NRB (67.95%) was unused.

In 2012 Mrs Smith married Mr Hall and then died in 2016 leaving an estate worth £750,000 with a gift to her own children of £500,000 and the rest to Mr Hall.

Mrs Hall's (formerly Smith's) personal representatives can claim her NRB of £325,000 and a TNRB of a further 67.95% of £325,000 (£220,837). The total NRB is £545,837 so no IHT is due on the £500,000 left to the Smith children.

Mrs Hall has unused NRB of £45,837. The TNRB available when Mr Hall dies is a fraction of the £325,000 basic NRB available at Mrs Hall's death or 41.11%. Note that this is a fraction of the basic NRB *not* a fraction of the increased NRB actually given on Mrs Hall's death.

Example 3.3: Multiple marriages

Mr Singh married Miss Jones who then died leaving half of the NRB at the date of her death to her sister and the remainder of her estate to Mr Singh.

Mr Singh then went on to marry Miss Jackson who died leaving 30% of the NRB at her death to her children and the remainder to Mr Singh.

The personal representatives of Mr Singh's estate could potentially claim a TNRB of 50% relating to Miss Jones's estate and 70% of Miss Jackson's estate, but this would exceed 100% and the TNRB claim is limited to 100%.

In summary:

- The TNRB provisions mean that on death there could be up to a maximum of two NRBs available to reduce the IHT liability.
- The first spouse to die must be married to the second spouse – they must not have been divorced.
- If the second spouse subsequently remarried, they are still able to claim the unused NRB from their first spouse.

3.2.4 Pre-1986

Deaths before 18 March 1986 were subject to capital transfer tax or estate duty. The claim to transfer the unused NRB of the first spouse may still be made where they died before the introduction of IHT, provided of course that the survivor died on or after 9 October 2007.

Capital transfer tax and estate duty applied to lifetime transfers and transfers on death differently from the way that IHT applies. If there is no available record of the position, for example, there is no estate return or knowledge of the position, a review of the old rules will be necessary to calculate the TNRB available.

Estate duty was charged on deaths between 2 August 1894 and 12 March 1975.

There was no spouse exemption until 22 March 1972. There was a limited spouse exemption from 21 March 1972 of £15,000. The £15,000 limit was removed for deaths occurring after 12 November 1974.

Capital transfer tax was charged between 13 March 1975 and 17 March 1986.

Finding accurate records may be the most difficult aspect to the claim. The personal representatives should carry out whatever searches they can do to obtain the documents and provide HM Revenue and Customs (HMRC) with as much information as possible.

3.2.5 The figures

The amount of available NRB is calculated as a percentage up to three decimal points of that unused on the first death. The percentage is then multiplied by the value of the NRB in the tax year of the survivor's death.

It does not matter if the value of the first to die's estate was more or less than the NRB. For example, Mr Smith dies and passed his estate of £800,000 to Mrs Smith. When Mrs Smith dies, her personal representatives can claim 100 per cent of the unused NRB.

Tax year	NRB	Combined NRB
2017/18	£325,000	£650,000
2018/19	£325,000	£650,000
2019/20	£325,000	£650,000

3.2.6 The procedure

A formal claim must be made, and this is generally done by the personal representatives of the surviving spouse. The allowable portion is the TNRB and is claimed against the survivor's estate. If the personal representatives do not make a claim, any person who has to pay tax because of the death can make a claim. This claim can only be made once the time period for the personal representatives to submit a claim has expired.

The time limit for personal representatives to make a claim is two years from the end of the month the person dies. If no claim is made, the personal representatives can make a request to HMRC for permission to make a late claim. In these circumstances, it must be shown that the reasons for delay were outside their control and that they had done everything in their control to progress matters. Alternatively, HMRC must be convinced that the personal representatives were unaware and could not reasonably have been expected to be aware that they were entitled to make a claim. If a person who has to pay tax as a result of the death wishes to make a claim, then HMRC has discretion over the time limit.

The personal representatives claiming the TNRB will first have to establish what percentage of the NRB was unused on first death. This is done in practice by establishing the terms of the will or intestacy rules; reviewing the estate documents such as a copy of the inheritance tax form, the death certificate, a copy of the marriage certificate, the grant of probate and estate accounts; and establishing how much passed to chargeable and non-chargeable beneficiaries. If a deed of variation was executed, this will also need to be lodged with the claim.

As part of the claim, HMRC may ask for details of specific assets that will have qualified for relief on the first death such as agricultural property relief (APR) and copy valuations. Where deaths occurred prior to 9 October 2007, documents may be difficult to obtain – but HMRC will still expect to see the death and marriage certificate, the grant and the will.

In practice, the claim is made using either form IHT217 (claim to transfer unused nil rate band for excepted estates) or form IHT402 (claim to transfer unused nil rate band). Form IHT216 (claim to transfer unused inheritance tax nil rate band) is used if a claim is being made by a person other than the personal representative.

3.2.7 Practical tips

HMRC has published guidance on the TNRB provisions, and this can be found in its *Inheritance Tax Manual* at IHTM43000 (20 March 2016, updated 28 August 2020). HMRC has also produced a table of historic NRBs to assist personal representatives.

HMRC has published an Inheritance Tax Toolkit to assist in the preparation of the inheritance tax accounts for deaths occurring from 6 April 2019, which can be found at: **https://assets.publishing.service.gov.uk/government/uploads/system/uploads/attachment_data/file/803009/Inheritance_Tax_toolkit_-_IHT400__2019_to_2020_..pdf**.

3.3 RESIDENCE NIL RATE BAND

RNRB is available when, on an individual's death, all or part of their home (a 'qualifying residential interest' (QRI)) passes to a descendant.

It is an additional allowance against the whole estate on death, including any aggregable trust, not just against the value of the QRI. In contrast to TNRB it cannot be set against the value of lifetime gifts.

The allowance is restricted, and, in many cases, lost altogether, for those whose assets are worth more than £2 million when they die.

The allowance is available only on deaths after 5 April 2017. It has been phased in and is the lower of the value of the QRI and:

- £100,000 in 2017/18;
- £125,000 in 2018/19;
- £150,000 in 2019/20;
- £175,000 in 2020/21.

If, at the time they die, the individual does not have a QRI sufficient to use the allowance in full, or no longer owns a QRI, they can usually add the value of an interest in a more valuable home that they previously owned, provided that was at some time on or after 8 July 2015 (the 'downsizing addition').

Widows and widowers (and those whose civil partners have died) can claim an extra allowance if it was not 'used' on their spouse's earlier death, whenever that deceased spouse died. At the moment, many widows and widowers have double RNRB, because a spouse who died before 6 April 2017 could not use an allowance that did not exist.

Only QRIs given so that they are 'closely inherited' are eligible for this new allowance. This starts with lineal descendants (children, grandchildren, etc.) but extends to adopted children, natural children who have been adopted, stepchildren and spouses, widows and widowers of 'lineal descendants' (provided they do not remarry), including some forms of trust for these descendants.

Unmarried partners of the deceased lose out. No RNRB is available on gifts to them or their children.

See further details of RNRB in **Chapter 16**, and more of the planning points in **Chapter 17**.

CHAPTER 4

Inheritance tax planning anti-avoidance

Anthony Nixon

4.1 KEY POINTS

- Any inheritance tax (IHT) planning needs to take into account these anti-avoidance provisions – to avoid the traps these present.
- Many provisions have been introduced over the years to thwart attempts to avoid liabilities for IHT. We cover here the main ones:
  - Restrictions on deducting liabilities – introduced in 2013 (see **4.3**).
  - Associated operations – introduced in the Inheritance Tax Act (IHTA) 1984 (see **4.4**).
  - Reservation of benefit – introduced with the change to IHT in 1986 (see **4.5**).
  - Pre-owned assets tax (POAT) charge – introduced in 2004 (see **4.6**).
  - General anti-abuse rule (GAAR) in 2013 and disclosure of tax avoidance schemes (DOTAS) in 2011, but extended in a major way in 2018 (see **4.7**).
- This chapter also discusses the Professional Conduct in Relation to Taxation (PCRT) rules (**www.tax.org.uk/professional-standards/professional-rules/professional-conduct-relation-taxation**), and the accompanying Solicitors Regulation Authority (SRA) guidance (**www.sra.org.uk/solicitors/guidance/tax-avoidance-duties/**) (see **4.2**).

4.2 SRA GUIDANCE AND THE PROFESSIONAL CONDUCT IN RELATION TO TAXATION RULES

Solicitors, and anyone regulated by the SRA, should also be careful to comply with the PCRT rules, and the accompanying guidance (**www.sra.org.uk/solicitors/guidance/tax-avoidance-duties/**). PCRT was first introduced for members of STEP, CIOT, ATT, ICAEW and other professional bodies, but the SRA said in September 2017 that all solicitors should also comply. The guidance was updated in November 2019; the SRA says: 'We therefore expect you to be familiar with the PCRT and adhere to its standards.'

The context for the PCRT rules, and all these anti-avoidance measures, is a growing pressure from HM Revenue and Customs (HMRC) to limit the scope of 'tax planning' and to seek to outlaw increasing amounts of planning as morally reprehensible 'tax avoidance'.

Care must be taken with the PCRT rules, as to breach them could be disastrous for professional reputations, and of course it is necessary to help clients avoid ever engaging in 'tax evasion', which is illegal. However, it is important to uphold genuine tax planning, which we try to outline in this handbook, and enable our clients to plan appropriately.

4.3 RESTRICTIONS ON DEDUCTING LIABILITIES

4.3.1 Introduction

Provisions introduced in 2013, and added to IHTA 1984 as ss.162A, 162B and 175A, prevent certain liabilities from being set against the value of assets liable to IHT. The restrictions apply, from 17 July 2013, to any IHT charge on death, or, in the first two cases, at the time of any other IHT charge, to the extent that:

- the liability was incurred to acquire, maintain or enhance excluded property (i.e. non-UK assets owned by non-UK domiciled persons) (s.162A);
- the liability was incurred to acquire, maintain or enhance agricultural property, business property or woodlands (s.162B);
- the liability is not repaid on death (s.175A).

4.3.2 Liabilities incurred to acquire, etc. excluded property (IHTA 1984, s.162A)

The object of this restriction is clear. If a non-domiciled person owns assets both within and outside the UK, the UK assets suffer IHT while the non-UK assets are free of IHT as excluded property. In the past, it was possible to reduce the taxable value of UK assets by setting against their value borrowings used for property outside IHT. This was helped by IHTA 1984, s.162(4) which provides that, where a liability is secured against an asset, it is deducted from that asset's value.

Section 162A reverses the normal rule of deducting a liability from the value of the asset against which it is secured, by looking at the use made of what was borrowed. If the funds borrowed were used to acquire, maintain or enhance the value of non-UK assets, the deduction must be made from the value of those assets. As a result, the borrowing will usually not save any IHT.

The restriction applies irrespective of when the liability was incurred.

The legislation uses the words 'to the extent that' so that liabilities incurred for more than one purpose can be apportioned on a reasonable basis. Of course, it may be necessary to justify the apportionment to HMRC.

Where a debt is incurred to purchase excluded property and that property later ceases to be excluded property (perhaps because the individual becomes domiciled or deemed domiciled in the UK, or because of the 2017 changes bringing non-UK assets whose value is derived from UK residential property into IHT) the deductibility of the debt is capped at the value of the property.

For example, suppose a non-domiciled individual borrows £1,000,000 to buy a house in Spain, but later becomes domiciled in the UK and dies when the Spanish house is worth £800,000 – only £800,000 can be deducted from the value liable to IHT.

In contrast, if a UK liability, charged on UK property, is incurred to purchase excluded property and that property remains excluded, then any excess liability over the value of the excluded property at death can be deducted from the value of the UK property, provided the excess did not arise from:

- an arrangement under which one of the main purposes was to obtain a tax advantage;
- a roll up of interest or the use of an index (or similar) calculation to increase the value of the debt; or
- the disposal or partial disposal of the original asset.

There are also specific measures to prevent the value of the non-UK asset being artificially depressed with the object of increasing the deduction.

4.3.3 Liabilities incurred to acquire, etc. relieved property (IHTA 1984, s.162B)

These rules largely mirror those for excluded property in IHTA 1984, s.162A and much that is said under that heading could be repeated here. In the past it was fairly standard practice for individuals or trusts owning a variety of properties, some qualifying and some not qualifying for business or agricultural relief, to ensure that liabilities were charged against unrelieved assets.

One important difference is that, in this case, liabilities will only be caught if they were incurred after 5 April 2013. While loans dating from before then will become increasingly rare, this date may prove important in some cases.

If existing loan agreements are varied to allow further funds to be drawn down, the variation is treated as a new loan and so treated as made after 5 April 2013 (see Finance Act (FA) 2013, Sched.36, para.5(3)(a)).

Where there is no written loan agreement, the date of the loan is the date when funds were received by the borrower.

If a liability has been incurred to acquire relievable property and there is then a lifetime chargeable transfer or a failed potentially exempt transfer (PET) of that relievable property, the liability has to be set against the gift for IHT purposes, even if actual responsibility for the liability remains with the donor rather than being passed to the donee. This means that the liability cannot then be set against the IHT value of the donor's estate. However, if the gift is exempt from IHT, perhaps because it is a PET which the donor survives by more than seven years, the liability does not attach to the gift.

Example 4.1

Suppose Gordon takes out a loan of £1,000,000 secured on his house to acquire company shares that qualify for business property relief (BPR) and, at a later time, gives those shares to his daughter, without removing the charge on his house. If Gordon survives another seven years, he may offset the whole of the borrowed £1,000,000 against his chargeable estate. If he fails to survive by seven years, then none of the liability can be deducted from the value of his estate; instead it will be treated as reducing the value of the failed PET.

In contrast, if Gordon settles the shares into a trust then, even though the shares qualify for BPR (and therefore there is no entry charge) he will lose the ability to deduct the liability from the value of his estate as it will have been 'used up' in reducing the value of the chargeable transfer between Gordon and the trustees.

4.3.4 Liabilities outstanding on death (IHTA 1984, s.175A)

IHTA 1984, s.175A prevents liabilities not actually repaid out of the estate being deducted from the taxable estate on death.

This is particularly directed at liabilities owed to family members, trusts and family companies, intended to reduce the IHT estate at death. Repaying these liabilities may mean another tax charge (usually income tax) for the person or entity receiving the repayment.

In the days before the TNRB was available between spouses, it was common for a trust set up by the first spouse to die to have the benefit of a charge or other loan arrangement for the value advanced to the survivor. That charge or loan would often be 'inflation-proofed' so that the amount repayable increased with indexation as time passed. The increased amount now usually suffers income tax if it is paid; but if it is not paid, s.175A prevents it being deducted for IHT.

'Estate' has its normal IHT meaning of all the property to which the deceased is entitled (see **1.4**), so includes, for example, jointly owned assets and the value of an aggregated qualifying interest in possession (QIIP). Section 175A(1)(a) extends the definition of 'estate' to excluded property owned by the deceased, but HMRC has said that 'owned' in this context is not as wide as 'estate'; so excluded property that is held in trust, even where the trust is for the deceased's benefit, cannot be used for repayment (*Inheritance Tax Manual*, IHTM28028 'Liabilities: restricted deductions: meaning of "out of estate"', HMRC).

There might be a trap if the deceased has taken out life insurance to repay a loan and arranged for that insurance to be held in a trust outside his estate. However, if the estate has limited liquid assets, HMRC's guidance confirms that the personal representatives can borrow money from a third party lender to repay the debt and, provided that new loan is a liability of the estate, this will be accepted. HMRC says that it is not concerned about the source of any new funds in this case (IHTM28028). So it appears that funds could be lent to the estate from a non-aggregable trust or excluded property settlement with the personal representatives, as necessary, joining with the trustees concerned to balance the interests of beneficiaries.

Personal representatives should ensure that their administration accounts show that the liability has been repaid rather than simply transferring the liability for a debt owed at death to a beneficiary. They should also ensure that there is an audit trail showing an actual payment.

In certain circumstances, non-repayment of a liability may be acceptable. However, this is subject to a number of conditions, in particular that the main purpose, or one of the main purposes, of leaving the liability or part of it undischarged is not to secure a tax advantage. The lender must usually be an unconnected third party. An example would be a jointly owned property, against which a commercial loan is secured, where one joint owner dies, but the surviving owner wants to continue with the loan.

4.4 ASSOCIATED OPERATIONS

The concept of associated operations, which are defined by IHTA 1984, s.268, is, on the face of it, very wide. Section 268 says:

> (1) In this Act 'associated operations' means, subject to subsection (2) below, any two or more operations of any kind, being–
>
> (a) operations which affect the same property, or one of which affects some property and the other or others of which affect property which represents, whether directly or indirectly, that property, or income arising from that property, or any property representing accumulations of any such income, or
>
> (b) any two operations of which one is effected with reference to the other, or with a view to enabling the other to be effected or facilitating its being effected, and any further operation having a like relation to any of those two, and so on,
>
> whether those operations are effected by the same person or different persons, and whether or not they are simultaneous; and 'operation' includes an omission.
>
> . . .
>
> (3) Where a transfer of value is made by associated operations carried out at different times it shall be treated as made at the time of the last of them . . .

Section 272 brings the concept of associated operations into the definition of 'disposition', by providing that it 'includes a disposition made by associated operations'. So, in practice, associated operations are usually involved only where a case turns on the interpretation of IHTA 1984, s.3 or s.10:

- Section 3 defines 'transfer of value' as a disposition, so confirming, as s.268(3) provides, that a transfer of value can be made by associated operations carried out at different times (and, of course, by different people or entities).

- Section 10 provides, broadly, that, where there is no 'gratuitous' intent, a disposition (including, of course, a disposition made by associated operations) is not a transfer of value.

In *Macpherson* v. *IRC* [1988] STC 362 the House of Lords considered the predecessor of s.268, commenting:

> The definition in s44 [of the Finance Act 1975] is extremely wide and is capable of covering a multitude of events affecting the same property which might have little or no apparent connection between them. It might be tempting to assume that any event which fell within this wide definition should be taken into account in determining what constituted a transaction . . . However, counsel for the Crown accepted, rightly in my view, that some limitation must be imposed.

The limitation was, the House of Lords ruled, that in order to be relevant to the associated operations rules the particular operation must have been a contributory part of arrangements to confer a gratuitous benefit. The operation does not itself have to have conferred a benefit but must have been a contributory part.

The distinction is not at all an easy one. This is demonstrated by the different interpretations arrived at by the various judges in *HMRC* v. *Parry and others* [2020] UKSC 35. A taxpayer had moved her pension out of an old scheme that would have meant that her undrawn benefits fell into her taxable estate; under her new pension scheme, benefits on death were payable at the discretion of trustees, so, ostensibly, were free of IHT. The Court of Appeal overruled both First-tier Tribunal and Upper Tribunal judgments to find that the transfer from one scheme to another, and the taxpayer's decision not to take any pension payments for herself before her death, were associated operations. Two judges in the Supreme Court agreed with the Court of Appeal, but were outvoted by the three in the majority, so that s.268 did not apply.

Two cases clearly set out where the associated operations rules do not apply.

First, in *Reynaud* v. *IRC* [1999] STC (SCD) 185 two leading Special Commissioners, Dr Avery Jones and Mr Everett, ruled that the Revenue (HMRC was at the time known as the Inland Revenue) was wrong to invoke the associated operations rules where three of the owners of shares in a private trading company qualifying for IHT business relief made gifts of shares to trusts and, on the following day, the company bought the shares back from the trustees. The Revenue's argument was that, since the gifts and buyback were both operations which affected the same property, and because s.268(3) provides that a transfer of value made by associated operations is treated as made at the time of the last of them, the buyback was the last, converting the assets given to cash, so that no business relief should be available.

The Special Commissioners ruled that an associated operation was relevant only if it contributed to the reduction of the value of the estate of the transferor. In this case the transfers of the shares into trusts were the only relevant operations. The company's purchase of the shares was not an operation contributing to the reduction of each transferor's estate. So the IHT disposition could not be treated as taking place any later than the actual gifts, which therefore qualified for business relief.

Second, in *Rysaffe Trustee Co (CI) Ltd* v. *IRC* [2003] EWCA Civ 356 the Court of Appeal confirmed that s.268 was irrelevant in calculating the appropriate 10-yearly IHT charges on five separate settlements to which similar assets had been transferred. The Revenue had argued that s.268 meant that the five separate gifts to five trusts should be treated as a single disposition. Mummery LJ, giving the single judgment, pointed out (at para.23):

> The inclusion of 'associated operations' in the statutory description of 'disposition' is not intended for cases, such as this, where there is no dispute that there was a 'disposition' of property falling within s. 43(2). They are intended for cases where there is a dispute as to whether there was a relevant 'disposition' at all.

4.5 GIFTS WITH RESERVATION OF BENEFIT

4.5.1 Introduction

Until 18 March 1986, when capital transfer tax became IHT, all lifetime gifts (subject to exemptions and reliefs) were chargeable transfers. IHT introduced PETs for the first time. This made it possible to make unlimited gifts to individuals (and, in those days, many trusts) without immediate IHT.

To avoid opening a yawning cavern of a loophole, Finance Act (FA) 1986, s.102(1) restored the old estate duty concept of reservation of benefit where:

> ... on or after 18th March 1986, an individual disposes of any property by way of gift and either –
>
> (a) possession and enjoyment of the property is not bona fide assumed by the donee at or before the beginning of the relevant period; or
>
> (b) at any time in the relevant period the property is not enjoyed to the entire exclusion, or virtually to the entire exclusion, of the donor and of any benefit to him by contract or otherwise . . .

The 'relevant period' means any period after the gift concerned which is in the seven years before death.

If, immediately before the death of the donor, there is any property which, in relation to the donor, is property subject to a reservation then, to the extent that the property would not, apart from this section, form part of the donor's estate immediately before death, that property shall be treated for the purposes of IHTA 1984 as property to which the donor was beneficially entitled immediately before death (FA 1986, s.102(3)).

So the gift with reservation of benefit (GROB) rules bring into IHT an asset which is not completely given away. It is essential to remember that a GROB can be triggered at any time from the date of the gift onwards. The rules are not limited to benefits that the donor receives in the seven years after the gift.

To take the simplest example, if Mrs Brown gives her house to her daughter but carries on living there, she has reserved a benefit. For IHT, the house still belongs to her. Unfortunately, it also belongs to her daughter, so that there can be an IHT charge if either of them dies.

If there has been a reservation of benefit, which comes to an end within the 'relevant period' (the seven years before death), it comes into account on death as if the donor had made a PET when the reservation of benefit came to an end.

To continue the previous example, suppose Mrs Brown, five years after giving her house to her daughter, while continuing to live there, moves to a care home and sells the house. The proceeds are paid to her daughter, so that Mrs Brown's reservation ends. If Mrs Brown dies four years after that, her estate pays IHT as if her gift had been four, rather than nine, years before her death.

4.5.2 Gifts and transfers of value

One result of importing the estate duty concept of a GROB into IHT was the mismatch between 'gift' (the trigger for a GROB) and 'transfer of value' (the trigger for an IHT charge). Pretty much all gifts are transfers of value, but not all transfers of value are gifts.

For example, if trustees exercise a power, under the terms of their settlement, to end an interest under which the beneficiary is deemed to own some or all of the trust assets, the beneficiary is deemed to make a transfer of value, when they have not made a gift. Until 22 March 2006, this gave trustees the ability to take assets out of a beneficiary's IHT ownership, while leaving them still a potential beneficiary of the trust concerned, without a GROB.

This was changed by FA 1986, s.102ZA, so that, from 22 March 2006 onwards, when their interest is ended in their lifetime, the beneficiary concerned is deemed to have made a gift.

4.5.3 GROB and trusts

If Mrs White gives her home to a trust for the benefit of her children and either:

(a) carries on living there; or
(b) remains a potential beneficiary of the trust (even if she does not actually live in her home or receive any actual benefit from the trust),

there is a GROB.

There used to be a technical argument that a settlor who did not actually receive anything from a trust they had created, but was a merely a potential beneficiary of the trust, did not reserve a benefit, but the courts long ago disposed of this.

4.5.4 Partial gift is not a GROB

If Mrs Green owns 2,000 shares in Shell and gives 1,500 of these to her children while keeping the other 500, this is not a GROB.

For the same reason, the House of Lords ruled in 1998 (*Ingram* v. *Inland Revenue Commissioners* [1999] STC 37) that, where Lady Ingram gave away the freehold of her valuable home, subject to a rent-free lease which, a day or two before the gift, she had reserved for herself, there was no GROB. She had divided beneficial ownership of her home into separate assets – the lease and the freehold – and kept one while giving the other away. The important factor was that she did not receive a benefit from the asset she gave away, she benefited only from an asset that she had never given.

FA 1986, s.102A took effect on 8 March 1999 and effectively blocks a repeat of Lady Ingram's plan, but a kind of mirror version of the plan survives in the reversionary lease, perhaps better called the deferred lease. The property owner creates and gives away a rent-free lease, for, typically, 299 years, which does not take effect until (usually) 20 years after creation; for those 20 years the donor still owns the unencumbered freehold; but, when the lease term begins, virtually the entire value of the property has left the donor's estate.

The case of *Buzzoni* [2013] EWCA Civ 1684 confirms that a deferred lease is not a GROB, in the context of a sub-lease given away out of an existing leasehold. However, beware the facts in the similar case of *Hood* [2018] EWCA Civ 2405 where the sub-lessee agreed to pay the rent under the donor's head lease and the donor was held to have reserved a benefit.

4.5.5 Other ways of making gifts outside GROB

- A gift of a part share of a home shared by donor and donee (FA 1986, s.102B(4)). The property does not have to be the donee's main home (for capital gains tax (CGT), say) but the donee must genuinely share occupation. The donee must not pay more than their fair share of outgoings on the home, because this would be allowing something to be returned to the donor from their gift and so make the gift a GROB.
- A gift of a part share of land or buildings not occupied by the donor (FA 1986, s.102B(3)). This appears to include property that is let out, so, for example, a donor could keep more than their proportionate share of rent following a gift of a part share of an investment property.
- For land, buildings and chattels, payment of a market rent by the donee. This can be a gift either of a whole property, or of a part share. The rent must be regularly reviewed (at least every three years it is suggested) and actually paid. The recipient will have taxable income as a result.

4.5.6 Liabilities owed to recipients of gifts

This provision, in FA 1986, s.103, was introduced at the same time as the GROB rules, to prevent a deduction on death of a liability owed to someone to whom the deceased had previously made gifts. Clearly the objective was to prevent individuals claiming a reduction in IHT when all they had done was made a gift and then borrowed back some or all of the subject matter of the gift. However, it also extends the disallowed liabilities to those owed to anyone who has assets of any kind derived from a gift by the deceased.

The case of *Phizackerley* [2007] STC (SCD) 328 demonstrates the wide ambit of FA 1986, s.103. As was common in the days before the transferable nil rate band (TNRB) was available, a married couple each had wills including discretionary trust gifts of the maximum that could be given away on the first death without IHT. The wife died first and her executors accepted from the surviving husband a promise to repay the £150,000 value of the gift in return for all of the wife's assets being transferred to him. The Special Commissioners agreed with HMRC that FA 1996, s.103 disallowed deduction of the £150,000 from the husband's estate on his death. This was because the husband had previously provided all the funds for the joint purchase of their home, so that the wife's executors owned assets deriving from a gift by the husband to the wife.

4.5.7 Excluded property and GROBs

The estate of an individual who is not domiciled in the UK is 'excluded property', and so outside any charge to IHT, to the extent the assets comprising the estate are outside the UK (IHTA 1984, s.6(1)).

Similarly, non-UK assets of a trust settled by a non-UK domiciled individual are excluded property, even if the individual has subsequently become UK domiciled or deemed domiciled (IHTA 1984, s.48(3)). So only UK assets are within the scope of IHT. This means that the settlor of an excluded property trust can remain a beneficiary of the trust without being taxed as if they had made a GROB. HMRC accepts that the rules on excluded property trump the GROB rules.

For some non-UK domiciled settlors, there was a fundamental change from 6 April 2017. For many years it was common for non-UK domiciliaries to own assets in the UK through shares in a non-UK company that owned the UK assets. The shares in the non-UK company were non-UK assets and so (until 2017) excluded from the scope of IHT. Usually those shares were owned by a trust settled by the individual while he was non-UK domiciled, because the exclusion from IHT could then continue even if the individual became UK domiciled.

From 6 April 2017, where the value of shares in a close company, or similar vehicle, is attributable to the value of UK residential property, that value is no longer excluded property. If the settlor of a trust with these shares remains a beneficiary they fall squarely within the GROB rules, and so the value of the residential property falls into IHT.

The trust will often also be within the IHT relevant property regime. This means that there are 10-yearly and exit charges as well as charges on transfers of value by the settlor. There is no relief from this double IHT charge for a trust in which the settlor has reserved a benefit.

4.5.8 Relief for double IHT charges

Regulations made in 1987 (Inheritance Tax (Double Charges Relief) Regulations 1987, SI 1987/1130) relieve some of the problems given by the application of the GROB rules. Broadly speaking, they provide that, in certain circumstances where there might be a double charge, only the charge that gives HMRC the higher amount of tax applies and the other is disapplied.

The rules most commonly apply where an individual has made a GROB within seven years of death, so that both the gift itself and deemed ownership of the asset at death are liable to IHT.

Relief from double charges can also apply:

- where a GROB made within seven years of death also ends within the seven years before death;
- where assets which were the subject of a GROB are given back to the donor so that they are taxable as actually in his estate at death, as well as on the occasion of the GROB; and
- where FA 1996, s.103 disallows deduction of a liability but a transfer of value was made by the deceased in the seven years before death to the person to whom the liability is owed.

As already noted, however, where a settlor has reserved a benefit in a trust they have created, there is no relief from the fact that the trust assets are treated as owned by the settlor, because of the GROB, and are also relevant property and suffer 10-yearly and exit charges.

4.6 PRE-OWNED ASSETS TAX (POAT) CHARGE

4.6.1 History

The income tax charge on benefits received by a former owner of assets (usually called pre-owned assets tax, or POAT) was introduced by Finance Act (FA) 2004, s.84 and Sched.15 specifically to counter certain IHT saving schemes not caught by the GROB rules:

- the 'Ingram scheme' (see *Ingram* at **4.5.4**) – reserving a rent-free lease and giving away the freehold;
- the 'Eversden scheme' – exploiting the exemption for inter-spouse gifts;
- the 'reversionary' or 'deferred lease scheme' – keeping the freehold but giving away a long rent-free lease to take effect on a fixed date in the future;
- the 'double trust scheme' (sometimes known as the 'lifetime debt scheme') – a property owner sold their home to an interest in possession trust for their own benefit, leaving the purchase price outstanding as a loan and then gave away the benefit of the loan, usually to a trust for their children and grandchildren.

Amendments to the GROB legislation brought most versions of the Ingram and Eversden schemes into the GROB rules from March 1999 and June 2003, respectively, but did not affect those schemes put in place before these dates.

4.6.2 POAT – took effect 6 April 2005

POAT is an income tax charge on all of these arrangements (including pre-1999 Ingram and pre-2003 Eversden schemes).

There are separate but similar charges on:

- land and buildings;
- chattels;
- intangible assets.

In broad terms, POAT taxes *enjoyment* of an asset, where IHT taxes *ownership*. The POAT legislation is partly modelled on the income tax rules that charge income tax on loans made to employees at concessionary rates of interest.

4.6.3 POAT on land and buildings

If an individual has given land away, or contributed to its purchase, they may have a POAT charge as a result of occupying the land. In some circumstances, POAT can even apply where there was a previous sale; for example a family equity release arrangement is caught, even if on fully commercial terms.

Where POAT applies, the right to occupy land is treated as a taxable benefit. The taxable benefit is calculated by reference to rental value, and may be apportioned where the taxpayer's earlier gift/sale/contribution represents only part of the total value of the land.

The taxable benefit is also reduced if the taxpayer pays a rent – to nil if it is a full market rent, and proportionately, to the extent the rent is below market value.

For arrangements already in place when POAT came into effect on 6 April 2005, the relevant valuation date both for rents and apportioning values was 5 April 2005. In later years it is 6 April of the tax year when the relevant arrangements come into effect. There is then a revaluation every five years.

4.6.4 POAT on chattels

The rules are very similar to those for land, except that POAT applies where the taxpayer 'is in possession of, or has the use of, a chattel'.

Rather than applying to a rental value the charge is linked to the official rate of interest (currently 2.5 per cent) applied to the capital value of the chattel(s). This is the same rate of interest used to tax beneficial loans to employees.

4.6.5 When POAT does not apply to land and chattels

There is no POAT to pay in the following cases:

- Where the land or chattels (or assets representing some or all of the value of the land or chattels) are within the taxpayer's IHT estate, whether as a result of:

  (a) outright ownership;
  (b) an 'old-style' interest in possession; or
  (c) reservation of benefit.

- Where the earlier transfer was a variation within IHTA 1984, s.142.
- Where the earlier transfer was a gift of a part share of a property within the exclusion in FA 1986, s.102B(4).
- Where there would have been a reservation of benefit, but there is not, because the taxpayer pays a full market rent – a useful exception in the case of chattels, where rents are not common, but are thought to be significantly less than the 2.5 per cent official rate of interest.
- Where the earlier transfer was to the taxpayer's spouse (or, by court order, to a former spouse).
- Where the land or chattel was bought with an outright gift of cash made more than seven years before the taxpayer's occupation or enjoyment.

In the case of land, there is no POAT charge on land which the taxpayer does not personally occupy (for example, property which the taxpayer lets out commercially).

There is an exemption from POAT if a taxpayer's taxable benefit is no more than £5,000 in any tax year.

4.6.6 POAT on intangible property

The rules on POAT on intangible property are different from those for land and chattels. Instead of being linked to actual enjoyment of the asset, they (broadly) follow the income tax rules on settlor interested trusts.

Most of the same exclusions apply as for land and buildings, but note there is no exclusion from POAT on intangibles for a gift to a spouse, transfer to a former spouse or gift of cash more than seven years before.

As under the chattels rules, tax is payable on a deemed benefit equivalent to the official rate of interest (currently 2.5 per cent) on the value of the assets.

The rules most often come into operation where land or chattels previously within POAT are sold and the proceeds reinvested.

Where POAT applies to intangibles, the rules can be very unfair, and it is best to take action to avoid them.

4.6.7 Opting in to IHT

POAT probably raises very little money for HMRC. It appears that it was not designed as a tax intended to raise money, but aimed to discourage people from planning to reduce IHT.

So the legislation includes a specific power to allow taxpayers to escape POAT by opting back in to IHT. An election under FA 2004, Sched.15, para.21 has the effect that the assets concerned are treated as if there was a reservation of benefit, even though, under IHT rules, there is not.

It is still an open question whether a para.21 election over a double trust scheme has the result HMRC wants. This is likely to be ruled on by the courts and it is understood that a case on this has been heard by the First-tier Tribunal.

Depending on the age and circumstances of the taxpayers, paying POAT may nevertheless be significantly cheaper than opting in to IHT. It does not, for example, 'put the clock back', and opting in to IHT may give rise to a double tax charge as CGT 'uplift' on death, or main residence exemption, may still be lost.

4.7 GAAR, DOTAS AND INHERITANCE TAX

4.7.1 GAAR

GAAR is the general anti-abuse rule introduced with effect from 17 July 2013. The rule is designed to counteract tax advantages arising from abusive tax arrangements.

Arrangements are 'abusive' if they 'cannot reasonably be regarded as a reasonable course of action in relation to the relevant tax provisions' (often referred to as the 'double reasonableness test') (FA 2013, s.207). If, however, the tax arrangements accord with established practice, and HMRC has indicated its acceptance of that practice, this will usually indicate that the arrangements are not abusive.

The result of GAAR being applied to IHT is not at all clear, because the usual consequence of a transaction being caught by GAAR is that it is reversed. If an IHT transfer of value is reversed, that will usually mean there is no transfer of value and no IHT.

It is hard to imagine cases where GAAR will bite on IHT planning. It seems to be a rule designed to frighten taxpayers away from planning rather than to place an effective barrier in their way.

In April 2013, with the help of an advisory committee, HMRC published guidance notes on GAAR which include a number of examples relating to IHT. These guidance notes are updated from time to time (see **www.gov.uk/government/publications/tax-avoidance-general-anti-abuse-rules**). Many of these examples have been superseded by other legislative changes, including some of the other anti-avoidance provisions considered in this chapter.

The author considers that most mainstream IHT planning, and all of the IHT planning suggested in this book, is outside the scope of GAAR.

4.7.2 DOTAS

The disclosure of tax avoidance schemes, or DOTAS, legislation requires 'promoters' of schemes to which it applies to make appropriate returns to HMRC, which must be referenced in tax returns made by taxpayers concerned.

When it was first introduced in 2004, DOTAS did not apply to IHT. An extension of the rules in 2011 applied the DOTAS rules to IHT for the first time, but only on transfers into trust where arrangements were entered into to reduce the lifetime IHT entry charge on the transfer to the trust. Even then, an exception was made for arrangements which were the same, or substantially the same, as arrangements first made available for implementation before 6 April 2011.

A small extension was made in 2016, but the major change came with the implementation of the Inheritance Tax Avoidance Schemes (Prescribed Descriptions of Arrangements) Regulations 2017, SI 2017/1172, which took effect from 1 April 2018. These apply DOTAS to arrangements which *both*:

(a) enable one or more of the following IHT advantages:

  (i) avoiding or reducing the entry charge on a lifetime transfer to a trust;
  (ii) avoiding or reducing 10-yearly or exit charges on trusts or the charge on participators in close companies;
  (iii) avoiding or reducing IHT charges resulting from the application of the GROB rules where there is also no POAT charge;
  (iv) reducing the value of someone's IHT estate without there being a chargeable transfer or PET,

and:

(b) involve one or more contrived or abnormal steps, without which the IHT advantage would not be obtained.

Both of these conditions need to be considered from the perspective of 'an informed observer' who has studied the arrangements and had regard to all relevant circumstances.

This time there is an exception for arrangements which are substantially the same as 'related arrangements'. Related arrangements are arrangements entered into before 1 April 2018 of which HMRC had indicated its acceptance. This is clearly narrower than the 2011 exception, but it is not altogether clear how much narrower.

HMRC published guidance notes on the 2017 regulations only a few days before they came into force on 1 April 2018. Unfortunately, these do not go far beyond the obvious. For example, gifts both in lifetime and on death to take advantage of the spouse exemption, regular gifts out of income and making disclaimers are all confirmed to be outside DOTAS. It would be very surprising if they were not.

There is also confirmation that a gift of land where the donor continues to occupy in return for full consideration is in order, as is a gift of a part share in land which both donor and donee occupy. However, for a gift of a part share, HMRC's guidance note suggests: 'The analysis might be different where the donor only retained a very small proportion of the property in comparison to their level of occupation.'

As with GAAR it is unlikely that many readers of this book will need to be too concerned with DOTAS, although HMRC's guidance identifies three circumstances where it expects a notification:

1. A gift of shares qualifying for business relief into a trust which are then sold back to the settlor, so allowing the settlor, effectively, to settle cash without an IHT entry charge.
2. The creation of a reversionary lease in circumstances where POAT is not payable; this appears to be limited to (a) a reversionary lease created over let property and (b) a reversionary lease where POAT would not be payable because the taxable amount fell below the £5,000 per annum de minimis level.
3. Certain uses of employee trusts.

See also **14.3** regarding DOTAS and deeds of variation.

CHAPTER 5

Forms of trust for inheritance tax purposes

Vicky Day

5.1 KEY POINTS

- In this chapter, the terms 'trust' and 'settlement' are used interchangeably. The word 'trust' is used more commonly in texts, general usage, precedents and in HM Revenue and Customs (HMRC) guidance, but the word 'settlement' is used in the Inheritance Tax Act (IHTA) 1984. Different types of trust have different inheritance tax (IHT) treatment and sometimes the same type of interest has different IHT treatment depending on whether it was created in the taxpayer's lifetime or on their death.
- There were major changes in 2006 and different IHT charges can apply to the same type of interest depending on whether it was created before or on or after 22 March 2006 (the date of the budget when the changes were announced). In this chapter, references to pre-2006 and post-2006 mean pre- and post-22 March 2006 respectively.
- The sections of IHTA 1984 relating to settlements are mainly found in Part III (ss.43–93).
- This chapter:
  - discusses what constitutes a settlement for IHT purposes;
  - sets out the different types of trust that can be created – first categorised by type of trust (i.e. by the underlying beneficial interest) and then categorised by their IHT treatment and whether they are created in lifetime or on death; then
  - discusses the treatment of trusts still in existence but created before 22 March 2006 ('pre-2006 trusts'); and
  - finishes with the treatment of disabled person's trusts (DPTs).

5.2 WHAT IS A SETTLEMENT FOR INHERITANCE TAX PURPOSES?

A settlement is created when property is given away by a person (settlor), not outright to an individual, but to persons (trustees) to hold for the benefit of others (beneficiaries). The term 'settlement' is defined in IHTA 1984, s.43(2). A settlement can be created by a written document, by word or by operation of law (for example on intestacy). The term includes:

- trusts for named beneficiaries with successive interests, for example to A for A's lifetime, then to B (interest in possession trust);
- trusts held for a number of beneficiaries or classes of beneficiaries at the discretion of the trustees (discretionary trust);
- property given to one individual but charged with regular payments out for the benefit of another individual in that other's lifetime; and
- arrangements made outside the UK which are equivalent to or would be settlements if made in the UK.

The settlor is the person who has made the settlement whether directly or indirectly. The definition is very wide and includes anyone who has provided funds for the purpose of the settlement, or in connection with the settlement, or has made a reciprocal arrangement with another person to make the settlement. So:

- If A gives money to B to set up a trust for C, A is the settlor.
- If A excuses B from repaying B's debt to A, so that B can set up a trust for C with that money, A is the settlor.
- If A agrees to set up a trust for B's children in return for B setting up a trust for A's children, A is the settlor of the trust for A's children.

If there is more than one settlor of a settlement, for IHT purposes each settlor is treated as having created their own settlement.

For example, if A and B each pay £200,000 into a settlement, for IHT purposes there are two separate settlements with an initial value of £200,000, not one settlement of £400,000.

5.3 CATEGORIES OF TRUST BY BENEFICIAL INTEREST

Trusts can be categorised by the type of interest the beneficiaries have. They may have an entitlement to the income, or the capital, or both. Their interest may be vested, i.e. they are currently entitled to it; or contingent, i.e. they are entitled to it only once some condition is fulfilled. Or, their interest may be discretionary, i.e. they are a potential beneficiary with no more than the right to be considered by the trustees.

5.3.1 Bare trust

A bare trust usually has one beneficiary who is entitled to both the income and the capital. Multiple beneficiaries will be entitled to an equal share of the income and capital. Bare trusts are commonly used where a beneficiary is a minor or under some form of disability. Effectively, the trustees are nominees.

5.3.2 Interest in possession trust

There is an interest in possession (IIP) trust where a beneficiary has an entitlement to the income from the trust (or the right of occupation of a trust property or the right to use a trust asset). A beneficiary of an IIP trust is generally known as a 'life tenant' although the interest may not necessarily be for the whole of their life.

Common examples are where a trust has an investment portfolio and the interest and dividends generated in the portfolio are payable to the life tenant. Or the trust holds a property and the life tenant has the right to occupy the trust property for their lifetime. An interest in possession can be for life or limited to a specific date or a specific age of the life tenant; or it may end on a specific contingency, for example on the beneficiary remarrying.

The interests in the trust that follow the IIP do not have to be fixed. They can be variable at the discretion of the trustees. And sometimes trustees are given the right to vary or end the IIP beneficiary's interest. There is still an IIP trust while that interest lasts.

NB: A beneficiary of a bare trust also has an interest in possession of both the income and the capital, but in common usage, where people refer to an interest in possession trust, they are referring to a trust where a beneficiary has an entitlement to the income only.

5.3.3 Discretionary trust

Some trusts are created for the benefit of a number of beneficiaries or a class of beneficiaries at the discretion of the trustees. These trusts can now exist for up to 125 years and are usually created for the long term, for example to benefit several generations of the same family.

The beneficiaries may be referred to by name or by class, for example 'for my children and their descendants'. None of the beneficiaries has any entitlement to the income or capital of the trust and the trustees have wide discretionary powers to decide which of the beneficiaries receive income and/or capital, in what amounts and when. The trustees are usually guided by a detailed letter of wishes written by the settlor but they are not bound by it.

5.4 CATEGORIES OF TRUST BY IHT TREATMENT

How a trust is taxed to IHT depends on:

- the type of trust;
- whether it is created on death or during lifetime;
- whether it is a pre-2006 trust or not;
- the relationship between the settlor and the beneficiary; and
- whether a beneficiary of the trust is a disabled person.

The types of trust (categorised by how they are taxed for IHT) are as follows.

5.4.1 Bare trust

A bare trust (see **5.3.1**) can be created during lifetime or on death. It is important to avoid any contingency, such as surviving to the age of 18, to be a bare trust.

5.4.2 Qualifying interest in possession (QIIP) trust

A qualifying interest in possession (QIIP) is an interest in possession trust (see **5.3.2**) that can be created either during lifetime (but, post-2006, only for the benefit of a disabled person) or on death (for the benefit of any person). When created on death, the trust is known as an immediate post-death interest (IPDI). Some trusts that were in existence pre-2006 continue to be taxed as QIIPs. These are pre-2006 interest in possession trusts, transitional serial interests (TSIs) and DPTs.

5.4.3 Relevant property trust (RPT)

Relevant property trusts (RPTs) were, prior to 2006, usually full discretionary trusts. They can be created during lifetime or on death. Lifetime trusts created post-2006 giving a beneficiary an interest in possession are also taxed as RPTs. Former accumulation and maintenance trusts, where the beneficiaries did not become entitled outright to capital at 25 (for example, they received a right to the income at 25 but not the capital) are also taxed as RPTs.

An RPT is the default form of trust; most new lifetime trusts and many will trusts, that do not comply with other requirements, will be RPTs. So while all discretionary trusts will be RPTs, many RPTs will not be discretionary; for example a life interest will trust that does not meet all the tests for an IPDI will be an RPT.

5.4.4 Bereaved minor's trust (IHTA 1984, s.71A)

Bereaved minor's trusts (BMTs) are created by will, for the benefit of a child of the deceased, or on intestacy (and include trusts created under some compensation schemes). A trust is a BMT if the bereaved minor is or becomes entitled to both capital and income at 18 years of age and the trust income or capital cannot be applied for any other person (other than £3,000 a year). The statutory trusts for a minor which arise on the death of their parent who dies intestate are also BMTs. The bereaved minor must be under 18 and the deceased must be their parent, step-parent or a person with parental responsibility for them (so that the one time a grandparent can set up a BMT is if they have parental responsibility).

5.4.5 Age 18-to-25 trust (IHTA 1984, s.71D)

Post-2006 age 18-to-25 (18–25) trusts can only be created by will for the benefit of a child of the deceased (and include trusts created under some compensation schemes). Some accumulation and maintenance trusts created pre-2006 are now taxed as 18–25 trusts. A trust is an 18–25 trust if the beneficiary becomes entitled to both capital and income at an age greater than 18 but no more than 25 and the trust income or capital cannot be applied for any other person (other than £3,000 a year). The deceased must be the beneficiary's parent, step-parent or a person with parental responsibility for them. So a trust created by a will for grandchildren at 25 is an RPT and not an 18–25 trust.

5.4.6 Accumulation and maintenance trust (s.71)

Since 22 March 2006, it is no longer possible to create an accumulation and maintenance (A&M) trust. Prior to that date, they were commonly created to benefit children or grandchildren because they enjoyed favoured treatment for IHT. They were a hybrid trust, which was discretionary among a class of beneficiaries (largely limited to the grandchildren of a common grandparent) until a child reached a specified age (maximum 25 years old) when the child had to receive either their share of the capital or an interest in possession in their 'share'.

Post-2006, a trust is only an A&M trust if it was in existence pre-2006; the beneficiaries will become entitled at 18; there is no interest in possession before that age and the income must be accumulated or used for the beneficiaries' benefit; and the trust has existed less than 25 years or all the beneficiaries are the grandchildren of a common grandparent.

5.4.7 Disabled person's trust

Special rules apply for trusts for the benefit of a beneficiary who qualifies as being disabled within the meaning of IHTA 1984 (see **5.12**.)

5.5 QUALIFYING INTEREST IN POSSESSION TRUSTS – WHAT ARE THEY?

The expression 'interest in possession trust' most commonly refers to a trust where a beneficiary has the right to income from the trust capital or the right to use a trust property (see **5.6**).

- An interest in possession trust is a QIIP trust only if it is:
  - an IPDI under a will;
  - a pre-2006 interest in possession trust, whether created in lifetime or under a will;
  - a TSI; or
  - a DPT.

- An IPDI. This arises where a beneficiary is given the right to income under a will or the right of occupation of a trust property. It does not need to be a right for a lifetime and can include a beneficiary who is due to inherit capital at 25 but under the will has an income entitlement from the outset.
- A pre-2006 interest in possession trust is a trust in which the interest in possession that existed on 22 March 2006 continues for the same beneficiary.
- A TSI. This is an interest in possession arising in very limited circumstances as part of the transitional provisions made when the law was changed in 2006:
  - Where there was a pre-2006 interest in possession trust with a life tenant (L/T) and L/T's interest came to an end in the period between 22 March 2006 and 5 October 2008 and another person (B) became entitled to an interest in possession in the trust property on that occasion, B's interest is a TSI.
  - Since 6 October 2008, a new TSI can arise in only one set of circumstances. That is where a life tenant (L/T) has an interest in possession in a pre-2006 interest in possession trust and L/T's spouse or civil partner becomes entitled to an interest in possession on the occasion of L/T's death. L/T's spouse's or civil partner's interest is a TSI.
- DPTs (s.89) are dealt with in more detail at **5.12**.

5.6 QUALIFYING INTEREST IN POSSESSION TRUSTS – IHT TREATMENT

The beneficiary (or life tenant) entitled to the QIIP is treated as being beneficially entitled to the capital of the property in which their interest subsists (IHTA 1984, s.49). There are no IHT charges in the trust during the lifetime of the life tenant but, on their death, the value of the assets of the QIIP trust is aggregated with the value of the life tenant's free estate for the purpose of calculating IHT. The life tenant's available nil rate band (NRB) is apportioned between their free estate and the QIIP trust and the total IHT calculated on the aggregate value. The IHT is then payable by the executors of the free estate and the trustees of the QIIP trust in the proportions which the values bear to one another.

Example 5.1

L is the life tenant of a trust set up under the will of her late mother who died in 2002. The trust asset is a property in which L lives. The property is valued at £300,000. On L's death, the property passes to her younger sister, Y. L has £400,000 of her own assets. On L's death, the value of the trust assets and her free estate are aggregated making a total of £700,000. L has her whole NRB of £325,000 available so her aggregated taxable estate (£700,000 less £325,000) is £375,000. Tax at 40% is £150,000. The trustees pay £64,290 (i.e. 42.86% of the tax or 300,000/700,000) and the executors pay £85,710 (i.e. 57.14% of the tax or 400,000/700,000). (For more detail see **Chapter 6**.)

The measure of the transfer of value when a QIIP ends during the beneficiary's lifetime is a notable exception to the rule that the value for IHT is the difference between the value of the transferor's IHT estate before and after the transfer. IHTA 1984, s.52 provides that, on this occasion, the transfer of value is only the value of the property in which the interest in possession subsisted.

Example 5.2

Suppose Mrs Evans has 25% of the shares of an investment company but also has an IPDI in another 26% of the company under her late husband's will. If, in her lifetime, she gives 2% of the shares from her personal shareholding to her children, her transfer of value is the difference between the value of a controlling 51% shareholding and a minority 49% – valuation conventions on the loss of control of a private company might mean she is deemed to give away half the value of her shares. If, on the other hand, she gives up her life interest in 2% of the shares, her transfer of value is of only the value of 2% (a very small, heavily discounted, minority).

The idea in **Example 5.2** might not be such good planning if Mrs Evans's husband died before 13 November 1974. These were the days of estate duty, when the spouse exemption worked the other way round and it was common practice to leave a spouse only an interest in possession which was free from estate duty on death. That estate duty exemption is carried forward into IHT.

5.7 RELEVANT PROPERTY TRUSTS – IHT TREATMENT

RPTs are:

- discretionary trusts;
- most post-2006 trusts created in a settlor's lifetime;
- any will trusts which do not come within the specific requirements of the other forms of trusts in wills (IPDIs, 18–25 trusts, BMTs or bare trusts); and
- former A&M trusts where the beneficiary's interest continues beyond the age of 25.

RPTs can last as long as 125 years. As the trust assets are not subject to IHT at 40 per cent in anyone's estate, they are subject to their own specialised IHT regime for 'relevant property'. The regime is complex and set out in more detail in **Chapter 7**. In essence, they are subject to 'periodic charges' on every 10th anniversary of the trust's creation and to 'exit charges' when trust assets are distributed out to a beneficiary.

5.7.1 Periodic charges (IHTA 1984, s.66)

Under the periodic charge, also known as the '10-year anniversary' (TYA) charge, the trustees are taxed at a rate of up to six per cent on the value of the assets on every 10th anniversary of the trust's creation.

The 10-year charge is based on the value of the trust assets at the date of the TYA. The value of income received more than five years before the TYA, and still held by the trustees, is included. The historic value (i.e. the value at the date of creation) of relevant property in trusts created on the same day ('related settlements') and of trusts to which 'same-day additions' have been made is aggregated as part of the calculation (see **7.2.6**). A NRB is usually available, but is reduced by the value of the settlor's chargeable transfers in the seven years before they created the trust and by the total capital paid out of the trust in the preceding 10 years. The value in excess of any available NRB is charged to IHT at six per cent. (See **7.2** for more detail.)

5.7.2 Exit charges (IHTA 1984, ss.68–69)

Exit charges are charged on the value of the assets leaving the trust. The rate of tax is based on the rate paid on the last TYA (recalculated to take into account the NRB at the date of exit) and is as many 40ths of that rate as the number of complete quarters that have passed. Often, only a minimal amount of tax is payable (although the calculation can be complex).

Where the trust property was under the available NRB on creation, it will not be liable to IHT on exit within the first 10 years. Where the rate of IHT at the last TYA was nil, there will be no exit charge in the following 10 years.

Example 5.3

In 2010, John gave an investment portfolio valued at £310,000 into a discretionary trust for his grandchildren. At the time of the gift, John had his whole NRB of £325,000 available so the chargeable transfer into trust was taxed to IHT at 0%. In 2018, the value had increased to £450,000. The trustees pay out the whole portfolio to John's granddaughter Sally. Even though the value paid out is well in excess of £325,000, the exit charge is 0%. (See **7.3** for more detail.)

5.8 BEREAVED MINOR'S TRUSTS – IHT TREATMENT

There is no IHT charge while the beneficiary is under 18, nor on the exit from the trust:

- when the bereaved minor reaches 18 and becomes absolutely entitled; or
- if they die under that age; or
- if assets are distributed to them under that age.

5.9 18–25 TRUSTS – IHT TREATMENT

There is no charge while the trust continues and no IHT charge on exit if the beneficiary receives capital at 18 or it is applied for their benefit under that age or they die under that age.

There is an exit charge if the beneficiary receives capital between the ages of 18 and 25 or dies after the age of 18. The maximum rate payable will be 4.2 per cent, representing 28/40 quarters multiplied by six per cent, and that rate builds up over the seven-year period with each quarter that passes.

The rate is often much lower than this, because a NRB is usually available. The NRB effective at the date of the exit charge is set against the value of the assets when they first went into the trust – perhaps more than 20 years before. The calculation involves applying a six per cent charge to the original value of the assets, to the extent they exceed the present NRB, and calculating the overall rate on the total (the 'settlement rate'). The 'settlement rate' is then multiplied by the 'relevant fraction' which is as many 40ths as the number of quarters that have elapsed from the date the beneficiary turned 18 to the date of the exit. A quarter is three months.

So, once three months have passed from the beneficiary's 18th birthday (or, if later, the date of the parent's death when the beneficiary's interest in the trust first arose) the rate is at 1/40th of the settlement rate; after six months it is 2/40ths; and so on, reaching a maximum 28/40ths on the beneficiary's 25th birthday.

As with the 10-year and exit charges on relevant property trusts the NRB brought into the calculation is reduced by the value of the settlor's chargeable transfers in the seven years before they created the trust and, in calculating the settlement rate, the historic value of other 18–25 trusts (but not, apparently, RPTs) created by the same settlor on the same day must be aggregated.

5.10 ACCUMULATION AND MAINTENANCE SETTLEMENT – IHT TREATMENT

A pre-2006 A&M trust will have become an 18–25 trust or a relevant property trust on 6 April 2008 (and sometimes earlier) unless the beneficiary was to become absolutely entitled at 18.

There is no IHT charge on assets leaving a pre-2006 A&M trust still in existence when the beneficiary reaches 18 and becomes absolutely entitled or if they die under that age or if assets or income are distributed to them under that age.

5.11 REVERTER TO SETTLOR TRUSTS

There is a reverter to settlor trust where, pre-2006, a settlor created a life interest trust and, on the ending of that life interest, the capital reverts back to the settlor. The IHT treatment described in this section can only apply to a post-2006 trust if the life tenant is a disabled beneficiary. In all other circumstances, a trust with these provisions would now be a RPT and the settlor would be treated as having reserved a benefit.

However, existing reverter to settlor trusts where, during the lifetime of the life tenant, the trust is taxed as a QIIP, have a specific IHT treatment. On the life tenant's death, the capital value of the trust is not aggregated with the life tenant's free estate and there is no IHT charge on it. The same treatment applies if the trust assets revert to the settlor's spouse or civil partner (or the settlor's widow, widower or former civil partner within the two years after the settlor's death).

For capital gains tax (CGT) purposes, there is no deemed uplift to market value on reversion to the settlor and the settlor's acquisition value for CGT will be the market value at the date the assets were transferred into the trust. Where the life tenant has few or no other assets, this may waste their available NRB and trustees may need to consider the position and take action prior to the death of the life tenant to achieve the most tax-efficient outcome for the settlor (as beneficiary).

5.12 DISABLED PERSON'S TRUSTS (TREATED AS IF THEY WERE QIIPS)

Lifetime trusts set up with specific provisions for the benefit of a disabled person have a special treatment for IHT and are taxed in the same way as pre-2006 interest in possession trusts, i.e. the transfer into trust is a PET and the underlying capital value of the trust assets is treated as being in the disabled person's estate for IHT purposes.

5.12.1 Meaning of disabled

A 'disabled person' is defined (Finance Act (FA) 2005, Sched.1A) as a person who is, at the date of the transfer into the trust, one of the following:

- incapable by reason of mental disorder of administering their property or managing their affairs;
- in receipt of attendance allowance;
- in receipt of disability living allowance by virtue of entitlement to the care component at the highest or middle rate;
- in receipt of personal independence payment by virtue of entitlement to the daily living component;
- in receipt of constant attendance allowance;
- in receipt of armed forces independence payment; or
- in receipt of increased disablement pension.

5.12.2 Types of disabled person's trust

There are four types of DPT:

1. **Section 89 trust.** Commonly described by reference to IHTA 1984, s.89, this is effectively a discretionary trust for the benefit of the disabled person. The terms of the trust must be that there is no interest in possession in the trust and the terms must secure that if any of the income or capital is applied for the benefit of a beneficiary while the disabled person is alive, it is applied for the benefit of that disabled person. A limited amount, of up to £3,000 (or three per cent of the trust property if lower) can be applied each tax year for the benefit of a beneficiary other than the disabled person.

   The great value of a s.89 trust is that the discretionary trust structure stops the income being taken into account, for means-tested benefits, but the simpler tax treatment of a QIIP usually works well for IHT. There are also some CGT advantages, and in many cases the disabled person will not have assets to use their own NRB on their death, as this trust can do.
2. **Section 89A trust.** Under IHTA 1984, s.89A, this is a self-settled trust by a person (A) who has a condition (at the time of transfer into the trust) that it is reasonable to expect will cause A to become a disabled person within the meaning set out above. The terms of the trust must be that, while A is alive, there is no interest in possession in the trust and must secure that if any of the income or capital is applied for the benefit of a beneficiary while A is alive, it is applied for A's benefit. The terms of the trust must also secure that if the trust is brought to an end in A's lifetime, either A or another beneficiary will be absolutely entitled to the trust property or it will continue as a s.89 trust or as a post-2006 interest in possession trust for a disabled person, i.e. continue as another disabled person's trust.
3. **A post-2006 interest in possession trust for a disabled person** which secures that while the disabled person is alive, only they can benefit from the trust.
4. **A post-2006 self-settled trust** by a person (A) who has a condition (at the time of transfer into the trust) that it is reasonable to expect will cause A to become a disabled person within the meaning set out above. The terms of the trust must secure that while A is alive, only A can benefit from the trust.

The rules about DPTs have changed over the years and careful attention needs to be given to DPTs created before 2013 (and particularly before 1981 as the taxation of pre-1981 trusts is significantly different). The details of the taxation of these trusts which are still in existence is beyond the scope of this handbook.

5.13 CLASSIFICATION OF TRUSTS BY IHT TREATMENT – A SUMMARY

- **Lifetime trusts created after 22 March 2006:**
  - discretionary trust – RPT;
  - life interest trust – RPT;

- discretionary trust for disabled person – DPT;
- life interest trust for a disabled person – DPT.

- **Trusts created on death after 22 March 2006:**
  - discretionary trust – RPT;
  - life interest trust (IPDI) – QIIP;
  - trust for child of deceased person where child's interest ends by 25th birthday – 18–25 trust;
  - trust for child of deceased person where child's interest ends by 18th birthday – BMT;
  - interest in possession trust for a disabled person – DPT;
  - discretionary trust for a disabled person – DPT.

- **Trusts created before 22 March 2006 still in existence:**
  - discretionary trust – RPT;
  - life interest trust, where the life interest in place on 22 March 2006 continues – QIIP;
  - TSI; there must have been a life interest in place on 22 March 2006; the present interest is a TSI only if, on the ending of the life interest in place on 22 March 2006, either another life interest came into existence before October 2008 or that earlier life interest ended on the original beneficiary's death and that beneficiary's spouse then became entitled to a life interest – QIIP;
  - former A&M trust where beneficiary's interest ends by 25th birthday – 18–25 trust;
  - former A&M trust where beneficiary's interest continues in trust beyond 25th birthday – RPT;
  - discretionary trust for a disabled person – DPT;
  - interest in possession trust for a disabled person – DPT.

CHAPTER 6

Aggregable trusts

Tanya Wadeson and John Bunker

6.1 KEY POINTS

This chapter will cover:

- What is an aggregable trust, and how they work, with examples.
- The inheritance tax (IHT) effect of terminating an aggregable trust, in whole or part, with an example.

6.2 WHAT IS AGGREGABLE

When a trust is a qualifying interest in possession (QIIP) trust, the assets are aggregated with the life tenant's personal estate to determine the value chargeable for IHT purposes on their death (see **Chapter 5**).

As the trust is aggregated with the life tenant's estate for IHT purposes, these trusts are not subject to 10-year charges or exit charges (as for relevant property trusts).

If the life interest trust is wound up, or the life interest is terminated in part, prior to the death of the life tenant then these are treated as potentially exempt transfers (PETs) by the life tenant and there is no IHT reporting requirement. These might take the form of capital payments being made by the trustees, during the life tenant's lifetime, using an overriding power of appointment. If capital payments are made to the life tenant, that has no effect for IHT as these are still taxable for IHT with the life tenant's estate.

6.3 HOW AGGREGABLE TRUSTS WORK

When the life tenant dies, the market value of the capital element of the trust must be ascertained. This is then reported to HM Revenue and Customs (HMRC) on the deceased's form IHT400 (application for probate or confirmation if there's IHT to pay, or if the deceased's estate does not qualify as an 'excepted estate') and a form IHT100 (reporting chargeable events when IHT is payable on a trust or gift) is completed by the trustees.

If the beneficiary is only entitled to a proportion of the trust income, then it is only the proportion to which they are entitled that is aggregated with their estate.

The assets in the trust are added to the life tenant's free estate with any nil rate band (NRB), transferable nil rate band (TNRB) or residence nil rate band (RNRB) deducted from the total. In practice this means that these NRBs are shared in proportion to the respective values of the aggregable trust and the free estate. Once the available NRBs have been deducted, the death rate (see **Example 6.1**) is applied to the net value. The IHT payable is then apportioned between the free estate and the aggregated trust.

Example 6.1

Jack died in 2019/20 leaving his free estate valued for probate purposes at £400,000. He was also entitled to the income from a qualifying life interest trust which was valued for IHT purposes at £250,000. He had a full NRB.

	£	£
Free estate	400,000	
QIIP (life interest trust)	250,000	
Total chargeable estate	650,000	
Less NRB	(325,000)	
Net chargeable estate	325,000	
IHT at 40% (death rate)		130,000
Apportioned as follows:		
Free estate (130,000/ 650,000x400,000)		80,000
QIIP trust (130,000/ 650,000x250,000)		50,000
		130,000

You can see from **Example 6.1** that trustees must determine the value of the free estate (and the personal representatives of the estate the value of the trust) before any distributions are made. In this case, the value of the trust is below the NRB but is still liable to IHT of £50,000. It is therefore essential that the trustees and personal representatives, or their respective professional agents, liaise closely over both the initial values and any changes that will affect the final total IHT on the combined estate and trust.

If the trust or free estate holds a property, or other assets qualifying for payment of IHT by instalments, then the IHT is also apportioned between instalment option and non-instalment option property.

Example 6.2

Following on from the example above, say Jack's free estate held a property valued at £175,000 with the balance of £225,000 being held in cash and investments and the qualifying life interest trust held a property valued at £100,000 with the balance of the trust assets being held in cash and investments. The calculation would be as follows:

	£	£
Free estate – property	175,000	
Free estate – cash and investments	225,000	
QIIP trust – property	100,000	
QIIP trust – cash and investments	150,000	
Total chargeable estate	650,000	
Less NRB	(325,000)	
Net chargeable estate	325,000	
IHT at 40%		130,000
Apportioned as follows:		
Free estate – instalment option (130,000/ 650,000x175,000)		35,000
Free estate – non-instalment option (130,000/ 650,000x225,000)		45,000
QIIP trust instalment option (130,000/ 650,000x100,000)		20,000
QIIP trust non-instalment option (130,000/ 650,000x150,000)		30,000
		130,000

If the life tenant was living, or had previously lived, in the trust property, and the property is passing to a direct descendant, then the estate may have the benefit of the RNRB (see **Chapter 16**). The RNRB is claimed by the executors of the estate even where the property to which to the RNRB applies is held by the trustees of the life interest trust. If there are two residential properties, which had both been residences of the life tenant, then the choice as to which is the qualifying residential interest

(QRI) for RNRB is solely for the personal representatives and the trustees have no formal say in the choice. The personal representatives will always be wise to choose the more valuable.

The choice of property makes no difference to the benefit that the free estate and the QIIP trust obtain from RNRB. IHT is apportioned between the free estate and the QIIP trust in exactly the same way. Therefore there may still be IHT to pay on a property which is valued at the same amount as the available RNRB.

Example 6.3

	£	£
Free estate (with £200,000 property left to children)		400,000
QIIP (life interest trust)		250,000
Total chargeable estate		650,000
Less NRB	(325,000)	
RNRB (£175,000 in 2020/21)	(175,000)	
	(500,000)	
		(500,000)
Net chargeable estate		150,000
IHT at 40% (death rate)		60,000
Apportioned as follows:		
Free estate (60,000/ 650,000x400,000)		36,923.08
QIIP trust (60,000/ 650,000x250,000)		23,076.92
		50,000.00

The deadline for the submission of the IHT100 forms to report the aggregable trust is 12 months from the end of the month in which the life tenant died; however, the tax is due to be paid six months from the end of the month in which the life tenant died. Therefore, it is important to establish contact with the executors at the earliest opportunity.

6.4 TERMINATING AN AGGREGABLE TRUST, IN WHOLE OR PART

Where a QIIP trust is ended during the lifetime of the life tenant this is treated as a PET by the life tenant. This could be in part or in full.

If the life tenant dies within seven years of the PET then there could be a charge to IHT and as this utilises the NRB before the free estate this could inadvertently load the IHT charge on the free estate. **Example 6.4** shows the effect of £100,000 worth of assets in the QIIP being distributed to the residuary beneficiary a year before the death of the life tenant. (This assumes that the lifetime annual exemptions have been used elsewhere.)

Example 6.4

	£	£
Free estate – property		175,000
Free estate – cash and investments		225,000
QIIP trust – cash and investments at death		150,000
Total chargeable estate		550,000
Less NRB	(325,000)	
Less partial lifetime termination of QIIP	100,000	
		(225,000)
Net chargeable estate		325,000
IHT at 40%		130,000
Apportioned as follows:		
Free estate – instalment option (130,000/ 550,000x175,000)		41,363
Free estate – non-instalment option (130,000/ 550,000x225,000)		53,182
QIIP trust non-instalment option (130,000/ 550,000x150,000)		35,455
		130,000

You will see there is an increase in the IHT payable by the estate and the amount due to be paid by the trustees has reduced due to the allocation of the NRB.

Note also the rules which can reduce the value of a lifetime transfer of value when that is on the occasion of ending a QIIP (see **5.4.2**).

CHAPTER 7

Relevant property trust (RPT) regime

Tanya Wadeson

7.1 KEY POINTS

This chapter covers:

- An introduction to the inheritance tax (IHT) treatment of relevant property trusts (RPTs), with the 10-year charges (periodic charges) and exit charges (proportionate charges) and examples.
- A brief introduction to the complex issue of 'grossing up'. This being a planning handbook, rather than an IHT textbook, this is a very brief comment to help understanding in this context.

7.2 10-YEAR CHARGES (PERIODIC CHARGES)

7.2.1 Basic rules

An RPT is revalued at each 10-year anniversary (TYA) and a maximum IHT charge of six per cent of the value is levied. The 10-year charge is sometimes called a periodic charge. In this chapter we look at the basic calculation together with the various traps of which you need to be aware.

The starting point for the trustees is to obtain an open market valuation of the trust assets on the day before the TYA. The trustees will also need to determine any outstanding capital liabilities at this date, which are deductible from the assets for IHT purposes, such as an outstanding capital gains tax (CGT) liability. Any allowable claims for business property relief (BPR) or agricultural property relief (APR) can be deducted at this stage. Therefore, if the sole asset is a shareholding in an unquoted company with 100 per cent BPR, the 10-year charge is nil.

Where the trust holds an interest in land or buildings, the element of the IHT attributed to that can be paid by the instalment option over 10 years. Interest is paid if the trustees elect to pay by instalment option but it may be their only choice if there are insufficient liquid assets and they do not wish to dispose of the property.

The instalment option is also available for IHT on most forms of business and agricultural property, where 100 per cent relief is not available; for most unincorporated businesses there is no interest provided the instalments are paid on time.

The legislation (Inheritance Tax Act (IHTA) 1984, s.66) bases the rate of tax on a notional lifetime chargeable transfer by a notional transferor and directs one to take 3/10ths of the effective rate of tax that would be payable.

When the rules were first put in place in the early 1980s there would have been a number of different rates. Since 1989 the rate of IHT on a lifetime chargeable transfer is always 20 per cent and 3/10ths of this is always six per cent. The rules would be much less confusing if they referred to six per cent.

The notional transfer will, in most cases, have some nil rate band (NRB) available, which brings the actual rate of tax below six per cent.

Example 7.1

	£
Market value of assets less capital liabilities	500,000
Less current NRB	(325,000)
Net value	175,000
IHT at lifetime rate – 20% of the net value	35,000
Effective rate (35,000/500,000)	7%
IHT due = 500,000 x 7% x 3/10	£10,500

This is equivalent to 6% of £175,000 or an overall 2.1% tax rate.

7.2.2 Undistributed income

Until 6 April 2014, the 10-year charge was on capital of the trust only. From that date, the trustees are obliged to add to the amount liable to IHT any income that has been held by the trustees for at least five years, without being formally accumulated with capital or distributed.

As will be seen in **7.2.7**, any assets which are not relevant property for the full 10-year period can have the charge reduced in proportion to the number of complete quarters which had expired before the assets became relevant property. Therefore, alert trustees can significantly reduce this charge by accumulating undistributed income with capital shortly before a TYA.

7.2.3 More than one settlor?

One point to watch out for is where a different person from the original settlor pays something into the trust; this person will then be treated as the settlor of that proportion of the trust fund for IHT purposes. This could be something as simple as someone paying the trust administration fees rather than these being settled from the trust assets. This may happen where there are no liquid assets to settle the funds. This person has then settled the balance of the trust fees.

> **Tip**
>
> One alternative to the addition to the trust is for the person settling the fees to make a loan to the trust which is repayable. This should be documented by the trustees and the person should be shown in the trust accounts as a creditor.
>
> The same occurs if two spouses jointly create a trust, perhaps for the benefit of their grandchildren and subsequent generations. Each is treated as the settlor of a separate settlement.
>
> Where there is more than one settlor, the settlement created by each has its own NRB for IHT purposes. Separate IHT forms may be required and, where the dates assets were added to the trust were different, there will be different TYAs for the different portions settled by each settlor.
>
> There is an oddity if a trust, at the time of its creation, initially gave the settlor's spouse a qualifying interest in possession (QIIP). Under IHTA 1984, s.80 the trust is, for the RPT rules, treated as created by that spouse.

7.2.4 When do the 10 years date from?

The date from which TYAs are reckoned is the date assets were first put into trust (IHTA 1984, s.60) even if the original trust has been varied, closed down or subdivided, as long as the assets have not become any individual's outright property:

1. Where assets are settled by will, the trust is treated as beginning on the date of the testator's death, even if the trust is not constituted for some time afterwards (IHTA 1984, s.83).
2. Where assets are settled by a two-year variation of an absolute inheritance in a will, even though the trust may not actually be created until nearly two years after death, for the purposes of the RPT rules the trust is treated as starting on the date of the death.
3. Where assets are moved from one trust to another, they are still treated as being in the original trust and it is the date of that original trust that fixes the dates of 10-year charges. This can go on through any number of separate trusts (IHTA 1984, s.81).

Accumulation and maintenance (A&M) trusts, which were created before 2006, but have now moved into the RPT rules, still date their TYAs from the date of the original settlement.

Where, as a result of IHTA 1984, s.80 the settlor's spouse is treated as the settlor, because of an initial QIIP, the starting date for TYAs is still the original date of settlement.

Example 7.2

Suppose Mr Jenkins died in 2011, creating a discretionary trust over part of his estate and a life interest for his widow over the rest. Mrs Jenkins died in 2018 and, under the terms of her husband's will, the residue was then added to the other trust in the will. All of it continues to be held on discretionary trusts.

This is treated as two separate settlements: one made by Mr Jenkins in 2011 and one by Mrs Jenkins when she died. However, the TYAs for both trusts are dated from Mr Jenkins's death in 2011, and there will be a 10-year charge on both in 2021. (See **7.2.6** for the reduction in the charge on what Mrs Jenkins is deemed to have settled.)

7.2.5 Adjustments to available nil rate band

When calculating the 10-year charge the trustees must look back both at the previous 10 years, to determine the value of any capital distributions, and at the value of the chargeable transfers made by the settlor in the seven years prior to the creation of this trust.

The NRB is reduced by the total of these values. Varying **Example 7.1** but introducing chargeable transfers of £75,000 in the seven years before the trust was created and previous capital distributions totalling £50,000 the calculation will be as follows:

Example 7.3

		£
Market value of assets less capital liabilities		500,000
Less current NRB	(325,000)	
Reduced by:		
capital distributions in previous 10 years	50,000	
chargeable transfers in 7 years before settlement	75,000	
Net value		(200,000)
		300,000
Lifetime rate – 20% of the net value		
		60,000
Effective rate (60,000/ 500,000)		
		12%

IHT due = 500,000 x 12% x 3/10	
	£18,000

To put this another way, this is 6% of the £300,000 above the NRB band.

If the settlor added assets to the trust at any time after its creation and, at the date of that addition, his chargeable transfers in the previous seven years were more than those in the seven years before the creation of the trust, then that larger total is added.

Remember that, for a trust created on death, the history of chargeable transfers in the seven years before death will include lifetime gifts that may have been potentially exempt transfers when they were made.

The value of capital distributions made in the previous 10 years does not include those made in the three months immediately following the creation of the trust or the last TYA. In the case of a will trust, capital distributions made within two years of death are also ignored, since IHTA 1984, s.144 deems them to have been part of the original provisions in the will.

As noted at **7.2.3**, where there is more than one settlor, there is deemed to be more than one settlement and the history of each is looked at separately.

7.2.6 Related settlements and same-day additions (SDAs)

Trusts created on the same day by the same settlor are related settlements for IHT purposes. These trusts will have the same TYA.

A separate calculation for each related settlement is required. The NRB is adjusted in just the same way as set out in **7.2.5**, but this time the effective rate is based on the total of:

- the market value on the TYA of the trust liable to the 10-year charge;
- the value originally introduced, at the outset, to any related settlement.

Example 7.4

Suppose two separate trusts, Trust A and Trust B, were established in the same will. £150,000 went to Trust A at the outset, and £100,000 to Trust B. On the TYA of both, Trust A's assets are worth £300,000 and those of Trust B are worth £175,000.

In this case the testator made no chargeable transfers in the seven years before his death and no capital has been paid out of the trusts.

Charge on Trust A

Trust A value on TYA	300,000
Trust B value on creation	100,000
	400,000
Less available NRB	(325,000)
Net value	75,000
Lifetime rate – 20% of the net value	15,000
Effective rate (15,000/400,000)	3.75%
IHT due on Trust A = 300,000 x 3.75% x 3/10 = £3,375	

Charge on Trust B

Trust B value on TYA	175,000
Trust A value on creation	100,000
	275,000

This is less than the available NRB.

Therefore there is no IHT due on Trust B.

Bear in mind that related settlements can be made by IHTA 1984, s.142 variation and may have nothing to do with each other. For example, three siblings might each receive a third of a parent's estate and use s.142 to settle their part on to a relevant property trust, each with different trustees. The settlor for IHT purposes is, in every case, the deceased parent and all are deemed to have begun on the date of the parent's death, so that they are related.

Same-day additions (SDAs) have been relevant since they were introduced by Finance (No.2) Act 2015 on 18 November 2015. The object was to counter a perceived loophole in the original RPT rules. A practice had grown up of taxpayers creating a number of separate settlements, with only nominal initial gifts, on separate days. Substantial funds were then added on a single date, or perhaps on the taxpayer's death. These were not related settlements and there was no provision bringing the different transfers to separate trusts into account, in the way the related settlements rules did.

The changes mean that where, on or after 18 November 2015, there are SDAs, the trusts to which SDAs have been made are all treated as if they were related settlements and both the original assets of those trusts and the amounts of the SDAs are brought into account accordingly.

7.2.7 Additions to relevant property

Where there was a period during the previous 10 years in which all or some of the trust assets were not relevant property, then the charge is reduced in proportion to the number of complete quarters which had expired before the assets became relevant property. This might be an addition to the trust by the original settlor (remember: an addition by another person is treated as a separate settlement) or the ending of another interest, such as a QIIP, when the trust assets were not relevant property while that previous interest existed.

Example 7.5

Using **Example 7.2**, say Mr Jenkins died on 1 May 2011 and Mrs Jenkins on 21 October 2018.

The 10-year charge on the TYA on 1 May 2021 on the portion of the trust funds deemed to have been settled when Mrs Jenkins's life interest ended on her death will not have been relevant property for the 29 quarters from 1 May 2011 to 1 August 2018, so only 11/40ths of the charge is made on the TYA.

7.3 EXIT CHARGES (PROPORTIONATE CHARGES)

7.3.1 Basic rules

An exit charge arises when there is a distribution or appointment of assets out of a relevant property trust. As with the 10-year charge there are various traps to watch out for.

There are different calculations for the exit charge depending on whether the exit charge occurs in the first 10 years of the trust or after a TYA. Exit charges are also known as proportionate charges, because the rate of tax is usually a proportion of the rate paid at the previous TYA (or, in the first 10 years, a deemed rate based on the trust's initial value).

The value taxed on the exit is the loss to the settlement, i.e. the value by which the relevant property in the settlement has decreased. This may, or may not, be the same as the value of the assets actually leaving the trust. (This mirrors the 'loss to estate' principle that applies to a 'transfer of value', the measure of a gift by an individual for IHT purposes. See **1.3**.)

If the exit charge is paid from trust funds, then that tax payment is itself subject to the exit charge so that the charge is 'grossed up'.

If you are claiming BPR or APR on the asset leaving the settlement then this is deducted from the loss to the trust to determine the amount on which the exit charge must be paid; for example if a trust holds cash of £100,000 and assets which attract 100 per cent BPR then the exit charge is on £100,000.

Where the trust holds an interest in land or buildings, and the donee is paying the exit charge, the element of the IHT attributed to that can be paid by the instalment option over 10 years. Interest is payable.

The instalment option is also available for IHT on most forms of business and agricultural property, where 100 per cent relief is not available; for most unincorporated businesses there is no interest provided the instalments are paid on time.

7.3.2 The calculation in the first 10 years

The starting point is to look at the value of the trust assets settled and, as for the 10-year charge, calculate the rate of tax on a notional lifetime chargeable transfer of those assets by a notional transferor. When looking at the assets settled, you must add the value of any additions made before the occasion of the exit charge. If there are related settlements or if there have been SDAs, the values of these must also be added.

Again, as with the 10-year charge, there is a NRB for this imaginary transfer (which may be reduced by gifts by the settlor in the seven years before creating the trust). This is the NRB at the date of the exit, rather than the NRB when the trust began.

Example 7.6

Value of assets settled	600,000
Less current NRB	(325,000)
Net value	275,000
Lifetime rate – 20% of the net value	55,000

The effective rate is calculated by taking the lifetime rate and dividing this by the value of the assets settled. This is then multiplied by the given fraction of 3/10. Following on from the example above:

Effective rate (55,000/600,000)	9.2%

3/10 of effective rate is 2.76%

If there are no additions after the initial gift to the trust, this effective rate, and 3/10ths of it, will be unchanged for the first 10 years.

If the value of the trust assets and additions brought into account on the notional transfer is less than the available NRB, there is no exit charge. However, there is no deduction to reflect that the settlor may have had business or agricultural relief on their transfer to the trust. This is different from the treatment where the trust assets have qualified for relief on the last TYA.

The actual rate of IHT on the exit is between 1/40th and 39/40ths of that 3/10ths rate, according to the number of quarters (periods of three months) that have elapsed since creation of the trust. If less than one-quarter has passed since creation, then there is no exit charge.

If there have been additions, then the quarters brought into account are reduced by the number of quarters the assets distributed were not settled property, although never to below 1/40th.

Example 7.7

Say £600,000 was settled as in **Example 7.6** and there was an addition to the trust of £200,000 after one year (four quarters). The trust was ended, when its value was £1,200,000, just after the ninth anniversary (36 quarters) of its creation.

Value of assets settled	600,000
Add addition	200,000
Less current NRB	(325,000)
Net value of notional transfer	475,000
Lifetime rate – 20% of the net value	95,000

The effective rate is calculated by taking the lifetime rate and dividing this by the total value of the assets settled. This is then multiplied by the given fraction of 3/10.

Following on from the figures above:

Effective rate (95,000/800,000)	11.875%

3/10 of effective rate is 0.035625

Three-quarters of the exit charge will be at 36/40ths, representing the original £600,000 settled.

The other quarter of the exit charge will be at 32/40ths representing the £200,000 settled a year after creation of the trust.

IHT due is the total of (a) and (b) below

(a) 3/4 of value leaving trust x 3/10 x effective rate x (complete quarters (36))

(£900,000 x 3/10 x 11.875% x 36/40) = £28,856.25

PLUS

(b) 1/4 of value leaving trust x 3/10 x effective rate x (complete quarters (36) less quarters before addition (4))

(£300,000 x 3/10 x 11.875% x 32/40) = £8,550.00

TOTAL = £37,406.25

7.3.3 Exit after a TYA

Where there has already been a TYA, the effective rate of tax on exits in the following 10 years is the same as the overall rate of tax on the TYA, subject to three adjustments:

1. The value of any additions made since the last TYA, but before the occasion of the exit charge, must be brought into account.
2. The rate of tax must be adjusted to reflect the NRB at the date of exit, rather than that on the TYA (in the 10 years up to 2020/21, of course, this has not been necessary, since the NRB has been unchanged since 6 April 2009).
3. The reduction for any period in the 10 years before the TYA when any property was not relevant property (see **7.2.7**) is added back.

In many cases the effective rate, and 3/10ths of it, will be unchanged throughout the 10 years.

As with exit charges in the first 10 years, if the value of the trust assets on the TYA and additions is less than the available NRB, there is no exit charge.

In addition, if the trust had 100 per cent business or agricultural relief on all its assets on the last TYA, there will be no exit charges in the following 10 years, whether or not what is distributed qualifies for relief at the time. Note that this does not apply to exits in the first 10 years, even if the settlor had 100 per cent relief on transferring assets to the trust.

When the effective rate has been ascertained, the actual rate of IHT on the exit is calculated in the same way as in **Example 7.7**. So the rate is between 1/40th and 39/40ths of the 3/10ths rate, according to the number of quarters (periods of three months) that have elapsed since the TYA. If less than one quarter has passed since the TYA then there is no exit charge.

If there have been additions since the TYA but before the date of exit, then the quarters brought into account are reduced by the number of quarters the assets distributed were not settled property, although never to below 1/40th.

7.3.4 Grossing up

The final point to look at is grossing up. When the payment of IHT is made from the remaining trust funds, in effect the loss to the trust is greater than the value of the capital distribution made and therefore the value of the benefit to the beneficiary is greater. In the example below, assuming a distribution of £100,000 just over three years after the last TYA (or the creation of the trust), the IHT is borne by the trustees and therefore 'grossed up'.

Example 7.8

Value of assets settled/previous TYA	600,000
Less current NRB	(325,000)
Net value	275,000
Lifetime rate – 20% of the net value	55,000
Effective rate (55,000/600,000 x 100)	9.167%
Actual rate (9.167% x 3/10 x 12/40)	0.825%
Grossing up distribution of £100,000	
100/(100–0.825) x £100,000	100,832
IHT due (100,832 x 0.825%)	832

Note that there is no requirement to gross up on the termination of a trust. Nor is there any grossing up of 10-year charges.

CHAPTER 8

Compliance

Tanya Wadeson and John Bunker

8.1 KEY POINTS

While this is an inheritance tax (IHT) planning handbook, it is worth taking note of some compliance aspects, so in this chapter we outline some of the issues relevant to IHT, estates and trusts (**Chapter 9** covers more of the issues re estates):

- The IHT account forms needed, and those trusts and estates that are excepted from the obligation to account.
- Payment of tax obligations, including situations where an instalment option is available and when interest is payable.
- An introduction to the Office of Tax Simplification (OTS) reports on IHT in November 2018 and July 2019, the first of which was concerned with the process of accounting for and paying IHT.
- An outline of a number ways that HM Revenue and Customs (HMRC) helps online with notes, toolkits, newsletters and manuals. These can all help both compliance and understanding of HMRC practice when considering planning options.

8.2 INHERITANCE TAX FORMS

8.2.1 Relevant property trusts

There is a suite of forms which support the form IHT100 for trustees to report an event for IHT purposes. For relevant property trusts (RPTs) the deadline for the submission of these forms is six months after the end of the month in which the chargeable event occurred.

The two supplemental forms which trustees of relevant property trusts will use are:

- IHT100c to report an exit charge; and
- IHT100d to report the 10-year anniversary (TYA).

If you do not already hold a reference for the trust, you will need to apply for one using form IHT122.

The IHT forms are very out of date and are, as at July 2020, in the process of being reviewed but are unlikely to be updated for some months. They have not been properly updated since the trust changes in 2006, to reflect references to age 18–25 trusts and relevant property trusts (RPTs) (rather than discretionary trusts), let alone the more recent same-day additions (SDAs). HMRC advises there are difficult issues with access requirements that are preventing as easy solution. There is also no form for reporting exit charges on 18–25 trusts.

Excepted settlements?

There are conditions that need to be met by trustees to determine whether a settlement can be an excepted settlement. These are:

- The settlor was UK domiciled at the time the settlement was created, and has continued to remain UK domiciled throughout the existence of the settlement until their death or the chargeable event in question, whichever comes sooner.
- The trustees of the settlement are and always have been UK resident.
- There are no related settlements.
- The value of the chargeable transfer at the date of chargeable transfer does not exceed 80 per cent of the current nil rate band (NRB).

If all these apply, then no report to HMRC is required. This allows for assets such as property which may have a subjective value.

The chargeable transfer value is the value either at the date of the TYA or on creation, depending on the event you are reporting. When determining the value of the trust for these purposes, any reliefs must be ignored.

8.2.2 Aggregated trusts

Form IHT100b is used to report the death of a life tenant for an aggregated trust and is submitted alongside the IHT100. When completing the IHT100 for this event, you will be required to complete the life tenant's details on the front page of the IHT100 and the IHT reference will be the same as the one used by the executors for the deceased life tenant. The deadline for the submission of this form is one year after the end of the month in which the life tenant died.

8.2.3 IHT205 (excepted estates) or IHT400?

An IHT205 form is used to report estates where the deceased was UK resident and there is no IHT to pay due to one of the following conditions:

- The total value of the estate was less than £1 million and all or part of the estate passes to a surviving spouse, civil partner or a charity.
- The value of the estate is equal to or less than the excepted estate limit (the available NRB, including a full transferable nil rate band (TNRB) or residence

nil rate band (RNRB)). If the TNRB is not a full NRB, for example a legacy has been made to reduce the NRB of the first death, then the executors can't complete an IHT205.

Where the deceased made lifetime gifts in excess of £150,000 the executors will be required to complete the IHT400 and not the IHT205. There are other, sometimes quirky, rules that can mean you need to do an IHT400 and sometimes one starts drafting the IHT205 and then finds something that requires a switch to the full form. HMRC recognises there is a problem with the huge number of estates that do not pay IHT but still have to complete a full IHT400 – see re OTS report below (**8.5**).

The IHT205 is not submitted to HMRC due to the fact that there is no tax payable. This form is submitted directly to the Probate Registry. HMRC will then complete random checks on IHT205s to ensure these are being reported on the correct form. Because of this, there is no time limit for the submission of the form, but probate will not be granted without it.

An IHT400 must be completed for all estates where the conditions for the completion of an IHT205 are not met. This form has a main form together with various supplemental pages to provide the details of the assets and liabilities of the estate together with details of chargeable lifetime gifts and aggregated trusts.

The deadline for submission of IHT400 is one year from the end of the month following the death; however, the tax is due to be paid six months from the end of the month in which the death occurred. Therefore, as you are collating the information to pay the tax, in the majority of cases, it is easier to have the forms completed at this time.

The IHT400 is submitted to HMRC with IHT417 and the tax paid. HMRC will return IHT417 to the practitioner, confirming receipt of the payment. This IHT417 will then need to be sent to the Probate Registry.

HMRC has issued a timeline for its response to the submission of the IHT400 (*Trusts and Estates Newsletter*, April 2018). It will contact you within 12 weeks of issuing its initial calculations (the IHT421) if it proposes to raise further queries, including queries from the Valuation Office Agency, or if HMRC intends to carry out a compliance check.

In weeks 1–2 after submission, HMRC will create a detailed record of the assets and liabilities of the estate detailed in the IHT400. In order to avoid any delay ensure you have answered all the relevant questions, completed the relevant schedules and forwarded a copy of the will and codicil(s).

It can then take up to 12 weeks for HMRC to confirm if it can close the record. If you have not heard from HMRC by the deadline provided in its letter, you can assume it has no further questions.

If the executors have been selected for a compliance check, then in weeks 15–20 you will be informed what is being checked and may be asked for more information. Once the values have been agreed then new calculations will be issued.

The executors can inform HMRC of small changes to the probate values in a single letter, either when the estate values are final, or 18 months from the date of death, whichever is earlier. You will only need to inform HMRC earlier if:

- there is a change in value to land, buildings or unlisted shares;
- a claim for loss relief is made (see **8.2.4**);
- assets are sold on which IHT payments were made using the instalment option;
- the total increase or decrease in value is more than £50,000 (before any exemptions have been claimed).

If you require formal clearance, this is not normally issued within a year of the date of death. Also if there is an aggregable trust, clearance will not be issued on the estate until the trust IHT position is also finalised. As a clearance letter is not always issued, if reassurance is needed it is best to submit a formal application for a Clearance Certificate in form IHT30. In August 2020 HMRC introduced a new process whereby instead of stamping and returning the IHT30 form, it will send a letter to discharge the applicants, with a unique authorisation code which has the same effect as a stamped IHT30 (**www.gov.uk/government/publications/hm-revenue-and-customs-trusts-and-estates-newsletters/hmrc-trusts-and-estates-newsletter-august-2020**). This will bring a natural closure.

8.2.4 Loss relief claim

If a property or investments are sold for a loss within the time limit, then a claim for loss relief can be made. The claim will be made on:

- IHT38 for property – the time limit: four years from the date of death; or
- IHT35 for investments – the time limit: one year from the date of death.

If more than one asset is disposed of, then all assets of the same type, sold by the personal representatives in the same capacity, must be included on the claim, regardless of whether there was a gain or loss. Where a portfolio of investments is sold all investments must be included, so the executors must determine whether there is an overall loss before making the claim. Alternatively it may be worth considering some more planning – see **9.5** and **9.6**.

Any costs of sale are not included on the loss relief; the loss is calculated by deducting the probate value from the gross sale proceeds.

8.3 PAYMENT OF TAX – INCLUDING INSTALMENT OPTION AND INTEREST

8.3.1 Relevant property trusts

The payment of tax on an RPT is due at the same time as the deadline for the submission of the forms, i.e. six months after the end of the month in which the chargeable event occurred.

8.3.2 Aggregated trusts

The payment of the tax on an aggregated trust is due six months after the end of the month in which the life tenant died.

Grossing up on lifetime gifts – see **Chapter 23**.

8.4 INSTALMENT OPTION AND INTEREST

IHT attributable to an interest in land or buildings can be paid by the instalment option over 10 years. Interest is payable, but this may be the only choice if there are insufficient liquid assets.

The instalment option is also available for IHT on most forms of business and agricultural property, where 100 per cent relief is not available; for most unincorporated businesses there is no interest provided the instalments are paid on time. In the case of stocks and shares, interest is payable on the same basis as for land or buildings if the business of the company concerned is mainly in investments.

The instalment option is available on lifetime gifts and RPT exit charges only when the donee pays the IHT.

The payment of the first instalment is due on the same day as the non-instalment option tax is due, i.e. six months after the end of the month in which the chargeable event occurred. Subsequent payments are due annually thereafter.

The interest on each instalment continues to run throughout the 10-year period and is calculated on the full value of the IHT remaining to be settled, i.e. all remaining instalments not just the instalment currently being settled.

If the property is sold within the 10-year period, it is important to pay the IHT in full as soon as the property has been sold to stop interest and penalties accruing.

8.5 OFFICE OF TAX SIMPLIFICATION REPORT ON INHERITANCE TAX

The OTS reviewed IHT in two parts – its first report was in November 2018 and the second in July 2019, with the first concerned with the process of accounting for and paying IHT. It reflected the wide-ranging concern within HMRC to 'improve the customer journey' to help to make it easier for customers to pay the right amount of tax at the right time. The OTS is a semi-independent body, based within HM Treasury (HMT), and not HMT or HMRC itself, but its proposals in the first report are being seriously considered by HMRC. The major focus of the November 2018 'Inheritance Tax Review – first report: Overview of the tax and dealing with administration' was the many estates that needed to have a full IHT400 completed even though there was no IHT payable.

The OTS's proposals were sensibly designed, with eight recommendations that could be implemented without the need for primary legislation.

HMRC has been looking at the recommendations to see whether, and how, they might be implemented. It has also started a specific review of the IHT100 forms, to make them easier to use, and that review is still ongoing in September 2020. Updating the forms is proving frustratingly difficult, due to the government's detailed rules regarding equal access requirements. See **20.4.1** for comment on the second OTS report in July 2019.

8.6 HMRC ONLINE HELP

HMRC maintains a valuable range of online resources that can help with the compliance burden, including details of how to complete forms, risk areas where problems arise in practice, and changes to practice of which to be aware. They are a great starting point for dealing with compliance, and finding answers in practice to queries, and should be used regularly.

When searching for the most recent versions of form IHT400, the IHT Toolkit, IHT400 Notes or any forms, it is usually better to use your usual search engine than searching in GOV.UK.

8.6.1 Inheritance Tax Toolkit for IHT400

Each year HMRC updates its IHT Toolkit, typically between June and August, for deaths arising from that April, to provide a valuable guide and reference resource for practitioners. The latest edition (published April 2020, for deaths from 6 April 2020) contains 25 key questions, each of which outlines 'Risk', 'Mitigation' and 'Explanation'. (See: **www.gov.uk/government/publications/hmrc-inheritance-tax-toolkit**.)

The 'Risks' are the main ones that HMRC finds in practice, reflecting its experience of mistakes made in practice, including mistakes by solicitors and other professional advisers. Following the 'Mitigation' greatly helps if anything goes wrong, for example information is missed or a valuation is wrong. This can help with mitigation of interest and penalties – if you follow the advice, it should reduce (or even eliminate) any penalty.

There is a handy four-page checklist at the start which sets out in summary these 25 risks. This Toolkit is worth referring to for internal training, e.g. in team meetings; in practice on any estate where you have something new, unusual or difficult; and in any event from time to time to ensure that your processes are in keeping with HMRC good practice.

8.6.2 IHT400 Notes

The IHT400 form is updated each year, typically around August, and with it the IHT400 Notes that take you through each section of the IHT return. These Notes supplement what is in the Toolkit and give specific guidance on the completion of the many extra pages of the IHT400. Again, it is worth referring to when completing anything new or unusual. It's important to ensure you always use the up-to-date version for the estate you are administering.

8.6.3 Trusts and Estates Toolkit – for income and gains and SA905

While in practice beyond the scope of this handbook, it is worth being aware of this second Toolkit which does not cover IHT but simply income tax and capital gains tax (CGT). There are 30 questions in a checklist, each with the same risk mitigation and explanation as for the IHT Toolkit, which reflect four areas of risk identified in completing returns for trusts and estates:

1. Establishing whether there is a trust or estate and/or the type of trust – always a crucial question for IHT, as well as for CGT and income tax.
2. Applying the correct legislation, rules and practice.
3. Incomplete information.
4. Capital gains – with a companion 'Capital Gains Tax for trusts and estates supplementary toolkit'. This includes a further checklist with 28 questions about, for example, main residence (principal private residence (PPR)) relief, gift relief, losses and valuations. At a time when we (from April 2020) adjust to paying CGT on residential properties within 30 days of disposal, this checklist could be increasingly valuable. The biggest area of risk on CGT remains valuations – which are also key for IHT.

While not specifically on IHT, these are helpful further toolkits that can help with better tax compliance and planning on estates. Updates of the toolkits, which are 'refreshed' annually, are also flagged up in the newsletters – see **8.6.4**.

8.6.4 Trusts and Estates Newsletters

The *Trusts and Estates Newsletters* are published by HMRC, giving updates and guidance on IHT and trusts (**www.gov.uk/government/publications/hm-revenue-and-customs-trusts-and-estates-newsletters**). The newsletters are produced online normally three times a year, for example, April, September and December. They have important updates on HMRC practice, changes in forms, technical and procedural developments, making them a 'must read' to keep up to date. They also have links to relevant documents, including updated forms, to click on for ease of access.

In January 2020 the newsletter announced that the 'new micro-service' version of the Trust Registration Service will be available to invited users via the 'private beta' testing. This enables agents to have access, updates to the process for the IHT421 Probate Summary form and changes to agent letters issued when the IHT400 is processed – following the timescales introduced by the April 2018 newsletter.

8.6.5 Inheritance Tax Manual

The HMRC manuals, including the IHT Manual (**www.gov.uk/hmrc-internal-manuals/inheritance-tax-manual**), are guidance for HMRC staff on how to assess and administer the tax, and give the official HMRC view about the law and procedure. They are not necessarily always right, and could be challenged by a brave person – HMRC always being bigger than you! – but it is always worth knowing how HMRC interprets the law. Apart from some rare examples, where the text is redacted under exceptions to the Freedom of Information Act 2000, it enables you to see what you need to do to satisfy HMRC in practice.

The Trusts, Settlements and Estates Manual (TSEM) covers details of income tax and CGT, though there is also a CGT Manual.

The manuals are updated regularly and it's sensible to get the up-to-date version online, whenever you need to rely upon it, and to print a copy as a record of the details on which you rely on that specific date. At the top of the manual is an index of updates, irritatingly not showing the most recent update first – though professional bodies are (in September 2020) lobbying HMRC about changing this. Looking up technical points in the manual can be a good way of learning.

PART II

Practical probate and trusts

CHAPTER 9

Probate

Emma McCann and John Bunker

9.1 KEY POINTS

This chapter covers the following:

- Alongside the inheritance tax (IHT) planning in this book, it is valuable to note practical compliance issues, starting with completion of IHT forms and paying IHT by instalments.
- Claiming the downsizing addition for the residence nil rate band (RNRB) – an introduction to one of the most complex areas of IHT law.
- Losses and gains in estates: claiming loss relief for IHT and how this interacts with capital gains tax (CGT) and the gains of the estate and individuals.
- Appropriation: analysing a key tax planning tool in estates, the form of appropriation, the nature of the power and values at which assets are appropriated; as well as the key role in dealing with losses and gains post-death.

9.2 PRACTICAL COMPLIANCE ISSUES

9.2.1 Introduction

When calculating the liability to IHT on death, the total value of all the assets in the deceased's name, and any qualifying interests in trusts, must be obtained, together with comprehensive debt and liability information, lifetime gifts in the preceding seven years and any gifts out of income information. In addition, consideration needs to be given to any exemptions and reliefs – for example, spousal and charity exemptions, and business property and agricultural property reliefs, which are the most regularly used ones. Further consideration is given to these in the next section. Comprehensive information is needed if any of these are to be claimed.

This process of investigating and collating the information, to be able to competently complete the relevant IHT forms, must be thorough and can take anything from a number of weeks to several months depending on the size and complexity of the estate. Care must always be taken to obtain the appropriate true open market valuations at date of death (there is no such thing as 'probate value') that are going to satisfy HM Revenue and Customs (HMRC) requirements, and decisions need to be made as to whether form IHT205 (either with or without IHT217), IHT207 or IHT400 needs to be completed, dependent upon the asset make up, value and the specific circumstances of the estate. Further information is available from HMRC in the IHT400 Guidance Notes (**www.gov.uk/government/publications/inheritance-tax-inheritance-tax-account-iht400**) and IHT400 Inheritance Tax Toolkit (**www.gov.uk/government/publications/hmrc-inheritance-tax-toolkit**).

Needless to say, considerably more detail is required to accompany an IHT400 application than for the other forms, albeit that the personal representatives must be satisfied in all cases that the figures disclosed represent the true valuation of the particular asset at the date of death and that there is no 'guess work' involved. Never forget that personal representatives are 'self-assessment taxpayers', required to report the details and amount of tax they consider is payable, with HMRC then able to ask any questions of the personal representatives to justify and evidence their figures. So, you must always be prepared with the evidence to back up any figures you include in any account.

9.2.2 Reliefs and exemptions

It is essential that prior to the completion of the appropriate inheritance tax return, the personal representative has considered what reliefs and exemptions may apply.

The main reliefs are as follows (see **2.7**):

- business property relief (BPR): at 100 per cent or 50 per cent of the value of the property being transferred, depending upon the type of asset/property and the minimum ownership requirements;
- agricultural property relief (APR): as for BPR this can be at either 100 per cent or 50 per cent of the value, and again dependent upon satisfaction of the criteria;
- woodlands relief: the value of the trees themselves or the timber. Tax payment can be deferred until disposal;
- heritage property relief: can be exempt from IHT if HMRC agrees and you comply with conditions (see HMRC IHT400 Guidance Notes);
- successive charges relief: the relief, also known as quick succession relief (QSR), is available if a transfer of assets takes place within the preceding five years prior to the death, on a sliding scale basis.

The main exemptions include (see **2.2–2.5**):

- annual gifts exemption of £3,000 for the current tax year and previous tax year (if unused);
- spousal/civil partner exemption (which together we will refer to simply as 'spouse' for the rest of this chapter) (including transferable nil rate band (TNRB) and transferable residence nil rate band (TRNRB));
- gifts to political parties;
- charitable exemption;
- gifts for public benefit;

- gifts of shares to employee trusts;
- death in service exemption;
- community amateur sports clubs.

A personal representative should ensure that they are fully conversant with the estate and any reliefs and exemptions that may apply before the IHT account is completed and submitted to HMRC.

9.2.3 Completion of the forms

There are a number of traps to watch out for when completing the returns, and it is important to be aware of them in order to ensure that you don't spend time completing an IHT205 only to discover that an IHT400 is required. There are some quirky rules about when a full IHT400 is required.

IHT205

An IHT205 is required in estates where the deceased died domiciled in the UK and the gross value of the estate for IHT is less than or equal to:

- the excepted estate limit which currently (2020/21) is £325,000;
- twice the excepted estate limit if form IHT217 'Claim to transfer unused nil rate band for excepted estates' is being included;
- £1 million if there is no IHT to pay because of the spouse or charity exemption.

IHT207

An IHT207 form is to be used where the deceased died domiciled abroad and the following conditions apply:

- the deceased has never been domiciled in the UK nor treated as domiciled in the UK at the date of death;
- the deceased's UK estate consists only of cash or quoted shares or securities, the value of which does not exceed £150,000.

IHT400

An IHT400 is always required if there is any IHT at all that is payable with the return or at a future date.

However, there are also a number of examples where completion of an IHT400 is required, even though no IHT may be payable:

- If the deceased made gifts or chargeable transfers in the preceding seven years prior to their death that totalled more than £150,000. However, if after deducting any applicable annual gift exemptions this value reduces to below £150,000, then the IHT205 may be completed.

- If the deceased made any gift(s) with reservation of benefit (GROB).
- If the taxable 'estate' comprises assets held in trust where the gross value exceeds £150,000, or from more than one trust.
- If the estate includes foreign assets where their gross value exceeds £100,000.
- If the gross value of the estate together with any specified transfers exceeds the IHT threshold and no spouse/charity exemption applies. This is the case even if the net estate reduces the value to below the threshold.

It is possible for HMRC to insist on the completion of an IHT400, and this is selected on a random basis. This would tend to be most likely in cases where the estate value nears the IHT threshold, which carry the greatest risk of underpayment of tax. Any request of this type would, usually, be directed to the personal representatives themselves, rather than to any solicitor acting on their behalf. It is prudent, therefore, to ensure that clients are aware should they ever receive any correspondence of this type direct from HMRC that they should immediately pass it on to their solicitor, rather than assume that the solicitor will have already received it.

If an IHT205 has been submitted and the personal representatives subsequently discover that in fact an IHT400 account should have been submitted instead, then they have the period of six months from the date of that discovery to submit a full IHT400 return to HMRC. This should include comprehensive details of the changes and any tax that subsequently falls due.

The same also applies if a deed of variation is executed and causes tax to become payable. There is an obligation on the personal representatives to submit a full IHT400 return and make the position clear to HMRC.

Personal representatives have a legal duty to ensure that the information submitted to HMRC is correct and have the responsibility to calculate the tax themselves. In the same vein, they have the legal responsibility to ensure that any changes are notified to HMRC as soon as they are recognised. It can often be the case that lay personal representatives, acting without any legal assistance, fail to recognise their obligations and the responsibility that they are taking on when dealing with an estate administration themselves. Lack of knowledge is no excuse to HMRC and personal representatives should be mindful to take advice, to ensure they have properly read and understood the HMRC guidance and read the appropriate manuals to avoid making mistakes, and note that they have to personally account to the estate and the beneficiaries for any loss made as a result. Failure to do so may result in penalties being applied for incorrect or incomplete information being submitted to HMRC.

9.2.4 Claiming transferable allowances

Personal representatives should be prepared to claim 'unused' allowances for the NRB and the RNRB.

Questions should be asked of the family at the earliest opportunity surrounding the estates to see if a deceased's spouse had died earlier and if so, what happened at that point in terms of succession and values. It is important to collate as much information as possible as early as possible in the administration. This includes:

- spouse's name, dates of birth and death and copies of will, probate and deed of variation, if applicable;
- date and place of marriage;
- any IHT reference from the first spouse to die;
- gifts made by the first spouse to die in the seven years prior to their death;
- the value of the estate of the first spouse – if this was more than £2 million the transferable residence nil rate band will be reduced, perhaps to nothing;
- the devolution of the estate – did it simply pass to surviving spouse or were some of the nil rate bands used?
- whether a property was disposed of to 'direct descendants' or not in the spouse's will or passed by the will (or survivorship) to the surviving spouse or became part of a trust arrangement for example, life interest or discretionary trust.

Once you have that information, you can complete the relevant IHT forms:

- IHT402 to claim the transferable unused NRB allowance; or
- IHT436 to claim the transferable unused RNRB allowance.

IHT436 and the RNRB

The RNRB (see also **Chapter 16** for more details) is applicable where the deceased died on or after 6 April 2017 and left their interest in their home to 'direct descendants', either outright or on certain forms of trust. Subject to the downsizing provisions, the RNRB applies where at the deceased's death the estate included a 'qualifying residential interest' or otherwise an interest in a property that had been the deceased's residence at some point while comprised in their estate.

The 'qualifying interest' must also be 'closely inherited' by a direct descendant which for these purposes includes children, grandchildren, and their issue, as well as the spouse of a lineal descendant (and their widow(er) provided they have not remarried).

The RNRB allowance has been phased in and is currently £175,000 for the 2020/21 tax year. The allowance tapers by £1 for every £2 over the £2 million taper threshold which is calculated as being the value of the estate (including any aggregable trust) net of liabilities but before the deduction of any exemptions and reliefs.

Any unused RNRB may be claimed on the death of the surviving spouse in a similar way to the transferable as NRB. It does not matter when the first spouse died providing the second death occurred after 6 April 2017 and that the other conditions of the relief are met.

Key factors to consider with form IHT436:

- If the death of the first spouse occurred before 5 April 2017, then the RNRB cannot have been used so should be available to transfer (subject to any taper).
- If the value of the first spouse's estate was over £2 million, the amount of transferable RNRB will taper at the rate of £1 for every £2 over £2 million.
- Once the calculations have been made, just like the NRB transfer it is the per cent unused value that transfers to the second estate, not the actual amount of 'unused' allowance.
- It is possible to claim multiple transferable RNRB (TRNRB), and transferable NRB (TNRB), if a person has been widowed twice or more, provided the total TRNRB does not exceed 100 per cent and the total TNRB does not exceed 100 per cent. See **Chapter 17** regarding potential for planning for use of more RNRB and NRB allowances.

9.3 PAYING INHERITANCE TAX BY INSTALMENTS

IHT may be paid by instalments in respect of specific assets. These include:

- land and buildings (IHTA 1984, s.227);
- a business or an interest in a business (IHTA 1984, s.227);
- shares and securities (as defined by IHTA 1984, s.228);
- woodlands (as defined by IHTA 1984, s.229).

If the personal representatives wish to pay tax in this way, then they must elect to do so with HMRC. This means that the tax on those specific assets only may then be paid via the instalment option over the period of 10 years from the date of death, unless the asset is sold, in which case the personal representatives have an obligation to discharge the tax in full. The personal representatives can pay off the unpaid instalments voluntarily at any time.

The first instalment will be due at the end of the month following the period of six complete months from the date of death (but will always be due on the first of the month). Interest is accrued daily where the instalments of IHT relate to land and buildings, but this may be the only option if there are insufficient other assets to be able to pay the tax or if the estate doesn't wish to look at other alternatives, for example an executors' loan. Interest is calculated on the full amount of IHT remaining to be paid on the date when each instalment is due.

Where IHT is paid by instalments on most forms of business and agricultural property (if 100 per cent relief is not available), there is no interest provided the instalments are paid on time. In the case of shares and securities, interest is payable on the same basis as for land or buildings, if the business of the company concerned is mainly in investments. Instalments of IHT on unincorporated businesses are almost always free of interest, even for mainly investment businesses.

Instalments after the first are due annually on the anniversary date of the first payment. When the asset is sold, then the amount of the IHT payable on that asset must be settled in full. It is important that the tax be paid immediately in order to stop the interest accruing and to avoid any penalties for late payment. If only part of an asset is sold, then only part of the IHT liability falls due, which is calculated proportionally according to the value of the asset which has been sold.

The election to pay by instalments can continue if the asset is transferred to a beneficiary, rather than being sold; however once it is sold, then again the IHT falls due for payment straightaway.

Tip

Because of the interest payments which become due by paying using the instalment option, it is always better to look at other ways of funding the tax due first on those assets, bearing in mind that other sources of funding (for example, executors' loan) will also be subject to interest and costs which may be more or less favourable than HMRC interest rates. Discussions should be had with the personal representatives as to the best way to proceed.

9.4 DOWNSIZING ADDITION: CLAIMING RNRB WHERE THIS RELIEF APPLIES

9.4.1 Overview

For further information on where RNRB relief applies, see **16.5**.

A unique feature of the RNRB relief is that there is an additional provision for downsizing addition. This is available if the estate did not include a qualifying residential interest (QRI) at the date of death but the deceased had an interest in a former property which had subsequently been disposed of on or after 8 July 2015. Alternatively, they still had an interest in a property that qualified as a QRI but it was of lesser value than one held since 8 July 2015. The equivalent of the asset or assets (whether this be a less valuable property or whether the deceased no longer owned a property at all) must then, in the estate, be closely inherited by descendants. The allowance cannot be more than the maximum RNRB available at the date of death.

The following example is one given by HMRC to demonstrate how downsizing works (*Inheritance Tax on main residence nil-rate band and downsizing proposals: technical note*, October 2015: **www.gov.uk/government/publications/inheritance-tax-on-main-residence-nil-rate-band-and-downsizing-proposals-technical-note/inheritance-tax-on-main-residence-nil-rate-band-and-downsizing-proposals-technical-note**):

> A widow sells a home worth £400,000 in August 2020 and moves to a home worth £210,000. At the time of the sale the available RNRB is £350,000 as, had she died at that time, her executors would be able to make a claim to transfer all the unused RNRB from her late husband. By downsizing, she has potentially lost the chance to use £140,000 or 40% of the available RNRB which could have applied had the more valuable home not been sold.

When the widow later dies in October 2020, the [new] home is worth £225,000 and is left to her children together with £500,000 of other assets. The estate can [potentially] use an RNRB of £225,000. However, the widow was eligible for a RNRB of £350,000 had she not downsized. The estate can therefore claim an additional RNRB of 40% of the available RNRB (40% × £350,000) or £140,000. This would give a total RNRB of £365,000 (£225,000 + £140,000). But this is more than the maximum available RNRB (£350,000) so the additional RNRB is restricted to £125,000 to ensure that the total amount used does not exceed the maximum available [£225,000 + £125,000 = £350,000].

In addition, the existing nil-rate band together with any transferable nil-rate band claimed from her late husband's estate can be applied to the remaining assets in the estate.

9.4.2 Form IHT435 – claiming downsizing addition

Key points to consider when completing form IHT435 to claim downsizing addition:

- The net value of the property on disposal must be given, so you should deduct any mortgage owing at that date to show the disposal value. Costs of sale are ignored.
- The RNRB can only be claimed if the property was a QRI for RNRB at the date of disposal.
- A QRI can be a life interest in an aggregable trust, or indeed both a personal interest and such a trust interest in the same property. A classic jointly owned property where a widow owns one half and her late husband's immediate post-death interest (IPDI) trust the other half, could both be included.
- The proceeds of sale should be in the estate at death. If less than the value of the property sale proceeds (or the RNRB allowance, whichever shall be the lesser) remains, then only the amount left to pass to direct descendants can be claimed as the RNRB.
- It is recommended to visit the online HMRC RNRB calculator which gives a step-by-step calculation: **www.gov.uk/guidance/inheritance-tax-residence-nil-rate-band**.
- If grossing up applies (where part of the estate is exempt from tax and part non-exempt – see **7.3.4**) or interaction applies (where the estate is claiming BPR or APR and part of the estate is exempt) then the calculation is done by HMRC. Fill in as much of form IHT435 as is possible and submit for assessment.

This is an extremely complex provision, and care should be taken when submitting a claim of this nature. Lay personal representatives may not even be aware of its existence, and expertise is required in order to fully understand the provisions and how they may apply in a range of circumstances.

9.5 LOSSES AND GAINS IN ESTATES

A major area of tax planning in estate administration arises from the combination of losses and gains after the date of death. This is a mixture of IHT and CGT planning, which can be a relatively simple way to mitigate the tax payable on an estate, including the tax position of the estate beneficiaries. We are looking here to utilise:

- loss relief for IHT;
- capital gains annual exemptions and deductions;
- variable CGT rates payable; and
- a combination of IHT loss relief and using CGT exemptions/lower rates.

9.5.1 Loss relief for inheritance tax

Loss relief is used to reduce the IHT payable at 40 per cent on an estate, by substituting reduced prices on sale for the probate values. See **8.2.4**. For investments (a one-year period) and property (four years), this is relatively straightforward if the sales have all produced losses, but in many estates there will be a mixture of gains and losses. In those cases there is greater potential for careful tax mitigation.

The key point to note is that loss relief needs to take into account all sales made by the personal representatives acting in that capacity, i.e. as personal representatives of the estate, whether those sales realised a gain or loss. This does not include sales by personal representatives as bare trustees for beneficiaries of a trust after an appropriation.

One way to preserve loss relief is to only sell those investments or properties that are showing a loss, so that no gains are offset against the losses. Another is to only sell investments with a loss in the first year, and delay sales with gains until after 12 months from the date of death. In practice this will not often work, timing wise, as personal representatives will want to get on with sales before the year is out. It is also not usually wise to delay selling investments, once personal representatives are ready to sell, as they are on a hiding to nothing if values fall and they end up losing money as a result of a tax-driven delay in selling.

So, better planning options are needed. See **9.6**.

9.5.2 Capital gains annual exemptions and deductions

- **For the estate:** A full exemption (equal to a personal one) in the year of death and the two following tax years. In 2020/21 this is £12,300. While a limited number of estates might be able to utilise three such exemptions, many will have the opportunity to use two.
- **For individual beneficiaries:** If an asset is appropriated (see **9.6**) to a beneficiary it is, from that date, held by the personal representatives as bare trustees for that beneficiary. Thus any sales after appropriation will utilise gains or losses for the beneficiary personally, and will not be included in the estate's tax

figures either for CGT or for IHT loss relief. The individual's annual exemptions, for example, £12,300 in 2020/21, can thus be utilised if not otherwise used.

- **For any trust arising from the estate:** Once assets have been transferred to, or simply appropriated to, any trust that arises under a will or on intestacy or a deed of variation (see **Chapter 11**), any disposals of assets by the personal representatives as bare trustees for that trust will realise losses and gains for the trust. Most trusts have an annual exemption of half the personal one, for example £6,150 in tax year 2020/21.
- **Deductions from gains for expenses:** Can also be made by both the personal representatives and beneficiaries, for costs of sale and, for personal representatives only, 'allowable expenditure' of a proportion of costs in obtaining probate (see HMRC Statement of Practice 2 (2004), *Allowable expenditure – expenses incurred by personal representatives and corporate trustees*, **www.gov.uk/government/publications/statement-of-practice-2-2004–2**).

9.5.3 Variable CGT rates payable

- **Any estate gains that exceed the annual exemptions:** These gains will be taxed at the CGT rate payable by personal representatives, either 28 per cent on residential property (including the eight per cent surcharge) or 20 per cent on shares or other assets including other (non-residential) property.
- **Beneficiaries pay CGT at variable rates according to their other income and gains:** Gains are taxed as if a top slice of income, on top of all other taxable income, to see if the gains are within the basic rate band or exceed that. For residential property gains are taxed at 18 per cent in so far as within the basic rate band, 28 per cent where over that band; for other assets it's a 10 or 20 per cent rate. This means that individual beneficiaries do not pay a higher rate of CGT than the personal representatives, who only pay at 20/28 per cent, but may benefit from having a lower rate to pay.

Any gains passed on to beneficiaries may thus have the potential to utilise personal annual CGT exemptions – as in **9.5.2** – and lower CGT rates. Trusts will pay CGT at the same rates as estates, so that there is no saving (unless exemptions to use) or additional CGT on trusts.

9.5.4 A combination of IHT loss relief and using CGT exemptions/lower rates

Our ideal is to make the maximum use of IHT loss relief while minimising any CGT payable as per **9.5.2** and **9.5.3**. The challenge is to realise cash, where needed – for example, for paying tax, debts, estate expenses or legacies – without creating unnecessary tax liabilities or missing the opportunity to reduce the IHT payable.

A crucial element in this process is the personal representatives seeing clearly the figures they are working with, and two tools are really valuable to help this:

- **Draft estate accounts:** Up-to-date details of the likely estate available for distribution, which would ideally come in the form of draft estate accounts showing all the projected outgoings on tax, debts, fees, etc. and the assets left (whether in a balance sheet, or some similar form) available to meet outgoings and then for beneficiaries.
- **Up-to-date valuations of investments showing gains and losses since death:** If there is an investment manager or broker managing the portfolio, it is ideal to ask them to load the probate values of the investments on to their 'system' so that they can produce revised valuations at any time, showing in each case the probate value and current market value for this exercise. Most companies will do this, as an opportunity to show their services to other potential clients – beneficiaries who choose to retain some of their inherited shares. You will need current market values, to do the appropriations, in any event.

Once you know roughly how much you have for distribution to each beneficiary, and the investment values, it may be appropriate to consult with the residuary beneficiaries as to whether they might want to keep any investments. If you have some gains, you can also ask them whether they have used their annual CGT exemptions this year and, if appropriate, whether any gains in excess of exemptions are likely to be taxed initially at 10 per cent or at 20 per cent.

Before considering planning further, we need to understand appropriations, which are crucially important.

9.6 APPROPRIATION: A KEY TAX PLANNING TOOL

9.6.1 Introduction

The power of appropriation is a key power of personal representatives in the administration of estates. It is for two purposes – (a) to achieve fairness in distribution of the estate and (b) for tax planning. The former fits with the fundamental legal duty to distribute fairly.

Appropriation involves allocating specific assets – such as specific shares or investments or a specified equitable share of a property – in part or full satisfaction of an entitlement from an estate. It could be a significant sized legacy, but more commonly is a share of the residuary estate. In the absence of any power, personal representatives would simply have to sell everything or divide it all into the shares of the estate.

Once appropriated, assets (investments, property or whatever) are held by the personal representatives as bare trustees for the beneficiary. Thus, any income or gains are the beneficiary's personal income and gains. This has implications for the accounting process, as any income after appropriation, and any gains realised, will need to be reported to the beneficiary separately from the estate's income and gains. More importantly, it opens up possibilities for capital tax mitigation.

9.6.2 Form of appropriation

There is no magic to the form of appropriation, simply that it should have these ingredients:

- detail of the asset (for example, number/full description of shares, units or proportion of property);
- both the probate value of that asset and the market value at which appropriated;
- signed by the personal representatives and dated before the sale of the asset – for example, for property before the exchange of contracts. Once a sale is contracted, it is too late to do any appropriation, however much some practitioners might wish they had done one – and many of us have been there! That is why it so helps to have an early draft estate account if that is possible –see **9.5.4**.

9.6.3 What power of appropriation do the personal representatives have?

Most wills include an express power, or an extension of the statutory power in Administration of Estates Act 1925, s.41 so that no consents are required, as the statutory power is limited by the need to obtain the consent of other residuary beneficiaries to the proposed distribution.

Example 9.1

Jim leaves his estate to three children equally, and it includes a holding of 30,000 Marks & Spencer shares. This would be divided into three holdings of 10,000 each if there were no other power. If Jim's personal representatives were reliant on the statutory power, they would have to divide the holding that way even if two of them wanted the shares and one didn't, if the third did not give their approval. With the normal extended power, the personal representatives could choose to let two of them have 15,000 each.

If Jim's estate also included 1,000 Glaxo shares, a holding which does not divide equally into three, it would need to be split 333/333/334, as nearly to equal as possible. The wide express power enables the personal representatives to consider if one of the children really wanted the Glaxo holding, to appropriate to them as part of their 1/3 share of residue.

9.6.4 Appropriation value?

It is necessary for the personal representatives to revalue assets for appropriation purposes, so that they appropriate at the current market value rather than at probate value. This is to achieve the fairness between different beneficiaries.

Example 9.2: Jim and Judi (continuing Example 9.1)

If the Marks & Spencer holding were valued at, say, £60,000 at date of death but had seen a significant rise in value to £90,000 after death, it would be unfair to appropriate 1/3 at £20,000 to one child when that holding was worth £30,000. If, say, daughter Judi wanted to have 1/2 of those shares they could be appropriated to her at £45,000.

However, the beneficiary acquires the shares for CGT purposes at their probate value, so for example Judi would have a holding worth £45,000 with a probate value of £30,000, a built-in gain of £15,000 which she could then realise in her own time. If none of the beneficiaries wanted to have any of this shareholding, so that it was all to be cashed in, then there would be a few options:

- The £30,000 gain can be realised, free of CGT, if split between the three children who are residuary beneficiaries. Each can use part of their £12,300 CGT exemption in 2020/21.
- If the estate needs some of the cash from the share sale for expenses, and has the personal representatives exemption still available, 10,000 Marks & Spencer shares (or even a little more) could be sold with a £10,000 gain within the personal representatives £12,300 exemption. The estate can sell to utilise its exemption in any event. The personal representatives will appropriate the relevant shares to beneficiaries and keep back some in the estate.
- If one of Jim's children has used their annual CGT exemption, the personal representatives could appropriate to the other two, so that they don't have to sell for the child whose gains would in practice be subject to paying some CGT.
- If, however, there were losses on shares in the estate, and the personal representatives wished to claim loss relief, they could avoid selling any shares as personal representatives with a gain, which would simply reduce the benefit of loss relief. All the shares could be appropriated to beneficiaries and sold for them as bare trustees, so that the loss relief is maximised.

9.6.5 Losses and gains post death: using appropriations to minimise tax liabilities

Whether it is land or shares, if selling assets with losses and gains there is a normal principle:

- sell assets with losses as personal representatives in estate within time limit for loss relief; and
- realise gains post appropriation as bare trustees for a beneficiary.

In that way, the 'losses' are kept pure, not reduced by any gains, and you maximise loss relief.

Always be aware of the comparable tax rates, which currently (2020/21) are:

- **IHT:** Estates pay at 40 per cent, so loss relief is a means of reducing the 40 per cent charge.

- **CGT – estates:** Estates pay at 28 per cent on residential property, or 20 per cent on investments or any other assets; but even if at 28 per cent this is always less than the 40 per cent, so you are better off paying CGT. You also have the potential to deduct annual exemptions and allowable expenses (such as sale costs) from the sale proceeds.
- **CGT – beneficiaries:** Beneficiaries pay CGT at rates of 10 or 20 per cent; or 18/28 per cent on residential property – see **9.5.3**. So possibly even lower than the estate pays CGT. Again, they have potential to deduct exemptions and expenses.

Conclusion: It is always worth considering whether you can claim loss relief to reduce the higher tax charge.

> **Tip**
>
> Do be careful to consider the costs of a claim at the outset. There's no value in claiming loss relief to reduce the IHT by £500 if it costs you fees of £600 to do so. However, if the cost/benefit analysis shows this is worth doing, do agree any extra fees with the personal representatives before you secure the benefits!

9.6.6 Appropriations for charities and non-resident beneficiaries

While not an IHT or CGT planning point, it's worth highlighting an appropriation point that is vital for the relevant beneficiaries. If you are acting for either of these types of residuary beneficiaries, you must appropriate before selling any investments or properties:

- **Charities:** As charities are not liable for CGT, it is simple to appropriate any investments or shares of properties to the charity, for its proportion of the estate, to ensure that there is no CGT issue arising on a charity's share of an asset. If you want to upset a charity legacy officer, try missing this point! You can upset the personal representatives too if you 'waste' part of an estate's annual CGT exemption by realising a gain using that exemption when the gain should have been exempt anyway. It is unfortunately the case that many solicitors and other professional advisers do miss this simple point.
- **Non-resident beneficiaries:** Non-resident beneficiaries are likewise not liable for CGT in the UK, so again always complete an appropriation before selling, so that the post-death gain is taxed as theirs and thus exempt in any event.
- **Mixed beneficiaries:** If part of the residuary estate goes to a charity or charities, and part to beneficiaries who pay CGT, you can appropriate assets with gains to a charity, and then:
  - if there is no IHT payable in practice (after allowing for the exempt part to charity): appropriate assets with losses to taxable beneficiaries who might

be able to utilise those losses against personal taxable gains; or

- if there is IHT to pay on the estate, maximise the loss relief claim by realising losses in the estate without any gains – which should then be realised post appropriation, as in **9.6.5**.

CHAPTER 10

Practical trust compliance and administration

Kirstie Williamson

10.1 KEY POINTS

While this handbook's focus is inheritance tax (IHT) planning, trusts are a major part of planning so it is helpful to note some trust compliance aspects, including some very practical administration points. Practitioners who don't do much trust work might feel able to do more basics themselves, even if referring to specialists on some aspects. This chapter covers the following:

- Starting with trust creation: choosing the form of trust, the choice of trustees and beneficiaries.
- Trust registration: an introduction to the HM Revenue and Customs (HMRC) Trust Registration Service (TRS) for online registration to deal with HMRC's relationship with the trust, including a brief reference to the changes due in 2020/22 with the Fifth Money Laundering Directive (5MLD) (EU Directive 2018/843).
- Investing trust funds and trusts with property: some technical and practical issues.
- Trusts with property: rental or occupied property.
- Trust tax returns and accounts: sometimes outsourced by solicitors to accountants, but below are some key points.
- Some thoughts on when trusts reach vesting and the winding-up of a trust.
- The master documents that might, as a matter of good practice, be kept on a separate 'permanent file'.

10.2 TRUST CREATION: CHOOSING YOUR TRUST

The decision to create a trust can be driven by a number of factors and so a careful evaluation of these factors is required when determining the type of trust to employ in any given situation.

Clients often decide simply that they want a trust because they have heard that it will resolve tax planning or succession issues. Trusts can also be vehicles for asset protection and are very effective in relation to minor children and other vulnerable beneficiaries. It is important, therefore, when discussing the possible establishment of a trust with a client, to try to understand their underlying objectives and any other planning arrangements which may already be in place. Below we discuss:

- discretionary trusts;
- life interest trusts;
- disabled person's trusts; and
- bare trusts.

See **Chapter 5** for the types of trust for IHT purposes; **10.2** addresses the choice of trust in the context of this chapter.

10.2.1 Discretionary trusts

In terms of flexibility, a discretionary trust often provides the greatest options with regard to the freedom of the trustees to determine investment strategy and distribution schedules. Distributions can be tailored to match individual beneficiary needs taking into account personal financial circumstances as well as individual temperament, health and other pertinent circumstances. Given the freedom of the trustees to make distributions at will, subject to the guidance in any 'letter of wishes', it is important that independence is maintained and in particular that a preference is not shown for any particular beneficiary or class of beneficiaries without justification. For this reason, a professional trustee is often recommended either as sole trustee, or as co-trustee with a lay trustee, in order to maintain impartiality.

10.2.2 Life interest trusts

In certain circumstances a life interest trust may be more appropriate than a discretionary trust. This is often the case where there is a desire to benefit a particular beneficiary in the short term but with the underlying capital ring-fenced for other beneficiaries. These trusts are often created in a will and used to benefit a surviving spouse with income, or the right to occupy a property, for life and the capital asset passing to adult children on their death. This can be particularly useful where there are children from earlier relationships who may otherwise be disinherited by the surviving spouse, or see their assets absorbed by the costs of providing long-term care for them.

10.2.3 Disabled person's trusts

A special type of discretionary trust is available if the beneficiary qualifies as either physically or mentally disabled using the criteria specified in Inheritance Tax Act (IHTA) 1984, s.89. These types of trust enjoy inheritance tax privileges which other types of discretionary trust do not. There are restrictions on the value of distributions which can be made to beneficiaries other than the disabled person, but these can be a useful vehicle to provide for a vulnerable beneficiary.

10.2.4 Bare trusts

The other main type of trust is a bare trust, which is where the trustees effectively act as nominee for the beneficiary. Such trusts can be used to hold assets for minors and benefit from the more generous tax rates and allowances available to individuals as the trusts are effectively 'looked through' for tax purposes. However, it must be borne in mind that minor beneficiaries will become absolutely entitled to the trust assets at age 18, which may not be appropriate in all circumstances, unless a power can be exercised to advance capital for example, on a trust to give the beneficiary income only.

Bare trusts are also often used to hold personal injury settlement monies in order to provide protection against means testing for various state benefits. Thought should be given as to the personal tax effect on the beneficiary when creating this type of trust as trust assets will be amalgamated with the beneficiary's own assets for all tax purposes including income tax, capital gains tax (CGT), IHT and stamp duty land tax (SDLT).

10.3 APPOINTING AND REMOVING TRUSTEES

10.3.1 General procedures

The settlor will usually name the trustees in the trust deed, which for will trusts will normally be the will or a codicil, possibly with the addition of a 'deed of variation' if that created or varied the trust – although this may be done at a later date using a 'deed of appointment'. (All references to the 'trust deed' in this chapter will include the will and any deed of variation for will trusts.) It is good practice for the trust deed to specify who has the power to appoint and remove trustees for the avoidance of doubt. For lifetime settlements, this will often be the settlor during their lifetime but provision should also be made in the event that the settlor loses capacity and this issue is often overlooked. For wills, it is often not specified and then will simply be the current trustees at the time.

By virtue of Trustee Act 1925, s.36 a trustee may be removed and a new one appointed, in the following circumstances, unless stated otherwise in the trust deed:

- death of a trustee;
- a trustee staying out of the UK for more than 12 months;
- a trustee who desires to be discharged;
- a trustee who refuses to act;
- a trustee who is unfit to act;
- a trustee who is incapable of acting;
- a trustee who is a minor.

Such a removal should be effected by a deed executed by the following:

- the nominated person as defined in the trust deed; or if there is none,
- the continuing trustee(s); or if there is none,
- the personal representatives of the last surviving trustee.

It should be noted that an executor who intends to renounce may still exercise the power of appointment even if they do not accept the executorship. Where there is more than one executor, then they must all have the intention to renounce in order to exercise the said power.

Where a trustee lacks capacity and also has a beneficial interest in trust property, then an application must be made to the Court of Protection in order to remove them as trustee and secure a replacement.

10.3.2 Overseas issues

Appointing a trustee who lives overseas can bring an additional layer of complexity to the management of the trust. The practical difficulties of holding trustees' meetings may largely be overcome by the judicious employment of modern video conferencing technology. However, documents which require wet signatures may have to be couriered to ensure safe arrival and then a local notary or other professional engaged to provide an appropriate witness. Specialist local advice should also be sought on the legal and taxation effects of accepting the appointment, as in some jurisdictions the trust will be 'looked through' and the underlying assets treated as belonging personally to the trustee. Trustees living in the US should exercise particular caution in this regard. It should also be borne in mind when making trust investments that many investment providers will not accept non-resident trustees due to money laundering concerns.

10.4 BENEFICIARIES

It is very important that trustees are familiar with the trust's beneficiaries, and their circumstances, if they are to manage the trust equitably. This is particularly important with discretionary trusts where they may be able to make decisions to appoint capital and income to a wide and varied class of beneficiaries.

First, the trustees should closely examine any 'letter of wishes' left by the settlor to ascertain whether any specific guidance has been left with regard to who should primarily benefit from trust assets, in what way and to what extent. They should enquire into the current circumstances of the beneficiary in case these have changed substantially since the trust was created. If the beneficiary no longer has capacity then they should correspond with any attorney or deputy appointed to act on the beneficiary's behalf in respect of their financial affairs.

When making decisions about whether to make payments to beneficiaries, it is important to be mindful of such issues as:

- whether the payments will affect means-tested benefits;
- whether the beneficiary has demonstrated any financially irresponsible behaviour which may be exacerbated, such as gambling or giving away excessive amounts of money;
- whether the beneficiary has demonstrated any addictive behaviours, such as to drugs or alcohol, which may be exacerbated by access to additional funds;
- whether the beneficiary is in the process of a relationship breakdown, whether marriage or otherwise, which may allow a former partner to make a claim on assets released from the trust;
- whether the beneficiary is having financial difficulties which may lead to bankruptcy;
- whether the beneficiary is facing prosecution likely to lead to a custodial sentence; such a beneficiary could become vulnerable in prison if it is known by other inmates that they have access to large sums of cash.

In some cases it may be more appropriate and more beneficial to make payments to third parties on the beneficiary's behalf, such as to creditors, in order to provide financial security without the risk of temptation to spend the funds elsewhere.

Beneficiaries should always be advised to take their own tax and legal advice regarding any entitlement to trust assets, particularly if they live outside the UK. Residents of the US should be especially careful, as the US tax regime is not favourable to non-US based trusts.

Beneficiaries should be contacted at least annually to ensure that contact details are up to date. Be careful of the risk of fraud, especially with emails that may get out of date or 'hijacked' by fraudsters, and the risk of paying funds to any new account.

Where the beneficiary is a minor, it is appropriate to contact the parent or guardian to advise them of the existence of the trust, unless advised to the contrary. If any funds are required, to reimburse payments for the minor, then proof of expenditure should be requested.

10.5 TRUST REGISTRATION

Trusts which are not bare trusts are treated as separate legal entities for tax purposes and are subject to their own regime for income tax and CGT.

At the time of writing, trustees must notify HMRC by 5 October following the tax year end of the existence of the trust by completing the online trust register on HMRC's Trust Registration Service (TRS) (**www.gov.uk/trusts-taxes/registering-a-trust**) – but completion of the register has only been required if the trust had a specific tax liability. A tax liability includes income tax, CGT, IHT, SDLT, stamp duty reserve tax (SDRT), and in Scotland land and buildings tax and in Wales land transaction tax. (The inclusion of SDRT has meant many charitable trusts have had to register as they have paid SDRT on shares.) This is in accordance with the EU Fourth Money Laundering Directive (4MLD).

The Fifth Money Laundering Directive (5MLD) was introduced from January 2020, but with a delay for the trust register regulations, to allow for consultation, to be introduced later in 2020. These regulations took effect in October 2020, with a schedule of trusts that were 'excluded' from the need to register – Schedule 3A. Many new trusts will need to register on TRS even though no tax liability arises at this stage, and they may in many respects be 'dormant trusts'. This may include some life policies or pensions written in trust for IHT planning, as well as jointly owned property, and some trusts arising on death where the trust continues beyond two years from the date of death. There are some specific exclusions here, and at the time of writing no guidance is as yet issued, but is likely in early 2021, with registrations due from March 2022. So the key point is to note that this needs considering with any new trust created on death or in lifetime planning.

The trust register requires extensive details of the settlor, trustees and beneficiaries, including names, addresses, dates of birth and national insurance numbers. If a national insurance number is not available – for example, if the beneficiary is under the age of 16 – then passport details may be substituted.

Once the trust is registered, HMRC will issue a unique taxpayer reference (generally known as a UTR) for the trust to allow tax returns to be filed.

From May 2020, trustees are also obliged to update the register online to advise HMRC of any relevant changes to the trust such as in relation to the following:

- settlor;
- lead trustees;
- other trustees;
- beneficiaries.

If there are no such changes, then the trustees must still complete an 'annual declaration', also online, to confirm such. The annual declaration must be completed by 31 January following the tax year in which the changes took place, if any tax was payable in that tax year. Trustees who file annual tax returns should also confirm in the tax return that the annual declaration has been completed. The requirements for 5MLD are slightly less onerous.

10.6 INVESTING TRUST FUNDS

10.6.1 Overview

One issue which trustees must consider very carefully is how to invest the trust's funds in order to match the objectives of the trust. The investment of trust funds is governed by the powers contained within Trustee Act 2000, Part II which must be read in conjunction with any specific powers provided in the trust deed and any letter of wishes.

Trustees are required by Trustee Act 2000 to take professional advice, but their responsibilities do not end here. They must be confident that their chosen adviser understands the specific investment requirements of trusts and the particular trust on which they are being asked to advise. In turn, the trustees must be sure to give clear instructions to the adviser about the trust's requirements and any investment restrictions.

The following are some examples of the details that should be supplied to the adviser to allow him to provide appropriate advice:

- whether, and to what extent, to invest for capital growth and/or income;
- tax position of trust;
- age and life expectancy of beneficiary;
- tax position of beneficiary;
- tax residence of beneficiary;
- period to vesting date if applicable;
- beneficiary's likely needs for income/capital in short and long term.

Trustees should review investments at least annually, preferably in conjunction with the original adviser, to monitor performance and to ensure that they still fulfil the requirements of the trust in the light of any changes.

It is best practice for trustees to prepare a 'statement of investment objectives' which are agreed and signed by them all which the adviser may use as a reference point. Such objectives should also be reviewed annually.

If a trust is established from the residue of an estate, it is often tempting for the executors to appropriate the existing investments to the trustees without any professional input. This is to be avoided, as investments which may have suited the lifestyle of the deceased are unlikely to be suitable for the needs of the trust and may not have been reviewed for several years. It should also be remembered that certain investments, such as ISAs, cannot be held by trusts and will require liquidation before transfer in any event. However, if advice is taken first, there may be circumstances where some investments can be retained and transferred to the trustees to avoid dealing costs.

10.6.2 Investment managers and financial planners

While typically trustees have instructed investment managers to advise on/manage investments, increasingly trustees are starting with an independent financial planner (FP). An FP can consider the investment objectives and requirements of the trust, the risk approach, etc. and advise both on whether an investment manager is required and, who that might be. In many cases, where there is a sufficient amount to invest, trustees are having a 'beauty parade' between two or three firms, to see what approach they would bring, and their outline ideas for investment. It can be a valuable approach worth considering.

10.7 TRUST WITH PROPERTY

It is very common for trusts to own property either in full or in part ownership. Such assets can bring their own challenges.

10.7.1 Rental property

A trust may purchase a property as an investment to be let to third parties. The trustees should be careful to take advice regarding the SDLT implications of such a purchase as in many cases the SDLT surcharge will apply. (See **Chapter 25**.)

Letting income will be taxed in the hands of the trustees unless mandated directly to a life tenant; however, in this case consideration should be given as to how the costs of repairs and maintenance are to be borne. It is wise to maintain a capital reserve fund in such cases.

If a will trust is designed for, or likely to include, a property, it is worth encouraging a testator, where possible, to include a capital sum as well as the property in the trust. Any such sum may then produce income to help an income beneficiary pay their share of expenses as well as providing capital for expenses and fees where needed.

The trustees should also consider the appointment of a letting agent to manage the property on a day-to-day basis and deal with any minor repairs. The trustees will be responsible for ensuring that adequate buildings insurance is in place.

10.7.2 Occupied property

Frequently a property or property share is left in trust by will, often for the benefit of a surviving spouse or child to be occupied for life. The terms of the trust usually provide for the occupant to maintain and insure the property but issues can arise if such instructions are not observed. If a property is not maintained, then this can affect its value and the capital beneficiaries may look to the trustees for a resolution if they believe that they have lost out financially as a result. Equally, a property which has not been comprehensively insured could leave the trustees at a real risk of a claim by affected beneficiaries.

A trust which contains only an occupied property and no liquid funds will be unable meet any form of expenditure including professional fees and for this reason when such a trust is drafted it is recommended that a sum of cash is included as a fees and maintenance fund.

In addition, trustees should be proactive about checking the property on a regular basis, preferably annually, in order to ensure that it is being kept in reasonable repair and condition. A record of the property should be maintained by taking photographs when the property is first acquired and keeping an inventory of any furnishings. If the trustees are not responsible for insurance then the trustees should request a copy of the relevant policy annually from the occupant, and ensure the insurers have noted the trustees' interest in the property on the policy and that it is insured for a sufficient sum, together with receipts and warranties for any repairs undertaken.

It is also important to ensure that the occupant is still living in the property; if they have moved out, then this may invalidate any insurance and a specialist policy may be required. It is best practice to write to the occupant annually and ask them to confirm in writing that they continue to occupy the property.

10.8 TRUST TAX RETURNS

Trusts which generate income or gains are obliged to file tax returns (form SA900) under the self-assessment system. If payments are made to beneficiaries, then the trustees may also be obliged to prepare forms R185 for each beneficiary. The form R185 shows the net amount of the income received (or treated as received), together with an associated credit for the tax paid by the trustees.

If the trustees are not confident in preparing the returns themselves then a professional should be engaged. Some solicitors and accountants are confident in, and do a lot of, this work, but many are not. If you are unsure, note that some solicitors' firms, accountants and tax advisers offer a service that can include 'white labelling' accounts and tax returns for other firms. In this case it is worth developing good working relationships with your fellow professional firm to ensure that you understand what each of you is doing, and needs, and to ensure the most effective liaison and the least duplication of time and cost. If accounts are being prepared (see **10.9**), the tax returns can follow naturally after the accounts are completed.

If returns are filed on paper then this must be done by 31 October following the end of the tax year on 5 April. Returns filed online must be submitted by 31 January following the tax year end. Returns filed after these deadlines will be subject to a late filing penalty of £100. If the trust has an income or CGT liability then this must be paid by 31 January following the tax year end. Tax paid after this date will accrue interest, and tax paid after 28 February will attract a late filing penalty of five per cent of the unpaid tax.

Additionally, trustees of relevant property trusts may be required to file form IHT100 and supplementary forms in respect of periodic and exit charges.

10.9 TRUST ACCOUNTS

Although there is no statutory obligation to prepare trust accounts, it is considered best practice to do so. If there are investments, or a property where some expenses are capital and some income, if accounts are not prepared it is easy for a trust to get into difficulties. Confusion and mistakes can easily arise – for example, with the split between income and capital.

There should be sufficient detail within the accounts to provide a basis for the trustees to make informed financial decisions and answer relevant questions.

The STEP Accounting Guidelines (3rd edn, 2018) (which establish common standards in England and Wales for the preparation of accounts for estates and trusts) suggest that the following questions should be addressed:

- What are the terms of the trust?
- Who are the beneficiaries, their ages and vesting dates as appropriate?
- What are the assets, their acquisition costs and current values?
- What cash does the trust hold, and what are the outstanding liabilities?
- How much income has been received?
- What income and capital distributions have been made to beneficiaries?

The format of the accounts should be discussed with the person preparing the trust accounts but the following sections would be expected:

- summary of trust – details of settlor, trustees and beneficiaries;
- notes on trust – history of trust to date, including vesting dates and changes to trustees;
- balance sheet;
- capital account;
- income account;
- distribution account;
- trustees' approval.

The accounts should be circulated to all trustees for approval and signature. Copies of the accounts may be requested by beneficiaries or their advisers to assist in financial planning.

10.10 VESTING

Where a beneficiary has a contingent interest in a trust, then it is important to diarise the vesting dates so that matters can be dealt with promptly.

The trustees should contact the beneficiary well in advance of any vesting date, advise them of their interest and ask for instructions as to how they wish to receive their entitlement. If the funds are invested in property or shares, for example, then the beneficiary may wish to leave the assets intact rather than encash them. The beneficiary should be advised to take their own independent legal and financial advice before deciding on a particular course of action. The trustees should give the beneficiary all necessary financial information so that informed advice can be given, for example the base cost of any assets subject to a holdover claim for CGT purposes.

Once a decision has been made, then the trustees can proceed with encashing or transferring the assets. Sufficient funds should be retained to meet any outstanding liabilities such as tax or fees.

Before making any payments to a beneficiary, the trustees should ensure that they have up-to-date identity and address information and preferably check that the beneficiary has not declared bankruptcy. This can be more difficult with beneficiaries living overseas, and specialist advice may be required.

A 'deed of advancement' should be prepared in relation to any payments of capital to which a beneficiary is absolutely or contingently entitled. If the capital is coming from a life interest trust, which is a qualifying interest in possession (QIIP) trust, then it is deemed to be a potentially exempt transfer (PET) by the life tenant. If the life tenant fails to survive for seven years, then the value of the PET will be amalgamated with their free estate for IHT purposes and the trustees could find themselves with an unexpected liability. They should therefore retain sufficient funds to meet the liability; take insurance; or obtain an indemnity from the recipient of the funds to ensure that they are covered.

Forms R185 should be prepared in respect of income payments.

Beneficiaries should always be asked to provide a receipt for payments made.

10.11 WINDING UP A TRUST

There are many reasons why a trust may be wound up and the trustees should be careful to document their reasons in the trustee minutes and prepare a trustee resolution for retention with the trust documentation.

Assets will then need to be valued, and arrangements made for their sale or transfer. Beneficiaries should be notified and discussions held as to how they wish to take any distribution. Final tax returns (SA900 and IHT100) should be prepared, tax paid and tax clearance requested from HMRC. Final payments should not be made to the beneficiaries until clearance has been received.

Final distribution accounts should be prepared and agreed/signed by all trustees before circulation to the beneficiaries for information.

Deeds of advancement (for contingent or absolute payments) or appointment (for discretionary payments) should be prepared.

10.12 MASTER DOCUMENTS

Best practice dictates that trustees should keep a master file to hold trust documents to contain the following:

- details of trust – trust deed or will; grant of probate; any deed of variation creating the trust; death certificate of settlor (if applicable); any deeds of appointment/advancement;
- trustee details – names; addresses; copy ID; deeds of appointment/retirement;
- beneficiary details – names; addresses; copy ID, personal information, birth certificate and any marriage certificate, adoption certificate or deed poll;
- copies of signed trust accounts;
- copies of signed trust tax returns;

- investment details – letters of instruction to, and advice from, any financial planner and investment adviser; and terms of business for third party providers;
- property details – copy title deed; insurance policy; photographs of property; valuation;
- estate accounts if trust arose from a will.

PART III

Estate planning, wills and variations

CHAPTER 11

Introduction to variations: changes within two years of date of death

John Bunker

11.1 KEY POINTS

- Variations within two years of death are a crucial part of inheritance tax (IHT) planning, to ensure that the right provisions operate 'with the benefit of hindsight', to mitigate the IHT payable either on that death or on a future occasion.
- This chapter outlines the crucial basics of the three forms of variation, including some examples illustrating how this can work, and then **Chapter 14** explores more fully the planning potential. The two intervening chapters work through lifetime planning (**Chapter 12**) and the crucial issue of will planning for spouses which is central to so much planning within the two-year period (**Chapter 13**).
- There are three sections of the Inheritance Tax Act (IHTA) 1984 – ss.142–144 – headed 'Changes in distributions of deceased's estate':

  - s.142 Alteration of dispositions taking effect on death;
  - s.143 Compliance with testator's request;
  - s.144 Distribution etc. from property settled by will.

- Which statutory provision applies and what powers are used to effect the variation? It is always important to be clear about the difference between:

  - the statutory provision that applies, especially IHTA 1984, s.142 or s.144; and
  - the powers used to achieve the variation, which may depend on the powers given to executors and trustees in the will, which often extend statutory powers, or the limited statutory powers themselves, which are crucial for s.144; and
  - the rights of beneficiaries under any will or intestacy, and any agreement to amend those rights – as under a s.142 variation.

Deeds of variation (DOVs) under IHTA 1984, s.142 (see **11.2**) are the most widely used of the three forms, and they are crucial to effective IHT planning, so this chapter aims to introduce the basics, before we look at planning in more detail in **Chapters 13**, **14**, etc. They are also invaluable in planning to make the most of the residence nil rate band (RNRB) – see **Chapters 16** and **17**.

- **Rearrangements of trusts under IHTA 1984, s.144** (see **11.3**) are increasingly important with RNRB, being a key way to ensure the right form of trust or absolute ownership is in place to utilise the benefits of RNRB. A rearrangement can be a means of correcting a form of trust that doesn't qualify for RNRB, for example by an advancement or appointment so that it does, which can be a very simple process. It also includes changing the form of trust, from one tax system to another – for example, from a discretionary trust taxed as relevant property to an immediate post-death interest (IPDI) trust (a qualifying interest in possession), or vice versa.

  However, it is important not to lose sight of two key points on both s.142 and s.144 variations:

  - Variations are often made for good non-tax reasons, e.g. to put right a problem with the estate, or a personal consequence of the way the will is drafted or that the intestacy rules work, or to meet personal needs. It is not just a tax planning tool – any beneficiaries can agree between themselves to change what they were to have, or to pass on something to another. This can be very simple, with different beneficiaries ensuring they inherit the right things – but it can be the end result of a dispute over the will or a claim under the Inheritance (Provision for Family and Dependants) Act 1975.
  - Whatever the driver for the rearrangement, it is important to ensure it is done in the most tax-effective manner possible; or that, at the least, clients have a chance to make an informed choice whether they wish to pay for advice on the tax effects of their proposed actions and any alternative structuring that may be better. It may be that a client is not prepared to pay for the tax planning advice, but the issue should always be brought to their attention. A will or trust dispute may be handled by a litigation lawyer, or a contentious private client specialist, but the tax planning effects ought to be considered by the relevant person.

- **Precatory trusts under s.143** are the oft-forgotten variation, 'compliance with a testator's request' most typically coming in the form of a 'letter of wishes' regarding personal possessions. It is easy to forget the effect of s.143, and care is needed with a regular provision in wills and estates that may be relevant to future IHT liabilities (even if not tax payable immediately on the estate), as set out in **11.4**.

  While the main IHT planning is secured through ss.142 and 144, it is good to be aware of how s.143 works and what impact that will have on other planning, and occasionally it might offer an effective form of planning itself.

11.2 DEEDS OF VARIATION UNDER IHTA 1984, S.142

11.2.1 Overview

Some of the main points to note about DOVs under IHTA 1984, s.142 are:

- They are also known as 'instruments of variation' (as HM Revenue and Customs (HMRC) refers to them) or deeds of family arrangement (as traditionally known).
- DOVs may be entered into by any beneficiaries of an estate, whether inheriting by will or by intestacy rules, to rearrange their inheritances, subject to two provisos:
  - all those giving up any rights are of full age and capacity; and
  - they are together fully and absolutely entitled to the assets or share of estate being varied.
- For the variation to be effective for IHT, s.142 requires a statement in the DOV that the parties intend s.142(1) to apply to the variation. Then it will be 'read back' to the date of death, as if the provision was made by the deceased in a will.
- A separate issue is whether the variation will apply for capital gains tax (CGT) purposes, and if so an additional statement should be included in the deed. Most DOVs are done for personal and/or IHT planning reasons and many will not need to apply for CGT. There was a time when 'elections' needed to be made, for IHT and CGT, and this is no longer the case, but a choice is still needed. This needs to be considered separately from the IHT position, and will be commented on briefly in planning, though largely beyond the scope of this book.
- There is no reading back to date of death for income tax purposes, so the income tax treatment simply changes with effect from the date of the DOV. So, the three main taxes (IHT, CGT and income tax) are all different here.
- DOVs must be signed by all those giving up anything from the estate, and by the personal representatives where there is any additional tax to be paid.
- DOVs are generally in one of three forms (discussed below):
  (i) beneficiaries carving up their inheritances in a different way;
  (ii) variations to pass on some benefit to others;
  (iii) beneficiaries with different settled interests carving up the trust fund.

11.2.2 Beneficiaries carving up their inheritances in a different way

Where different people entitled to a specific asset, legacy or share of a residuary estate under a will or on intestacy want to divide up the estate in a different way, they can do so as a legal document in any event. If there is no special tax treatment required, this does not need to be done before the second anniversary of death.

However, for the IHT benefits, if done within two years of death, IHTA 1984, s.142 enables them to 'read back' the new provisions to the date of death, as if the deceased had made that varied provision in a will.

If there is any contingency, so that say one beneficiary is not fully entitled to an inheritance unless and until something happens, this would in practice restrict what can be done in a variation. There may be powers in the will, and/or statutory powers, that the executors and trustees can use to help the situation. For example, if a will provided for a grandchild if they attain the age of 21, a power of advancement could be used to advance the capital to the beneficiary, which if done within two years of death would be treated as done by the deceased under s.144. The grandchild, assuming over the age of 18, could then join in a DOV in respect of their inheritance which was now theirs without any contingency.

There is no restriction on the use of s.144 and s.142 in the same case, such as this – the commonly understood restriction is not having two variations under s.142 in respect of the same asset.

Example 11.1

Sisters Erica and Rasha were each left a valuable item of jewellery by their mother, Julia, as specific gifts in her will, in addition to being residuary beneficiaries with their brother Lenny. Erica was left a diamond ring worth £20,000 but really wanted Julia's gold necklace worth £10,000 which went to Rasha. As Rasha preferred the ring, they agreed a DOV that gave Erica the necklace and £10,000 cash to come out of Rasha's share of residue.

Example 11.2

Anna, who had no children, left her property to her sister Thea, thinking she wished to live there, and the residue of her estate to her brother David. By the time of her death, Thea had moved to another part of the country but David was getting a divorce and wanted to live in Anna's home. The net values were similar, even though not the same, and they agreed a DOV for the mutual convenience.

11.2.3 Variations to pass on some benefit to others

Some simply do not want or need all they have inherited and would prefer to give some away to their loved ones, or to a charity or other body. This is, in effect, like a deed of gift but in the form of a DOV so that the gift can be treated as made by the deceased and not be a lifetime gift by the person giving up their inheritance.

But for IHTA 1984, s.142, it would be a potentially exempt transfer (PET) (if to a beneficiary outright) or a chargeable transfer (if to a trust) by the original beneficiary who gave up their rights. This is important as many DOVs do not have any immediate effect on IHT on the deceased's estate, but are designed to avoid any IHT consequences for the effective 'donor', through the deceased being treated as the donor for IHT purposes.

Example 11.3

Ruby, who has inherited from her mother Gloria, has a son Eddie whom she wants to help, but his life has many difficulties and leaving him money outright would be problematic. By contrast, her daughter Ella is well able to handle an outright inheritance. So you advise Ruby to do a DOV giving funds to Ella outright, and leaving an IPDI trust for Eddie to have the income, with power to advance capital but thereafter for his children.

Example 11.4

Wes, Ruby's husband, has just died, and he didn't do any tax planning by his will, everything coming to Ruby. She thinks she can manage without the full estate, and wants to leave Wes' nil rate band (NRB) in trust. She could set up a NRB discretionary trust, to put in the £325,000 NRB on Wes' death, of which she can be a beneficiary with her children. (See **14.2.1** – this is a major element in planning for spouses.)

The DOV can set up the trust with all its management powers and include the appointment of trustees. No IHT is saved on Gloria's estate, but the gift to Ella is treated as from Gloria (not a PET by Ruby) and Gloria is also the settlor for IHT purposes of the trust for Eddie.

Example 11.5

Julia (in **Example 11.1**) had a second son Freddie, who had not been left anything in the will, as he had fallen out with his mother some years ago as he had been taking drugs. His three siblings all wish to give him an equal share of the residue. They can therefore do a second DOV, as it's a different asset from the change regarding jewellery that Erica and Rasha are making, or it could be all in one document.

Freddie is being *given* something, not giving anything up, so doesn't need to be party to the DOV but could be for completeness. Of course, the provision for Freddie may follow a formal claim against the estate, with the DOV for IHT purposes to effect the agreed change. Advice should be sought from a litigation specialist about anything that needs signing from that perspective.

11.2.4 Beneficiaries with different settled interests carving up the trust fund

If the beneficiaries who are together absolutely entitled to the income and capital of a trust (set up by will or intestacy) wanted to rearrange their interests within two years of death, for example to carve up the capital between them, they could do so by a DOV. The deed could involve all swapping their interests in income, or in reversionary capital, for an outright share of capital. This is often done to avoid the costs, and frustrations that some feel, with running a trust. In an appropriate case, where an ongoing trust is not needed, it can be a very sensible arrangement.

This is effectively a deed of partition and can be done at any time, as a matter of legal entitlements, but if done within two years of death that arrangement can be read back to the date of death for IHT. If the initial entitlement is an income one, and that amounts to an IPDI, IHTA 1984, s.144 for trust rearrangements will not apply and one must use s.142 DOVs. This may also be a case where it would make sense for the DOV to apply for CGT too, so that for both taxes there is no complication with valuations on the partition.

11.3 REARRANGEMENTS OF TRUSTS UNDER IHTA 1984, S.144

The main points with regard to rearrangements of trusts under IHTA 1984, s.144 are:

- The heading to IHTA 1984, s.144 – 'Distribution etc. from property settled by will' – reflects the fact that this may be a distribution out of a trust, or might be a rearrangement into a different form of trust.
- A classic use of s.144 is to rearrange a discretionary trust into an IPDI for a surviving spouse, by giving that spouse a life interest (whether or not revocable) in order to utilise the spouse exemption. This is classically done by a deed of appointment by the trustees.
- A second major means of processing a change is by a deed of advancement to correct the form of a trust, for example so that it qualifies for the IHT treatment required, or to make an absolute gift.
- Section 144 is available to 'rewrite' the terms of any trust in a will, or indeed any intestacy trust, provided no IPDI arose in the meantime, i.e. a life tenant and reversionary beneficiaries would need to do a deed of variation under s.142.
- Section 144 will apply automatically, for the rearrangement of the trust to be read back to the date of death, and s.144 does not require a statement that the section is intended to apply.
- Great care is needed not to make any change, within the two-year period after death, that is inadvertently within s.144 and which is read back when it is not needed. This can lead to unexpected and unwanted consequences.

Example 11.6

Ravi has died and left his whole estate on a discretionary trust. He has fully used his NRB with gifts during his lifetime and so the spouse exemption needs to be utilised to avoid any IHT on his death. So the trustees can do a deed of appointment to appoint out the capital to his widow Sunita either absolutely or on an IPDI trust with a revocable life interest. The latter is preferable for asset protection purposes. It helps that Ravi has left a clear and full letter of wishes about how his trustees should use their powers.

Example 11.7

Sam had left a NRB discretionary trust in his will, with an IPDI trust of residue for his widow Marlene. He was widowed before and has a double RNRB to use if a suitable interest is left to a trust for his children direct from his estate. The trustees can use their powers in the will to appoint out of the NRB discretionary trust, to take effect under s.144, or can convert the discretionary trust to an IPDI trust which qualifies for the spouse exemption. Or the NRB discretionary trust can be kept as such, for the various IHT planning advantages – see **Chapter 13**.

11.4 PRECATORY TRUSTS UNDER IHTA 1984, S.143 – THE 'FORGOTTEN' VARIATION

IHTA 1984, s.143 is the third section in the part of IHTA 1984 concerned with 'changes in the distribution of deceased's estate'. It is the oft-forgotten variation, but it is actually relevant to many estates. While not limited to this situation, its regular application is to wishes regarding personal chattels.

Many testators leave a 'letter of wishes' regarding personal possessions, or personal chattels, with a clause in the will requesting executors to follow the wishes in any such note. This can cause confusion among practitioners, let alone clients, as the will clause will usually say the gift to the spouse and/or the executors is an absolute one with no obligation to follow the wishes. However, this is a classic example of 'compliance with a testator's request' and, if followed, should be read back under s.143.

It is easy to forget the effect of s.143, and just to assume, especially where this is left to a surviving spouse to arrange, that the chattels passed on by the spouse will be lifetime gifts. Great care is needed with such a provision in estate administration, as this may be relevant to future IHT liabilities (even if not to the tax payable immediately on the estate).

Example 11.8

Brenda has died leaving her husband, Tom, the classic gift of chattels to divide as per any list of wishes she left. Brenda had some rather lovely, valuable items of jewellery, totalling £25,000, and also some other personal items worth £40,000 which were her personal property and not jointly owned with Tom. As the latter were family heirlooms, and Tom did not need them, she wanted her children and grandchildren to have these. Tom follows Brenda's wishes and passes on the specified items to the family.

The effect of IHTA 1984, s.143 is that Brenda has made gifts totalling £65,000, or 20% of her NRB of £325,000, to children and grandchildren, i.e. non-exempt beneficiaries. This uses 20% of her NRB and if there were a legacy for example, to a NRB discretionary trust, assuming no other legacies the balance of £260,000 would be available for the trust.

However, in many estates the remainder would simply go to the spouse, Tom, with the benefit of a spouse exemption.

The question of how much of the NRB had been 'used' would then arise on Tom's death, when the transferable NRB (TNRB) would be considered. 20% has been used on the chattels, so that if the NRB at Tom's death were still £325,000, it would leave £260,000 for the TNRB. However, if the NRB had then increased, to say £350,000, the 80% TNRB would be £280,000. (It's easy to forget, when the NRB has been 'frozen' at £325,000 for so long, that the TNRB is a percentage of the new NRB not a set figure.)

What might be the alternative treatment, if Tom said he wanted to decide for himself whether to follow Brenda's wishes, and make the gifts himself as lifetime gifts to the children and grandchildren? If Tom was still relatively young, and felt he had a good chance of living for seven years after these gifts, he might feel that is a better option. It is not straightforward, and there are practical and valuation/tax issues to consider.

Practically speaking, it would be necessary for Tom to take responsibility for the process, the handing over of the items, etc. If he were to ask the estate solicitor to deal with this, to arrange receipts from each child and grandchild for the items received, etc., that would risk looking like a continuing part of the estate, and a potential tax avoidance. He would need to get his paperwork in very good order, to back up the choice he had made, to show how he had received the items himself and then later made a decision to give the items. Ideally this should be later, if possible after the second anniversary of Brenda's death, to bring the tax treatment and practical reality into line.

What steps would be needed by a surviving spouse, such as Tom, who chose to make the gifts later, personally?

1. An up-to-date valuation, or confirmation that all the values were unchanged, not simply the total value, should be obtained – for two reasons. First, for IHT, Tom needs to know the value of each item he has gifted. Second, for CGT, if any item worth at least £6,000 were to have increased in value since the date of death, there is a potential liability for CGT on the increase. If IHTA 1984, s.143 is followed, the items are treated as given by the deceased spouse, Brenda, at probate value. That would then be the acquisition cost for the beneficiary for future CGT purposes.
2. A total value gifted to each beneficiary is needed, to see the amount of the lifetime gift to each from Tom. Some of the values may be £250 or less, in which case they could be exempt within the small gifts exemption, subject to whatever other gifts Tom has given that person in that tax year.
3. If the total value of the chattels gifted to any one beneficiary, plus all cash or other gifts in the tax year, was not more than £250, it would be exempt. However, if the value exceeded £250, then the whole amount would count towards the annual exemption or, if that had already been used, it would be a PET.
4. Thus, Tom would need to break down the £65,000 of items gifted, according to the recipients; consider the other relevant gifts; and then keep records in case he died within seven years.
5. Tom would also be well advised to get each person to sign a receipt and acknowledge the value gifted, to give each of them some record for their own future tax purposes.

Altogether, it is rather simpler to treat the gifts as made by the deceased, as well as being the way to follow IHTA 1984, s.143. As s.143 will apply in any event, as for s.144, it is important to show, as a matter of fact, that this has not been followed, if the different tax treatment outlined above is intended to apply.

CHAPTER 12

Planning with lifetime gifts

Vicky Day

12.1 KEY POINTS

- This chapter sets out practical ways to reduce inheritance tax (IHT) on death by making lifetime gifts. It also identifies potential traps when certain gifts are made.
- The small gifts exemption and the annual exemption, although relatively small, can prove useful.
- Normal expenditure out of income (Inheritance Tax Act (IHTA) 1984, s.21) is explored in some detail, as it is both an exemption with huge potential and one that is easy to get wrong, with crucial elements that need to be satisfied.
- Interaction with capital gains tax (CGT) is considered, as to gifts to trust with the benefit of holdover relief and the traps with residential property, which are important in practice – both for planning and for trust compliance if running any trusts.
- Bare trusts are an underutilised tool but may be beneficial for minors, people with a mild disability or those who may be potentially vulnerable.
- Reservation of benefit, such a major issue in IHT planning, is addressed to illustrate how this can operate as 'the worst of all worlds'.
- Death-bed CGT planning is a very niche aspect of lifetime planning, but can be very useful in the right circumstances – for example, where one spouse has a terminal illness and seeks to do some planning to benefit their spouse when they have died.

12.2 SMALL GIFTS AND ANNUAL EXEMPTION

Although relatively small in value, the small gifts exemption (£250 per year to any number of people) (IHTA 1984, s.20) and the annual exemption (£3,000 a year) (IHTA 1984, s.19) can mitigate tax if used consistently over a number of years. For example, two spouses between them using the annual exemption every year for 10 years will save £24,000 tax for their estates. If they each used the small gifts exemption to give £250 a year to, say, 10 grandchildren over the same period, they would save an additional £20,000 tax.

Example 12.1: To illustrate the interaction of small gifts, annual exemptions, PETs and taper relief

Hilary is married to Bill and they have a son Joe and a daughter Al; and each 6 April Hilary makes gifts to Joe and Al of £1,500 each (total £3,000) and £250 to each of their grandchildren (in place of gifts at Christmas and birthday).

However, the Christmas before she dies Hilary gives each of her four grandchildren £100, which is not exempt but also means that the sums of £250 given on 6 April are also no longer exempt as small gifts, so are now PETs. 4 x £350 PETs = £1,400 total.

Her husband Bill doesn't give to Joe and Al each year. Why doesn't Bill give £3,000 between Joe and Al, to use his annual exemption; or jointly give £6,000 with Hilary? This is allowed if from a joint account to which both make payments or receive income. Bill then gives Al £306,000 in June 2010, and he dies five years later in June 2015. Bill had used no annual exemptions, so has his £3,000 exemption for 2010/11 and the 2009/10 exemption brought forward, which reduces the amount of his PET to £300,000.

Hilary gives Joe £400,000 in 2011 to buy a house, which is all a PET as she has used all her annual exemptions, and she dies five years later in 2016.

Bill's PET to Al of £300K is a failed PET when he dies five years later in 2015. It uses most of his NRB, leaving £25,000 unused NRB transferable. All his estate of £400,000 goes to Hilary so is spouse exempt.

Hilary's PET to Joe of £400,000 is a failed PET when she dies five years later.

- Ignoring transferable NRB of £25,000 in 2016:
  - Would be £75,000 over NRB = IHT on gift £75,000 at 40% = £30,000.
  - Taper relief of 60% (= £18,000) reduces tax on the gift to £12,000.
- But taking into account the £25,000 transferable NRB from Bill:
  - This reduces the IHT on the gift: £75,000 – £25,000 = £50,000 at 40% = £20,000.
  - Taper relief of 60% (= £12,000) reduces the tax payable to £8,000.
  - Then the rest of the estate is all taxed at 40% as there is no NRB/TNRB left.

12.3 NORMAL EXPENDITURE OUT OF INCOME

12.3.1 Definition

This provision (IHTA 1984, s.21) is sometimes overlooked, as it relates to a series of gifts out of excess income rather than capital. It is worth setting out the wording of the relevant section:

(1) A transfer of value is an exempt transfer if, or to the extent that, it is shown –

(a) that it was made as part of the normal expenditure of the transferor, and
(b) that (taking one year with another) it was made out of his income, and
(c) that, after allowing for all transfers of value forming part of his normal

> expenditure, the transferor was left with sufficient income to maintain his usual standard of living.

In summary, if a taxpayer makes gifts, or makes a commitment to make gifts, as part of their everyday expenses and out of taxed income, these are not subject to IHT.

Unlike other exemptions which are given automatically, this exemption must be claimed by the executors on the taxpayer's death, and therefore careful thought needs to be given to planning use of the exemption and providing enough evidence to show compliance with all the conditions necessary to claim the relief.

12.3.2 'Normal expenditure'

In considering what is 'normal', HM Revenue and Customs (HMRC) will look at the frequency; the amounts given; the nature of the gift; the identity of the recipients; and the reasons for the gifts (see IHTM14243, first paragraph):

- **Frequency:** The gifts do not have to be regular or even annual, but regular gifts are more likely to meet the normality test.
- **Amount:** Gifts must be comparable in size. Sometimes gifts can be made by reference to a source of income that is variable (for example, share dividends from a private company); sometimes gifts can relate to specific costs which vary (for example, different school fees for grandchildren). A taxpayer can, for example, resolve to give away 10 per cent of their excess income (which may vary in amount from year to year depending on what income was received). If a particular gift is in a different category from those which are normal because of its size, HMRC will want further evidence to show whether and how it fits into the pattern of normal giving.
- **Nature of the gift:** The gifts will usually be transfers of money. A gift of a specific asset can meet the condition if it can be shown that it was bought out of excess income specifically allocated for that purpose (for example, a car for each grandchild on their 18th birthday).
- **The identity of the recipients:** The gifts in question must be given to people or organisations in one category, but there can be more than one category. The gifts can be made to a category by need (for example, to the poor and needy, which might include impecunious relatives and charities). Or, they can be made to a category by relationship (for example, children/grandchildren).
- **The reason for the gifts:** The circumstances around the gifts and the reasons for them show whether the taxpayer habitually makes gifts in such circumstances (for example, to reduce IHT on the taxpayer's estate; to help his children by paying grandchildren's school fees; to help children get a foot on the housing ladder by paying the deposit for their first house). The gifts must be comparable (for example, a large gift to set a son up in business is not comparable with modest birthday gifts to the other children).

12.3.3 Income (taking one year with another)

> Income is not defined in the IHTA84 but should be determined for each year in accordance with normal accountancy rules. It is not necessarily the same as income for income tax purposes. Income is the net income after payment of income tax.
>
> It is usually clear whether payments received are income in nature.
>
> *Inheritance Tax Manual*, IHTM14250, HMRC
> **(www.gov.uk/hmrc-internal-manuals/inheritance-tax-manual/ihtm14250)**

Withdrawals from investment bonds, typically using the five per cent per annum allowance, involve cashing in capital, and will not normally be accepted as income for this purpose even if drawn regularly – say monthly.

Where income has accumulated from previous years, it is likely to be treated as capitalised unless the taxpayer can show that it had been set aside for the purpose of gifts within the meaning of IHTA 1984, s.21 – for example, the case of *McDowall (McDowall and others)* v. *Commissioners of Inland Revenue* [2004] STC(SCD) 22) where income had been put aside in a separate account over three years for the purpose of making a gift of £12,000 to each of five children.

Income that has been saved for many years and has been invested or saved into a form that now itself produces income is likely to have been capitalised. HMRC's current view is that income is deemed to have been capitalised after two years, and documented evidence will be required to show anything different (IHTM14250, paragraph headed 'Available Income').

'Out of income' does mean that it must be paid out of income in practice, rather than out of, for example, capital repayments.

Tip

Clients could pay their income into a bank account and then make the gifts out of the same account. If the gift is to come from both of a couple, then the account should be in their joint names and income from both should be paid into it. If it was only coming from one source, then HMRC might question whether it was a genuine joint gift, if the details were investigated.

For example, if a savings plan involved capital payments being made (such as redemption of gilts or withdrawals from an investment bond), and then gifts out of income (for example, payment of premiums on a whole life policy), the capital should go into the main bank account, which also receives income, rather than into a separate account out of which the gifts are made. Otherwise, HMRC will say the payments were not, as a matter of fact, made out of income. This can be the case even if there is other surplus income available elsewhere in the person's funds.

12.3.4 Maintenance of usual standard of living

The taxpayer must retain sufficient income, after making the gifts, to maintain their usual standard of living. The test for standard of living is a subjective test, personal to each taxpayer. When the relief is claimed, HMRC requires a detailed analysis of the income and expenditure for each year the exemption is claimed. Form IHT403, one of the supplementary pages to the form IHT400, is the current form that the executors are required to submit when claiming this relief.

Tip

If a client is making gifts to utilise the normal expenditure exemption, give them the IHT403 form and invite them to complete it with details of their expenditure each year. In practice it is very difficult, and time-consuming.

What is normal for one taxpayer will not be normal for another. Take holidays as an example. The cost of a holiday will not be normal expenditure when a taxpayer goes on holiday once every few years on an ad hoc basis. However, if a taxpayer regularly takes two holidays a year, the costs of those holidays can form part of their normal expenditure.

If a taxpayer changes their car every eight years, that is unlikely to form part of their normal expenditure – unless the taxpayer pays for it by taking out a loan/lease agreement which they pay by monthly instalments. Capital purchases such as TVs or computers made once every five or six years are likely to be just that, capital purchases.

12.3.5 Written resolution

A written resolution can set out the taxpayer's intention for future payments and also secure past payments, to the extent to which they qualify. This can be very varied, so the taxpayer will need to think carefully about their particular circumstances. Many solicitors find clients say that a gift should be exempt as it was paid out of income – but it is not that simple!

Tip

To maximise the chances of a successful claim, the taxpayer should decide what income they want to give, the reasons why they want to make the gift and to whom – and set these out in writing. This written statement, or resolution, should be reviewed and updated if necessary every few years to ensure that it remains current and evidences the taxpayer's intention. They can make outright gifts from income to individuals or into trust. Where income is variable each year, what percentage does the taxpayer intend to give?

Where there is overpayment, HMRC will still allow the amount that qualifies for the relief, but the taxpayer may be inviting more investigation into their affairs the more they try to claim.

Once the taxpayer has recorded their intention and set out their plan, it is important then to adhere to that plan as recorded to minimise the chance of a successful challenge by HMRC. They then need to set up the payment mechanism (for example, standing orders from their current account to the donees of their choice in the frequency of their choice). A simple regular payment (out of surplus income) is the best way to comply with the conditions of IHTA 1984, s.21.

12.4 INTERACTION WITH CAPITAL GAINS TAX

Generally, IHT and CGT are taxes which counter each other – i.e. when one is payable, the other usually is not.

12.4.1 Gifts to trusts with benefit of holdover relief

As we saw in **Chapter 5**, a lifetime gift into a substantive trust (other than a disabled person's trust (DPT)) is a chargeable transfer for IHT. A taxpayer can currently (2020/21) give £325,000 into trust without paying tax (assuming they have made no gifts into trust (chargeable transfers) in the previous seven years. The transfer into trust is still chargeable, but at the 0 per cent rate. Any value in excess of that (cumulated) threshold will be subject to an immediate 20 per cent lifetime inheritance tax charge.

A disposal into trust is also a disposal for CGT purposes, but there is a relief under the Taxation of Chargeable Gains Act (TCGA) 1992, s.260 where the gift is a chargeable transfer for IHT. Then the CGT does not have to be paid but can be deferred if the transferor and trustees claim holdover relief. The gain is held over into the trust and the trustees acquire the asset at the settlor's original acquisition value, rather than at the market value at the time of the gift.

Trustees also pay CGT on the gain on disposal of an asset within the trust. The trustees' rate is 20 per cent (28 per cent for residential property) and they have only one-half of an individual annual exemption. However, any gain can also be held over on an exit from the trust. The beneficiary will acquire the asset at the trustees' acquisition value. (If the gain has been held over going into the trust, that acquisition value will therefore be the settlors' acquisition value.)

12.4.2 Traps with residential property

CGT payable on the gain in a residential property is subject to an eight per cent surcharge. The gain on a residential property can be held over on a transfer into a relevant property trust. However, if it is intended that a beneficiary of the trust will occupy the property as their main residence, careful thought should be given to the position at the outset. This is because no claim can be made for main residence relief by the trustees where a gain has been held over – so if it is intended that the property in trust is to be any beneficiary's main residence at any point, a careful analysis of the position to ascertain which is the most tax advantageous should be undertaken.

Trustees need also to be mindful of exercising their powers of appointment to create life interests in relevant property trusts which contain residential property. Although this planning might be undertaken to mitigate income tax payable in the hands of the trustees, it can affect stamp duty land tax (SDLT) that the beneficiary with the life interest may pay when they buy residential property for themselves. An interest in possession is treated as ownership for SDLT purposes which may result in the additional three per cent surcharge being paid by the beneficiary. The interest in possession does not have to be a qualifying interest in possession (QIIP) for SDLT purposes. The trustees may have powers to override such an interest in possession in these circumstances (see also **Chapter 25**).

12.5 BARE TRUSTS

Bare trusts are an underutilised tool in the box. Perhaps because they are not a substantive trust at all and are transparent for tax purposes, i.e. the beneficiary is treated as the beneficial owner of the trust assets for all tax purposes. Because of this, any gift to a bare trust is akin to a gift to an individual, and therefore a potentially exempt transfer (PET). There is an obvious benefit to using bare trusts for minors as a way to start the seven-year period for the donor while protecting the assets in trust until the minor comes of age.

Bare trusts are also a useful tool for adults under a mild disability or who are financially or emotionally vulnerable in some way. Their disability may not be enough to qualify them as a beneficiary of a DPT, but it might be significant enough to warrant protection in some way. Although an adult beneficiary of a bare trust who has capacity is able to call for the assets of the trust to be transferred into their direct ownership, the adult beneficiary must still call for them. There is therefore an occasion when a conversation must be held. Consider a situation where a young adult is about to turn 18, or a vulnerable adult is aware that they have fair-weather friends – they might be grateful for the layer of protection that holding their funds in a bare trust entails, with the support of the trustee to manage those funds and help with the use of them as appropriate.

See also **10.2.4** for focus on compliance.

12.6 RESERVATION OF BENEFIT ISSUES

12.6.1 Introduction

Gifts with reservation of benefit (Finance Act 1986, ss.102–102C), commonly called GROBs, are the worst of all worlds. A GROB results in the legal transfer of an asset from donor to donee and is effective for CGT purposes but ineffective for IHT. The donor therefore loses access to the asset, but their estate is still liable for the IHT on the value of that asset. (See also **Chapter 4**.)

Example 12.2

James lives in Bournemouth in his home worth £700,000. It is his only asset of any value. As a divorcee, he is aware that he has only one nil rate band (NRB) and residence NRB (RNRB) so there will be at least £80,000 IHT payable on his death. In June 2019 he gives his property to his daughter Anne who lives in Manchester with her children. He however continues to occupy the property. Suppose James dies 10 years later when the property is worth £900,000 and assume no change in value in the NRBs. Because James continued to live in the property, he reserved a benefit. Therefore the value of the home is included in his estate for IHT purposes (and HMRC will take the higher of the values at the date of the gift and the date of death). In addition, he has lost main residence relief for CGT as Anne does not live in the property as her main residence. Therefore not only will Anne pay IHT on the £900,000 property (less any NRBs) but on the sale of the property she will also pay CGT on the increase in value from £700,000 in 2010 to £900,000 10 years later.

To avoid the GROB rules, possession and enjoyment of the gifted property must be bona fide assumed by the donee to the exclusion or virtual exclusion of the donor (although in practice the de minimis benefits that can be retained under the 'virtual' exclusion are too negligible to be of practical value). Therefore, where the donor pays a market price for use or possession of the gifted property, no benefit has been retained (because of the consideration paid) and there is no GROB.

Example 12.3

Joan lives in a beautiful manor house just outside Leeds with a large collection of paintings and artworks. She gives the collection to her daughter but keeps it in her home. This would be a GROB. So Joan has the collection valued and pays a market rent to her daughter for the lease of the artworks from her daughter. Provided that the rental value is reviewed regularly (rule of thumb – at least every three years or as provided for in the rental agreement to ensure it is sustained at market value), the gift will be effective and fall out of account after seven years. Joan must continue to pay market rent for the duration of the time she continues to hold the artworks in her house and benefit from enjoying them.

Tip

As the example demonstrates, although it is often forgotten by clients, it is vitally important that the market rent is kept current. Regular reviews of the rent are required and the necessary increases made. The payment of rent is a useful way of donors getting further assets out of their estate for IHT purposes.

12.6.2 Joint ownership

Although it may be difficult to give away an entire property which the donor wishes to continue to use, the legislation allows for a gift of an undivided share in land to be given in some circumstances and for there to be no reservation of benefit (Finance Act 1986, s.102B). For the exception to apply, both donor and donee must either (a) both not occupy the land, for example where it is rented to a third party; or (b) both occupy the land and the donor does not receive any benefit from the arrangement. If the latter, it is not necessary that the donee occupies as their main residence, but they must actually be in occupation.

Tip

For a residential property where the donor is enjoying and requires the income but needs to consider disposing of the capital for IHT purposes, (a) above could be used to carve out a gift of a significant amount of the capital value of the property to the donee while the donor retains a significant amount of the income. Provided you come within the rules, this should not be seen as a GROB. Care, however, must be taken with CGT. This solution is helpful if the property is not already pregnant with gains.

12.7 DEATH-BED CAPITAL GAINS TAX PLANNING

There is an opportunity to undertake some tax planning where one spouse is terminally ill. (The term 'spouses' in this chapter includes both married couples and civil partners and where both or neither of the couple are domiciled in the UK.) This utilises the reliefs for both IHT and CGT where one spouse transfers assets to the other.

The usual position is that gifts between spouses (who are living together) are tax neutral for CGT, i.e. neither the gifting spouse nor the receiving spouse makes a gain or a loss on the gift (TCGA 1992, s.58). Therefore, the gifting spouse has no gain to report and the receiving spouse acquires the asset at the gifting spouse's acquisition value for the purpose of calculating future CGT. The gift must be fully effected before the receiving spouse's death for this to apply.

On the death of the receiving spouse, the transferred asset will form part of their assets which will pass to their personal representative, who will be deemed to acquire them at the market value at the date of his death (TCGA1992, s.62(1)).

The receiving spouse's will can then give the asset to the surviving spouse who will then once again own the asset but with a new acquisition value which is the value of the asset at the date of the receiving spouse's death (TCGA 1992, s.62(4)).

Example 12.4

Mrs Bott, a higher rate taxpayer, owns an investment property which she inherited from her mother 10 years ago when it was worth £200,000. It is now worth £400,000. If Mrs Bott sells it now, she will be liable for CGT on the gain at 28% (which will include the 8% surcharge on residential property). Mr Bott has been given a terminal diagnosis and given less than six months to live. Mrs Bott gives the property to Mr Bott. There is no CGT on the disposal and Mr Bott acquires the property with Mrs Bott's acquisition value of £200,000. There is also no IHT, as it is a transfer between spouses. *NB: The income from the property will be payable to Mr Bott from the date the property is transferred to him.*

On Mr Bott's death, the property forms part of the residue of his estate, which under the terms of his will goes to Mrs Bott, again free of IHT. As Mr Bott's estate will have had all its assets uplifted to market value for CGT purposes, Mrs Bott has a new acquisition value of £400,000. She can now sell the property and there will be no CGT.

Too good to be true? The general anti-abuse rule (GAAR) was introduced in 2013 to target abusive tax avoidance schemes, i.e. where HMRC considers that the taxpayer is entering into an abusive arrangement which is beyond anything which could reasonably be regarded as a reasonable course of action. If HMRC considers that a course of action is abusive, then there will be a tax adjustment which is just and reasonable in all the cases.

The action set out in **12.7** is given as a specific example of an arrangement that does not fall within GAAR.

CHAPTER 13

Spouses/civil partners: will planning with trusts

John Bunker

13.1 KEY POINTS

- **To use, or not to use, the nil rate band (NRB), the residence NRB (RNRB), or both?** That is the question. The key question in inheritance tax (IHT) planning for spouses. Along with how to use the spouse exemption. The planning changed greatly with the introduction of the transferable NRB (TNRB) in October 2007. Then again with the advent of the RNRB in April 2017.
- **The NRB discretionary trust (NRB D/T) is hugely important** – see **13.3**. Its purpose has changed since 2007, but it has had a new lease of life with the RNRB with reference to planning around the £2 million threshold. Using the NRB with this form of trust takes assets out of the potential 'estate' for the purpose of the £2 million threshold, above which the RNRB is tapered away, and thus serves a major role – see **Chapter 17**.
- **IHT planning for spouses who cannot claim RNRB:** what can be done? One of the answers is the use of the NRB D/T, as this can help secure many tax benefits, even when there are no descendants to claim RNRB or the estate is well over the £2 million threshold and so the RNRB is bound to be tapered away. These include securing a third NRB (see **13.3.3**), securing a valuable discount on the appropriation of a property interest to the D/T (**13.3.4**) and assets likely to increase significantly in value (**13.3.5**).
- **Variations: It is increasingly important to consider variations within two years of death to secure the best structure:** variations of both estates and trusts – see **Chapter 14**. While variations are normally not the best option, and can have some drawbacks, they are often the only way to secure reliefs after the first spouse dies, where up-to-date planning was not entered into prior to death. Changes in law and practice, and uncertainty about the value of estates, mean that spouses often do not have the more sophisticated wills incorporating trusts for the most effective IHT structure.
- **Clients considering the costs of a better structure?** See this comment in full in **14.1**. So long as a simple form of cost/benefit analysis shows the extra value

offered by a better structure, clients can decide whether to incur the extra fees for a variation. It is even better if that analysis can be offered in the joint lifetimes of the spouses, to encourage a better structure to be set up in both wills – see **14.3.3**.

- **Any retrospective planning for the deceased's estate can still be done by variation, but the main focus is on the surviving spouse's own estate planning.** The new thinking to maximise the benefits of RNRB includes a great deal of new spouse planning (see second point above).
- One advantage of including the surviving spouse in the trustees' planning is that, assuming the surviving spouse and the trustees are working towards the same outcome, that outcome can be achieved by the surviving spouse varying their absolute entitlement, or the trustees exercising their powers contained in the will trust.
- There may be practical difficulties with varying other trusts or arrangements if there are insufficiently wide powers for the trustees within the terms of the will trust. It can mean having to obtain beneficiaries' consent to a variation and if beneficiaries are underage or incapable (for example, because of lack of mental capacity) the variation may not be possible. It's always better to advise clients to appoint trustees that they absolutely trust and then give those trustees wide, flexible powers, wherever possible!

NB: In this chapter, for simplicity we will use the word 'spouse' to also denote a civil partner.

13.2 SPOUSE EXEMPTION AND INHERITANCE TAX PLANNING

13.2.1 The spouse exemption

The spouse exemption applies to both:

- outright gifts to a husband/wife/civil partner; and
- gifts by will to an immediate post-death interest (IPDI) trust where that spouse has an income entitlement.

It also applies to a less-used form of lifetime gift into trust for a disabled spouse which qualifies under Inheritance Tax Act (IHTA) 1984, s.89 (as this is another form of qualifying interest in possession trust). This special provision under s.89 is an exception to the rule that a gift into any lifetime trust with a life interest for a spouse would now normally be into a relevant property trust (RPT) where the spouse exemption would not apply.

Since the introduction of the TNRB, common provision for spouses in wills has been by outright gifts or within an IPDI trust, in each case relying on two IHT elements (and now, with RNRB, on a third element):

(a) the spouse exemption means no IHT is immediately payable;
(b) the TNRB will be available to use on the surviving spouse's estate, and any aggregable trust; and now
(c) the carry-forward of RNRB (sometimes called TRNRB as if it is also being 'transferred') means there can be a double RNRB set against the surviving spouse's estate (and any aggregable trust).

At the rates applicable in tax year 2020/21 that means the following tax-free or nil rate allowance:

2 NRBs @ £325,000 = £650,000

2 RNRBs @ £175,000 = £350,000

Total = £1 million!

2020/21 is the tax year when we reach the magic target figure which is at the heart of RNRB, that two spouses are able to leave £1 million tax-free to their descendants. There are of course conditions which must be met (for which, see **Chapter 16**), but this chapter highlights the big proviso that the aggregable total of estate and trust must not exceed £2 million, otherwise the RNRB is 'tapered away' by £1 for every £2 over the limit.

The taper threshold over £2 million means that, in practice, there is a 60 per cent marginal IHT rate on the capital over that limit, when 40 per cent IHT and the lost benefit of the RNRB are added together. This is a very high marginal rate of tax, exceeding even the 55 per cent rate on pension death benefits that was withdrawn in 2015 (and that had been a penal rate where pensions had not been drawn as they were supposed to be, to compensate for the tax benefits enjoyed by pension schemes).

We therefore explore some alternative planning ideas in this chapter, and come to the key question: To use, or not to use, the NRB, the RNRB, or both?

13.2.2 To use, or not to use, the NRB, the RNRB, or both?

'To use' here means making a gift in the will of the first to die which is not an exempt gift, so that the NRB or RNRB is utilised and not transferred or carried forward, and the spouse exemption is not used. We use the word 'use' regularly throughout this chapter (and the whole book). It also works with the adage 'use it or lose it'. We will cover the using of the NRB in **13.3**, but the using of RNRB is best left to **Chapter 17** on RNRB planning, after the basics of RNRB are explored in **Chapter 16**.

The important point for IHT planning is that these alternatives to the main practice since 2007 need to be considered carefully, as part of a rethinking of how spouses arrange their estates, plan to use their assets and then leave their assets on their deaths. This also extends to the whole estate planning review covered in **Chapter 18** and the financial planners' perspective referred to in **Chapter 19**.

13.3 NIL RATE BAND DISCRETIONARY TRUSTS

13.3.1 Setting up a NRB D/T on the first spouse's death

A NRB D/T in a will usually has these main key features:

- **It is expressed to take effect** only if the testator dies before their spouse.
- **The beneficiaries** of the trust include the surviving spouse, the children, grandchildren, etc. (Whether 'in-laws' are included is a difficult issue, but on balance it is advisable not to include them but to give the trustees the power to add beneficiaries.)
- **The trust fund** comprises the maximum amount that can be left free of IHT, typically one NRB, i.e. £325,000 in 2020/21. The precise wording is best left to a precedent/drafting book or resource, but there are some important drafting points to note:

  - **TNRB:** It is best to allow for the TNRB to be included in the trust. This will allow a testator who is already a widow to put say £650,000 (two NRBs) into their will trust and if the TNRB from the widow's first spouse is not used on the death of the widow, it will be lost – see **13.3.3**.
  - **Agricultural property relief and business property relief (APR/BPR):** If there are any farm or business assets, it is best to include such assets in the trust, or at least those that qualify for APR or BPR. Any assets with 100 per cent APR or BPR can be included in the trust in full, in addition to assets up to £325,000 in value. Any assets with 50 per cent BPR or APR can be included up to a value of £650,000 – reducing to a value of £325,000 for IHT purposes. If these assets are not specifically gifted to the trust, you cannot have the benefit within the trust of the APR or BPR value on top of the NRB.
  - **Uncertainty as to whether APR or BPR applies**? **Chapters 15** and **20** explore some issues about the extent of any relief and, in particular, whether a business is mainly trading or mainly an investment – if the latter, BPR would be denied. So if you are not sure, it is worth putting the whole farm or business into the trust, not limiting it by reference to the relief, and then HMRC will need to assess the eligibility for the relief. See **20.5.2**.

- **The spouse can benefit from the trust as much as they need** by the use of the property, or from income. It would ideally operate as a form of 'reserve fund' on which the spouse could draw if needed, but not otherwise. Certainly if capital is to be drawn on it is better (IHT-wise) for the spouse to draw on their own estate, rather than on the capital of the D/T which is outside their estate for IHT purposes all the time it is a RPT.
- **There is the two-year period from the date of death**, in which to review the D/T, to decide whether to keep it as a relevant property trust (RPT), or to appoint out on IPDI trusts to the spouse (or, even, if asset protection is not an issue – to the spouse absolutely).

- **If the D/T is kept as an RPT (for example by staying as a D/T) on the first death, it is not subject to IHT on the second death.** The trustees can give the spouse a life interest after the period of two years has passed from the date of death, at which point it is not 'read back' to that date of death under IHTA 1984, s.144 – see **Chapter 14**.
- **If a NRB D/T is not set up in a will, it can be set up by a deed of variation.** It should work fully for IHT, but see the comments on disclosure of tax avoidance schemes (DOTAS) in **Chapter 14**. Do note, as set out in **Chapter 14**, the different rules that will apply for the other taxes whereby the spouse will be treated as the settlor for income tax and (if they had been entitled to the capital) for capital gains tax (CGT).

13.3.2 A recap on purpose

NRB D/Ts were a major tax planning vehicle until October 2007, when the TNRB was introduced, as a way to get two bites of the cherry – to use two NRBs rather than waste one of them. The introduction of the TNRB means there are fewer circumstances where NRB D/Ts are needed for the sole purpose of securing the TNRB and some clients and solicitors see them as superfluous.

However, there is still a real value in having a NRB D/T, for the right client and potential estates, even before the new value added by RNRB – see **Chapter 17**. Solicitors and tax advisers should still encourage the use of NRB D/Ts by clients in appropriate circumstances (even though they may be more difficult to 'sell' to clients) for all the good reasons set out below. It is worth noting that, while there is an added RNRB factor, this option is also one of the few that is open to clients who don't qualify for RNRB. Spouses who wish to mitigate IHT but don't have the direct descendants to benefit from the RNRB can still benefit from these planning ideas.

13.3.3 Securing a third NRB?

- **Use it or lose it!** One important principle of TNRB is that the maximum amount that can be transferred is 100 per cent of a NRB. No matter how many times a person has been widowed, and how many unused NRBs there have been, the unused parts of NRBs to be transferred can only add up to 100 per cent. Thus if a NRB is not used, it is lost. It really is a case of 'use it or lose it'.
- **Possibility of a third NRB if it is used well.** There are two situations where a third NRB could become usable:

  1. **If a spouse (spouse B) had been previously married to spouse A and was then widowed before this marriage to spouse C.** If spouse A had left their full estate to spouse B, then B's estate can claim A's TNRB and there is the potential to use two NRBs. If only part of A's estate was left to B (disregarding any charitable or other exempt gift), any other non-exempt legacy or gift that A had left would potentially use part of A's NRB so that

only a reduced percentage of A's NRB would be transferable. If B had been widowed more than once, the unused percentages of TNRB can add up to the 100 per cent maximum.

Tip

- **Always check whether either spouse has been widowed before, and whether the NRB was 'used' on the death of that previous spouse.** Clients often forget details of how the estate passed that may be relevant to whether any part of the NRB has been 'used'.
- **How can you tell whether the NRB has been used?** You can tell to some extent from seeing the earlier spouse's will, grant of probate and estate accounts; but, as important as these are, you do need to know other elements. Were there any lifetime gifts that were caught by death within seven years? Was there an aggregable trust and did that leave part of the trust to another chargeable beneficiary on the death of the spouse (for example, part going to children or grandchildren)? Finally, had a life interest in a trust been brought to an end in whole or part?

2. **If the widow(er) remarries, there can also be a third NRB.** As there is a maximum claim of two NRBs in one estate, the deceased's own and one transferable (whether this is from one previous spouse or a combined total of 100 per cent from more than one previous spouse), a third NRB becomes available if the TNRB is used on the first death. Using the example above, if on B's death you ensure that A's TNRB is utilised, for example by a NRB D/T, the survivor C then has both their own and B's NRB that can be used or transferred if C remarries and then dies first. Or if their second spouse (D) also dies before them, D's NRB can be transferred to C's estate.

13.3.4 Putting a share of the property into the NRB D/T, claiming a discount

This is a major IHT planning opportunity that can work for many surviving spouses, and provide a solution to the operation of the D/T that is very manageable and cost-effective. It can stand alone, as a valuable arrangement in any event, or be part of a wider plan to 'use' the NRB to reduce the estate value for RNRB purposes ahead of the second death. It is an arrangement that has been used a great deal since the trust tax changes in 2006.

The arrangement that now works well for jointly owned property, to use the NRB D/T for the main residence owned by spouses (or potentially a second property), is as follows:

- When the first spouse dies, they leave a legacy equal to the NRB (or double NRB – see above) to the NRB D/T.
- Then, all or part of their half share (or it could be any share) is appropriated to

the NRB D/T, in satisfaction of the legacy, normally with a small cash balance to cover costs. In appropriating the property share to the trust, the executors of the estate can make a discount of 15 per cent in the market value of the property. This discount is 15 per cent because there is a co-owner in occupation, and is possible because it is a valuation for the purpose of appropriation, not for IHT on death. The 'related property' rules (in IHTA 1984, s.161) do not apply because at the point of appropriation, the property is no longer co-owned by spouses (as the marriage ends on death).

- On the death of the surviving spouse, the remaining interest in the property can be valued with a 10 per cent discount. It is 10 per cent because at this stage there is no co-owner in occupation, but the property is jointly owned with a RPT. If the D/T had been changed into an IPDI then, of course, the trust would be aggregable with the spouse's personal estate and there would be no discount.
- The 15 per cent discount causes some uncertainty, as it cuts across a principle well known to many. However, the arrangement does work, and the writer's firm has seen many cases work through the second death with the second discount claimed and the whole interest dependent on the first 15 per cent discount.
- As it happens, HMRC has helpfully confirmed in the context of RNRB that appropriation is an administrative power and 'is not a disposition' (IHT Manual IHTM46033). For RNRB purposes, this is so that it is not possible to rearrange an estate to be 'read back' for IHT purposes to the date of death. See **Chapter 16**.
- The combined effect of the two discounts, of 15 per cent and 10 per cent, is that IHT on the property can be reduced by 12.5 per cent of the value. If it were a second investment property, it would be a straight 10 per cent discount on each death and thus a 10 per cent reduction in the value of the property.

Example 13.1

Harry and Wendy are married and own a cottage valued at £760,000 when Harry dies in 2020 with a £325,000 NRB. Wendy lives for a further eight years, and when she dies the property has increased in value by 30% to £988,000. We will also assume the NRB is up 30% to £420,000, although that is optimistic and the potential tax savings would be even better if it had increased by less.

There are two ways of dealing with Harry's property interest:

1. If Harry's 1/2 share goes to Wendy, on Wendy's death:
   - Wendy's estate has a double NRB (2 x £420,000) = £840,000;
   - to set against the full property value = £988,000;
   - so 40% IHT on £148,000 = £59,200.
2. But if Harry's 1/2 share goes to the NRB D/T:
   - Harry's executors claim a 15% discount on 1/2 share on appropriating the share to the trust;
   - £380,000 discounts to £323,000 so that all Harry's 1/2 goes to his NRB D/T;
   - the balance of the legacy is £2,000 cash towards expenses;

- on Wendy's death her 1/2 = (£988,000 ÷ 2 less 10% discount) = £444,600;
- deducting £420,000 leaves only £24,600 over NRB x 40% = £9,840.
- **IHT saving on Wendy's estate = £49,360.**
- **Therefore 12.5% of value of the house taken out of IHT.**

This arrangement has in practice replaced the old arrangement of putting the property into the name of the surviving spouse, subject to a debt or charge to the trust – see **13.3.6**.

NB: Caution is advised in using the 15 per cent discount in planning involving a discretionary trust created by a deed of variation. See **14.3.2**.

13.3.5 Other tax planning benefits of NRB D/Ts

Investing to beat the frozen NRB

With the NRB threshold frozen as it has been for 12 years at £325,000, until 5 April 2021, and the real prospect that this could be extended because of the need to raise more tax from taxpayers (following the impact of the coronavirus pandemic), one simple idea is to try to invest to beat the frozen NRB.

Assets in a NRB D/T may grow, in the short term, to a value higher than the NRB. So some trustees might aim to invest the £325,000 in, say, investments to be managed, in the expectation that they will grow in value, with the growth being outside the surviving spouse's estate. The future for the NRB beyond April 2021 is unclear, but it may be worth considering as some further freezing is quite likely. The author had a client who decided to take this course in the early days of the frozen NRB of £325,000, when it was anticipated it would be retained at that level for another three or four years, since when it has in fact been frozen for many more years, illustrating the potential here.

Assets likely to increase significantly in value

It is possible to appropriate an asset to a NRB D/T at a low market value applicable during the estate administration and then, if that value should increase significantly over a period of 10 years, see some added tax benefits.

If the asset does appreciate significantly before the 10th anniversary of the date of death (when the 10-year periodic charge on the RPT first arises) it is possible to secure that increased value free of IHT by taking it out ahead of the 10-year anniversary date. Any 'exit charge' in the first 10 years of a NRB D/T should be nil, so that there is no IHT to pay.

So the asset could be appointed out to beneficiaries, so that it is outside the RPT before the 10-year charge arises. The capital gain could be 'held over' to the beneficiaries so that they themselves would pay the CGT when they dispose of the asset, and in many cases the beneficiaries' personal CGT exemptions (£12,300 each in 2020/21) will be available. The rates of CGT payable, after any exemption, would then be the marginal rates of those beneficiaries, with some potentially at lower rates than the 45 per cent rate of CGT that would be payable on the gain on assets disposed of by the trustees in the trust.

This arrangement can work especially well with land that has development potential, but starts with a relatively low value. A piece of agricultural land will have a low value, but if planning permission is acquired, there will be a significant increase in value. Some clients hold small pieces of land which are unlikely to be developed on their own and so have minimal value now, but have good prospects for an increase in value if adjoining land should be developed. They are often described as 'ransom strips', valuable as they give better access to other land which then opens up the scope for development. Where land in an estate is relatively low in value (and within the NRB threshold), giving it into a NRB D/T by will can be good planning.

Example 13.2

Sam had some land, a run-down shop which was no longer trading, adjoining a site used as a car park, in an area of town where there was potential for development for some town-centre homes, to help the council's housing targets. On Sam's death, the land was put into Sam's NRB D/T under his will at the market value of £50,000. Eight years later, planning permission for the development of the car park was granted and the developer approached the trustees to buy the site owned by Sam's trust. The trustees plan to sell it in the ninth year after Sam's death, having had an offer for £1 million, and seek your advice on tax planning.

The land is owned in the NRB D/T of which the discretionary beneficiaries are Sam's widow, his three children and 10 grandchildren. With a value of £1 million, it can be appointed out of the D/T to a number of these beneficiaries, with the gains held over, before the sale (pre-exchange of contracts). This could be done any time before the 10-year anniversary, but the commercial considerations of securing the sale mean action is needed quickly with reference to the £950,000 gain. The distribution from the trust to the beneficiaries is effectively free of IHT, and the capital gain is held over to the beneficiaries, to pay tax at their lower rates, thus mitigating overall CGT.

13.3.6 What about the debt/charge scheme for the main residence?

Historically, the debt/charge scheme was widely used in the 1990s and early 2000s, but is not recommended for new arrangements, as noted in **13.3.4**. (This has been included as, although it is now rarely used, it was used a lot in the past and you may come across historical arrangements with this structure.)

It worked as follows:

- On the death of the first spouse, the property was transferred into the name of the surviving spouse subject to a debt to the NRB D/T equal to the NRB.

- To create a return on investment and give security to the arrangement, sometimes the debt was secured by a charge on the property; and sometimes the debt was index-linked so that it rose in line with inflation.

This old arrangement had the advantage that the whole property was then in the estate of the surviving spouse who remained in occupation and had the benefit of main residence relief for CGT. However, there were complex issues about whether, when and how the debt was repaid and the income tax treatment on any return on the 'investment'.

In addition, new anti-avoidance provisions were introduced in 2013/14 relating to liabilities outstanding on death and the extent to which they could be deducted (IHTA 1984, s.175A) – see **4.3.4**. Essentially, unless a debt of an estate was actually repaid to the estate, it could not be treated as a deduction for IHT, which was an indispensable part of the debt/charge arrangement. So there was a choice, to repay and deduct or to waive the debt and not repay.

If the debt was index-linked, the decision was whether to repay the indexation (as well as the loan) and pay the income tax HMRC claimed was due on it, and then claim that as an additional deduction from IHT; or to waive the loan, not pay any income tax but not deduct the value of the loan from the estate to reduce the IHT. At that time, HMRC argued that the increase in value on the loan created by the indexation was subject to income tax at the trust's rate, but this was disputed by many lawyers and academics. An HMRC *Trusts and Estates Newsletter*, in April 2017, made it clear that HMRC wanted to put an end to continuing academic speculation that the indexation was not taxable, and estates having outstanding issues about this. It said, effectively, 'put up or shut up'.

Either make a formal appeal and let the tax tribunal decide, or accept that the indexation is subject to income tax. The 45 per cent income tax charge on the trustees (unless the surviving spouse was treated as the settlor for income tax because the NRB D/T had been created by a deed of variation) could, potentially, be offset by distributing income to a number of different members of the family who were nil or basic rate tax payers, who could then reclaim some or all of the income tax paid. If you encounter any of these arrangements now, this is the principle of how they work, but the author does not recommend implementing a NRB D/T using the debt/charge arrangement now.

The changes in legislation in 2006 removed the risk there had been that the surviving spouse might be treated as having a qualifying interest in possession (QIIP) in the share of the property in the NRB D/T, where the trustees jointly owned the property with the surviving spouse. That was the concern that led to the debt or charge being developed in the 1990s.

Once again, this shows the need to keep alive to changes in practice, so that the arrangement you are recommending to clients is current, appropriate and workable, and so that old arrangements can be reviewed and updated if needed.

13.3.7 A trust structure to enable a claim for main residence relief for CGT

While this book is focused on IHT, it is helpful to consider how any trust structure might also enable the trustees to claim main residence relief, often referred to as principal private residence (PPR) relief, to avoid an unnecessary CGT liability.

PPR relief can be claimed by the trustees of a will trust where the trustees co-own a property with a surviving spouse in one of two ways:

1. Where the part share of the property is held in a NRB D/T, and after the second anniversary of the death (so that it is not read back into the disposition of the estate under IHTA 1984, s.144):
   - the trustees create an income entitlement or right of occupation for the spouse; and
   - the trustees can then claim PPR relief under Taxation of Chargeable Gains Act 1992, s.225. (HMRC will permit the relief to apply also for the relevant part of the previous two years that the surviving spouse, as beneficiary of the trust, has occupied as beneficiary.)
2. Where the part share of the property is held on an IPDI for the surviving spouse, who remains in occupation, the trustees can claim PPR relief on the whole of the trust's share in the property:
   - where the deceased's share of the property is left part in an IPDI trust and part in a NRB D/T, for example, if the trustees hold 90 per cent of the deceased's half share of the property in a NRB D/T and 10 per cent of the deceased's half share of the property on an IPDI for the spouse, they can claim PPR relief on the whole 50 per cent trust interest without the need to create an income entitlement in the share held in the NRB D/T. (See also **Example 14.5** in the next chapter.)

CHAPTER 14

Planning within two years of death

John Bunker

14.1 KEY POINTS

- **Variations:** It is increasingly important to consider variations within two years of death to secure the best structure –variations of both estates and trusts. While variations are normally not the best option, and can have some drawbacks, they are often the only way to secure reliefs after the first spouse dies, where planning was not considered recently prior to death. Changes in law and practice, and uncertainty about the value of estates, mean that spouses often do not have the more sophisticated wills incorporating trusts for the most effective inheritance tax (IHT) structure.
- **Clients considering the costs of a better structure?** Whatever the reason why a variation may be needed (for example, lack of advice or failure of clients to take the advice or clients not wanting to spend the money for the advice at the time of making the will), practitioners should never be afraid to proactively suggest an improved structure that could work more effectively. So long as a simple form of cost/benefit analysis is given, showing the extra value offered by a better structure, clients can decide whether to incur the extra fees for a variation. It is even better if that analysis can be offered in the joint lifetimes of the spouses, to encourage a better structure to be set up in both wills – see **14.3.3**.
- **The two-year window offers an opportunity to switch between two trust regimes**, that of the relevant property trust (RPT) and that of the qualifying interest in possession (QIIP). The different IHT treatment each offers means this is a crucial choice, according to the specific circumstances, and we explore this in **14.4**.
- **Any retrospective planning for the deceased's estate can still be done by variation, but the main focus is on the surviving spouse's own estate planning.** The new thinking to maximise the benefits of the residence nil rate band (RNRB) includes a great deal of new spouse planning (see next point). See a fuller comment in **13.2**.
- **Two crucial points for spouse planning are key features of post-death planning** (set out more fully in **13.2**):

- **To use, or not to use, the NRB, the RNRB, or both?** This is a key question in IHT planning for spouses, along with using the spouse exemption (see **14.5**).
- **The nil rate band discretionary trust (NRB D/T) is hugely important** – see **13.3** – for both RNRB planning (see also **Chapter 17**) and those who don't qualify for RNRB.

NB: In this chapter, for simplicity we will use the word 'spouse' to also denote a civil partner.

14.2 INTRODUCTION

We outlined the main elements of variations in **Chapter 11**, including Inheritance Tax Act (IHTA) 1984, s.143 for precatory trusts. In this chapter, we will explore some of the planning issues with reference to the two main forms of variation, as a great way to secure the right structure for IHT planning purposes. By way of recap, IHTA 1984, ss.142 and 144 can be used to achieve the right end result within two years of death. Two different points to consider:

1. Which statutory provision applies?
   - IHTA 1984, s.142 if beneficiaries are varying their entitlement under the terms of will/ intestacy, by deed of variation (DOV).
   - IHTA 1984, s.144 if trustees are varying the terms of a trust created by will or intestacy.
2. What powers are being used?
   - Beneficiaries varying their entitlements by DOV, if they are of full age and capacity and are not compromising anyone else's rights.
   - Trustees using powers under the will, or statutory powers, and properly drafted wills will normally give the trustees powers to do so without obtaining consent of the beneficiaries.

14.2.1 Deeds of variation under IHTA 1984, s.142

Inheritance tax

Beneficiaries of an estate can vary their entitlement to income and/or capital. If they comply with the provisions of IHTA 1984, s.142, for IHT purposes the variation is 'read back' as if it were the result of a disposition by the deceased. The DOV has been a staple part of IHT planning for so many years; it has survived because it works. A Conservative Chancellor of the Exchequer famously tried to abolish it in the 1990s, but had to withdraw the plan. The reality is that DOVs are not mainly used by the supremely wealthy (who generally take timely advice getting effective plans into place in their lifetimes), but DOVs are particularly useful for three situations:

1. First, where changes in law and practice mean that tax planning provisions in wills and trusts need updating, to take advantage of new opportunities – for example, with RNRB.
2. Second, where clients have not addressed the tax planning opportunities when they were alive, either because these were not brought to their attention or they didn't ask, or in many cases the possibility was raised but they did not wish to spend money on advice or more complex wills and trusts.
3. Third, where disputes arise because of the terms of the will, including cases where family members are disgruntled and want to make a claim about the will's terms, a DOV can record the resolution of the dispute and ensure the end result is as tax effective as possible.

Once the DOV is executed, the terms of the DOV are 'read back into the will' as if the varied disposition had been made by the deceased, with effect from the date of death. That 'reading back' is critical to the planning. Any legacy or trust then takes effect from the date of death for all IHT purposes. This is where we must remember that each of the three taxes is different. For income tax, the variation is never read back, and for capital gains tax (CGT) it may be (if it is stated in the DOV that it applies, but the legislation for CGT is different and it does not apply for all CGT purposes (as for IHT)).

Capital gains tax

While CGT is beyond the scope of this book, it's worth noting in passing the key point in planning. While DOVs are executed almost always primarily for IHT purposes, it is not always appropriate for CGT to apply. It may be best for a 'disposal' to take place at the date of the DOV, crystallising any gain at that point, especially if there is an unused CGT exemption in the estate. That disposal – if, say, a transfer to a trust – can result in the trust acquiring the assets at a higher base cost, which can be valuable on a later disposal given trustees have only half the annual CGT exemption compared with individuals (i.e. only £6,150 cf. a full annual exemption £12,300 in 2020/21).

Income tax

There are no special rules for income tax. The income of the estate is due to the beneficiary of the will from the date of death up to the date of the DOV, even if the capital is then gifted by the DOV to another person or into a trust. The new beneficiary/trust receives income only from the date of the DOV. So income tax is rarely an issue in the planning process.

14.2.2 Variation of trusts under IHTA 1984, s.144

Under IHTA 1984, s.144 the varying of the terms of a trust, whether created by a will or on intestacy, also involves 'reading back' the variation to the date of death. Section 144 only applies to a trust with no interest in possession. The variation depends upon the terms of the will, or statutory powers, but can involve the trustees making the change:

- by a deed of appointment, under powers in the will – for example, the classic step of appointing out of a discretionary trust a life interest for the widow(er), to be an immediate post-death interest (IPDI) trust using the spouse exemption;
- by an advancement to a beneficiary absolutely, or on a more tax-effective form of trust, using powers under the will or statutory powers – for example, to advance to a grandchild who was left a contingent interest, so that they inherit absolutely, or on bare trust, in part to 'closely inherit' for RNRB.

Section 144 can be used to 'rewrite' a will or any intestacy trust, within the two years, provided that no IPDI or other QIIP arose in the meantime. If there was an IPDI/QIIP on death, the income beneficiary (if they had mental capacity) would need to liaise with the capital beneficiary or beneficiaries to vary their entitlements by a DOV under IHTA 1984, s.142.

14.3 DOTAS AND DEEDS OF VARIATION

14.3.1 DOTAS regulations introduced 1 April 2018

The regulations to extend the disclosure of tax avoidance schemes (DOTAS) with reference to IHT (see **4.7.2**) from 1 April 2018 substantially extended the scope of DOTAS, particularly with specific reference to DOVs. As a recap, disclosure to HM Revenue and Customs (HMRC) under DOTAS is required if it is reasonable to expect 'an informed observer' (having studied the arrangements and having regard to all relevant circumstances) to conclude that two conditions have been met:

1. Condition 1 is that the main purpose, or one of the main purposes, of the arrangements is to enable a person to obtain one or more of the following tax advantages:
   (a) the avoidance or reduction of a charge on a transfer into an RPT, such as a NRB D/T;
   (b) the avoidance or reduction of an IHT 10-yearly or exit charge from a RPT;
   (c) the avoidance or reduction of a charge to inheritance tax by avoiding a gift with reservation of benefit (GROB) in circumstances where there is also no pre-owned assets tax (POAT) charge to income tax (income tax charge on benefits received by a former owner of property);

(d) a reduction in the value of a person's estate without giving rise to a potentially exempt transfer (PET) or chargeable transfer.

And:

2. Condition 2 is that the arrangements involve one or more contrived or abnormal steps without which the tax advantage could not be obtained.

14.3.2 HMRC's guidance on DOTAS

In HMRC's guidance on DOTAS (2014, updated April 2018: **www.gov.uk/government/publications/disclosure-of-tax-avoidance-schemes-guidance**), the only example given on this subject – example 6 in section 13 – says it is not a breach of Condition 1 to redirect a gift to an exempt beneficiary, such as a legacy to the deceased's surviving spouse. On the spectrum from illegal tax evasion, through the grey areas of tax avoidance to legitimate tax planning, this is so far at the safe, planning end as to be virtually meaningless. When two representatives of HMRC spoke at STEP Tax conferences in spring 2018 and said that some DOVs might be caught by DOTAS, it raised some concerns.

Questions were raised with HMRC, through the Capital Taxes Liaison Group (CTLG), in April 2018, for clarification of the DOTAS position where a surviving spouse varied an outright gift to themselves from their deceased spouse's estate into a NRB D/T, with the surviving spouse as a beneficiary of that trust. HMRC was asked to confirm whether this would by itself be a breach.

HMRC's response four months later, in an appendix to the CTLG minutes, was that IHTA 1984, s.142 means a DOV cannot be caught by Condition 1(d), but could be caught by Condition 1(a) or (c). It's not clear to the author why it would be a breach of Condition 1(a) or (c), when not 1(d). HMRC says that s.142 means the person whose interest is being varied is treated as never acquiring the property, so that by s.142 it is treated as coming from the deceased.

What form of DOV might be in breach of Condition 2? What might be 'contrived or abnormal steps'? When advising a client, it is sensible to avoid any extra steps or complexity. Given HMRC's current stance, it may also be advisable not to use the 15 per cent discount referred to in **13.3.4** on the appropriation of a share of property to a NRB D/T where that trust was created by a DOV of the surviving spouse's legacy.

However, let's not give up on making simple DOVs to create NRB D/Ts, which is mainstream tax planning, has been for many years, and is perfectly legitimate! That said, let's also encourage clients to plan by will and not leave it to their beneficiaries to have to consider planning by DOVs. Some advisers recommend that planning is left to a variation after death, which is unfortunate advice. A variation is a good arrangement to put things right, but for this reason (DOTAS) as well as for others (for example, some other adverse tax treatment, such as income tax and CGT), it should not be a first option. Variations are invaluable – but they are always a second-best option!

DOTAS may make DOVs vulnerable, especially if there is any 'retained interest', such as being a beneficiary of a NRB D/T, but does not have the same effect on wills. Wills cannot be challenged in the same way under DOTAS, as taxpayers do still have testamentary freedom and any tax planning through a will will have been undertaken, by definition, by a deceased person, not a living person. Trustees of will trusts with wide powers are free to exercise their powers, guided by any letter of wishes left by the deceased.

14.3.3 Encourage married/civil partner clients to plan by will – to do what?

Typical planning for married couples and civil partners (now together referred to as spouses), subject to any specific requirements (for example see **14.5** re using the RNRB), is to write wills containing:

- a NRB D/T including:
  - business/agricultural property relief (BPR/APR) provisions – if applicable;
  - any transferable NRB (TNRB), if a spouse has been previously widowed and their late spouse's NRB is transferable; followed by:
- a flexible IPDI of residue, to the surviving spouse, with:
  - an overriding power of appointment – for maximum flexibility;
  - so that trustees can exercise their flexible powers;
  - which cannot be attacked under DOTAS;
- guided by a comprehensive 'letter of wishes' to the trustees:
  - including the express wishes to achieve specific tax planning objectives;
  - and, if appropriate, including a comment from the clients on any specific reason for wanting to appoint an independent professional as an executor and trustee.

14.4 TWO-YEAR OPPORTUNITY TO SWITCH BETWEEN TWO TRUST REGIMES

It's always good to hold on to the picture of the two parallel trust regimes we can work with, and whether to stay in one or move into the other during the two-year window:

1. RPTs are subject to IHT:
   - every 10 years (10-year anniversaries (TYAs)); or
   - on exits in between anniversaries (exit charges),

   at a maximum rate currently of six per cent (30 per cent of the current lifetime rate of 20 per cent).

The aim of RPTs, as the author always understood them, was that the effective IHT payable is the lifetime rate 20 per cent over 33 1/3 years, the equivalent of a generation. It should be noted, however, that the HMRC review of the taxation of trusts in 2019 threw doubt on this, as to whether this rate was indeed sufficient (see **www.gov.uk/government/consultations/the-of-taxation-of-trusts-a-review**).

2. QIIPs are subject to IHT:

    (a) on the death of the life tenant (L/T) entitled to the income, when the trust capital in the QIIP is aggregated with the L/T's own estate for IHT purposes; or

    (b) if any change in the life interest is made in the L/T's lifetime, for example it is revoked in whole or part, when a deemed gift is made by the L/T, which will have IHT consequences; the gift becomes either:

        – a PET, if an outright entitlement replaces the life interest, so that no IHT is payable straightaway but it will affect the total IHT position in the event of the L/T's death within seven years of the deemed gift; or
        – a chargeable lifetime transfer (CLT) if the life interest is replaced by another contingent or trust interest. At that point, the trust will normally become an RPT, as it cannot be any other form of trust unless it is for a disabled person or is a genuine bare trust (i.e. really an absolute interest).

The main examples of switching between these two trust regimes are:

- **Moving from RPT to an IPDI for a spouse (a QIIP):**
    – where the will creates a NRB D/T and the trustees conclude that is not needed, but a switch to an IPDI trust (or an outright appointment to a spouse) allows the executors to claim the spouse exemption and the surviving spouse's estate will rely upon the TNRB rather than 'using' the NRB of the first to die at the point of their death; or
    – where an estate starts with a full discretionary trust of residue, but an IPDI or outright gift to the surviving spouse needs to be carved out to benefit from the spouse exemption for the remainder of the estate in excess of the NRB; or
    – where a NRB D/T includes the whole of a farm or business, to test whether APR or BPR applies in full, or not, and especially whether or not BPR at 100 per cent applies to a business or farm (the parts that can qualify for BPR rather than APR) where there may be a question as to whether it is 'mainly trading' or not. If HMRC disallows APR or BPR on any part of the assets in the trust, those assets can be appointed out to an IPDI trust for the spouse within the two years so spouse exemption can be claimed instead.

- **Moving to an RPT from a QIIP:**
  - A will may start with an IPDI trust of the whole estate for a spouse, but it is changed to use the NRB to achieve one of these example objectives:
    - to reduce the second spouse's 'estate' to avoid going over the £2 million limit for RNRB purposes on the death of the second spouse;
    - to maximise the amount taken out of the second estate, both NRB and BPR/APR assets;
    - to bank APR and/or BPR at 100 per cent on the first spouse's death, where the farm or business may be sold, before the second death, or there may be some issue with whether it will qualify for 100 per cent relief – see **Chapter 20**.

NB: Because a switch from an IPDI trust to an RPT trust does not benefit from the provisions of IHTA 1984, s.144, it will sometimes be better to draft a will with a full discretionary trust where there is a need to retain flexibility.

14.5 TO USE, OR NOT TO USE, THE NRB, RNRB OR BOTH?

For spouses, this is the crucial question of the moment: which of either (or both) of the NRB and RNRB to 'use' on the death of the first spouse. Each potentially links to a second, transferable allowance, if the spouse had been widowed before and has an unused TNRB or transferable RNRB (TRNRB) to bring forward. For the good reasons given above, this is best done by will, but in many cases may need to be sorted by a variation within two years of death.

Advisers need to review the planning between spouses, in terms of what one passes on to the other, and the prevailing pattern for many clients of leaving the estate to the surviving spouse outright or in an IPDI trust. That does not use the NRB or RNRB and relies upon both being transferred or carried forward to the survivor's estate.

14.5.1 RNRB – risks

For RNRB, there are two risks to watch out for:

1. **To ensure neither estate on its own is over the £2 million limit.** Where the RNRB could have been claimed on the first estate but instead is transferred to the second estate, and if that second estate is then over the £2 million limit when the first spouse's estate/trust is added to it, it might mean that neither RNRB can be claimed when both could have been in practice. This could result in an unnecessary extra IHT liability in 2020/21 of £140,000!
2. **If the first estate is over the £2 million limit and the second wasn't over the limit but becomes so when the value of the first estate is added to it.** In

practice, this means that capital passed to the second spouse is 'caught' twice, denying relief on both estates. RNRB on the first estate could not be claimed anyway, as that first spouse's estate was over £2 million and after tapering it loses RNRB. However, if the second estate was not over the limit until augmented by assets from the first, increasing its value to over £2 million, the second RNRB is lost. A 'cost' in extra tax of £70,000.

14.5.2 What provisions to include in wills to take effect on the first death

Spouses have these choices to consider, as to what provisions to include in their wills to take effect on the first death:

- **To use the NRB – for example, by a NRB D/T:**
  - retain as a RPT (beyond the second anniversary of the death);
  - so the D/T uses the NRB, though it cannot use the RNRB;
  - but may help preserve the future RNRB, by taking the second estate below the £2 million threshold.
- **Or, to use the RNRB – for example, by an IPDI to children (and the spouse as a beneficiary):**
  - and not relying on carrying forward the RNRB;
  - or if previously widowed and has a TRNRB from that previous spouse's estate, could use two RNRBs on the first death, so the TRNRB from that previous spouse's estate is not 'lost';
  - in either case taking some of the value out of the estate to protect the second RNRB.
- **Or, to use both the NRB the RNRB – for example, by an IPDI to children:**
  - for example, by a gift of £325,000 + £175,000 in 2020/21;
  - recognising that a NRB can be 'used' not solely by a D/T (the form of trust used most as it provides the best security and use of assets for the surviving spouse);
  - but that an IPDI trust to children can also 'use' the NRB, in addition to using the RNRB;
  - this arrangement uses the maximum value taxed at 0 per cent on the first death to reduce the value of the estate of the surviving spouse, to protect from the loss of RNRB by tapering over the £2 million limit.

14.5.3 Examples to illustrate the use of NRB and/or RNRB, helped by a variation

---

Example 14.1: Rosie and Jim (simple use of a NRB D/T)

Jim's whole estate of £600,000 was left to his widow Rosie absolutely. Rosie is concerned that her estate, being larger than Jim's, might go over the £2 million limit for RNRB. Rosie therefore varies her entitlement from Jim's estate to put £325,000 into a NRB D/T to 'use' Jim's NRB, with the residue of £275,000 going to an IPDI trust for Rosie for her lifetime, then to their two children Alice and Bob. The D/T remains an RPT, as it is kept in place for more than two years from death, having been 'read back' under IHTA 1984, s.142.

The spouse exemption applies to the IPDI, as it would have done had Rosie received the residue outright.

Had Jim left his whole estate on an IPDI trust for Rosie in the first place, with the remainder to Alice and Bob absolutely, then Rosie, Alice and Bob could together have signed a DOV to create a NRB D/T of £325,000. To be able to do this, the three of them would have to be together absolutely entitled to the estate – this is an example of where it is important that Alice and Bob don't have contingent interests, with the potential for an interest passing to the next generation if they did not survive Rosie (they only needed to survive Jim).

Example 14.2: Fred and Ginger (using a NRB with BPR and APR)

Fred and Ginger own a top dance school as partners, the business value of £500,000 qualifying for 100% BPR. The business operates from premises worth £1 million owned by Ginger personally and used by the partnership so the value of the premises qualifies for 50% BPR. If Ginger could put the premises into the partnership with Fred, all other things being equal, she could secure 100% BPR on the premises which would then be a partnership asset. Ginger dies first and before she has taken any action in relation to the premises which can't be changed after her death.

Ginger leaves her whole estate to Fred. He varies Ginger's will so as to set up a NRB D/T including BPR provisions (to leave all the assets that qualify for 100% relief and any other assets that can be included in the value of the NRB including those that have 50% relief up to the amount of the NRB) and the residue of the estate to Fred absolutely. Ginger's half share of the business, i.e. value £250,000, goes into the D/T at nil % for IHT. In addition, the executors can transfer 65% (valued at £650,000) of the premises (the whole of which is owned by Ginger outside the partnership) which equates to a value for IHT of £325,000 after claiming 50% BPR. The whole of Ginger's NRB has been used with £900,000 of assets in the trust.

Example 14.3: Henry and James (using the NRB with a share of the home included)

Option A

Henry dies in 2012 leaving his whole £1.3 million estate to his civil partner James. This includes a half share of their home valued at £750,000 (total £1.5 million). James dies of COVID-19 in 2021 when his total estate is £2.5 million. This is £500,000 over the £2 million threshold. His estate loses £1 for every £2 over the limit so a double RNRB (£175,000 x 2 = £350,000) tapers to £100,000, with a loss of £250,000 of RNRB and an extra £100,000 IHT to pay.

Option B: which James can secure by a DOV

If Henry had left a NRB D/T in his will, half of his half share of the house could have been appropriated to the discretionary trust. This quarter share of the whole house would have been valued at £375,000 value, but reduced for appropriation purposes by a 15% discount to £318,750 so that the discounted value is within the £325,000 legacy to the NRB. The 15% discount can be claimed because it is a valuation for appropriation only, not for paying IHT on death (see **13.3.4**). No RNRB was used when Henry died in 2012, as the RNRB legislation had not then been introduced.

On James's death in 2021, his estate can claim a double RNRB of £175,000 x 2 = £350,000, i.e. James's RNRB and Henry's TNRB (which is still available to James's estate even though Henry died before the legislation was in place). Assume that by 2021 the house has increased in value to £2 million, with three-quarters, i.e. £1.5 million, in James's estate. The other quarter share is in Henry's will trust and now worth £500,000. James's estate is no longer valued at £2.5 million (because one-quarter or £500,000 of the property is in Henry's D/T). Because of Henry's planning through his will, James's estate is £2 million, i.e. it has reached the threshold for RNRB but is not over it, so there is no excess for the relief to be tapered. Thus the double RNRB of a total £350,000 is preserved provided the property passes outright to Henry and James's children, etc. under the terms of James's will. So the IHT saving compared with option A = £250,000 x 40% = £100,000.

Example 14.4: Roger and Sunita (using both the NRB and RNRB)

Roger dies in 2021 leaving his whole estate to his wife Sunita, with a value of £1.2 million, including his £500,000 half share of their home. When Sunita dies a few years later, her estate is worth £2.7 million, including the whole house, now worth £1.4 million. As a result, there is no RNRB as it is all tapered away. So what could Sunita have done to vary Roger's estate?

If Roger's half of house had gone to the children on flexible IPDI trusts, with Sunita still a beneficiary of the residue of his estate, there would have been no IHT payable on Roger's death. The half share of the house valued at £500,000, the subject of his gift into trust for the children, would have utilised both the £325,000 NRB and the £175,000 RNRB. As well as using the NRB, the gift would have qualified for RNRB as the gift to the children's trust qualifies as 'closely inherited' as it is an IPDI. So Sunita can vary Roger's estate on these terms. Her own estate will then be valued at £2.2 million so her own £175,000 RNRB will be tapered away unless she reduces the value of her estate to £2 million by spending or making lifetime gifts.

Example 14.5: Roger and Sunita but with main residence relief for CGT

Following the comment in **13.3.7**, **Example 14.4** can then be tweaked to enable the trustees to claim the principal private residence (PPR) relief on the full trust interest in the property as owning part of the PPR (which would not otherwise be available if the children did not occupy the property as their main residence).

Sunita could vary Roger's will to leave part of Roger's property share on an IPDI for herself as the occupying spouse. The value of the half share in this example equates to the combined NRB and RNRB, so in practice part of the NRB will need to be left 'unused' and transferred or carried forward.

The answer is to leave say a 5% share of the property (or 10% of Roger's half share) to the IPDI for Sunita and 45% (or 90% of Roger's half share) to the IPDI for the children. Then if the value of Roger's half share at his death is £500,000, £50,000 is held on the IPDI for Sunita and £450,000 for the children's IPDI. That would leave, say, £50,000 or 50/325 of the NRB not 'used' to be transferred on Sunita's death. There would be a judgment here on the particular facts as to whether the greater tax saving might be relieving CGT at 28% by claiming PPR relief or relieving 40% IHT. If this arrangement only meant more IHT being payable, especially given the tapering of RNRB on Sunita's death, it might not be worth doing.

Example 14.6: Denis and Pamela (using three or four RNRBs by IPDI trusts)

If a spouse was previously widowed and has a brought-forward RNRB from the estate of that previous spouse, their estate can claim two RNRBs on their death and if a TRNRB is not used at that point, it is lost. Only one unused TRNRB can be claimed, even if a spouse is widowed more than once, as one estate can claim a maximum of two RNRBs only. Use it or lose it! So if each previously widowed spouse can use their two RNRBs on their own death, by leaving an IPDI to their children – with their spouse as a potential beneficiary – there is a potential for a couple to claim three or four RNRBs.

Denis and Pamela were each widowed in the early 2000s and married each other in 2012. Both their late spouses had set up NRB trusts in their wills, fully utilising their NRBs, so there were no TNRBs. Denis and Pamela live together in Denis's house, worth £500,000, and Pamela's old home, worth £400,000, is let out producing an income. They have £450,000 in total joint savings.

The first of them to die (in 2020/21) could leave a £350,000 'slice' of their own house to an IPDI for their own children. (As Denis and Pamela are married, they could also benefit each other's children as 'stepchildren' can also closely inherit but that flexibility is not needed in this example.) If Denis dies first, as they live in Denis's house, worth £500,000, he could leave an IPDI to his children of 70% of the house, with an IPDI to Pamela of the remaining 30%.

If Pamela died first, Pamela's old home, worth £400,000, is let out. It was her residence before, so can still be her qualifying residential interest (QRI) now. (Denis could not claim it as such, as it never was his home, but Pamela can.) If Pamela gave part of her property to the value of £350,000 into an IPDI for her children that would equate to 7/8 of her property leaving 1/8 in an IPDI for Denis. While this would secure Pamela's double RNRB for IHT, the adviser would need to ensure that Denis was not reliant on the income from the property as he would only be entitled to 1/8 from Pamela's death. When Denis then subsequently died, he would have his own £350,000 double RNRB on his later death. There would also then be a double NRB (including a TNRB) of £650,000 and thus no IHT to pay on a joint estate of £1,350,000.

This could also apply if Denis and Pamela owned one property worth say £900,000 (owned as tenants in common in equal shares) whereupon the first to die could leave the double RNRB to an IPDI so that 350/900 of the property was held on the IPDI for the children of the first to die and 100/900 on an IPDI for the surviving spouse. The surviving spouse would retain their own 450/900 share in their outright ownership to pass down to their own children on their death.

In either case, the surviving spouse would need the protection of a good, strong 'letter of wishes' to the trustees of the IPDI explaining the need to protect the surviving spouse's security of occupation and giving the trustees the power not to require rent be paid for the occupation of the part owned by the IPDI of the children; and, ideally, a good independent trustee to protect the relevant beneficiaries.

14.6 SECURING THE 36 PER CENT LOWER INHERITANCE TAX RATE WITH 10 PER CENT OF NET ESTATE TO CHARITY

14.6.1 Introduction

The 36 per cent lower IHT rate is a much underused form of IHT mitigation, little publicised and a real opportunity often wasted. We include the detail in this chapter as the planning will often arise within the two-year period, with the potential to vary an inheritance to leave the 10 per cent to charity and reduce the IHT payable on the rest of the estate.

The amount to be given to charity to meet the required 10 per cent will depend upon the value of the estate when finalised so that any changes, for IHT purposes, during the administration period will affect that figure. Higher values substituted by sales for more than the original probate figure, as well as claims for loss relief, will therefore change the calculation.

There is potential to save the beneficiaries money, even after giving increased amounts to charity, in certain cases. The figures below will illustrate how this can work, and show the potential to vary an inheritance as a residuary beneficiary and be better off. There is great scope for encouraging beneficiaries to consider a simple deed of variation to achieve this simple but effective tax saving.

14.6.2 10 per cent of the 'baseline amount'

Ten per cent of the 'baseline amount' is needed which, essentially, means the net value of the estate less any available NRB (including TNRB) but not including RNRB, and less any exemptions and reliefs on death (other than charity relief).

Example 14.7

Alice and her brother Brian are both unmarried and die leaving estates of the same size, £575,000. Alice leaves a little less to charity, less than 10% and misses the 36% tax rate. However, Brian secures it, as follows:

Alice dies leaving £575,000, and her will gives £20,000 to Age UK, and the rest to her nephew Peter. Who gets what? Age UK £20,000, HMRC £92,000 and Peter £463,000.

Brian also leaves £575,000 but gives £25,000 to his local charity the Sussex Community Foundation and the rest to his nephew John. SCF gets £25,000, HMRC £81,000 and John £469,000.

John gets £6,000 more than Peter, from the same-sized estate, the charity gets £5,000 more, and HMRC £11,000 less!

The 'baseline amount' for both examples is £575,000 – £325,000 = £250,000. So 10% = £25,000.

A key figure is 4% of the baseline amount, in this example £10,000.

- If the deceased gave more than 4% of the baseline amount to charity, and the beneficiary by DOV increases that to 10%, it will increase the value of the net estate passing to that beneficiary.
- If the deceased had left exactly 4%, that can be increased to 10% with no loss to the estate, the net residue being exactly the same.

In **Example 14.7**, if Peter makes a DOV of Alice's estate, to leave £5,000 more to any charity (it does not need to be the same one), he will end up £6,000 better off. Thus, even if he pays for a simple DOV he would still be better placed. That seems quite a neat result for IHT mitigation. The figures would be greater with larger estates, but even at this level it is worth considering with clients.

If Alice had left four per cent exactly, i.e. £10,000 to a charity, Peter could have increased that to £25,000 and been no worse off, save for any costs of the variation document. Some beneficiaries might feel a small variation might be worth paying for to give £15,000 more to a charity of their choice and save £15,000 IHT. In some cases, where a variation is being done for something else, there may be no extra cost.

The 10 per cent test applies to three component parts: the survivorship component (all assets held as joint tenants that pass by survivorship); the settled property component (all trusts which were aggregable with the deceased's estate); and the general component (essentially the free estate, except for any GROB assets). There are more complex rules about merging components, which are worth exploring but are beyond the scope of this handbook.

14.6.3 How best to use a deed of variation to secure the 36 per cent inheritance tax rate?

If clients wish to include the 10 per cent gift to charity in their wills to secure the lower tax rate on the remainder of the estate, it is clearly preferable to do so in advance, and many solicitors will advise their clients to include the relevant clause in their wills. The clause is typically complex with many detailed provisions; STEP has a model clause and precedent providers should all offer this option, even if the wording sometimes runs to a full page of A4 text.

So what provisions would you put in a DOV if seeking to secure this in the two years after death? If the estate values have all been finalised, and no further sales/adjustments of value are due, you could work out an exact figure required to meet the 10 per cent test and include that in the deed. However, do be careful that this is not premature. The discovery of an additional asset, or the sale of a property or chattels at a higher value, can change the figures and mean that the 10 per cent figure is not reached.

In **Example 14.7** with regard to Alice's estate: if Peter varies the estate to add an extra gift of £5,000 to charity, but then discovers that Alice had a holding of £10,000 of premium bonds that no one knew about his £5,000 would now fall £1,000 short. If he does the variation before selling Alice's chattels, and they then sell at auction for £1,000 more than the formal probate value, he will also miss the 10 per cent figure, which now needs to be increased by a further £100. So Peter should either wait until all is finalised or use a precedent formula of words for the extra gift to charity to reach the 10 per cent level.

14.6.4 Using a discretionary trust in a will (or variation) to secure the 10 per cent figure

A good alternative can be to use a D/T of residue, including charities as potential beneficiaries, with a letter of wishes to guide the trustees. This letter of wishes can specify both the wish to gift the 10 per cent figure, to ensure the tax saving is secured, and also the specific charities or causes the client wishes to support. One advantage of this arrangement is the flexibility to change those wishes in the testator's lifetime, by updating the letter of wishes, as needs and charitable concerns change over time.

An alternative way to have this flexibility for charitable concerns, in so far as they are local ones, is to use one of the network of Community Foundations (as with Sussex in **Example 14.7**) in counties across the country that are charities that exist to facilitate giving to other local charities. Most of them have the facility to gift to that foundation, then adapt the local charitable causes over the years in revised notes of wishes.

So if a will includes a D/T on this basis, take care with the appointments out to any charity to watch the timing issues noted in **14.6.3**. If for any reason the estate administration is running on beyond the two-year anniversary, consider appointing out a gift according to the formula for the 10 per cent, so that this can be finalised when the estate is completing.

In **Example 14.7**, if Alice's estate administration was protracted because her house would not sell, and you were mindful of the four years to claim loss relief, you might not want to finalise the figure before the two-year deadline. However, you might agree with Peter that any loss relief claim, made on a sale in the four years post death, would only reduce the estate, and thus the amount needed to reach the 10 per cent figure. Peter might be happy to proceed provided there was no risk of the 'probate value' submitted being treated as too low, more than two years on, and the executors were confident all the assets had been identified. Any increase to the probate value subsequently agreed with HMRC or the finding of new assets in the estate would increase the amount needed to reach the 10 per cent, but Peter may accept that as a risk worth taking.

A D/T for the 10 per cent gift to charity could be set up by a post-death variation, if it were helpful and worth incurring the extra costs for any other reason – but typically using the formula to ensure a 10 per cent gift is a better option at that stage.

CHAPTER 15

Reliefs for agricultural and business property (APR and BPR)

Anthony Nixon

15.1 KEY POINTS

- Agricultural property relief (APR) and business property reliefs (BPR) are extraordinarily generous. They are the most generous of any country in the developed world that has an equivalent to inheritance (IHT). Relief is most commonly given at 100 per cent, which means a complete exemption from IHT on the assets concerned.
- 100 per cent reliefs are not to be taken lightly, or for granted, and while they are available it is a waste not to utilise them as fully as possible. Careful planning is called for.
- At first glance the reliefs look very much the same. However, while they have many common elements, there are crucial differences. One common factor is that there is usually no relief unless the asset concerned has been owned for a minimum of two years.
- BPR can be given for any kind of business asset in any part of the world, but there is no relief for investment businesses. Business where there is both trading and investment activity can still obtain relief provided the business is not mainly investment.
- APR is given only to agricultural land and certain associated buildings, all of which must have been used for agriculture throughout a particular period. At one time only property in the UK qualified for agricultural relief, but this was extended in 2009 to land anywhere in the European Economic Area (EEA).

This chapter will explore the following key issues:

- Assets qualifying for both reliefs.
- APR: Basic conditions for agricultural relief; what is agriculture; minimum ownership and occupation periods; the split between 100 per cent and 50 per cent relief; that it is only on agricultural value and the special requirements for farmhouses.

- BPR: Basic conditions for business relief and what is a business; valuing a business or an interest in a business and how the loss to the donor applies for business relief; and restrictions on liabilities.
- Investment businesses and the bar to relief; how the 'mainly' trading concept works and analysis of the key cases of *Farmer*, *George*, *Pawson*, *Graham* and *Vigne*, and the *Balfour* case (also known as *Brander*), which is one of the most critical and contentious areas of IHT law.
- BPR and APR and wills for spouses; and lifetime gifts with relief.

15.2 ASSETS QUALIFYING FOR BOTH RELIEFS

Where an asset qualifies for both agricultural relief (Inheritance Tax Act (IHTA) 1984, ss.115–124C) and business relief (IHTA 1984, ss.103–114), agricultural relief is given first.

No business relief is given on the agricultural value (see below) of an asset that qualifies for agricultural relief, but this does not prevent value in excess of the agricultural value (for example, hope value, where land might one day be developed) obtaining business relief. Many farms will have significant elements of both reliefs.

On the other hand if an asset obtains only 50 per cent agricultural relief on its agricultural value, it is not usually possible to claim business relief on the other 50 per cent of the agricultural value.

Where a company owns land and buildings that would, in the ownership of an individual, qualify for agricultural relief, the relief is also given on shares owned by those who control the company.

15.3 AGRICULTURAL PROPERTY RELIEF

15.3.1 Basic conditions for agricultural property relief

APR is available: 'Where the whole or part of the value transferred by a transfer of value is attributable to the agricultural value of agricultural property' (IHTA 1984, s.116(1)). Under IHTA 1984, s.115 'transfers of value', for s.116, include 10-year charges and exit charges on relevant property trusts.

'Agricultural property' is defined as (IHTA 1984, s.115(2)):

> . . . agricultural land or pasture and includes woodland and any building used in connection with the intensive rearing of livestock or fish if the woodland or building is occupied with agricultural land or pasture and the occupation is ancillary to that of the agricultural land or pasture; and also includes such cottages, farm buildings and farmhouses, together with the land occupied with them, as are of a character appropriate to the property.

This covers agricultural land, agricultural buildings, farmhouses and farm cottages. However, because the definition requires the occupation of woodland and buildings to be ancillary to the occupation of land, some assets thought of as agricultural may be outside relief. For example:

- A building used for the intensive rearing of animals does not qualify for relief if no land is occupied with it.
- Nor can a farmhouse qualify for relief without a holding of land, in the same occupation, sufficient to make the farmhouse 'of a character appropriate'. HM Revenue and Customs (HMRC) used to argue that the house and land had to be in both the same ownership and the same occupation, but the Upper Tribunal decision in *Hanson (trustee of the William Hanson 1957 Settlement)* v. *Revenue and Customs Comrs* [2013] UKUT 224 (TCC) confirmed that this is not essential, provided there is a nexus between ownership and occupation of the separate properties.

15.3.2 What is agriculture?

There is no definition of 'agriculture' in IHTA 1984. HMRC seems to accept (see IHTM24220, *Inheritance Tax Manual*, 'Agricultural Holdings Act 1986: what is an agricultural holding?') the definition in Agricultural Tenancies Act 1995, s.38:

> 'agriculture' includes horticulture, fruit growing, seed growing, dairy farming and livestock breeding and keeping, the use of land as grazing land, meadow land, osier land, market gardens and nursery grounds, and the use of land for woodlands where that use is ancillary to the farming of land for other agricultural purposes, and 'agricultural' shall be construed accordingly.

This definition is not exhaustive, however. As HMRC says in IHTM24220, 'arable farming is not included in the definition but is evidently an agricultural use'. It is clear that vineyards, cultivated for the production of wine, must be agricultural – and this was recently confirmed in IHTM24061 (*Inheritance Tax Manual*, 'Agricultural purposes: qualifying uses of land'). The author has successfully argued that land used for beehives was in agricultural use.

HMRC is unwilling to accept that simply growing grass is agriculture, particularly on land grazed by horses, but there seems no doubt that, if a crop of hay is being taken, that is agriculture. If the predominant use is for horses used only for leisure activities to graze, it seems this may not be agriculture (see the First-tier Tribunal decision in *Personal Representative of the estate of Vigne (Deceased)* v. *Revenue and Customs Commissioners* [2017] UKFTT 632 (TC) at para.48: 'Equine activities are not usually characterised as agricultural. That is the reason why Parliament enacted section 115(4) of the [IHTA 1984] so as to provide that the breeding and rearing of horses on a stud farm and the grazing of horses in connection with those activities does, for the purpose of the statute, amount to agriculture').

While horses usually mean no relief, agricultural relief is specifically extended to land and buildings occupied for the 'breeding and rearing of horses on a stud farm' (IHTA 1984, s.115(4)). Of course, if the horses are actually among those few still being used as working horses on a farm, or if, dare one say it, horses are bred for meat, this would be occupation for agriculture.

15.3.3 Minimum ownership and occupation periods

APR requires not only a minimum period of ownership, but also that the land or buildings must have been 'occupied for the purposes of agriculture' throughout a minimum period. The period is different according to whether the owner has personally occupied for agriculture:

- two years is enough to qualify if the owner has personally occupied (IHTA 1984, s.117(a));
- seven years' ownership is needed if someone else occupied for agriculture; and the land or buildings must have been occupied for agriculture throughout those seven years (IHTA 1984, s.117(b)); it does not matter if there was only one or more than one occupier during those seven years, and it is fine for the owner to have been one of the occupiers for some of the time.

HMRC will question whether the landowner was occupying for agriculture if there is a grazing licence, but it seems that, if the landowner is sowing, fertilising, etc., they will be occupying. HMRC's view is that a landowner who has arranged a grazing licence and 'does nothing but collect the rent and maintain boundaries' is unlikely to be in agricultural occupation (see IHTM24074, *Inheritance Tax Manual*, 'Occupation: Definition of a lease as opposed to a licence'), but this is in conflict with the normal legal rule that a landowner who has granted a mere licence remains in possession and, perhaps, could be successfully challenged.

Succession to a spouse's ownership on death will pass on a spouse's ownership and occupation periods, but it is crucial to remember that this does not apply to lifetime transfers between spouses.

There are also rules allowing for replacement of formerly owned agricultural property with new agricultural property.

15.3.4 100 per cent or 50 per cent relief?

Historically 100 per cent relief was given only to in-hand farmers who occupied the land themselves, but 100 per cent relief is now more generous than this.

On 1 September 1995, farm business tenancies (FBTs) replaced the old-style Agricultural Holdings Act (AHA) 1986 tenancies, which could give security to successive generations. One hundred per cent relief was extended to land let on tenancies beginning on or after 1 September 1995.

In addition, 100 per cent relief can still be available where land remains with the old AHA 1986 regime:

- if a successor tenancy has begun since 1 September 1995, this will count as a new tenancy and the landowner can qualify for 100 per cent relief;

- Agricultural Tenancies Act 1995, s.4(1)(g) (introduced in 2006) allows a pre-1995 tenancy to be replaced by a new tenancy which gives the tenant the same protection as was available under the old AHA 1986 regime. This gives a landlord the opportunity to agree a new tenancy which gives a pre-1995 tenant exactly the same security as before, but increases 50 per cent relief to 100 per cent relief. Care needs to be taken over other tax issues if this is planned; there will usually be a stamp duty land tax (SDLT) charge on the new tenancy; the capital gains tax (CGT) position is helped by HMRC's concession ESC D39, but this will not assist in every case (see CG71240 'Scope of ESC D39').

There is also a transitional 100 per cent relief from the time when the present rules for APR came into force in 1981. This is capped at £250,000 of relief or 100 acres, whichever is the greater (so, with today's values, usually at 100 acres). It reflects the fact that, under the previous relief regime, it was common practice for an older generation of farmers to grant a tenancy to a partnership including both themselves and members of younger generations. It is surprising how many of these old arrangements are still in place.

A review of farming tenancies was started by the Department for Environment, Food and Rural Affairs (DEFRA) in 2019 (consultation from April to July: **https://consult.defra.gov.uk/ahdb-sponsorship-and-agricultural-tenancies/agricultural-tenancy-consultation/**), because of concerns about succession and the commercial realities of tenanted farms. It was said not to be concerned with the IHT issues but the IHT treatment in practice has a significant effect on values. Developments here need to be watched carefully.

15.3.5 Agricultural value only

A critical restriction on APR is that it is given only for the agricultural value of the land or buildings concerned.

Agricultural value is 'the value which would be the value of the property if the property were subject to a perpetual covenant prohibiting its use otherwise than as agricultural property' (IHTA 1984, s.115(3)).

There is no hard and fast rule on the practical effect of this restriction. In particular, there is disagreement as to whether a covenant of this kind would give a lower value or higher value than the common planning restriction on newly built rural properties that they should be occupied only by those engaged in agriculture. The one thing that is certain is that HMRC's District Valuer will argue that agricultural value is less than open market value.

It is also clear that, where there is evidence that agricultural land has a high value because of potential for development, or perhaps because of mineral rights, the development element does not qualify for agricultural relief.

After the Lands Tribunal case of *Antrobus 2* ([2004] DET/47/2004, unreported) which decided that the agricultural value of the farmhouse was 30 per cent less than its market value, HMRC's valuers seemed for a while to argue that a 30 per cent discount was a fixed rule, but every case should still be argued on its facts. It is essential to have valuation advice from a professional with experience of arguing with the District Valuer in agricultural cases. The valuer should be asked to include in the opinion specific advice on whether the agricultural value is the same as or less than open market value.

15.3.6 Farmhouses

IHTA 1984, s.115(2) gives agricultural relief to 'such cottages, farm buildings and farmhouses, together with land occupied with them, as are of a character appropriate to the property'.

In order to get agricultural relief, a residence must be either a cottage or a farmhouse. HMRC would probably like it to be the case that a single farm can never have more than one farmhouse, but the statutory definition is farmhouses, in the plural, and there is every reason for claiming that more than one can qualify when, say, parent and child or two siblings are in partnership.

HMRC has made lots of assaults on APR for farmhouses. There is no statutory definition of a farmhouse and the best summary is probably that in *Arnander and others (executors of McKenna, deceased)* v. *Revenue and Customs Commissioners* [2006] STC (SCD) 800 (para.88), citing various other cases:

> From those authorities I derive the following principles:
>
> - That a farmhouse is a dwelling for the farmer from which the farm is managed (*Rosser*);
> - that the farmer of the land is the person who farms it on a day-to-day basis rather than the person who is in overall control of the agricultural business conducted on the land (*Antrobus 2* and *Lindsay*);
> - that the status of the occupier of the premises is not the test but the proper criterion is the purpose of the occupation of the premises (*Whiteford*);
> - however, if the premises are extravagantly large for the purpose for which they are being used, or if they have been constructed upon some more elaborate and expensive scale, it may be that, notwithstanding the purpose of occupation, they should be treated as having been converted into something much more grand (*Whiteford*);
> - and that the decision as to whether a building is a farmhouse is a matter of fact to be decided on the circumstances of each case and must be judged in accordance with ordinary ideas of what is appropriate in size, content and layout, taken in conjunction with the farm buildings and the particular area of farm being farmed (*Korner*).

Once you have ascertained that you have a farmhouse, the next hurdle is to consider whether the farmhouse is 'of a character appropriate to the property'. Once again, the best description is to be found in the *Arnander* case (para.102):

> The Revenue relied upon *Higginson's Exors* for the principle that the price or value of the house relative to that of the agricultural land and the profitability of the agricultural land relative to the affordability of the house were relevant factors to be borne in mind. The appellants argued that the 'character appropriate' test related to the character of the house

> and not the price and the fact that the price would be a bad investment in terms of yield from the farm was not a relevant factor.
>
> In my view it is not appropriate to compile an exclusive list of relevant factors which are to be considered in deciding whether a farmhouse is of a character appropriate to the agricultural land. The question is one of fact and degree and any factor could be relevant. No one factor is determinative but relevant factors in this appeal are: the historical associations; the size, content and layout of the house; the farm outbuildings; the area being farmed and whether the house is proportionate to the land being farmed; the view of the educated rural layman; and the relationship between the value of the house and the profitability of the land.

As noted in *Arnander*, HMRC is keen to explore the relationship between the value of the house and the profitability of the land. In particular, would the house attract demand from a commercial farmer who has to earn a living from the land, or is its value significantly out of proportion to the profitability of the land? HMRC's arguments along these lines were dealt something of a blow by the delightful case of *Golding and Middleton (executors of the will of Dennis Golding deceased)* [2011] UKFTT 351 (TC), in which the deceased farmed only 16.29 acres of agricultural land. The tribunal ruled that the condition of the house was 'such that it would only be acceptable as a farm house' (para.27), observing that 'a working farm is not expected to be finished to the higher standards of a domestic residence' (para.28). The fact that the farm had only made small profits did not prevent the house from qualifying for relief.

Remember that, like the question of whether a house is a farmhouse or not, the character appropriate test is an 'all or nothing' test.

The farmhouse's agricultural value is then a separate question.

15.4 BUSINESS PROPERTY RELIEF

15.4.1 Basic conditions for business property relief

BPR is available: 'Where the whole or part of the value transferred by a transfer of value is attributable to the value of any relevant business property' (IHTA 1984, s.104(1)). Under IHTA 1984, s.103 'transfers of value', for s.104, include 10-year charges and exit charges on relevant property trusts.

'Relevant business property' falls into a number of different categories, set out in IHTA 1984, s.105 as follows:

- **'[P]roperty consisting of a business or interest in a business' (s.105(1)(a)):** This is the value of the business of a sole trader or the value of the partnership interest of a partner; relief is at 100 per cent.
- **Unquoted 'securities of a company which … gave the transferor control of the company immediately before the transfer' (s.105(1)(b))** and **'any unquoted shares in a company' (s.105(1)(bb)):** Both obtain 100% relief.

- Note the different wording of 'securities' and 'shares', according to whether or not the transferor has control.
- 'Unquoted' means not quoted on the London Stock Exchange or its equivalents in other countries; a full list is at **www.gov.uk/guidance/recognised-stock-exchanges**.
- Shares listed on the Alternative Investment Market (AIM) are unquoted and therefore can qualify for business relief.

- **Quoted shares or securities which give the transferor control (IHTA 1984, s.105(1)(cc))** obtain 50 per cent relief, but are not often met in practice.
- **'[A]ny land or building, machinery or plant which, immediately before the transfer, was used wholly or mainly for the purposes of a business carried on by a company of which the transferor then had control; or a partnership of which he then was a partner' (IHTA 1984, s.105(1)(d))**.
  - This has 50 per cent relief and is available regardless of whether or not the partnership or company pays rent to the individual owner. Note that relief is more generous for partnerships than companies. For example, if three sisters who jointly own land let to: (i) a partnership in which all three are partners, all have 50 per cent BPR on the land; but if they let to (ii) a company in which they are equal shareholders, none has control of the company and thus none has any BPR.
  - It may be possible to increase relief under this head from 50 per cent to 100 per cent by making the assets partnership or company assets, but there are other tax issues, particularly SDLT and CGT. Any restructuring would need professional input on these tax issues as well as advice on the commercial implications of, perhaps, exposing the asset to trading liabilities.
- **Land, buildings, machinery or plant which was settled property in which the transferor was beneficially entitled to an interest in possession** and which was used in their business attract 50 per cent relief (IHTA 1984, s.105(1)(e)).

Businesses mainly involved in investment activities get no relief (see **15.5**).

Relief can only be claimed if the assets concerned have been owned by the transferor throughout the two years before the transfer of value concerned. Succession to a spouse's ownership on death will pass on a spouse's ownership period, but it is crucial to remember that this does not apply to lifetime transfers between spouses. There are also rules allowing for replacement of formerly owned business property with new property.

15.4.2 What is a business?

Most of the recent IHT cases about whether or not a business is an investment business include a concession by HMRC that there is a business. However, this is, all the same, an important question.

The best guide is probably now in the CGT case of *Ramsay* v. *Revenue and Customs Commissioners* [2013] UKUT 226 (TCC), in which a taxpayer claimed CGT incorporation relief. The Upper Tribunal ruled that it was the degree of activity as a whole that was material to the question of whether there was a business. It was wrong to say, as the First-tier Tribunal had done, that activities ordinarily associated with management of an investment property were not to be regarded as referable to a business.

Note also IHTA 1984, s.103(3), '"business" includes a business carried on in the exercise of a profession or vocation, but does not include a business carried on otherwise than for gain'.

15.4.3 Valuing a business or an interest in a business

IHTA 1984, s.110(c) provides:

- the value of a business or of an interest in a business shall be taken to be its net value;
- the net value of the business is the value of the assets used in the business (including goodwill) reduced by the aggregate amount of any liabilities incurred for the purpose of the business.

Ninth Marquess of Hertford and others (executors of Eighth Marquess of Hertford, deceased) v. *Inland Revenue Commissioners* [2005] STC (SCD) 177 includes an interesting discussion of the expression 'assets used in the business' and draws attention to the fact that there is no requirement for the assets concerned to be exclusively used for the business.

Ragley Hall was open to the public as a business. While the whole exterior was accessible to public view, part of the interior (some 22 per cent by volume) was occupied by the Marquess and his family as their private residence. HMRC argued that only 78 per cent of the value qualified for BPR. While the Special Commissioners accepted that the margin was a fine one, they found that it was natural to consider a single building as a single asset. So100 per cent of it was 'the asset used in the business' and the whole of Ragley Hall qualified for relief.

15.4.4 Loss to the donor applies for business relief

Revenue and Customs Commissioners v. *Trustees of the Nelson Dance Family Settlement* [2009] EWHC 71 (Ch) is a reminder that, just as IHT is a tax on transfers of value, in other words the difference between what the transferor owns before a disposition and what is owned afterwards, so BPR applies to reduce the value of that transfer of value.

Mr Dance gave to a trust 359 acres and the two farm cottages, from his 1,735-acre farm. Although APR was available, the land given away had significant development value and, without BPR, a lot of IHT would have been payable. HMRC argued that the gift did not qualify for BPR, because it was not a gift of a business or an interest in a business. The High Court ruled that, because Mr Dance's gift had reduced the value of his interest in his business, relief applied to that reduction in value.

This contrasts with the CGT position for entrepreneurs' relief (and, in the past, retirement relief) where it is the nature of the asset disposed of that governs whether relief is available.

15.4.5 Restrictions on liabilities

The Finance Act 2013 introduced new restrictions, now in IHTA 1984, s.162B, on setting liabilities against assets when those liabilities relate to business property. These restrictions apply to all IHT events (death, gifts, charges on trusts) from and after 17 July 2013 (when the Finance Act 2013 received royal assent) and to borrowings made after 5 April 2013.

The basic IHT rule is that a secured liability is deducted from the value of the property against which it is secured (IHTA 1984, s.162(4)). So, in the past, it was possible to get an IHT deduction when unrelieved assets (commonly an individual's home) were charged as security for business borrowings.

Example 15.1

Suppose that Ron, in 2012, borrowed £800,000 from his bank, on the security of his £2 million home, to buy the shares in a company manufacturing widgets. £500,000 is still outstanding. If Ron has just died, his estate will get 100 per cent relief for the company shares *and* the taxable value of his house will be reduced by the £500,000 debt charged against it.

However, suppose Ron was offered a better deal on the outstanding borrowing and changed bank. A new loan after 17 July 2013 would prevent his setting the value of the loan against his home. The new rules require that a loan taken out to invest in assets qualifying for business relief has to be set against the value of relievable property. Since this qualifies for 100 per cent relief anyway, Ron has lost the deduction of £500,000, and in practice will be paying 40 per cent IHT on the borrowing, exposing his estate to an extra £200,000 IHT on his death.

Tip

Some business owners may have 'golden charges' dating from before 6 April 2013, which should not be changed.

15.5 INVESTMENT BUSINESSES AND THE BAR TO RELIEF

15.5.1 Overview

No BPR is given on the value of a business or on assets used in it if the business, in whatever form, 'consists wholly or mainly of [...] dealing in securities, stocks or shares, land or buildings or making or holding investments' (IHTA 1984, s.105(3)).

'Mainly' is interpreted as meaning 50 per cent or more, but, if a business falls the wrong side of the line, there is no BPR. If a company or partnership has a business that is 51 per cent trading and 49 per cent investment, 100 per cent relief is available on its shares; but if that company is 49 per cent trading and 51 per cent investment, no relief is given – it really is all or nothing.

15.5.2 The *Farmer* case

Farmer v. *IRC* [1999] STC (SCD) 321 is a guide to the different factors to be taken into account.

The deceased carried on a business of farming and letting properties on the farm. Two full-time employees spent most of their time on the farm. The deceased and his son spent about one day a week looking after the lettings, which were mostly of buildings formerly used by the farm.

A single set of business accounts was prepared for both farming and letting.

For most of the last eight years, farming turnover had been more than the gross rents received, but the net profit from the lettings had been more than the profit from farming. On the other hand, the value of the farmhouse, farm buildings and farmland was more than the value of the let properties.

The Special Commissioner ruled against the Inland Revenue's (as it then was) argument that relative net profits should be the critical factor in deciding whether the business consisted mainly of making or holding investments, pointing out that IHTA 1984, s.105(3) was concerned with what the business consisted of, so that it was necessary to look at the business and its activities in the round and to consider all the relevant factors. Although the lettings were more profitable than the farm, the overall context of the business, the capital employed, the time spent by the employees and business owner and the levels of turnover supported the conclusion that the business consisted mainly of farming, rather than investment, so full relief was available.

Tip

Two elements are really important for a 'mainly trading' business:

- to keep one composite set of accounts, as in *Farmer*, rather than separating out any rental properties or other 'investment' income; and
- to have a unified management, not separating out the staff or management of, for example, property producing rent and trading income.

15.5.3 The *George* case

The analysis in *Farmer* was expressly approved by the Court of Appeal in the leading case on what is and is not mainly investment, *IRC* v. *George* [2003] EWCA Civ 1763: *Farmer* v. *IRC* 'is particularly helpful, not least in its emphasis on the need to look at the business "in the round"' (para.13).

George itself was about a majority shareholding in a company which owned and operated a residential caravan site. The main components of the business were:

- letting pitches on the caravan park;
- providing a caravan storage area;
- running a club and shop for residents;
- selling of caravans.

The first two were regarded as investment activities, but the Special Commissioner held that the business did not consist 'wholly or mainly of making or holding investments'. The Revenue succeeded on appeal to the High Court, where the judge said that holding investments was 'the very business' of the company, but the Court of Appeal restored the Special Commissioner's original ruling that relief was available.

Part of the reason for the Court of Appeal's decision was its view that the Special Commissioner was the primary judge of facts and, in particular of what was and was not mainly investment. However, it also overturned the High Court's finding that connections to sewerage, water, electricity and supplies of bottled gas were 'ancillary' to the investment part of business; the caravan park was buying these services in and retailing them to the caravan owners. The Court of Appeal also ruled that one should not calculate the contents of an 'investment bag', into which were placed all the activities linked to letting pitches on the caravan park. Nor was it necessary to determine whether or not investment was the 'very business of the company'. The holding of property as an investment was only one component of the business, and on the findings of the Commissioner it was not the main component.

Although it is common ground that the exploitation of a proprietary interest in land for profit is in principle an 'investment activity', the author would agree respectfully with the Commissioner's comment as to the wide 'spectrum' involved (Carnwath LJ at para.12 of *George*, quoting the Special Commissioner in the same case):

> There is a spectrum at one end of which is the exploitation of land by granting a tenancy coupled with sufficient activity to make it a business, which may be activity in granting tenancies rather than activity in relation to the tenancy once granted. At the other end of the spectrum, while land is still being exploited, the element of services means that there is a trade, such as running a hotel, or a shop from premises owned by the trader.

Another influential feature of *George* is the Court of Appeal's discussion of *Martin* v. *IRC* [1995] STC (SCD) 5. *Martin* concerned a business letting industrial units on three-year leases. The taxpayers argued that the scale of activity in managing and maintaining the properties took it out of the 'investment' category. The Special Commissioner rejected that argument, ruling that 'active' rather than purely 'passive' property investment was still investment and the Court of Appeal, in *George*, described that ruling as 'unimpeachable'.

The Court of Appeal quoted with approval the Special Commissioner's categorisation of the landlord's various activities:

- those directed at 'making' the investment (finding tenants, negotiations over rent, granting leases, taking surrenders and the like);
- 'compliance activities' which the owner had to carry out as landlord (such as keeping the exterior painted and in good repair);
- 'management activities' (such as day-to-day maintenance of the exterior and the common areas, and 'policing' the common areas to ensure that tenants complied with the terms of their leases).

The first two of these were regarded as 'clearly activities of or attributable to the making or holding of investments'.

15.5.4 Furnished holiday lets: the *Pawson* and *Graham* cases

Some of these conclusions found their way into the Upper Tribunal's decision in *Pawson* v. *IRC* [2013] UKUT 050 (TCC). This has led HMRC to the view 'that furnished holiday lets will in general not qualify for business property relief' (IHTM25278). This is odd in the face of special income tax and capital gains tax rules which grant many holiday letting businesses what might be called quasi-trading status. Nor does HMRC's view follow from the cases referred to above, and a number of other cases, that make it clear that the particular business must be considered in the round.

While the *Pawson* decision seems correct on its facts, it is the author's opinion that the Upper Tribunal judge was wrong to reject the taxpayer's submission that 'a holiday letting business is inherently of such a nature that it falls outside the scope of a "normal" property letting business', and to go on to say: 'On the contrary, I consider such a business to be a typical example of a property letting business, albeit one of a fairly specialist nature' (para.46). Putting on one side the question of why an example 'of a fairly specialist nature' is still a 'normal' 'property letting business', surely, looking at the spectrum referred to in *George,* a holiday letting with significant input from the business owners is much closer to running a hotel than it is to granting a tenancy?

Is there not a significant difference between a business letting units for three years (as in *Martin*), where each 'sale' provides an income stream for, literally, years, and holiday lettings, where a new sale has to be made for every week or two's income? If a holiday letting owner employs an agent for all their lettings, it is probably right to describe the lettings as investment. But if the owner is directly involved in lettings and engaged in continuous marketing to achieve those week-by-week sales it seems to us to make no sense to call this investment.

Pawson was followed in two more recent cases about holiday lettings: *Ross* v. *HMRC* [2017] UKFTT 0507 (TC); and *Green* v. *HMRC* [2015] UKFTT 334 (TC), but *Graham (deceased)* v. *HMRC* [2018] UKFTT 0306 (TC) demonstrates that some holiday lettings businesses will not be mainly investment. The First-tier Tribunal, in this case, fought shy of criticising *Pawson* (para.61):

> We do not think that the appellants have any need to seek to dilute the effect of Henderson J's statement . . . Nevertheless we accept that we must be vigilant in having in mind the spectrum and assessing where [a] business lies on that spectrum; and we agree that there is no presumption which requires rebuttal that a business which involves the exploitation of land for profit is mainly an investment business: the facts must be looked at in the round.

HMRC initially appealed *Graham* but withdrew before the hearing. It seems likely that, for the time being, it will continue to refuse relief for holiday lettings, on the basis of *Pawson* and its conclusion that a holiday letting is 'a typical example of a property letting' and a reference by the judge in *Graham* to the case being 'exceptional'.

It is all too easy for HMRC to rule that particular kinds of business are investment. So it is essential that those arguing for business relief demonstrate how what may appear superficially to be the same kind of business will often be very different. The author's experience is that, as with holiday lettings, HMRC will usually regard providing stables and pasture for livery as investment. It seems to apply the same approach to storage businesses, and even to 'rent a chair' arrangements of the kind common in hairdressing businesses.

15.5.5 The *Vigne* case

The entertaining case of *Vigne* v. *HMRC* [2017] UKFTT 632 (TC) and [2018] UKUT 357 (TCC) demonstrated a fresh and welcome approach.

Most encouragingly, the First-tier Tribunal judgment began by looking at the two Court of Appeal cases in this area (*George* and *McCall* v. *HMRC* [2009] NICA 12) and only considered *Pawson* towards the end. Some comments from *Pawson* about services not being sufficient to prevent the business from being one of holding an investment are quoted, followed by (para.44):

> With respect to the learned judge, that is to transpose the statutory test. The essential question requires us to begin by asking the simple question: was the deceased carrying on a business, wholly or mainly, of holding investments. It is not correct to start with the preconceived idea that in any given situation, the business is wholly or mainly one of holding investments and then to ask whether there are factors that result in that preliminary view being altered. The proper starting point is to make no assumption one way or the other, but to establish the facts and then to determine whether, taken together, they indicate that the business is wholly or mainly one of holding investments.

HMRC was unsuccessful in overturning the First-tier Tribunal decision in the Upper Tribunal. Again this provides support to challenge, in appropriate cases, HMRC's comment in IHTM25278 'that furnished holiday lets will in general not qualify for business property relief'.

15.5.6 The *Brander* case and some conclusions

Our view is that the best guide to the law as to what is and is not mainly investment is currently in *Brander (PR of Balfour)* v. *HMRC* [2010] UKUT 300 (TCC), which is about a landed estate with a variety of business activities. This case established the following:

- What the term the 'business of holding investments' means is what an intelligent businessman would conclude and is a question of fact.
- The decision-maker must look at the business in the round and, in the light of the overall picture, form a view as to the relative importance to the business as a whole of its investment and non-investment activities.
- This exercise involves looking at the business over a period of time.
- Various factors should be considered, such as:
  - the overall context of the business;
  - the turnover and the profitability of various activities;
  - the activities of employees and other persons engaged to assist the business; and
  - the area and value of land dedicated to each activity.
- Not one of these factors is conclusive, as the exercise involves looking at the business in the round.
- The fact that the owner of an investment engages in activities to manage and maintain their investment does not of itself take the business out of the investment category.
- In looking at the question in the round, it is not appropriate in every case to compartmentalise the business and attribute management and maintenance activity either to investment or to non-investment as an ancillary activity.
- Because the question is a question of fact, the Upper Tribunal can interfere with the decision of the First-tier Tribunal only if an error of law has been demonstrated.

- In *Brander*, it happens that two-thirds of the property value was in let properties but the overall business, considered in the round, was considered to be mainly a trading one.

While we have looked at many cases here, to understand how the law in this difficult area works, it is not purely a theoretical technical area, but a very important practical one. With difficult economic times in recent years, many businesses have diversified out of necessity. Much of this diversity will have included moves to let out premises that previously had been trading.

Example 15.2

Fred and Ginger are in partnership running a chain of three dance schools, which they operate from premises that they own, but economic pressures lead them to concentrate their energies into two schools, and to let out the third. Later they decide the move is worth repeating, so they let out a second and focus their time on one elite dance school. Each of these changes the balance of the various factors in the *Brander* case, as set out above.

The problem with IHT and BPR is that one is not banking a relief that is then guaranteed, or secure, but setting up a structure that will be assessed at a future date, to decide whether it does or doesn't qualify for relief. The balance of the different factors will often change a great deal over the years. There is also not one decisive factor, such as net value or net profit, that you can turn to. These factors are considered in the round.

As ever, Fred and Ginger in this example, and other clients like them, will mainly focus on making a living now, and what can be done to mitigate their tax liability this year. The potential treatment of their business in the event of death will not be their key focus.

Tip

Encourage your clients and their tax advisers to take stock of their IHT position, on a regular basis, say 3–5 yearly, to consider how, for example, the last three years' accounts would look, and what factors they could utilise to support a claim for BPR in the event of death. This is not easy, but is worth trying.

15.5.7 Excepted assets

Excepted assets (IHTA 1984, s.112) are assets of a business or company that are either:

- not used for the purpose of the business; or
- not required for the future use of the business.

Where a business or company has excepted assets, the value that gets relief is the value that the business interest, shareholding, etc. would have if the excepted asset were not owned.

It was once thought that this only really affected 'playthings' within companies – yachts and racehorses were the usual examples. But HMRC has successfully used the provisions to challenge what it considers to be excessive cash within businesses and, today, will often look at a balance sheet, see a large sum of cash, and argue that it is not all needed.

It is important to be prepared for an argument of this kind. Is the cash held because the business operates in an uncertain market and the cash is an essential reserve? Is a cash balance being built up to invest in an expansion or a new line of business? Contemporaneous records are crucial here.

Tip

Encourage clients to review, when considering their annual accounts with their business advisers, the amount of cash held and the purposes for which it is needed. Where possible, a note can be included on the accounts to note the purpose for which the cash is being held. This valuable contemporaneous record has the great virtue of being the first place HMRC will look, and is easily reviewed in subsequent years if, in practice, the stated purpose does not materialise.

The rules barring investment businesses from relief and those on excepted assets are sometimes confused. They are completely separate provisions. An investment activity and its associated assets can get full relief, provided the investment activity is not the main business. So one solution to holding excess cash within a business may be to add an investment business stream, taking care that it does not cause the business as a whole to be mainly investment.

15.5.8 Groups of companies

The holding company of a group can qualify for relief if 'the business of the company consists wholly or mainly in being a holding company of one or more companies whose business does not fall within' the investment restriction in IHTA 1984, s.105(3) (IHTA 1984, s.105(4)(b)).

This means that it is necessary to apply the 'mainly investment' test to the group as a whole.

Even if the group as a whole passes the test, subsidiary companies which, in themselves, are mainly investment, lose relief. So, as with excepted assets, any relief available to the holding company must be reduced to reflect the value of those investment companies. It may be possible to increase relief by moving investment businesses from one company to another within the group, often up to the holding company.

There is an exception for subsidiary companies which own assets used by other companies within the group.

15.6 BUSINESS AND AGRICULTURAL RELIEF AND WILLS FOR SPOUSES

Where BPR or APR is available, it is always better, on the death of the first of a couple to die, for the asset with relief not to go to a surviving spouse (whether married or civil partner). It is a waste of IHT exemptions and reliefs to make an exempt gift of an asset that qualifies for relief in its own right.

In a case where there are doubts as to whether, or to what extent, assets qualify for relief, this is an opportunity to ascertain the position that is likely to apply on the second death, which will help the family and their advisers plan if relief is not available.

If the will of the first to die specifies the assets thought likely to qualify for at least some relief and gives those assets to a discretionary trust of which the surviving spouse, children and remoter descendants are all potential beneficiaries, and also makes a gift of a cash amount equivalent to any unused nil rate band, HMRC is forced to consider whether relief is available. If, as the two-year period after death is drawing to a close, it is clear that relief is going to be refused, the trustees can, in the exercise of their discretion, divert the relevant assets into the IHT ownership of the spouse, to get exemption on the first death, invoking IHTA 1984, s.144.

The introduction of the residence nil rate band (RNRB), which begins to be withdrawn once an individual has assets at death of more than £2 million, makes it more valuable than ever to keep assets out of the survivor's ownership. A trust in the first will achieves that, while still allowing the survivor to have access to all the assets of the first to die.

The worst option is to split assets with relief between the surviving spouse and children. Many years ago a kind of a double discount could be exploited in these cases, but this was blocked by IHTA 1984, s.39A, which frequently has the effect of disallowing a substantial part of the relief that would be available if the whole gift were made to a taxable beneficiary.

15.7 LIFETIME GIFTS WITH RELIEF

Assets qualifying for 100 per cent business or agricultural relief incur no inheritance tax when they are given to a trust, whatever the amount of the gift.

Relief on a lifetime gift is withdrawn if the settlor dies within seven years and either the donor no longer owns the asset given, or the asset no longer satisfies the conditions for relief. This withdrawal of relief is usually called 'clawback'.

Clawback works in a surprising way on gifts to trusts. If 100 per cent relief was available on the original gift, the gift never forms part of the settlor's cumulative total. So a full £325,000 nil rate band (NRB) remains available to set against other gifts, or on the settlor's death.

This is apparent from a comparison of IHTA 1984, s.113A(1) and (2), which apply clawback where BPR is available on the original gift (s.124A(1) and (2) contain identical provisions for APR):

> (1) Where any part of the value transferred by a potentially exempt transfer which proves to be a chargeable transfer would (apart from this section) be reduced in accordance with the preceding provisions of this Chapter [the business relief provisions], it shall not be so reduced . . .
>
> (2) Where –
>
> (a) any part of the value transferred by any chargeable transfer, other than a potentially exempt transfer, is reduced in accordance with the preceding provisions of this Chapter, and
>
> (b) the transfer is made within seven years of the death of the transferor,
>
> then . . . the additional tax chargeable by reason of the death shall be calculated as if the value transferred had not been so reduced.

So for failed potentially exempt transfers, in (1), BPR is simply cancelled. For chargeable transfers, under (2), it is only 'the additional tax chargeable by reason of the death' which is recalculated. No change is made to the transferor's lifetime cumulative total, which will not include the gift on which 100 per cent relief was obtained. So the donor obtains an extra, tax-free, NRB.

Even if there is no plan for assets with 100 per cent BPR or APR to remain in trust in the long term, it is actually better to make a chargeable gift to a trust than a potentially exempt transfer (PET) to an individual.

If there is a plan for a long-term trust and a possibility that the relieved assets will be sold during the life of the trust, separate transfers of portions of the business assets to separate trusts, created on different days, can significantly reduce future 10-year and exit charges. Each trust will normally have a full £325,000 NRB, unreduced by earlier relieved gifts to the other trusts. This strategy is not affected by the rules on same-day additions (SDAs) introduced in 2015.

CHAPTER 16

The residence nil rate band (RNRB)

John Bunker

16.1 KEY POINTS

- The residence nil rate band (RNRB) was introduced in 2017 on a phased basis with a target that was reached in 2020/21: to enable spouses (married couples and civil partners) to leave £1 million free of inheritance tax (IHT), by adding the RNRB of £175,000 (in 2020/21) to a nil rate band (NRB) of £325,000.
  - RNRB has built up to its full value over four years:
    - £100,000 in 2017/18,
    - £125,000 in 2018/19,
    - £150,000 in 2019/20,
    - £175,000 in 2020/21.
  - In 2020/21 the total IHT saving, with IHT being chargeable at 40 per cent, is £70,000, or £140,000 for two RNRBs, if the transferable RNRB (TRNRB) is fully claimed on the death of the second party to the marriage or civil partnership.
- **To claim RNRB there are four main requirements:**
  1. The taxpayer owns the right interest in a residential property, including a trust interest (see **16.4**); or can claim a 'downsizing addition' (see **16.5**).
  2. The taxpayer leaves that interest to children or remoter descendants who 'closely inherit', either outright or through the permitted form of trust (see **16.7**).
  3. The taxpayer's estate (including any aggregable trust) is not over £2 million, or if it is, the RNRB is tapered away by £1 for every £2 over that threshold (see **16.8**).
  4. RNRB does not take into account lifetime gifts, although they may come within the downsizing addition. Gifts can be made at any time before death, so long as they are completed, valid gifts. They can serve to reduce an estate below the £2 million threshold (see **16.9**).

- **Three notes on the controversial form of this tax:**
  - It was introduced to achieve a clear objective to enable spouses to leave that 'magic' total figure of £1 million before tax is payable. Many have said it is unfair, to those who don't have descendants, or a home of sufficient value, and others that it is biased towards parts of the UK that have higher property values. As advisers, our task is to make the most of this new opportunity for many clients to save significant amounts of tax.
  - It is incredibly complex. We set out below the 15 new clauses in the statute that were needed to bring this in. The original draft legislation needed three substantial amendments in 2015 and 2016 to reach this stage, and there are still a number of serious defects in the legislation. The author, in this book as in his lecturing on this over that five-year period, seeks to make it as understandable as possible in order that advisers can help clients maximise their opportunity.
  - Many wish for reform, to save complexity, and it may be reformed, or totally withdrawn, in the future. Until then, we have a duty to help clients make sense of what this means. Lawyers and other advisers who get to grips with it can help clients all the more in writing wills, tax planning, in estate administration and variations.

16.2 THE NEW SECTIONS IN THE INHERITANCE TAX ACT 1984 AND THE KEY DEFINITIONS

To bring in the RNRB, 15 new clauses in the IHTA 1984 were needed, as follows:

- s.8D Extra nil-rate band on death if interest in home goes to descendants, etc.
- s.8E Residence nil-rate amount: interest in home goes to descendants, etc. – generally known as 'residence nil-rate band', or RNRB
- s.8F Residence nil-rate amount: no interest in home goes to descendants, etc.
- ss.8FA–8FE Downsizing addition:
  - s.8FA Downsizing addition: entitlement: low-value death interest in home
  - s.8FB Downsizing addition: entitlement: no residential interest at death
  - s.8FC Downsizing addition: effect: section 8E case
  - s.8FD Downsizing addition: effect: section 8F case
  - s.8FE Calculation of lost relievable amount
- s.8G Meaning of 'brought-forward allowance'
- s.8H Meaning of 'qualifying residential interest', 'qualifying former residential interest' and 'residential property interest'
- s.8HA 'Qualifying former residential interest': interests in possession
- s.8J Meaning of 'inherited'
- s.8K Meaning of 'closely inherited'

- s.8L Claims for brought-forward allowance and downsizing addition*
- s.8M Residence nil-rate amount: cases involving conditional exemption

* Section 8L sets out the process for claiming the two elements of RNRB which must be formally 'claimed' within the permitted period, normally two years from the end of the month in which the deceased died. RNRB itself does not need to be 'claimed', even though you need to fill in the IHT435 form to get the RNRB, and if you don't fill in that form in time you don't lose the right to RNRB. By contrast, downsizing addition needs to be claimed, on that IHT435 form, and the brought-forward allowance (sometime called 'TRNRB') claimed on the IHT436 form within the time limits.

16.3 HMRC'S INHERITANCE TAX MANUAL, IHTM46001–46100

This section of the HM Revenue and Customs (HMRC) *Inheritance Tax Manual* on RNRB is invaluable, uses the correct technical language and cross-references to statute – but there are some cautionary notes:

- Always remember that the manuals are HMRC's interpretation of the legislation, not new legislation themselves. The 15 clauses above are quite enough new legislation. Any of the manual may be wrong, and it is open to anyone to challenge HMRC's interpretation, but in practice this is rare and difficult.
- The manuals are addressed to HMRC officers, telling them how to administer the tax, and make decisions. It is their perspective and, while the examples can be very useful, they may not have addressed all points.
- The manuals are regularly updated, with some minor changes of text, but sometimes of more significance. Do ensure that you refer to the up-to-date text and, if you are referring to the manual and relying on it, that you keep a copy of the IHTM at the relevant date so that you can refer to it if needed in correspondence.

16.4 QUALIFYING RESIDENTIAL INTEREST: OWNING THE RIGHT INTEREST AT DEATH

You need to own a residential property, or an interest in a property, either yourself and/or through the permitted form of trust.

16.4.1 Residential property interest

You have to have occupied a residential property (a dwelling-house or part of one, such as a flat) as a residence at the same time as you had an interest in that property in your IHT 'estate' (meaning in your own name or via an aggregable trust). It doesn't have to have been your main residence, just a residence, so that by the time of your death it could be let out.

Your 'estate' can have more than one residential property interest in one property, as you can have a personal interest and a trust interest where the trust is within the definition of 'estate' in IHTA 1984, s.5. Trusts here will be qualifying interest in possession (QIIP) trusts, in which you have a life interest or similar, including an immediate post-death interest (IPDI) or an old-style, pre-March 2006, QIIP which could include a life interest in a lifetime settlement.

16.4.2 Qualifying residential interest

If you have just residential property interests in one dwelling-house (or part) in your estate at your death, those interests will be a qualifying residential interest (QRI). It's not good English, but two interests (classically the personal and IPDI) become one QRI.

If you have residential property interests in more than one dwelling-house, at your death, the personal representatives of your estate nominate one of the dwelling-houses and the interests in that dwelling-house become that person's QRI. Thus the trustees of any aggregable trust will have no say in the choice of QRI, even if the QRI in the trust has a greater value and would be a better choice than the one in the estate.

If you are acting for both (the personal representatives and the trustees), you can of course advise on the right choice, but if not then it's worth liaising with the other advisers, or the clients if they are acting for themselves. Conversely, if you are only acting for the trustees, you may need to encourage personal representatives or those advising personal representatives to consider whether it is best for all to choose the trust property.

16.4.3 How is the benefit of RNRB set against the deceased's estate and any trust?

This is a critical question at this stage, as it is critical to the choice of QRI. The RNRB is not offset against the QRI, reducing the tax on that property, as agricultural property relief (APR) would be for a farmhouse. RNRB is set against the total IHT payable on death, on the personal estate and any aggregable trust, as for the NRB. Thus it reduces the IHT payable in proportion to the value of the estate and the trust. If an estate has two-thirds of the value, it will get two-thirds of the benefit of the RNRB. Likewise, the trust gets one-third of the benefit, through the overall reduction in the tax payable, even if the QRI is held in the estate.

16.4.4 Any mortgage is to be deducted from the value of the QRI

It is the value of the QRI net of the mortgage that is taken, so that, for example, a QRI worth £300,000 subject to a mortgage of £100,000 would provide a net value of £200,000. Thus it is enough to use a single RNRB, but not a double RNRB of £350,000. The QRI's value is less than the double RNRB but at least, if the mortgage were paid off, the full £300,000 value could be used. So, in advising clients on RNRB, always check the amount outstanding on any mortgage and consider whether there are other assets to pay off the mortgage – all other things being equal.

16.4.5 Examples of QRI

Example 16.1

Ainsley and Bertha share a house 10 Peel Street, they own 50:50 as tenants in common, and after Bertha's death Ainsley has a life interest in an IPDI trust under Bertha's will, the capital then due to their two children. Ainsley has two residential property interests (his own 50% share in Peel Street and his IPDI in the 50% held in the trust) which would form one QRI in the event of his death (assuming it was closely inherited).

Example 16.2

Ainsley meets Cassie two years after Bertha dies, and they decide to live together. Cassie has her own home, 'Hope Cottage', which they make their joint home and Ainsley buys a half share so they own it as tenants in common in equal shares. They keep 10 Peel Street as an investment property to give them income. They listen to your advice and decide it is sensible to be married for tax reasons as well as personal ones.

If Ainsley dies there will be two dwelling-houses, with his personal estate having a half share of Hope Cottage, which will go in trust to Cassie under his will; and also a half share of 10 Peel St which also has a second half share owned by Bertha's trust. Ainsley's personal representatives have to nominate which of the two dwelling-houses will have the QRI.

Hope Cottage is worth £300,000, so that Ainsley's half share is just £150,000. He has a double RNRB of £350,000 in 2020/21 available, as there is the RNRB carried forward from Bertha's estate. Using Hope Cottage as the QRI would potentially waste £200,000 of RNRB and result in an extra £80,000 IHT bill. By contrast, 10 Peel Street is worth £400,000 and the whole of it qualifies as a QRI for Ainsley as it was his residence and both the interests (i.e. including his one-half share IPDI in Bertha's trust) qualify for RNRB (again assuming it was closely inherited).

It would therefore be better for Ainsley's personal representatives to choose 10 Peel Street as the QRI. The author is often asked whether this is not unfair as there are different beneficiaries for his estate and Bertha's trust. It's easy to miss the point in **16.4.3** about how RNRB is set against the estate and trust. They share proportionately any reduction in IHT. The personal representatives should choose the higher value property, 10 Peel Street, that can use the full double RNRB of £350,000. Everyone is better off this way, the beneficiaries of both the estate and trust, as the IHT payable is reduced by the maximum £140,000.

Example 16.3

June is a widow, her husband died before RNRB was introduced, so she has a carried-forward RNRB, making a double £350,000 in 2020/21. She did live in a house worth £400,000 but moved in June 2015 (before the date for the downsizing addition – see **16.5**) to a property worth only £275,000. Thus she loses £75,000 of the RNRB she would be able to have on her estate.

Doreen is also widowed, with a double RNRB available, and she has two houses, each worth £250,000, so a total of £500,000 in residential property. She can only have one of the homes as her QRI, so it will be only £250,000 and thus £100,000 short of the £350,000 RNRB.

What advice can you give June and Doreen? If you bring to their attention the potential 'waste' of part of the double RNRB, and show how the figures work, each of June and Doreen can take that into account in making decisions about their home. While it is not suggested they should be advised to move house to secure the full tax relief, it is a factor that may then make a difference to life choices.

Suppose that June says, she is grateful for the advice, she has been thinking about moving closer to her daughter, April, but April lives in a more expensive area. Your advice might just help June make a decision she is contemplating for other, non-tax reasons!

Then suppose Doreen says, she has been talking to her sister about her proposed move, so can see more clearly that it is also a choice for her. She has been getting a bit fed up with having two houses to maintain and had been thinking she might sell them both and buy one bigger property for her family to come and stay. If you don't flag up this element to June and Doreen, they can't factor it into their thinking.

16.5 DOWNSIZING ADDITION

16.5.1 Introduction

The downsizing legislation was introduced, as one of the major amendments to IHTA 1984, with the aim of ensuring that there was no disincentive to downsize or sell a home. Otherwise, as envisaged in the early days of RNRB, some older people might feel obliged to stay in unsuitable, larger properties to protect the tax benefits for their family.

It was backdated to cover any changes since 8 July 2015, Budget Day when the new provisions for RNRB were first introduced. It is a quite horrendous bit of legislation, with new IHTA 1984, ss.8FA, 8FB, 8FC, 8FD and 8FE comprising about five pages of A4 text and some of the most convoluted technical provisions you could hope to see (or not see!). Fortunately, this is an IHT planning handbook, not a full IHT textbook, and so we will here focus on just a few details and planning points.

16.5.2 Downsizing basics

The main points regarding downsizing are as follows:

- All the provisions apply to changes on or after 8 July 2015.
- The former home would have qualified for RNRB if it had been held until death.

- The direct descendants must inherit at least some of the estate.
- The downsizing addition will usually be the same as the RNRB lost when the former home is no longer in the estate. It cannot be more than the maximum amount of RNRB available if the sale or downsizing had not happened.
- The personal representatives must make a claim for downsizing addition within two years of the end of the month of the deceased's death. (This is one of only two claims that are needed in RNRB – the other, the carry-forward of a deceased spouse's RNRB as RNRB itself, does not need to be 'claimed'.)
- Only one move or transaction can be included but, if the deceased had two moves on or after 8 July 2015, the personal representatives can choose which one to claim – it doesn't need to be the most recent.
- GOV.UK has a guidance note with a helpful five-step process to work out the lost RNRB, and some helpful examples (*How downsizing, selling or gifting a home affects the residence nil rate band: Check if an estate can get the residence nil rate band (RNRB) when someone downsizes, gifts or sells their home before they die*, 2017). While many GOV.UK guides are at a more basic level, not giving the information as technically as may be helpful, this one is very useful. See: **www.gov.uk/guidance/how-downsizing-selling-or-gifting-a-home-affects-the-additional-inheritance-tax-threshold**.

16.5.3 Selling, downsizing and gifting: the three downsizing addition situations

Downsizing addition can apply in the following situations:

- **'Low-value death interest in home':** The deceased was downsizing to a lower value property:
  - provided the new property and an equivalent value of 'lost' RNRB is left to descendants;
  - see IHTA 1984, s.8FA;
  - so, as a practical point, where this may need to be claimed, keep the completion statement, with the original will in the strongroom.
- **'No residential interest at death':** The deceased sold the only residence and moved to a care home or rented accommodation:
  - provided the sale proceeds or an equivalent value are left to descendants;
  - see IHTA 1984, s.8FB.
- **Gifted property and assets of equivalent value left to descendants:** The legislation does not have a separate category for gifts, but it does not refer to sales, so that a reduced interest can result from a gift as well as a sale.

16.5.4 Planning issues with downsizing

While downsizing will not normally be a planning tool, it is important to keep it in mind for cases where it is relevant and, for example:

- if any planning involves a gift of a main residential property, do take into account the gifting option here;
- take care to obtain further information from a client, about any moves since July 2015, if they might otherwise not fully utilise their RNRB but they are in fact within the provisions for the addition;
- downsizing addition calculations are horrendously complicated, and thus are really best for use if there are no other options available.

16.6 SHARES OF AN ESTATE, APPROPRIATION AND IHTM46033

16.6.1 IHTM46033

IHTM46033, a vital page in HMRC's *Inheritance Tax Manual*, tells us the following:

- The QRI does not need to be left as a specific legacy – it can simply be part of a share of residue.
- HMRC takes the view that each residuary beneficiary inherits a share of the property in the same proportions as they inherit the residue of the estate. However, if insufficient is closely inherited (see **16.7**), it is not possible for personal representatives to appropriate the property to those that are closely inherited to fix the availability of the RNRB.
- The QRI does not need appropriating to those closely inheriting.
- The actual home does not have to end up in (their) hands.
- The personal representatives can sell the property and pass the proceeds to beneficiaries.
- Once the property is inherited, there are no restrictions on what the beneficiaries have to do with it.

Example 16.4

Ravi left his estate with three equal shares of residue – a 1/3 share to each of three residuary beneficiaries, his two children A and B, and his sister C. The estate had a property with a value of £450,000. HMRC takes the view each inherits a 1/3 share of the property, and as A and B closely inherit but C does not, as she is a sister, it means only 2/3 of the QRI is closely inherited. So only £300,000 of the £450,000 property qualifies for RNRB. As Ravi is a widower, with £350,000 for two RNRBs in 2020/21, this means that £50,000 of RNRB is wasted and £20,000 more IHT is payable.

16.6.2 Appropriation is an administrative power

IHTM46033 tells us appropriation 'is not a disposition' and therefore can't be used to fix RNRB if the QRI is not left to qualifying beneficiaries. Ironically, the QRI could potentially be appropriated to the very beneficiary who does not closely inherit, as the RNRB application is not 'read back' into the will!

As a quick reminder, a power of appropriation is one of the key powers to include in a will. It is sometimes done as an extension of Administration of Estates Act 1925, s.41, but it's generally better to have an express power of appropriation. This crucial clause will allow the personal representatives to appropriate a specific asset to a beneficiary, or a trust, in whole or part satisfaction of the legacy or share of the estate left to that person/trust. The allocation of a specific asset, at its then market value, saves the need for the whole estate to be sold, and can really help the effective administration of an estate, including sensible IHT and capital gains tax (CGT) planning with losses and gains – see **Chapter 9**.

Example 16.5: Ravi's estate: a deed of variation by his three residuary beneficiaries

Following **Example 16.4**, how do we then advise the three beneficiaries? Ravi having left his estate with three equal shares of residue, his children A and B are only treated as 'inheriting' 1/3 each of the QRI, so only 2/3 is closely inherited. A, B and C would therefore need to agree a deed of variation that the property goes to A and B, and cash, etc. to C. This assumes there is sufficient cash in the estate to be able to do this and all the beneficiaries are of full age and capacity, and willing to co-operate! It is for their mutual benefit, as the RNRB reduces the tax payable on the estate for the benefit of all three of them, not simply the two who closely inherit.

16.7 CLOSELY INHERITING

You need to leave the estate to the right people, in the right way, to qualify for RNRB. Essentially it is only for children and remoter descendants, although widely defined, see **16.7.1**. Also it can be left outright or in the permitted form of trust – see **16.7.2**.

16.7.1 Meaning of 'closely inherited'

The meaning of 'closely inherited' is as follows:

- a property interest (QRI) would be 'closely inherited' by children, grandchildren and remoter descendants;
- this is widely defined to include:
  - stepchildren – but see **16.7.3**;
  - foster children;

- even natural children who've been adopted – changing the normal rule on the effect of adoption; and is extended to
- the spouses and widows of such descendants, provided they do not remarry, so that remarriage before the death of the parent-in-law (etc.) means they no longer qualify.

16.7.2 Closely inherited outright or through the right form of trust

The QRI or share of an estate can be left either:

- outright to a beneficiary who closely inherits; or
- in trust if in one of these forms of trust:
  - bare trust;
  - bereaved minor's trust (BMT);
  - 18–25 trust;
  - IPDI trust on/after 22 March 2006;
  - an old-style (pre-22 March 2006) QIIP trust, such as a lifetime life interest, that would be aggregated with the estate; or
  - a disabled person's trust (see **5.12**).

16.7.3 'Stepchildren'

Who is a stepchild for RNRB purposes?

- A 'stepchild' includes children of a spouse or former spouse.
- However, 'stepchild' does not include the children of an unmarried partner – to whom some clients loosely refer as 'their stepchildren', which is a misnomer.

Under IHTA 1984, s.8K(3): 'A person who is at any time a step-child of another person is to be treated, at that and all subsequent times, as if the person was that other person's child.' Therefore:

- your stepchildren's children, etc. are included; and
- the stepchildren of your children are included.

So, once any beneficiary is included, so are their descendants.

Example 16.6

Ana had a son, Ben, when she was 15, whom she gave up for adoption but who found her, his birth mother, when she was 45 and he was 30. Ana is now 65 and makes a will leaving her estate as follows:

- 1/4 share to Ben who is a natural child, so he does qualify to 'closely inherit'.
- 1/4 share to Chris who is the widow of her daughter Carrie who sadly died three years ago, and they had no children; Ana is very close to Chris. Chris has recently met

someone else and was remarried a week before Ana died. Chris does not closely inherit because he remarried just before Ana's death and so was then no longer Carrie's widow.

- 1/8 share to each of Dale's two children at 21, they currently being 14 and 16, Dale being the child 'who has gone off the rails', so that share is going to his children. Although for grandchildren, the trust does not qualify, as they are under 21 and the trust for them until that age is a relevant property trust (RPT) and not one of the permitted trusts that qualify as being 'closely inherited'. The trustees need to advance to the grandchildren outright or use their powers in the will to make it into an IPDI trust – see **Chapter 17** on how to correct this.
- 1/4 share to Emma, Ana's daughter late in life who is only 17, to be held in trust until she is 25. This would be an 18–25 trust, so she closely inherits.
- Result: 2/4 is fine, 1/4 is not, and the last 1/4 depends on the trustees' actions. So 3/4 should closely inherit.

16.7.4 No restriction on the use of IHTA 1984, ss.142 and 144 to achieve the right end result

You can vary an estate, within two years of death, to ensure that the estate qualifies for RNRB through the right people closely inheriting. See **Example 16.5**.

RNRB will not apply to a discretionary trust, as a discretionary trust is not the permitted form of trust that would qualify for RNRB being closely inherited. In order to qualify, such trusts would need to be appointed out within two years of the date of death, either absolutely or on appropriate trusts. This is a classic use of 'reading back' into the will, under IHTA 1984, s.144, within two years of date of death – see **Chapters 11** and **14**.

Do note, however, the trust trap that you can't use IHTA 1984, ss.142/144 on a discretionary trust following a life interest, where for example an IPDI and a discretionary trust of residue are used, a not uncommon arrangement for good legal reasons in wills.

Some draft discretionary trusts as a starting point and then rearrange as needed in the two years post-death. If there are any discretionary trusts arising under a will, you should advise if there is potential tax to save, that action needs to be taken and that it will not qualify for RNRB without that action. It would be ideal to flag up this need, saying that the discretionary trust needs to be rearranged within the two years, offering advice on restructuring the trust and the potential tax-saving benefit.

This would normally be additional detailed advice on top of the usual estate administration work and charged accordingly. Normally additional fees would need to be quoted, and approved, to reflect the complexity of this work, the work not being completed until the clients have agreed additional fees. (See **17.2.**)

16.8 THE £2 MILLION TAPER THRESHOLD

If an estate exceeds £2 million – the 'taper threshold' – it loses £1 of RNRB for every £2 over the threshold limit. Three keys points to note:

1. 'Estate' includes aggregated trust interests, i.e. trusts which are subject to IHT on death, including IPDIs and pre-22 March 2006 QIIP trusts.
2. It also includes gifts with reservation of benefit (GROBs) but not lifetime gifts where there is no reservation of benefit. Valid, completed gifts can be made on a 'death-bed' or at any time before death, and it does not matter that the donor does not survive for seven years – see **16.9**.
3. However, it disregards all exemptions and reliefs, including APR and business property relief (BPR), so clients have the difficulty of understanding that the full value of a business or farm is included.

Planning issues arise a great deal around the £2 million threshold, to preserve the full amount of RNRB or as much as is possible – see **Chapter 17**.

16.9 LIFETIME GIFTS: HOW THEY DO OR DON'T AFFECT RNRB

RNRB is not offset against, to relieve, lifetime gifts of property in itself, unless the gift was on or after 8 July 2015 and within the downsizing addition – see **16.5**. You can potentially lose RNRB if the gift was made and death occurred within seven years so that it is a failed potentially exempt transfer (PET) without the RNRB relief being available.

However, it does mean you can do death-bed planning – for now! – to reduce an estate below £2 million. As long as there is no GROB (no reservation of benefit), lifetime gifts are therefore a last resort for RNRB planning. While some people may make the regular making of gifts a tactical way of reducing their estate for RNRB purposes, in practice most will use this at a late stage in life, to reduce an estate below the £2 million threshold. Currently the £2 million estate figure takes no account of lifetime gifts that will be failed PETs or chargeable lifetime transfers (CLTs).

There are three potential traps to watch out for (discussed below):

- Was a valid, completed gift made?
- Did the donor have capacity?
- Note the very limited capacity of attorneys to make gifts.

16.9.1 Was a valid, completed gift made?

For example, if a cheque was given, was it cleared by the donee's bank? If it hasn't cleared, it is not a completed gift. In the author's experience, some children of a dying person are reluctant to pay in a cheque they are given, as if it seems mercenary, or in bad taste, and can therefore need encouragement to accept and pay in a cheque.

16.9.2 Did the donor have capacity?

It's important to watch the capacity of a person who is very ill or dying. Especially if the person is on a death-bed, do take care with fluctuating capacity, which can vary a lot from day to day and at different times of day. It is therefore important to keep detailed records of the process and conclusions to establish that a client had capacity.

The capacity required includes understanding the nature of your estate and the gifts you might be making, a similar capacity to that required for making a will. In practice, a lot of attention tends to be given to making a will, and whether a client is capable, but less so for lifetime gifts in practice.

If a client's capacity is declining, there is a valuable principle if instructions are given for a document, for example for preparing a deed of gift, when the client had full capacity, but it had declined by the time they came to sign a document. It is an extension of the longstanding rule in *Parker* v. *Felgate* (1883) LR 8 PD 171, affirmed in the 2010 case of *Perrins* v. *Holland* [2010] EWCA Civ 840 in relation to wills. This was applied to lifetime gifts by the 2011 case *Singellos* v. *Singellos* [2011] EWHC 2353 (Ch). If a person had sufficient capacity to understand that they were signing a document that carried out the instructions they had given at a time when they had full capacity, that can suffice.

16.9.3 Note the very limited capacity of attorneys to make gifts

If an attorney makes a gift for which they had no authority, the gift will be invalid and it will be a debt to the estate, so that it fails for IHT. See **Chapter 26**.

CHAPTER 17

Residence nil rate band (RNRB) planning

John Bunker

17.1 KEY POINTS

To secure the maximum inheritance tax (IHT) benefit from the residence nil rate band (RNRB), there are four main planning areas:

1. **Ensure the client owns the right interest in a residential property, including a trust interest (see 16.4), or can claim a 'downsizing addition' (see 16.5). There are three key planning issues for advisers:**

   (a) When making a will or advising on IHT, check the values of property:

   - that it is sufficient to use the RNRB, or double RNRB if applicable; and
   - that there is no mortgage on the property; or if there is, it does not reduce the equity too much to claim the RNRB.

   (b) When giving lifetime advice, check the ownership structure:

   - if the property is in trust, check it is one of the permitted trusts where RNRB can be claimed when the time comes; and
   - if there are two potential residential property interests (in the personal name and any trust) that it is clear which would be the qualifying residential interest (QRI).

   (c) When administering an estate, if there is any second estate (of a spouse or partner) to come in the future:

   - consider whether a variation of the estate or trust may be beneficial, so that the permitted form of trust interest is owned – to enable the life tenant's personal representatives to claim RNRB on their death; and
   - check the values, in case any planning is needed during the survivor's lifetime, as in (a) or (b) above or to reduce the survivor's estate below the £2 million threshold (see **17.4**).

2. **Ensure that the client leaves the right interests to children or remoter descendants, so that they 'closely inherit', either outright or through the right form of trust – see 16.7, with two main planning opportunities:**

   (a) In will drafting: to consider whether the testator's plans do cover those that sufficiently closely inherit:

   - If a specific gift of the proposed QRI is being made, will it work to use whatever RNRB (or double RNRB) is available?
   - If the QRI would be part of the residue, is that all left to people who closely inherit, or do some 'closely inherit' but others do not – for example siblings or parents, which might be called 'mixed residuary beneficiaries'?

   (b) In estate administration: with the values of the estate (and any trust) does the deceased's will (and any trust) leave the QRI satisfactorily for 1(a) or (b) above? If not, is there a variation that would work more effectively?

   In either case, can you ascertain what portion of the estate is closely inherited and the potential RNRB available to advise of any action possible – bearing in mind the practice points in **17.2**?

   The specific planning required, with reference to different situations, is considered in **17.3**. In looking at any planning, it is usually better to maximise the availability of the RNRB during lifetime (for example, in your advice and structuring the will). However, we do have, at present, the potential to 'put it right' by a variation within two years of death if the right structure has not been put in place during lifetime:

   - by a deed of variation read back under Inheritance Tax Act (IHTA) 1984, s.142; or
   - by a variation of a trust read back under IHTA 1984, s.144 – see **Chapter 14**.

3. **Ensure your IHT estate (including any aggregable trust) is not over £2 million,** or if it is the RNRB will be tapered away by £1 for every £2 over that threshold – see **16.8** and **17.4**. We will explore three main planning approaches to optimise the figures:

   (a) arrangements for passing assets between spouses, to maximise the use of RNRBs;

   (b) estate planning to use capital and income effectively, with an eye on the £2 million value, especially (but not only) spouses;

   (c) lifetime gifts, a strategy in itself for some, and death-bed planning as a valuable last resort, to make gifts to bring the 'estate' below £2 million at death.

4. Ensure you use lifetime gifts effectively. RNRB does not apply to lifetime gifts of property (although the value of the gift may come within the downsizing addition and tax relief be claimed at death), but gifts of any assets including property can be made at any time before death, to reduce the value of an estate for the £2 million threshold purposes – see **16.9** and **17.5**.

17.2 RNRB PLANNING PRACTICE

RNRB's complexities mean that clients will regularly need proactive advice, to avoid the traps and ensure the right structure of assets and inheritances to make best use of the relief. One problem is that many will just assume they get RNRB, take it for granted and not realise that action is needed. Many lawyers and other professionals will therefore need to show clients the following:

- You can do the work (will drafting, estate administration, etc.) as it is, for specified fees, but this is not the optimum arrangement.
- Greater IHT mitigation can be secured by a better structure:
  - on which you can advise; and
  - for which this additional documentation would be needed, for example a trust deed to change the form of trust;
  - for this specific estimated cost, and, if it helps, estimating the fees in two parts, for advice and implementation, so that the clients have a simple cost/benefit equation to consider as, e.g. required by Solicitors Regulation Authority (SRA) practice rules;
  - to secure an estimated benefit, but without giving away that advice or too much information so that clients can do the work themselves!
- The author would encourage practitioners with five practice points to make this work:
  - Do ensure that the offer of the potential added benefit is in writing so that, if the option is turned down, it is clear that the advice has been offered but not taken up.
  - Don't be too apologetic about the additional work and the extra fees that may go with that. This is complex law, and you are simply offering an opportunity – they don't have to take it.
  - Do not give 'off the cuff' advice, as this is complex work and you should be instructed and paid properly for your advice.
  - Be careful about clients getting the advice for free and then going off to do the implementation themselves, as some clients seem to be happier paying for a document, an end product, but not to value sufficiently the advice behind that!
  - There is an art in giving clients enough information to see the added value they will get, without giving away the advice, which needs to be tailored to

their circumstances – RNRB legislation is among the most complex in IHT practice and expertise in this area should not be given away for free!

RNRB planning will arise particularly in three areas of work:

1. **Will drafting:** A great opportunity to give proactive advice on IHT mitigation, when considering the IHT effects of the proposed wills; many clients will assume that their wills are 'simple', and may need clear advice of the disadvantage of the proposed terms and the cost/benefit equation referred to above. See especially **17.3**.
2. **IHT planning advice:** If clients specifically seek advice on mitigating IHT, then RNRB is for many a critical part; and we consider estate planning which addresses the planning for clients with capital up to, say, £5 million, so a lot greater than the £2 million threshold, where planning to secure RNRB may be feasible – see **17.4** and **Chapter 18** on estate planning.
3. **Estate administration:** Many estates will have the potential to make some change to secure a better tax treatment, either on that death or on a later death of a spouse, partner or another, such as a co-occupier of the home.

17.3 'CLOSELY INHERIT': WILL PLANNING AND VARIATIONS TO SECURE DIFFERENT TYPES OF RECIPIENTS

To secure RNRB, the right property interest needs to be 'closely inherited'. There is a major task for advisers to structure wills, or rearrange inheritances by a variation within two years of death, to ensure that the right beneficiaries inherit in the right form to 'closely inherit'.

17.3.1 Children and grandchildren

Children: what you can leave them to qualify for RNRB

For RNRB, you can leave children the following interests:

- an outright gift, of a specific legacy or part or share of estate; or
- a gift on one of the qualifying trusts:
  - bare trust;
  - bereaved minor's trust (BMT);
  - 18–25 trust;
  - immediate post-death interest (IPDI) trust;
  - disabled person's trust (DPT).

Note that all five of these forms of trust have specific requirements and, if the will does not meet that test, the default is a relevant property trust (RPT) which does not qualify for RNRB. So if, for any reason, a trust for a child defaults to an RPT, the trustees would need to use their powers in the will to advance out to the child(ren) on terms that would satisfy the above, for example outright as a bare trust, or an 18–25 trust or IPDI trust. This is so much easier if you have a wide power of advancement clause in the will – an invaluable tool in the executor's armoury.

Grandchildren: greater risk of trusts needing change to meet RNRB

For RNRB, you can leave grandchildren the following interests:

- an outright gift; or
- a bare trust (i.e. with no age contingency); or
- an IPDI trust, i.e. an income entitlement, whether to an age or for life;

unless the special circumstances of a DPT apply.

Any age contingency – such as attaining the age of 18, 21 or 25 – will mean it is not a bare trust, and unless the trust gives a right to income and satisfies all that is required for an IPDI, it will default to a RPT and there will be no right to RNRB.

Many wills provide for the children of the testator, with a gift-over if the child dies first, to go to that child's children at a specified age. If the grandchild has already reached that age when their grandparent dies, then there is no problem as no trust arises. However, if they are under the specified age, then action will be needed – as in 'Putting it right' below.

For will drafting, therefore, if you wish the gift to be eligible to claim RNRB, then the choice is a bare trust or an IPDI:

1. Avoid any age contingency; instead use words such as 'for those grandchildren in equal shares absolutely' so that it is clear it is a bare trust. Then you could rely on the 'get out of jail card', the express power or extended Trustee Act 1925, s.32 power of advancement to advance on a life interest trust before the grandchild reaches their 18th birthday, if needed, say because they have 'gone off the rails'.
2. Or use an IPDI, giving the grandchildren a right to income say for life, with a reversionary gift to any children of theirs, but including an overriding power of appointment and power of advancement so that the capital can be advanced to them when the time is right; and in most cases the capital will then be advanced say in their 20s and the trust wound up.

Putting it right

So many wills need to be reviewed, which is something worth suggesting to clients, with this choice in mind; or you simply rely on IHTA 1984, s.144 as a last resort, to sort it out in the two years after death.

In many cases the latter will be the only option – so to recap:

- IHTA 1984, s.144 will apply to read back to the date of death, to 'put right' a trust, within two years of the date of death, through the use of a power of advancement:

- under Trustee Act 1925, s.32 or extended s.32 power; or
- an express power of advancement;

- it is possible to advance either absolutely, or on appropriate trusts, i.e. a bare trust (if the beneficiaries are still under 18) or an IPDI trust, so that it qualifies for RNRB.

Example 17.1

Freda is Barry's widow, having inherited all from him. Her old will leaves her estate to their children Victoria, Michael and Julie equally; and if any of the three don't survive then their share goes to their children at 25.

Victoria's two sons Bobby and Jack are both over 25, and if Victoria dies before Freda, Bobby and Jack would get RNRB on Victoria's estate.

Victoria's will left all to them equally and if either died before her then a gift-over to such of his children 'as survive me and attain the age of 18'. A potential RPT which fails for RNRB.

Victoria could remake her will, to change those 'gift-over' provisions, or Victoria's trustees could use extended powers of advancement to appoint out to Bobby/Jack's children absolutely or on IPDI trusts, so that it is read back into her will under IHTA 1984, s.144.

Freda's other two children, Michael and Julie, each have their own children under 18. If Michael dies before Freda, what if his children are still under 18? Grandchildren contingent on surviving to 25 means an RPT unless they are entitled to income (and it meets all the requirements of an IPDI), so Freda can change her will to leave a 'gift-over' to her grandchildren to a bare trust or an IPDI, if needed to secure RNRB. If Freda died without changing will, her personal representatives could advance on a bare trust with the power in her will.

17.3.2 Stepchildren

'Stepchildren' are the children of a spouse or former spouse, but not the children of an unmarried partner –see **16.7.3**. So we need to be careful if clients talk loosely about their stepchildren, to be clear whether in their case they do qualify as such.

The options for stepchildren are as for grandchildren – see **17.3.1** – essentially an outright gift, bare trust or IPDI. Don't forget the categorisation of trusts for IHT, post-22 March 2006, differentiates children for a BMT or 18–25 trust, and all others fall back on bare trusts and IPDIs. (The same options apply, for example, for nieces and nephews, but with the crucial difference that they cannot claim RNRB – much to the frustration of many uncles and aunts.)

17.3.3 Unmarried partners and their separate children

The 'unfair' problem

There is a real unfairness about children of an unmarried partner, as that partner's child may be a 'child of the family', if brought up in the home by their parent's partner; so they would be able to make an Inheritance (Provision for Family and Dependants) Act 1975 claim for reasonable financial provision from the estate. That such a person does not then qualify as a stepchild for RNRB shows a real lack of join up between tax and legal rights. Just another reminder that tax law does not always deliver consistency or fairness!

This presents a huge issue for trusts in wills as unmarried partners might leave, for example, a share (typically a half share) in the shared home which is jointly owned by the unmarried partners. How can you provide for your partner's security, if they survive you, and also secure RNRB?

The classic life interest or right to occupy trust, included in so many wills, leaving a life interest or QIIP to your partner in your half share of the home, and then to your own children thereafter, just doesn't work because:

- your children are not your partner's stepchildren, when the capital comes to them, so they do not qualify as 'closely inheriting' and there is no RNRB on the partner's death;
- there is also of course no carry-forward of any unused RNRB as the partners are not married, so the RNRB is wasted on the first partner's death if it is left on a trust or outright to the unmarried partner; many unmarried couples do not marry, as one or both of them are widowed and do not wish to marry again, so there may be a double RNRB wasted here;
- the waste of IHT relief could be, in 2020/21 terms, £175,000 or £350,000, i.e. extra IHT payable of £70,000 or £140,000. It is worth looking at solutions.

Would a civil partnership be a solution?

Many practitioners have advised clients, over the years, to consider marriage as a tax planning solution. The option available, from 31 December 2019, to have a civil partnership whether of the same sex or a different sex, opens up a new opportunity. Some clients who do not wish to remarry, with all the 'baggage' and expectations that go with that, may be more willing to consider a lighter touch civil partnership.

Civil partners have all the tax advantages of a married couple, and hence we have used the term 'spouses' throughout this book to cover both, but in some terms of public perception, etc. they are rather different. Just as some same-sex couples were keen to move on from civil partnership to marriage, for all the extra symbolism that means, as well as for religious reasons, so for some people the prospect of a civil partnership might be palatable, or even attractive, in a way that marriage is not. So there is value in the choice people have.

Two points to note on civil partnerships:

1. There are different tax disadvantages, as well as the IHT advantages:
   - only one principal private residence (PPR) for capital gains tax (CGT) main residence relief, whereas two unmarried partners could each have had an election for their own PPR; and
   - stamp duty land tax (SDLT) allows only one main home for civil partners, when looking at the three per cent extra, higher rate for additional dwellings charge, which HM Revenue and Customs (HMRC) decides as a matter of fact, with no election as for CGT – see **Chapter 25**. So some careful planning ahead of a civil partnership is required where more than one home is owned.
2. There is no 'duty to consummate' a civil partnership, as there is for marriage, so that it is potentially an option open to some people living together as good friends, or in some form of platonic relationship.

A trust solution to protect the unmarried partner and enable an RNRB claim

Any solution needs to satisfy these elements:

- protecting the surviving partner, giving them security in the joint home for as long as required;
- protecting the children of the first partner to die, the ultimate beneficiaries of the capital, while showing them that their interest during the survivor's lifetime will be very limited (if anything);
- we have to use the first partner's QRI, i.e. their share of the joint home, unless they have a second residential property interest which might be a QRI – for example, because an old home is retained as a second, holiday home or investment;
- to manage the different interests means using a trust, and we are limited to using an IPDI trust for the first partner's children, as it is the only trust that could claim RNRB, or to have an outright gift to those children;
- if possible, we should have regard to CGT and claiming PPR relief on the trust interest as well as the IHT benefits.

A possible solution therefore looks like this:

- A gift to a flexible IPDI trust for the children of the first to die, as follows:
  - the amount of the RNRB, for example, 'of a part of my home with a value equal to the residence nil-rate amount that is taxable at 0% on my death under section 8D(2) of the Inheritance Tax Act 1984'; or
  - extend it to a double RNRB where the person is a widow with a carried forward RNRB unused by their late spouse; or
  - you could add in amount of the NRB to the gift so could leave, for example, £500,000 share of property to an IPDI trust in 2020/21.

- So the property is jointly owned by the surviving partner themselves and the trustees of an IPDI trust for their partner's children. How might it work?
- The surviving partner needs protection:
  - A strongly worded 'letter of wishes' setting out the detailed tax planning purpose and that the benefit to the children is in IHT saving, rather than rent or property use, unless they are still of an age when they are living in the property, and then that needs careful extra attention.
  - The trustees are requested to protect the surviving partner.
  - Trustees are given an overriding power of appointment, to rearrange the trust terms. If necessary, they can always revoke the life interest of the children to protect the surviving partner, for example if the children get too difficult about wanting some rent or occupation of the property. There are tax consequences of such a revocation, which would be a chargeable lifetime transfer by the children, but it is a valuable last resort, a threat to hold over the children if needed!
  - There is value in having a good independent trustee to ensure that all are protected, and it is good to set out any specific needs anticipated here, such as members of the family who might be unco-operative, in a letter of wishes.
- CGT: To enable the trustees to claim PPR relief on a trust property share, there could be a share of the property left on an IPDI for the surviving partner. See the examples of Roger and Sunita in **14.5.3**.

Example 17.2

Fatima and George are unmarried partners living together, each having two children from their previous marriage. Fatima was widowed, and her late husband left his whole estate to her, and George is divorced. Their main home is worth £1 million, in their joint names, and while they have a small holiday home it is only worth £150,000. George has a flat he used to live in, currently let out, worth £250,000.

- George could use his old flat as his QRI to claim his own RNRB of £175,000 in 2020/21. They could not use their holiday home as it does not have sufficient value to use the £175,000 single RNRB, let alone Fatima's double RNRB at £350,000.
- Fatima could leave a £350,000 share of her 1/2 of their joint home to an IPDI for her children. If she then left the balance of her 1/2 share, currently £150,000, to an IPDI for George, that would meet the need to provide security for him, while protecting the capital for them and also enabling the trustees to claim the PPR relief on the whole of the trust's 1/2 share of the property.
- If it were needed to extract more value from George's estate, if he dies second, Fatima could leave more of the 1/2 share to the IPDI for her children, to 'use' part of her NRB, but leave say a minimum of £50,000 (10% of her 1/2 share) to an IPDI for George.

17.3.4 Discretionary trusts as a starting point

If properties are given to, or the residue passes to, a discretionary trust, the trust cannot qualify as 'closely inherited', if it stays as such, and RNRB will be lost.

However, this can be rectified if an appropriate appointment is made by the trustees within two years of death. It can then be read back, to the date of death, under IHTA 1984, s.144. The trustees need to appoint out to a beneficiary (outright) who closely inherits, or on appropriate trusts that qualify, such as a BMT, 18–25 trusts and IPDIs.

A sensible, workable arrangement, quite often used, is to leave the whole residuary estate (after any legacies, and especially provision for chattels) to a discretionary trust. This can be a good way to enable the trustees to consider the family circumstances as a whole, anyone who may be going through marriage or financial difficulties, where, for example, a trust is needed to avoid the inheritance being lost in a divorce or business failure.

If advising on this route, do ensure that there are sufficient powers in the will, including powers to add beneficiaries if they might be needed (and that there isn't a too restrictive requirement for consent to adding, for example needing two beneficiaries to consent if there is a small family without many who would qualify).

This can be effective for the whole tax planning arrangement on death, not just for RNRB, with scope to cover a full range of planning options:

- use of the NRB as appropriate including, if applicable, business or agricultural property relief (BPR/APR) and transferable NRB (TNRB);
- leaving sufficient property to, for example, an IPDI trust for children to use the RNRB;
- claiming the spouse exemption, with either an outright appointment or an IPDI trust, for the residue after all NRBs and RNRBs are claimed.

Tips

1. Ensure the letters of wishes address this issue, of complying with RNRB, and so guide the trustees (and the family, etc.) in understanding what is being done and why. If the wills were written with discretionary trusts before RNRB was introduced, the letters of wishes, at least, will need updating.
2. After death, note the risk of executors taking the will away, to do a DIY probate, and not sorting out this issue within the two years. Consider having a standard letter to give out with the will, in this event, to explain the need for action within the two years if RNRB is to be claimed. This will both help to protect your position, if anything goes wrong, and gives a good opportunity for the executors to return to you for advice.
3. You can offer to help with the legal documentation and note that it is best not left too late before the second anniversary as it takes time to consider, draft the documents and get them signed. You want to avoid someone realising the day before that the two years is about to expire that something needs doing!

17.4 £2 MILLION THRESHOLD: ESTATE PLANNING TO AVOID TAPERED LOSS OF RNRB

17.4.1 Spouses arranging assets between them and on death

We have addressed inter-spouse planning in **Chapters 13** and **14**. Our task here is to apply that specifically to the RNRB threshold. In particular, we have addressed the big question of planning for spouses:

- To use or not to use the NRB, the RNRB, or both – see **14.5**, and the examples in **14.5.3**.

The aim is to avoid the two risks set out in **14.5.1**:

- Neither spouse's estate is over £2 million, but after the first spouse's death all is carried forward to the second estate, when the total is over £2 million and both RNRBs are lost.
- The first estate was over £2 million, so that RNRB is lost anyway, but the second need not be as below £2 million, until the first estate is added and takes the value over the threshold. One lot of capital ends up tainting both estates and losing £350,000 of RNRB.

The key here is to extract value from the taxable pot, on the first death, so that we avoid these risks. This means using the NRB or RNRB or both with the right form of trust. **Example 14.6** in **14.5.3** illustrates how one can secure four RNRBs for spouses who have both been widowed, if each uses the TRNRB carried forward to them. A classic case of 'use it or lose it'!

17.4.2 Estate planning with an eye on the £2 million figure

RNRB planning also requires a review of the whole use of assets, including pension funds, to see how to maximise the value of RNRB and avoid its loss by taper through the 'estate' going over £2 million. The marginal IHT rate on the band of capital over £2 million is effectively 60 per cent, if you add the 40 per cent IHT charge to a loss of £1 of relief for every £2 over the £2 million. If we can save clients this high rate, and protect a tax saving of up to £70,000, or £140,000 for a double RNRB, this is worth clients paying for the planning.

This is not just for financial planners (FPs), but for all involved in estate planning, as a vital part of IHT planning, working with FPs. While some clients will have ongoing arrangements with FPs that include annual reviews, which is one of the best elements for keeping on top of estate planning, the FPs' input is vital at two points:

(a) planning ahead for both spouses, as to how they structure their assets and draw their income, ideally ahead of retirement (before drawing down a pension); and

(b) a review on the death of the first spouse, when the survivor is able to plan with the benefit of hindsight, knowing then the value of assets and income available to them as a widow(er). They need to use the first two years as a time to take stock, not to rush into decisions, and in particular to reflect on their needs for a home and whether to move (which many feel is best not done in the first year after bereavement).

We address estate planning as a concept, with some of the ideas for effective operation, in **Chapter 18**. Our focus here is the specific issues that are relevant to the £2 million threshold.

Pensions written in trust are not part of the taxable estate for the £2 million limit. The pension death benefit taxation rules brought in in 2015/16 (Taxation of Pensions Act 2014) offer greater tax planning value in leaving the pension to the next generation (or two). So a surviving spouse should consider spending other capital in their estate, to meet their living needs, rather than drawing on a pension. In this way they can keep as much as possible of the pension with favourable tax treatment to pass on to the family, tax effectively.

Lawyers and tax advisers are sometimes anxious about straying into financial advice they are not allowed to give. There is one step that can be taken – to say 'stop' to clients in this situation. For example, if a client says something along the lines of, 'I'm retiring in three months so I can't wait to take my pension and …'. Your response can be: 'STOP. Take proper financial planning advice before you take your pension, as you may not want to start drawing down and you have options as to what to take, how and when – and you need specialist advice.' That is not financial planning advice, but good sensible advice to take detailed advice from an FP.

Three important points to note:

1. 'Estate' for the £2 million threshold does not include pension death benefits – in a pension scheme, written in trust, provided the client only 'nominated' benefits and there was no binding nomination. This is needed for the pensions to be IHT-free.
2. Suggesting that clients look at ways to spend capital over £2 million, which otherwise may be subject to 40 per cent IHT on death and count towards the £2 million estate threshold, is entirely logical and sensible advice. However, for many clients spending capital is an anathema, something they would never want to do. This is where most FPs have an invaluable tool in their toolbox: the cash flow programme described in **18.6**. If that can be used to illustrate the potential for capital to meet needs until a specified age, it can give them the comfort that they can afford to spend, or gift, assets.
3. The beneficial tax-effective way of passing on the pension death benefit, by flexi-access drawdown (FAD) at the marginal tax rates of beneficiaries, is fine so long as this tax advantage lasts. It is one area of tax law that is, perhaps, vulnerable, as it is quite generous. If it were changed, for example, to bring back in the old 55 per cent charge on undrawn pensions, this would need

further review. This shows again the value of flexibility, so that one can adapt according to the prevailing tax treatment and all the circumstances at the time.

See the example of Michael and Samira in **18.6.5** which illustrates how the pension might be passed on to the family while the widow gets the capital of an ISA to draw down. That kind of integrated solution is a good example of estate planning working well.

17.5 GIFTING AS A STRATEGY TO REDUCE AN ESTATE BELOW £2 MILLION

17.5.1 Lifetime gifting generally

Just as spending capital can be a sensible strategy (see **17.4.2**) so can gifting capital be a good way of reducing capital below the £2 million threshold. Cash flow modelling by an FP can help someone see that they can afford to gift specific amounts and still be comfortable and secure.

Any lifetime gifts are best made with reference to the IHT exemptions, so that these are utilised as well as possible. Anything that exceeds the exemptions is not a problem, so long as it's an outright gift, and therefore a potentially exempt transfer (PET), or lifetime IHT at 20 per cent is paid on any gift to a trust. Sometimes people think they can only make gifts within the exemptions, which can be an unfortunate misunderstanding.

With gifts to reduce an estate below the £2 million level it doesn't matter how long the donor survives, so long as they make a valid gift. See **16.9** and the three potential traps to watch out for.

17.5.2 Death-bed gifting: the last resort

You can do death-bed planning – for now – to reduce an estate below £2 million. As long as there is no gift with reservation of benefit (GROB), lifetime gifts are therefore a last resort for RNRB planning. While some people may make the regular making of gifts a tactical way of reducing their estate for RNRB purposes, in practice most will use this at a late stage in life, to reduce an estate below the £2 million threshold. Currently the £2 million estate figure takes no account of lifetime gifts that will be failed PETs or chargeable lifetime transfers (CLTs).

See **16.9**.

CHAPTER 18

Estate planning from lawyer/tax perspective

John Bunker

18.1 KEY POINTS

- Estate planning is the process of managing your estate to achieve your objectives in your lifetime and on death. It is a mix of three elements: legal; tax planning; and financial planning.
- Estate planning can help inheritance tax (IHT) mitigation by giving better integrated solutions for clients.
- It is important to explore client objectives and the elements to consider in seeking to achieve them.
- It is important to consider 'letters of wishes' and other tools available to advisers in this process.
- We must consider how advisers can work together for the benefit of clients.
- Referral of work to a select panel of financial planners can also be good for lawyers.

18.2 WHAT DO WE MEAN BY 'ESTATE PLANNING'?

Estate planning is the process of managing your income and assets, your estate, to achieve your objectives in your lifetime and on death. Typically, for most of us and our clients, this involves arranging your finances and affairs to be able to achieve the following objectives:

- to enjoy the comfort and security you wish for, during your lifetime, and that of your spouse/partner after your death;
- to consider how your own circumstances interact with not only your spouse/partner, but also any children or dependants; how that can be done more effectively; and how you can provide for those dependants and children/grandchildren, and any other loved ones;
- to make any provision for others in a way that provides security, etc. and protects assets and beneficiaries (for example, from themselves, or from others who might take advantage of them) as well as saving tax;

- to provide for any charities, organisations or causes you wish to support, either now or in the future (for example, on your death);
- to bring into consideration any benefits you and your loved ones may have in any trust or will, so that any inheritances of capital, or access to income or use of property, can be used/enjoyed as part of this process, to help achieve these objectives.

18.3 THE THREE KEY INGREDIENTS: LEGAL, TAX AND FINANCIAL

18.3.1 Legal planning

Wills, trusts and other structures, for holding property, businesses and investments are all crucial elements of effective estate planning. Other legal documents such as lasting powers of attorney (LPAs) are also important, to enable objectives to be fulfilled by ensuring that an attorney is there to pick up the reins if and when needed.

As a profession, lawyers have traditionally worked on transactions, in a reactive way, helping clients with advice when needed – but increasingly lawyers are seeking to work proactively, to help clients imaginatively. Some are even developing annual estate planning reviews with clients, just as financial planners (FPs) typically work with annual financial planning reviews.

So, instead of just waiting for clients to ask for advice, for example on reviewing a trust, a lawyer can suggest that a review might be helpful and obtain approval to the fees needed to do that. Lawyers are increasingly learning from others, such as FPs, the art of quoting a fee and preparing an initial report on options, for that set fee, and in that report to set out various further costs to implement specific aspects of the work proposed. Clients can then choose whether they wish to proceed with the various steps outlined. In doing so, they can consider a simple form of 'cost/benefit' analysis.

So the key is being proactive, but also doing it cost-effectively – see **18.6.2–18.6.3**.

18.3.2 Tax planning

Clients may have a tax adviser dealing with their personal tax compliance, whether a member of the Chartered Institute of Taxation (CIOT) (chartered tax adviser (CTA)) or the Association of Taxation Technicians (ATT), an accountant or in some cases someone employed by a solicitor, who may themselves be a CTA, a member of the ATT or an accountant. That person may be the expert in income tax and capital gains tax (CGT) compliance, but in thinking about tax planning we must be clear about the tax advice required.

For example, the tax advantages of individual savings accounts (ISAs) are income tax and CGT ones, nothing to do with IHT – so expertise in those two taxes is needed, not IHT planning. So tax planning advice may be needed from different sources, and in part that may be separate from tax compliance work.

The key question for someone dealing with IHT planning in, for example, a solicitor's office, is the limit of their personal expertise and of that of other members of the team. In many firms, teams will have a range of understanding and expertise to advise – for example:

- A junior person may be able to explain how IHT works in respect of a legacy in a will, or an estate, but not give advice on IHT mitigation.
- A more experienced fee earner may be able to advise on IHT planning through wills, and deeds of variation, including agricultural property relief (APR) and business property relief (BPR), and on the use of lifetime exemptions, but not be able to advise on CGT planning elements like business asset disposal relief (BADR – formerly entrepreneurs' relief (ER)) or more sophisticated lifetime planning regarding businesses.
- A more specialist tax lawyer may then be available for that specialist business advice, or the lawyers may need to bring in an outside specialist for that element.

Clients are increasingly sophisticated and become used to the concept of a team of people who can help them, with the appropriate person dealing with the right work at the most cost-effective level.

Tip

Explain to the client at the earliest stage who in the team is likely to be helping them, and how the charges for their advice will be worked out, as transparency is key to this teamwork. Matters often develop in unexpected ways, when, for example, a will-drafting exercise becomes complicated by the nature of a business interest, or elements of lifetime gifts or an aggregated trust, that were not known about at the outset, change the work on an estate. Hence the reference to advising 'at the earliest stage' possible. It is always best to agree additional fees in advance, as required by practice rules in any event, rather than proceeding without proper agreement and trying to negotiate after the event.

18.3.3 Financial planning

The one-time independent financial adviser (IFA) has generally morphed into a more highly qualified financial planner (FP). Following the Retail Distribution Review (RDR) at the end of 2012, which ushered in a world of transparency, a commission-driven world of IFAs advising clients to take up investments or schemes based on the commission payable has gone.

It has been replaced by FPs advising clients mainly on the basis of their time, at hourly charging rates, or for set fees, and then clients deciding whether or how to proceed on that advice. It is a major transformation and enables lawyers and accountants/tax advisers to work with FPs as fellow professionals who are also charging fees for their professional advice.

An increasing number of clients will now have three advisers to deal with their legal, tax and financial advice. In some cases, these are then linked with a fourth – a discretionary fund manager, investment manager or wealth manager. Many firms offer two or three of these advisers, under the same roof, in a few cases all four.

Cash flow planning, or modelling, using really helpful software, is key to the FP advice. This is described by the financial planner David Gooding in **19.3**, and he uses two examples of charts from financial planning software Voyant to illustrate this. This current chapter is designed to complement that one, to give you this tax lawyer's perspective, and to hopefully help the process of integrating advice on IHT mitigation.

The author's personal perspective is that the work of FPs has been transformed in the last 10 years, in a much needed way, and it's a shame it didn't happen many years earlier. If you are reading this with an old prejudice against IFAs, the author would encourage you to try the new world of FPs.

18.4 THE ELEMENTS TO CONSIDER IN HELPING CLIENTS ACHIEVE THEIR OBJECTIVES

If we are to meet the aims set out in **18.2**, we need to be able to bring into the picture the following elements (discussed below):

- client income from earnings;
- property income;
- capital gains on property;
- main and second homes – values;
- life policies and life assurance based savings schemes;
- stocks, shares and other equity investments;
- chattels.

18.4.1 Client income from earnings

We must consider client income from earnings, including any potential bonuses or other elements like share options, etc. This may be a given, that is not variable, or may involve elements that can be packaged differently. While that is largely a tax issue, for any tax adviser, there may be elements of wider estate planning on which a lawyer who does the IHT planning and the FP might have some input. For example, the use of the IHT exemption for normal expenditure out of income can be invaluable for gifting out of cash bonuses. See **12.3**.

18.4.2 Property income

Property has been a major part of estate planning over the generations, as people in the UK are often attached to the security and comfort of land assets and the income and gains they produce. Apart from homes, referred to below, many clients have one or more investment properties producing an income, and in some cases a portfolio of properties has built up, sometimes without a clear long-term tax strategy. As this can be slightly random, and without any professional adviser monitoring values and income (as, for example, share investments might be monitored) it can often be helpful to take stock of the values and income and who holds them. Clients sometimes lose track of all the bits of property they have, and the income produced, which may not all be 'needed'.

18.4.3 Capital gains on property

Capital gains on property are beyond the scope of this book, but are worth mentioning in the estate planning context as they can have a major effect on what can be done for IHT planning. Making gifts of property without other tax liabilities is quite a challenge, especially with stamp duty land tax (SDLT) as an additional factor (see **Chapter 25**).

Three specific CGT points are worth adding here:

1. **CGT is a tax on 'disposals' not sales**, so keeping under review the potential CGT on sale or gifting of all or part of property is therefore highly recommended. Gifts of property can be made by a declaration of trust of the beneficial or equitable interest, relatively simply, provided that the resulting share of income also follows the gift.
2. **Some clients don't use their annual CGT exemptions each year**, which in 2020/21 is £12,300 or £24,600 for a couple. If the income from property is not needed, the potential to save IHT by gifting shares of property using these exemptions is often undervalued.
3. **Elections for main residence (principal private residence (PPR)) relief for CGT** are critical, and the facility to make an election within two years of any combination of residences changing is most valuable.

18.4.4 Main and second homes – values

'An Englishman's home is his castle', goes the old saying, though it is also true that an English woman's home can be her castle. Likewise the Welsh and Scots can enjoy their homes. More than most European citizens, we in the UK do value owning homes and have had a great many tax reliefs supporting home ownership. Huge value has built up as a result, which reflects in the major element of homes in most estates.

For many, property is a core investment, not just a home, and many clients will have second homes – sometimes to facilitate working lives, but also to enjoy the freedom of living in your own place in a beautiful setting when you can. Planning can be used to save tax on second properties while being able to have good access to enjoy them, without breaching reservation of benefit rules (see **Chapter 4**).

18.4.5 Life policies and life assurance based savings schemes

If many have lost sight of the land they own, many more have no real idea of all the bits of life cover, or investments/savings schemes built around life cover, they have taken out over the years. From the days of the 'man from the Pru' calling at homes for regular investments in Prudential, through to all the products 'sold' by IFAs in the old commission days, an enormous amount of the nation's savings has been put into these products.

While today's FPs will build their work around regular (annual) reviews of all the client's finances, and even in the commission-driven days some IFAs did do this, many clients started paying premiums but lost track of what they were doing and why. Getting a full 'fact find' of all that a client has, and all the purposes it serves, is therefore crucial.

The life assurance industry has been hugely creative in designing savings, or 'wealth protection', or 'IHT mitigation' products, over the years. Many of them have involved capital investment bonds whose flexibility (and attractive commission structures) has contributed to many such arrangements. Getting to the bottom of the structures, the trusts often involved, etc. can be challenging, especially if the IFA who arranged it has long since gone. Reference to the original sales material can help explain how these are meant to work. It is important that these documents are carefully scrutinised to ensure that they do what they are supposed to do. Many a time, the client thinks a product passes to a particular beneficiary and it doesn't, or the client has a mistaken belief about the tax consequences or restrictions on such a product.

For the estate planning process, advisers will need to know what capital value there is; how and when it can be drawn; whether it is in a trust and if it is the terms and details of trustees; the amount of any premiums still being paid; and the purpose served. An innocuous-looking policy could easily be cancelled when it is, for example, providing security for loss of income in the event of death or serious illness while children are young.

18.4.6 Stocks, shares and other equity investments

We must consider long-term returns, of income and growth, for many clients depend upon some form of equity investment – whether through shares, or a collective investment like unit trusts, open-ended investment companies (OEICs) or an investment bond. Getting a complete record of these, and their acquisition record for tax purposes, is step one.

Step two, for most (assuming they are not really sophisticated investors who like to play the markets themselves), is having those investments managed by an investment manager. Most will now do so with nominee holdings and discretionary powers delegated to manage the investments. FPs may have a role to play in finding the right discretionary investment manager (DIM) or discretionary fund manager (DFM), and certainly in keeping the risk profile under review and seeing how the investments continue to fit in with the rest of the client's finances.

The FP is really the first stop, the DFM (sounds better than DIM would) the second stop, and they should complement each other. Some clients will be happy to simply have some collective investments managed by the FP, without the need for a portfolio managed by a DFM, and many solicitors will play a key role as the trusted adviser of the family in arranging this set-up.

One joy of a managed portfolio is that the admin is all with that manager, and the records should not be a problem, and at any time valuations can be produced to see the details of what capital and income returns are available. After the death of a client, it can be invaluable to get the DFM to load the probate values as the 'cost' figures, so that decisions can be made on raising cash and tax mitigation during an estate administration – see **Chapter 9**.

If one of the estate planning options considered is to spend capital in a planned way, the FP may be able to illustrate how this can be done, in terms of how long the capital might last, with the aid of cash flow analysis. Cash flow analysis is fundamental to any sort of lifetime estate planning to demonstrate client need and the risk that they need to take. The DFM would then need to make decisions on how and when to sell investments to enable cash to be released. This is good teamwork, when at its best, with the different professionals respecting each other's roles.

18.4.7 Chattels

Most people keep their personal chattels, or possessions, for their personal enjoyment and use, rather than as an asset of value. In most estates the value of personal chattels may be a few thousand pounds, but not tens of thousands. However, two points are worth noting.

1. **Insurance and market values:** Do help clients to be careful with valuations for insurance purposes, which typically will give a substantially higher figure, to allow for the costs of replacing items if needed, than a valuation for open market value on death. It is important for clients to have their personal possessions properly insured, in case of, for example theft or fire, so that a loved home can be restored.
2. **Watch out for the few items that may be of real value.** Some people, with otherwise normal possessions in their home, have one or two, or a few, items of real value. They may have been inherited, or bought as a bargain, and the success of TV programmes like *Antiques Roadshow*, and *Bargain Hunt*, illustrates the enthusiasm to find something of real monetary value. For most, it will be a case of making sure the special, much loved, items are well insured and protected for long-term enjoyment. If, however, there is scope to sell

something, as a fund-raising exercise, then great care should be taken to ensure good value is secured through the auctioneer or otherwise.

Cars are normally wasting assets, that are a value effectively 'written off' over a few years, and necessary for daily life rather than a significant element in estate planning. However, for some clients, collecting period cars, that may hold or increase their value, is a specialist factor to consider. Some wealthier clients may own or collect more substantial 'chattels' such as yachts (often bought by a group of people in shares), planes, etc. Some will own a yacht, or a share of one, simply for the personal pleasure of using it for recreation. It can help to identify with clients which assets simply represent a recreational pursuit and which they might see as a valuable investment that might appreciate. For any gifts here, watch valuation and the constraints of 'reservation of benefit'.

Gift and loan back of chattels may be seen as a good tax planning arrangement. It can enable someone to continue to enjoy the use of their personal possessions without a huge cost, as the 'market rent' for the use of chattels can be quite low, typically one or two per cent of the capital value. So it can be a good way to get significant value out of someone's estate, but there are three practice points to watch:

1. Arrange a full inventory of the chattels to be gifted and loaned back, which identifies only the more valuable ones and not all the lesser value items.
2. Ensure there is a proper element of negotiation between two qualified fine art auctioneers/valuers, to show that a real market rent is negotiated, and keep that rent under review in accordance with the terms of the 'leaseback' so that no reservation of benefit arises for IHT purposes.
3. The client must not forget that the items have been given away, and ensure insurance is used to replace lost or broken items, etc. so as to preserve the asset for the new owners – i.e. it's not an easy step just once, it has ongoing repercussions for home life.

18.5 THE TOOLS TO ENABLE CLIENTS TO ACHIEVE THEIR OBJECTIVES

18.5.1 Wills and letters of wishes

Lawyers will be comfortable with wills as a place to start, a key element in a long-term estate planning strategy, as the tool to ensure assets and income are dealt as wished after your own lifetime. It's easy to say 'keep them under review', as we often do, but this is really critical, not just for the will but also for any accompanying 'letter of wishes' (LOW). It's a criticism sometimes made of lawyers that we are better at reviewing wills than LOWs, or perhaps that we sometimes review and the client decides it is not worth paying for an updated draft.

Flexibility in the provisions of wills, which is an increasingly important element in estate planning, does require a good LOW which is kept up to date. If your client authorises you to share this, both the will and LOW should be shared with the FP (and the capital tax adviser, if someone separate is doing that part), as it contributes to the longer-term estate planning.

FPs also may become aware of changes that may need to be reflected in the LOW. Their regular contact with clients, including annual reviews, is invaluable and (as noted above) it would be great if lawyers also had an annual 'estate planning review' to take stock of everything and see whether anything needs attention. Many people don't know that something may be relevant, or a change in law or practice may affect them, until it arises in conversation with a lawyer or FP. If it's only the FP's annual review, do ensure you have a good rapport with the FP so that relevant changes are shared.

Tips

1. It can be really helpful to set out the tax planning strategy of the will in the LOW, to guide the trustees that this is what you are seeking to achieve, especially if circumstances or practice change and a trustee wonders why on earth you drafted such a complex trust!
2. If it's possible, it can help to show how the will and any trust fit in with other elements of what is divisible on death. (See also comments regarding the Law Society's Wills and Inheritance Quality Scheme (WIQS) in **18.5.2**.)
3. Do record changes in facts or circumstances that might be thought to have an impact on the LOW even if the end result is unchanged. It can be easy to think that the cost of amending this document is not needed as the ultimate division is the same, but see **Example 18.1**.

Example 18.1

Ada has left her estate to be divided between her three children, Lenny, Jacob and Kate. Her late husband Max left two trusts on his death, a nil rate band (NRB) discretionary trust (see **Chapter 13**) which owns a share of Ada's home, and a life interest for Ada in his residuary estate, and then for the three children. Ada's LOW, with her will, seeks to bring together the two trusts with her own estate, referring to the inheritance due from their late father as well the flexibility in the discretionary trust of which she is a trustee, with her solicitor.

While Max did say something of the planning strategy in his LOW, some circumstances have changed in the five years since he died. Ada is not sure if it's worth doing a new LOW. She helped Lenny out with a gift of £50,000 to help him buy a house as he is a nurse with a limited income, and she helped Jacob when he was divorced with a gift of £100,000 so that his children had a proper home. The end result of dividing equally between the three children is unchanged, but it's worth the LOW noting that these gifts have been made, and are not to be brought into account, as Kate is a high-earner in the City and Ada feels that she does not need compensating, nor is Lenny having any adjustment for his lower gift.

The other change is that Jacob has now remarried and has two young adult stepchildren, who are not to be provided for as their father is a high-earner and Ada feels that they don't need it. Noting their position, and why they are not included, will be helpful. Likewise, it will be helpful to confirm that Lenny's recently adopted child is a welcome addition to the family and is to be equally treated with the other grandchildren. While legally this is true, there's no harm in making this clear, and it is also a positive inclusive step for Ada.

18.5.2 Law Society's Wills and Inheritance Quality Scheme (WIQS)

Those solicitors who are members of the Law Society's Wills and Inheritance Quality Scheme (WIQS) have a tool that can be very helpful in estate planning. The author is not encouraging, or discouraging, the use of WIQS, as it can have real value if used in an effective way; for some it may seem a little too full and complex a scheme in practice – but if you have it then it's really sensible to make good use of it!

The protocol at the heart of WIQS includes reference to the 'standard advice to be provided as part of the will drafting retainer' and envisages a comprehensive overview of all the assets and income that will be part of the picture on the death of the person making the will. This includes advice on assets passing independently of the will, like assets owned as joint tenants, or written in trust. The proceeds of any life policy, assigned/written in trust for another, would be included in this full picture. It is an excellent process, although too time-consuming and costly for some, and definitely a marketing USP if you have it.

A negligence claim case, *Herring and another* v. *Shorts Financial Services LLP* [2016] EW Misc B12 (CC), illustrates the difficulty of taking into account the whole picture. It was a case against the FP, as for specific reasons the case against the lawyer could not proceed. There was a life policy written in trust for some beneficiaries, on which the FP did not advise, and the client said they should have advised on the terms of trust as they would have then changed their will. Leaving significant amounts to some of the family, through the life policy, meant that they need less from the estate. On the facts, the court said the FP was not liable as they had no obligation to advise on this aspect.

It is a good reminder that clients often forget what they have done, and life policies (see **18.4.5**) written in trust are a classic for client oversight! It also reminds us of the impact of one part of the picture, of what will happen on the client's death, on their estate. It enhances the case for a comprehensive review on assets passing independently of the will, whether by WIQS or otherwise.

18.5.3 Trusts: reviewing existing trusts for the client and their family

One of the greatest criticisms of lawyers is that we set up trusts that are often expensive to run, and lose sight of their purpose, so they end up continuing without a clear understanding of the purpose that they serve. In some cases, better communication of that purpose is the answer – but in many others, we (as a profession) simply don't keep trusts under review enough.

We need to keep under review the following (discussed below):

- changes of tax law and practice;
- changes of law and practice – non-tax issues;

- any benefits being received, whether still needed and possible planning options;
- changing circumstances and relationships of beneficiaries.

Changes of tax law and practice

For example, NRB discretionary trusts used to be set up with the main residence being transferred to the surviving spouse subject to an indexed-linked debt to the trust, prior to 2006. The trust law changes in March 2006 change the way that these tended to work in practice, and more often now a share of a property can be held by the trust without the risk (as there had been) of it being treated as subject to IHT on the death of the widow(er). LOWs then need revising.

The introduction of the transferable NRB (TNRB) in October 2007 changed a large amount of tax planning by will, as the need for the NRB discretionary trust to utilise a second NRB had gone; see **Chapter 13**. Many therefore felt the trusts could be wound up, as superfluous, but this might have missed two important estate planning opportunities. First, there might be real value in keeping a trust going for asset protection reasons, and thus the work and cost of drawing up more complex wills would not be 'wasted' if the trust could be used for a wholly different purpose. And a second planning option that might be lost is that in many cases a NRB discretionary trust is still worth doing, and is better for tax planning than simply using the TNRB. See **Chapter 13** for details.

Changes of law and practice – non-tax issues

Sometimes changes in the law might affect the technicalities of the trust, such as the extension of accumulation periods from 99 years to 125 years. Sometimes it might affect relationships and those who should be named in a class of beneficiaries or in a LOW to be included in the benefit.

Any benefits being received, whether still needed and possible planning options

Any income received is adding to the value of the recipient's estate and, if it's no longer needed, it may be a tax inefficient addition. More significantly, if the trust is aggregable with the estate of the life tenant, the capital value which is likely to be aggregated may be out of proportion to the benefits for the life tenant.

It may be that there is value in terminating a life interest, in whole or part, as a deemed lifetime gift (or transfer of value) to set the seven-year clock running on the deemed gift. If the life tenant survives seven years, the 'gift' is tax-free, and if outright and therefore a potentially exempt transfer (PET), it is totally out of the IHT net.

However, trusts may also be worth using for other purposes. If someone has a trust that is set up with, for example grandchildren as beneficiaries, and some trust provision for some of them is needed, it may be that the existing trust can be re-purposed to meet those needs. It might even be more tax effective for it to be a grandparental settlement than a parental one. I have seen clients about to set up a new lifetime trust at the very time they were planning to wind up the trust of a parent, when the two things could be brought together. Apart from anything else, there could be a terrible waste of costs on the new trust in this case.

Changing circumstances and relationships of beneficiaries

The changing circumstances and relationships of beneficiaries must be considered. Births, deaths, separation, divorce and new relationships are all part of so many family lives. So too are changes in personal financial circumstances, successful career development, new jobs and financial rewards with bonuses, etc.; or redundancy, unemployment and hard times; inheritances or good fortune such as winning in a lottery – these can all make a major difference in the lives of those our clients wish to support. Sometimes these things happen to or for children, grandchildren, etc., but also they apply to in-laws.

What difference does it make to the provision in a will or trust if good or bad financial developments happen to the beneficiaries themselves or their partners/spouses? There are no right or wrong answers, of course – it depends on the client's personal perspective how they treat family and whether such changes mean a revised LOW to guide the trustees in exercising their discretionary powers, or changes to the will or trust itself.

For the most part, individuals who are properly advised are still considering trust planning especially in their wills given the flexibility that it provides. In considering these difficult judgments so many clients look to their lawyer as a 'trusted adviser' whose judgment they respect and to whom they turn in confidence to consider their choices. This role is explored in **18.6.1**.

18.5.4 Reviewing life policy trusts

All the issues that arise in **18.5.3** also apply for existing life policy trusts. They can so easily be forgotten, as in the *Herring* case.

18.5.5 Pension policy nominations of benefit and letters of wishes

These also need careful consideration; see further in **Chapter 19**.

18.6 WORKING TOGETHER WITH FINANCIAL PLANNERS, TAX ADVISERS AND DISCRETIONARY FUND MANAGERS

18.6.1 The role of the lawyer in estate planning

We often refer to 'lawyer' rather than 'solicitor' as it is a more generic term that recognises that many chartered legal executives are very experienced and competent lawyers able to advise fully in this area. Indeed, some paralegals are also good lawyers who can fulfil a great role in this field. In either case, training with STEP (by exams or essays) to be a TEP (trusts and estates practitioner) is a clear sign of technical ability. **Example 18.3** illustrates the different contributions members of a team can offer on tax planning and teamwork is of great value here. For this purpose, exploring the role of the lawyer, we are likely mainly to refer to a solicitor or senior legal executive who is leading the client relationship.

While it is possible to simply work reactively, being available to assist clients with specific legal needs, as and when they arise, we are also anticipating a more proactive or ongoing role. This finds its ultimate form, where feasible, in an annual estate planning review – similar to the financial planner's annual review, but we do not mean to be limiting here, this can be done in many ways.

The 'trusted adviser' role referred to in **18.5.3** is a role that solicitors had fulfilled much more in former times, when practitioners seemed to cover a wide range of subject areas, and people with money would go to see their solicitor for a number of different issues. This was rather lost to bank managers and others in recent decades, at the same time as lawyers were becoming more specialised in areas of more limited scope, with the increasing complexity of the law. However, changes in banking practice and the provision of financial services mean there is an increasing opportunity here for lawyers as well as financial planners.

The writer has been training lawyers on IHT and estate planning with local law societies and elsewhere for some 10 years, aiming to help practitioners develop the understanding and skills to be able to advise more fully in this area. Lawyers ought to do this work but should have the skills to do so and not just 'dabble' without technical understanding. Having some real tax planning understanding, especially if working with FPs in the ways anticipated in this book, can open up real avenues to rebuild the trusted adviser role. The 'man (or woman) of affairs' is another old concept, that may sound dated, but has a good principle at its heart.

If you get to know your major clients, and their families, and can have a good understanding of all the elements in this chapter, with a good general knowledge of IHT planning, you can be well placed to fulfil the trusted adviser role, all the more so when you work well with the FP and/or DFM. The author has, in 23 years as a partner looking after clients, before moving into a technical and training role, acted for various families through more than one generation's legal needs. At a recent funeral reception, one grandchild said to me, 'Oh you're the Mr Bunker who Granny was always saying she needed to speak to first'. An example of the trusted adviser relationship encouraged.

If the lawyer is the first port of call, and can encourage the teamwork for a client with an FP, you can be in more of a driving seat. The ideal is where you have an opportunity to introduce the client to their FP. However it is being done, the next two questions are crucial: who is being paid to do what?; and, who is giving ongoing advice?

18.6.2 Who is being paid to do what?

It is always important to be clear who is doing what, and not only what they are doing but what they are not! Two cases illustrate this – first, *Herring* v. *Shorts Financial Services* (2016), where the FP was able to show that they were not instructed to advise on the life policy written in trust.

Second, *Mehjoo* v. *Harben Barker* [2014] EWCA Civ 358 is a cautionary tale of an accountant who was very helpful to his client and regularly raised issues proactively, but was then nearly caught out by his own helpfulness. A major tax issue arose (regarding capital gain concerning the client's residence status) on which the accountant did not have the expertise to advise and for which he should have referred the client to a specialist. In the High Court he was held responsible and liable for damages for professional negligence for the tax liability that could have been saved had the client taken the action that a specialist adviser would have suggested. The accountants won in the Court of Appeal, being not liable on the facts, as the test is 'what the reasonably competent practitioner would do having regard to the standards normally adopted in his profession' (para.69).

The *Mehjoo* case does, however, illustrate the importance of being clear about one's terms of business, and of referring the client for specialist advice where needed. A good client will normally understand that one adviser will not know everything but will need to bring in, or suggest, an expert in certain circumstances. Being clear and 'up front' about this really makes a difference.

So where we have say three advisers – a lawyer, a tax adviser and an FP – it is important that the client knows how the three fit together and to ensure that important elements do not 'fall between the three stools' or 'between the cracks' (pick your analogy!). Another cautionary tale comes in the following example, based on a case where the author was asked to advise on potential negligence.

Example 18.2

Jackie was a millionairess, with surplus capital and income whose bank referred her to an IFA (several years ago) to arrange some life cover for IHT. The IFA arranged an investment that was sold as a packaged scheme, and involved investing in some gilts, which were redeemed year by year and the proceeds put into premiums on a life policy written in trust to pay the IHT bill. As each of the premiums paid was a gift to the trust, and thus a chargeable transfer, the question arose whether they were within the 'normal expenditure out of income exemption' (see **Chapter 12**). While Jackie had surplus income, elsewhere, the payments were not actually 'made out of income' and thus were taxable. HMRC assessed the estate for the tax due on each chargeable transfer, with interest and penalties for non-declaration. It did not need to be that way. There could have been cash going into the bank account from the gilt redemptions, and payments out of other surplus income made for the life policy premiums, but it was done through a specific plan sold years ago but not these days.

So who was liable for the losses in Jackie's estate, as it appeared prima facie to be negligence somewhere? The bank manager had simply referred the client for advice. The IFA had arranged the product, but had then consulted a lawyer regarding the trust arising under the policy. It appeared to be the fault of the IFA, who should have been aware of the nature of the product they were 'selling' and how it operated with reference to the surplus income available. There was some uncertainty and that is always best avoided.

18.6.3 Who is giving ongoing advice?

Tip

Be clear who is giving advice on any continuing basis, such as annual reviews. There's some specific advice at a time when a major review is undertaken, but then who is doing what thereafter year by year? Has the lawyer completed their retainer or does the lawyer have an ongoing role and, if so, on what fee basis?

Typically, many clients will have these ingredients:

- a tax adviser (whether an accountant, a CTA or a member of the ATT) with a letter of engagement to deal with annual tax compliance work, for income tax and CGT, but not other tax advice unless specifically agreed;
- a DFM or a DIM, managing a portfolio for fees charged on the basis of the fund's value, but not dealing with other financial advice;
- an FP, charging annual fees for an annual review and some ongoing work in between, as defined in a letter of engagement, but who from time to time may carry out other specific work for additional fees;
- a lawyer who may deal with annual work in relation to the administration of a trust, which may include tax and accounting work for that trust (or that might be dealt with by an accountant or tax adviser), and other work from time to time.

As will be seen from the examples in this chapter, many situations are enhanced by different professionals bringing their expertise together. A good example is on death of a first spouse when the executors may include a professional, such as the lawyer, working with the surviving spouse, and being a lead adviser to the widow(er). The FP needs to be involved in advising on the pension provision and whether and when to draw on the pension death benefit. Even if the lawyer can give all the IHT planning advice, the tax adviser may have a role to advise on the other tax elements such as the level of personal income and gains, the tax position of an ISA and whether it should be transferred to the surviving spouse, etc. So the lawyer executor needs to liaise with two further advisers in giving advice to the widow(er).

18.6.4 Referral of clients/work between professional advisers on estate planning

While lawyers might be able to give all the IHT advice, and carry out the trust administration of any trust, in most cases they will not be able to offer financial planning services, so will need a separate FP. While some firms have a tax compliance person or team, this is still relatively rare and if tax compliance work is needed (e.g. preparing returns, advising on liabilities and assessments) it will normally need a separate person and letter of engagement even if the service is offered internally. Often there will be a need for a tax adviser or accountant outside the lawyer's firm.

So there may be an opportunity to refer a client to an FP and/or a tax adviser. In each case the needs of the client are clearly paramount, but there is real potential to develop goodwill with other firms with a view to referrals of work back to the law firm. The author's experience is that FPs are, like lawyers, concerned with long-term client relationships and very much complement the work of lawyers who are doing estate planning, specifically the legal and tax planning parts.

Tips

1. It's good to have a panel (even if in a rather informal way) of FP firms on which you have done some 'due diligence' and are satisfied of their qualities, know the key individuals and their strengths (and weaknesses), so that you can offer clients a choice. In some cases a client might wish to have a form of 'beauty parade' (as it is sometimes called) whereby they can meet, say, two or three individuals before deciding to instruct. In other cases it may suffice to meet one FP, to decide whether they feel comfortable with them and the way they share their expertise, and then may be happy to instruct without seeing anyone else. Most FPs will offer a first interview on this basis without any charge.
2. Three key qualities in an FP, apart from a good interpersonal manner, and ability to communicate technical financial information at the right level without being patronising, would be:
   (a) a good understanding of a holistic approach to estate planning, rather than a desire simply to recommend IHT saving products;
   (b) expertise with cash flow management software, as cash flow analysis is such a crucial part of estate planning;
   (c) good pensions expertise, either personally or within the firm, as pensions is such a technical area and it is so central to so much tax effective financial planning.
3. Have a clear understanding with the client and the FP as to the sharing of information, and when you will get updates from the FP. A good FP will also come back to you, where you have a good relationship (whether you introduced the client to them or not), when any new legal or tax planning needs arise. For example, if the client themselves were getting separated from their partner/spouse, so that you could offer advice as and when needed. Also, if one of the client's children were getting divorced or some other circumstance arose (such as in inheritance or an accident claim) where they might need new advice on their will, etc. If the relationship works well, the referral of work back and forth can help secure the

client relationship and build on the value of the FP's annual review whereby they often become aware of changes in the family before the lawyer does.

4. It's good to keep in touch with your FP contacts over changes in the law and tax planning, whether through seminars, newsletters, meetings for coffee or lunch, or simply an email or a telephone call. Letting your referrers know of a significant change can be really beneficial to show you are 'on the ball' and on top of important developments, and may help them to see openings for your services they would not otherwise have seen. In some cases with significant developments – like the pension death benefit changes and the introduction of RNRB – it is good to have technical discussions with your main FP referrers to consider the changes from your different perspectives. This is one of the best forms of training.

18.6.5 The benefits for clients of this co-operative interaction

What can be good for the professionals, for business development (BD) referring work opportunities, is also a real benefit for clients. The more good professionals know each other, and how each works, and can bounce ideas around, often proactively, the better. So tips 1–4 above will benefit clients. Clients also benefit if their professional advisers are actively talking to each other. It means that their affairs can be planned in a holistic way without things falling through the cracks and without any misunderstanding as to who is responsible for each piece of advice.

The big problem will be the extra cost involved in getting two (or more) people to look at something, which can seem like duplication, but which can produce better results.

Example 18.3

Michael has died leaving his pension in trust and a portfolio of stocks and shares including £650,000 in an ISA. He left a NRB discretionary trust in his will, together with a life interest trust of residue to his widow Samira, his second wife by whom he has two children at secondary school, in addition to the three grown-up children by his first, late wife Irene. His ultimate division of his estate after Samira's death is an equal split between the five children. You are an executor and trustee of both trusts and are advising on the IHT planning. There is no FP but you have recommended an FP who is able to advise Samira. They have a CTA who does their tax compliance work.

There are a classic trio of different legal, tax and FP issues to consider here:

1. **Tax planning (IHT):** You wish to help secure the RNRB on Samira's death, by avoiding the estate going over the £2 million taper threshold. You plan to keep the NRB discretionary trust in place, including the TNRB from Irene's estate as all her estate passed to Michael, and this will put £650,000 into trust and keep the aggregable estate down on Samira's death; but her estate and the potential immediate post-death interest (IPDI) trust is even so currently around £2.5 million, i.e. losing £250,000 of RNRB (of the current double RNRB of £350,000) and meaning an increase of £100,000 in IHT payable.
2. **Tax planning (income tax and CGT):** You consult the CTA over the use of the children's personal tax allowances, the tax value of having an extra £650,000 in Samira's ISA

(the tax benefits are all income tax and CGT, not IHT, after all) and Samira's potential 40% liability. She is using a large part of her annual CGT exemptions in any event, so the ISA makes good sense.

3. **Financial planning:** What options are there for the pension death benefit and how might they be drawn by Samira or any of the five children if they were designated to drawdown? Also, what does Samira need from investments and would it be good financial planning for her to have the investments in the ISA transferred in specie to her ISA as an additional permitted subscription (APS)? This depends on her personal saving/investments and risk profile, and for Samira, as a woman in her 50s who is happy to take a medium-term view and has already used her own ISA allowances, the FP supports the transfer of the ISA.

   The FP has also done some cash flow projections showing how Samira's extra £650,000 in an ISA could, with her other investments being used first, be 'spent down' over the next 20–30 years to reduce her capital below £2 million, to protect her RNRB, and then further reduce the assets subject to IHT on her death. The capital distributions could help pay for the education, and settling in first homes, of her two teenage children.

   In return, the FP and you discuss how the pension death benefits could be split between Michael's three children by Irene, all of whom are now having children themselves and will have substantial expenses in the next 10 years and could draw down the pension as 'tax-free' within the tax allowances of those grandchildren.

4. **Legal planning:** You have to have regard to Michael's will, with its two trusts, and the LOW he left as to how the relative merits of benefits to his five children and his widow might be balanced. You conclude that the IPDI trust would be about £700,000 and so the whole of the ISA could be advanced out to Samira, together with £50,000 cash, leaving just the one trust to be run. The NRB discretionary trust would then be satisfied by a share of the property, so that the running costs for the trusts would be minimal, once the IPDI trust has been wound up.

Your conclusion is that advancing the IPDI trust to Samira, for her benefit with her two children, is balanced by designating the pension death benefit to Irene's three children, to help them with their immediate needs. The end result brings together legal tax and financial planning into one integrated solution.

You consider carefully whether Samira needs separate legal and FP advice, given that under this plan the pension is being denied her, and conclude that she should have independent advice. You note that your primary role is to fulfil Michael's wishes as his executor and trustee and, while you are happy to act for Samira in the future, she needs to see someone else for one-off advice. So you present the legal, tax and financial planning proposal as a whole in a report for Samira to take along to another FP (to whom you introduce her after agreeing she would like that help) and a lawyer/tax planner, who basically approve the plan on her behalf, subject to minor tweaks.

CHAPTER 19

Estate planning – financial planner's perspective

David Gooding

19.1 KEY POINTS

Much of this book is based on legal planning, such as drafting wills, carrying out estate administration and the setting up, rearranging and winding up of trusts. For many lawyers, tax planning is inextricably linked with these legal structures – but *financial* planning is a vital third element.

A financial planner's (FP's) input can be important in five ways:

1. The financial planning process, including objective setting (see **19.2**), can be central to a client achieving their priorities. It can also help them to see how inheritance tax (IHT) mitigation fits in with meeting their own needs.
2. Cash flow analysis (see **19.3**), now offered by most FPs, can be an invaluable tool in identifying what clients can afford to do, and to do without, and to consider the consequences of different options for gifting and/or structuring their finances.
3. The RNRB and the £2 million taper threshold (see **16.8** and **17.4**) mean it is important to review the use of assets and sources of income to determine whether there would be a more efficient way to structure these. An FP may have a vital contribution to make, to help lower the IHT bill by avoiding the taper thereby increasing the amount that can be passed on tax-free.
4. Pension death benefits (see **19.4**) are now a vital tool in IHT planning, especially as they do not usually come into the equation for the £2 million threshold. While lawyers may be aware of some of the tax considerations, a good FP (who understands pensions well) is needed to explore the detailed options.
5. Life assurance products (see **19.5**), on which FPs can advise, offer specific solutions to IHT planning, as a key part of a wider plan for some clients.

This chapter also covers some specific life assurance based arrangements used widely in IHT planning: investment bonds, discounted gift trusts, loan trusts and reversionary trusts, as well as comments on business relief and long-term care. For many clients, an FP can play a key role in IHT planning even if none of these arrangements are appropriate or made, just simply through the review of objectives, attitude to risk, assessment of assets held and the invaluable cash flow analysis.

19.2 OBJECTIVE SETTING

The starting point of any good financial plan is to have a clear and accurate picture of a client's finances, as well as a good understanding of their objectives.

The first part is usually quite straightforward and is simply an information-gathering exercise. How much does the client earn? What investments do they hold? How much do they contribute to pensions? How much do they spend? etc. The client may not have this information readily to hand, but it can easily be obtained from copies of bank statements, policy valuations or from the various investment, pension or insurance providers directly.

The second part, understanding the client's objectives, is often much more difficult: When would they like to retire? What will that retirement look like? How much income will be needed? Do they want to purchase another property? Would they like their children to be privately educated? etc. These are questions that the clients themselves may not have fully considered yet, and this is where an FP can really add value, by starting the thought process and by challenging assumptions.

When discussing general financial planning objectives, clients often raise IHT mitigation as a concern. Who wouldn't want their estate to pass to their children and loved ones, rather than to the Chancellor of the Exchequer? For many, though, the timing may not be right and there can be other more pressing demands, such as mortgage repayment and school fees. Often, the ideal time to address IHT planning is when there is a major change in a client's life, which causes them to reappraise their lifestyle and focus on their objectives. This may be at retirement, when clients face a shift in mindset from saving money to spending it; or it could also be on the occasion of some other event, such as selling a business or inheriting money themselves.

The financial planning process should draw out all of a client's objectives and financial needs, and in doing this, the FP can start to test the willingness of the client to take action. Most clients will have a general wish to reduce IHT, but how committed are they to achieving this? Would they be willing to hand a cheque to their children if it meant a reduction in their own net income? How would the client feel if their children spent the money unwisely, or got divorced and the gift formed part of the divorce settlement?

These are the types of questions that an FP should discuss with a client in order to assess where IHT planning sits in the order of financial priorities. Once a client's willingness to undertake IHT planning has been established, the process of analysing what impact that IHT mitigation would have on the future financial security can start. If a client is considering gifting, there are a number of concerns that may prevent them taking action:

- How do they know how much money can safely be given away and how much needs to be retained in order to meet their own needs?
- What happens if they give away too much money and leave themselves short?
- What happens if the stock market falls and the value of their investments decreases?
- What happens if they get ill and need to pay for care costs?
- How do we establish the viability of IHT planning?

FPs are well versed in navigating these issues, and lifetime cash flow planning is one of the invaluable tools used to model the potential impact of the IHT planning proposals on a client's financial security.

19.3 CASH FLOW PLANNING PROCESS

In the past, the financial planning industry has been fairly heavily focused on product-based solutions to financial issues but, in recent years, a much more holistic approach has been adopted. This places the client's goals and objectives at the heart of the advice process and works out the most effective way of arranging finances to achieve these.

Cash flow planning, in its simplest form, is a budget of cash inflows and outflows, together with an estimation of the cash balance at the end of a given period. In the hands of a good FP, it can develop into a plan of how assets and investments are likely to be used over the course of a client's life.

At the start of the cash flow planning process, an account of assets, income and expenditure is required, together with details of any future changes in these. An estimate of all future lump sum receipts (such as bonuses or inheritances) and one-off expenditure (such as property purchase, weddings, new cars, etc.) is also needed.

Quite often, particularly while clients are still working, their grip on income and expenditure is looser than when they retire and have more time to spend on their finances. Sitting down with a client and going through expenditure in detail is therefore often a useful exercise in itself.

All of the information gathered is fed into the cash flow plan, which will then allow variables to be adjusted in order to assess the financial impact of different scenarios, such as:

- What happens if investment growth rates are lower than expected?
- What happens if inflation takes off?
- What happens if the stock market crashes?
- What would be the effect of downsizing?
- How would care costs affect the financial plan?

By running through all of these scenarios with a client, it is possible to obtain a good idea of the financial strength or otherwise of a client's finances and test whether they can actually afford to undertake IHT planning. For example, are their finances robust enough to allow outright gifts to be made? Would a more sophisticated solution, such as a trust that allows the settlor to access capital, be more suitable?

From an FP's viewpoint, the cash flow planning exercise is essential. It provides a reasonably accurate assessment (subject to the assumptions used bearing out in reality) of the amount of surplus capital and/or income. It also allows the client to see and understand the effect IHT planning options could have for their finances and other plans.

An example of a cash flow planning output is shown in the charts below, which illustrate the finances of a couple who are considering retiring in five years' time. The thick black line represents their total income requirements, and the dark grey bars indicate the extent to which they need to draw on their existing assets and investments in order to meet it. The clients' ages are on the horizontal axis, and in the first chart it is clear that their expenditure requirement is sustainable at least to age 100.

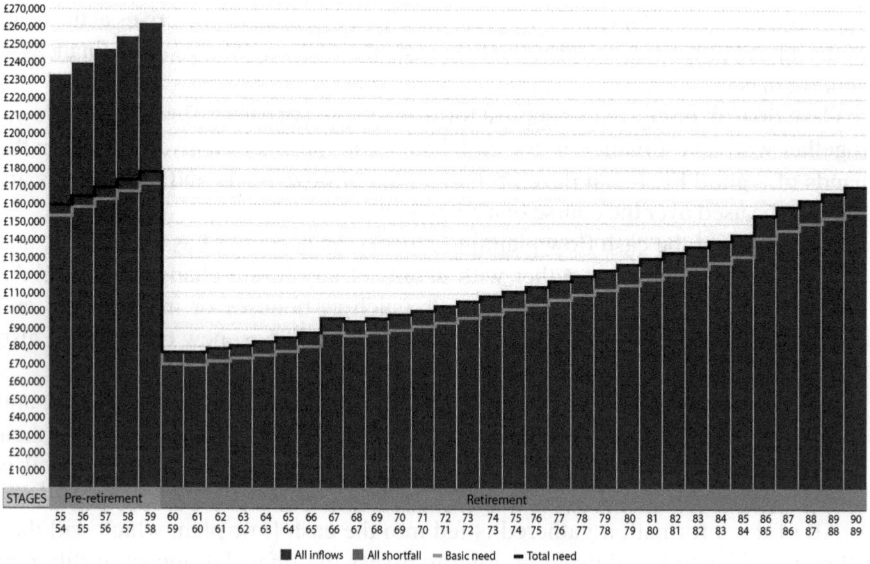

Figure 19.1 Cash flow planning output

Note: Chart produced using Voyant software.

The next chart shows how the same clients' plan would be affected if they gifted a lump sum to their children on retirement in order to mitigate IHT.

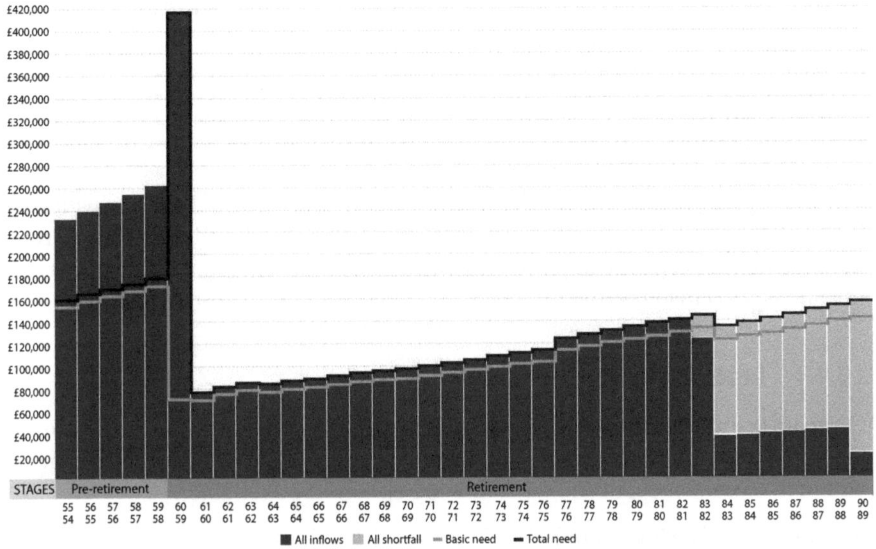

Figure 19.2 Cash flow planning output after gifting a lump sum

Note: Chart produced using Voyant software.

In this second case, it can be seen that the couple's income requirements can only be sustained to age 83 (where the bars turn light grey), when there would be a significant shortfall of income. This would prompt a discussion with the clients about the affordability of gifting and whether a lesser sum should be gifted and/or alternative methods of IHT planning such as trusts should be used.

Clearly, any cash flow plan is only as good as the assumptions made and a small change in the assumed rate of growth or inflation could have a dramatic effect over long periods of time. It is therefore essential to regularly review the plan and update and adapt it to reflect changes in the client's circumstances, tax rules, investment returns and inflation rates, etc. These reviews should be undertaken at least annually, or whenever there is a material change to a client's situation.

When you have established the affordability of IHT planning, the practical solutions can then be considered with more confidence. Some of the potential solutions are outlined in the following sections.

19.4 PENSION DEATH BENEFITS

Since the introduction of pension freedoms in April 2015, pensions have become one of the most important and simple methods of IHT planning.

Prior to April 2015, the tax applying to pension death benefits depended upon whether the fund was crystallised (i.e. the client has already started drawing funds from it) and whether the pension holder was under or over age 75 when they died. If the pension holder was under age 75, uncrystallised funds could be paid as a tax-free lump sum, but a lump sum paid from a crystallised fund suffered 55 per cent tax. Once a client had reached age 75, lump sum death benefits suffered a 55 per cent tax charge whether crystallised or not.

The tax treatment now is much more favourable. There is no longer a distinction between the crystallised and uncrystallised parts of the fund, and the only difference in tax treatment is between those clients under age 75 and those 75 and over. The rules are summarised below.

19.4.1 Death before age 75

On death prior to age 75, the pension fund is paid free of tax, whether payments are made as a lump sum or as a pension, provided that it is designated to the beneficiary within two years of death and the following options are available:

- take a tax-free lump sum;
- take tax-free income from a flexi-access drawdown (FAD) pension;
- buy a lifetime annuity with payments paid tax-free (although payments from a scheme pension in this situation would be taxable).

Designating the pension fund simply means notifying the pension provider which one of the above options the beneficiary wishes to select. If the fund is not designated within two years, then in most cases it will be subject to income tax at the recipient's marginal rates.

> **Tip**
>
> If the pension fund is in excess of the lifetime allowance, designating the fund after the two-year period could potentially result in a lower rate of tax because, while this will subject the fund to income tax, the lifetime allowance tax charge will no longer apply.

19.4.2 Death after age 75

On death after age 75, the value of the pension fund, whether paid as a lump sum or as a pension, will be taxed at the beneficiary's marginal income tax rate when money is withdrawn, and the following options are available:

- take a lump sum death benefit, which is taxable at the recipient's marginal rate of tax;
- take income from FAD, which is taxable at the recipient's marginal rate of tax; or

- buy an annuity or scheme pension, which is taxed at the recipient's marginal rate of tax.

Taking benefits under FAD can provide a planning opportunity, as the fund can be inherited as a pension and drawn upon as and when needed. Taking benefits over many years, or even leaving them inside the pension until later, could allow funds to be taken at a lower rate of tax. An inherited pension can even be left intact and passed through the generations and its tax treatment will then depend on the policyholder's age when they die. However, not all policies offer this option, and an FP will be able to investigate whether the existing policy is compatible with this type of planning, or whether a new one is required.

If the beneficiary is a discretionary trust, the trust rate of income tax (45 per cent at the time of writing (2020/21)) will apply, but the trust then has a tax credit that can potentially be reclaimed when distributed to a beneficiary who pays a lower marginal rate of tax. Where the beneficiary is a charity, the death benefits will be tax-free.

Pension funds are normally outside the client's estate for IHT purposes. There are some exceptions, however, which are considered at **19.4.6**. Lifetime allowance tax charges may also reduce the inheritable fund.

19.4.3 RNRB: pension death benefits and the £2 million threshold

A key feature of RNRB is the £2 million threshold over which the RNRB is reduced by £1 for every £2 over the limit. This in practice means a 60 per cent marginal IHT rate for estates worth more than £2 million (not only is IHT at 40 per cent payable on the assets that were above the various NRBs, but there is more tax to pay on other assets as a result of all or part of the RNRB being withdrawn). This results, in practice, in a marginal IHT rate of 60 per cent.

Pension death benefits are not normally included in the estate's value for the purposes of the RNRB and thus can be left in place without affecting the amount of RNRB due to the estate. This makes the decision whether to draw down on pension funds during lifetime a crucial part of IHT planning.

19.4.4 Pension planning opportunities

Given the beneficial IHT treatment of pensions, a sensible approach to IHT planning is often to draw all living expenses from non-pension assets, instead of taking withdrawals from the pension – at least until age 75. This will have the effect of reducing the value of assets within the estate and allowing the pension fund (which is outside the estate) to grow. This is also advantageous for maintaining RNRB – as noted in **19.4.3**.

Furthermore, when the beneficiaries finally inherit the pension they will benefit from the same tax rules on their death, which are based on their age, rather than the original policyholder's age. So for example, an individual dying at age 74 could leave a pension fund to their child tax-free. If the child subsequently died at age 76, the pension would be inherited as a taxable fund, but if the recipient subsequently died before age 75, the pension would again be inherited tax-free, and so on. It is therefore potentially possible for the pension fund to be passed down through the generations entirely tax-free.

If the pension is surplus to requirements, the expression of wish (or death benefit nomination) form provides a planning opportunity. If the surviving spouse is nominated, any lump sum received or benefits withdrawn would ultimately form part of their estate and suffer IHT on second death. However, if the surviving spouse is already financially secure and does not need the pension, or a certain percentage of it, the value could instead be transferred to others, such as the children or grandchildren, by nominating them on first death.

Depending on their age and income position, leaving a pension to grandchildren potentially offers an additional tax planning opportunity in that they may be in a position to draw income from the inherited pension within their personal allowance each year and, in effect, allow the pension to be drawn either tax-free or at a lower tax rate of say 20 per cent.

Tip

In order to take full advantage of tax planning opportunities, it is vital that death benefit nominations are up to date and that consideration is given to all family members. A death benefit nomination can be changed at any time. So, you could nominate the fund to your spouse and then update it to nominate your children if your spouse dies before you.

While a pension scheme administrator must have discretion over distribution of death benefits, there are some limitations to the scope of this discretion and it is better to make a clear nomination, that is kept up to date, in order to provide the best chance of the pension benefits ending up in the right hands.

19.4.5 Spousal bypass trusts

Prior to April 2015, when the pension freedom rules were introduced, pension death benefits were often paid to a spousal bypass trust, which permitted the surviving spouse to access the funds, while at the same time keeping the value outside their estate.

With the current favourable pension death benefit rules, it is possible to pass the pension fund through the generations via FAD without a spousal bypass trust, and clients with existing trusts should therefore review their suitability. If it is considered that the trust is no longer required, the nomination could be changed in favour of other beneficiaries. If, however, the pension holder wishes to have more control over the final destination of the funds, bypass trusts may still have a place. This will depend on the client's priorities, as bypass trusts they to be less tax-efficient than a straightforward nomination.

19.4.6 Pensions and inheritance tax

In the majority of cases, IHT will not apply to pension death benefits, as most pension funds are held in trust and are therefore outside the policyholder's estate. However, there are some exceptions:

- where the estate has a direct entitlement to the death benefits, i.e. from certain plans not written under trust, such as a retirement annuity contract;
- where the scheme trustee has no discretion over payment of benefits;

> **Tip**
>
> Always ensure that any death benefit nomination is clear, that it is not binding, and that it is only expressing wishes for the trustees to take into account.

- certain events occurring in the two years prior to death, such as a pension transfer or contribution.

Care should be taken when considering a transfer of pension rights where the pension holder is seriously ill and life expectancy is less than two years. In some circumstances HMRC may regard this as a lifetime transfer that is subject to IHT. The Supreme Court judgment in *HMRC* v. *Parry* [2020] UKSC 35 (generally known by the name of the deceased Mrs Staveley) has removed some of the uncertainty, but there are still circumstances where the transfer of a pension by a person in ill-health could be treated as a lifetime transfer.

Transferring out of a final salary scheme can result in a considerable increase in death benefits and IHT must be a part of the discussions and advice to a client when advising on these transfers, particularly where the client is in poor health.

19.4.7 Pension contributions

Contributions to a pension scheme are not usually lifetime transfers of value for the purposes of IHT, and will be immediately excluded from the member's estate.

However, if the contributions are made while the member is in poor health, a transfer of value may occur.

The underlying principle is that, where the member is likely to survive to take their retirement benefits, the payments are for their benefit so are not transfers of value. It is generally accepted in practice that contributions made more than two years prior to death are not transfers of value.

19.5 THE USE OF LIFE ASSURANCE

Insurance policies are often overlooked as a method of addressing IHT, but they can be a very effective solution in certain cases.

19.5.1 Life policies to fund the IHT bill, tax efficiently

Most methods of IHT mitigation involve gifting or losing rights over assets in some way, and many clients will have their wealth in illiquid assets, such as property, making gifting difficult. Others that do have liquid assets may be unwilling to make gifts because of uncertainty regarding their own future income and capital requirements.

Insuring the tax liability is therefore a simple way of addressing IHT while still retaining ownership and control over assets and investments. Although, to be clear, this strategy does not reduce the IHT payable but instead provides some cash to pay it, thereby increasing the beneficiaries' net inheritance.

A life assurance policy is taken out on the life or lives of the clients seeking to mitigate tax and, if written in trust, the proceeds payable on death will not be paid into the estate and should therefore be free from IHT. Furthermore, the payment should be more or less immediate once a claim on the policy has been made, as the proceeds will not have to pass through probate. This means the cash should be available to pay the tax needed to obtain the grant of probate and release the estate.

At the time of writing, the premiums for £100,000 of level (not inflation-linked) life cover for a healthy, non-smoking couple aged 65 are approximately £2,000 per annum. It is therefore 50 years before the amount paid in premiums would be equal to the amount paid out on death. This is a reasonable investment proposition in its own right, but when the IHT benefits are also taken into account, the advantages can be quite compelling, assuming the premiums are affordable.

Of course, if the policy is written in trust, paying the premiums could result in a series of transfers of value. Provided there is sufficient income to cover these without reducing the client's standard of living, they should be covered by the 'normal expenditure out of income' exemption (see **12.3**) and this can therefore be a very effective way of turning income into IHT-free capital outside the estate.

19.5.2 Type of policy and choice of trust

There are many different types of life assurance, but whole of life policies are usually the most suitable for funding an IHT liability on death. The policy is normally set up with the initial sum assured being equal to the IHT liability at the time the advice is given. This liability will of course change over time and it is important the level of insurance is kept under review. Some policies provide for the sum assured (and premiums) to increase each year, usually in line with the RPI (retail price index) and this can be a useful way to keep the sum assured in line with the potential liability.

For most married couples or civil partners, the IHT liability would arise on second death and the insurance policy would be written on a joint life, second death basis.

Where cover is required for a liability arising as a result of a client's death within seven years of making a lifetime gift, a term assurance policy should be considered.

This could either be a 'gift inter-vivos policy', where the sum assured reduces in line with the tapered tax liability or a series of term assurance policies to provide a similarly reducing sum assured.

If the gift to be covered is less than the available nil rate band (NRB), there will of course be no taper relief and the insurance should be level term rather than reducing.

19.5.3 IHT treatment of life policies

The premiums paid for a life policy written in trust will potentially be transfers of value. In most cases, these gifts will be exempt either under the £3,000 annual exemption or under the normal expenditure out of income exemption mentioned earlier. Larger premiums may not be covered by these exemptions. If the policy is written in a bare trust, the premiums will be 'potentially exempt transfers' (PETs), whereas the non-exempt premiums for policies in discretionary trust will be chargeable lifetime transfers (CLTs). CLTs that exceed the NRB will be subject to the lifetime rate of IHT, currently 20 per cent.

If written in trust, the proceeds of a life assurance policy will usually be paid to the beneficiaries free of IHT. If the policy is not in trust, the proceeds will be paid into the estate and subject to IHT.

In most cases, the proceeds will be used immediately to settle the IHT bill as intended. However, if they are left in the trust for the longer term, ongoing management may be required and there may be ongoing trust tax liabilities. If a bare trust is used, there are no ongoing tax complications. However, a discretionary trust (or any other trust subject to the relevant property regime) may be subject to tax charges in the future.

A relevant property trust is potentially subject to periodic charges every 10 years and tax will be payable if the value exceeds the NRB at each 10th anniversary, less any chargeable lifetime transfers made in the seven years prior. The value of the policy is taken to be the surrender value of the policy or the total of premiums paid in that 10-year period if greater.

> **Tip**
>
> In order to reduce the risk of a periodic charge applying, a series of separate life policies could be taken out and placed into separate trusts on different days. This strategy was established by *Inland Revenue* v. *Rysaffe Trustee Company (CI) Ltd* [2003] EWCA Civ 356, which confirmed that separate trusts established on different days would benefit from their own NRB.

19.5.4 Underwriting

Once a life policy application has been made, it will be submitted to the insurance company for underwriting.

As part of this process, the insurance company will usually write to the applicant's GP for a report on their medical history, and in many cases (certainly for larger sums assured), a medical examination will be required. The insurer will make an assessment of the client's insurability based on a number of factors including age, health, medical history, smoker status, hazardous activities, etc.

Once the underwriting is complete, the insurance company will offer to accept the clients on standard rates, or apply a rating (increase in premiums to reflect reduced life expectancy), or decline to offer cover.

Tip

Insurers can take different views of a client's life expectancy following underwriting and it is possible for one company to decline, yet another to accept on standard terms. It is therefore well worth making concurrent applications to more than one insurer, particularly where large sums are involved. It is possible to arrange for the client to attend one medical examination and have the results shared between several insurers (depending on each insurer's terms). If the applications are made concurrently, the fact that one company may decline cover is not something that needs to be declared to any other company.

19.6 INVESTMENT BONDS

Although they do not confer any inheritance tax benefits in themselves, investment bonds are often used as the investment wrapper within a trust. This is because their tax treatment is attractive for certain trusts:

- They are regarded as non-income producing, so there is no requirement for the trust to submit a tax return (unless a chargeable event occurs) if the bond is the only asset.
- Up to five per cent of the amount originally invested can be taken as a tax deferred withdrawal each year for up to 20 years, which can be useful if a regular sum is to be paid from the trust.
- They can be assigned without creating a tax charge, so when the trust is to be wound up, it is possible to assign to a beneficiary with a lower marginal tax rate than the trust itself would pay.

Investment bonds can be either offshore, in jurisdictions such as the Isle of Man, Ireland and Luxembourg, or onshore in the UK. Income and gains received in an onshore bond are taxed on an ongoing basis, whereas offshore bonds grow largely tax-free.

When the bond is surrendered, any increase in value will be subject to income tax at the policyholder's marginal rate, although in the case of an onshore bond credit will be given for the tax that has already been paid within the fund. Top slicing relief may also be used to reduce the tax charge, but this is not available to trustees. A financial adviser can recommend whether an onshore or offshore investment bond is likely to be most suitable.

The following sections give an overview of some specialist trusts commonly used by financial planners.

19.7 DISCOUNTED GIFT TRUST

19.7.1 Overview

A discounted gift trust normally comprises an investment bond written under a trust which provides for the settlor to be paid a specified level of income for life. On the settlor's death, the remaining funds are in trust for the beneficiaries.

When the trust is set up, the settlor's right to receive an income is subject to an actuarial valuation to calculate the notional capital value. As this entitlement is unlikely to have any value at the point of the settlor's death, this part of the fund is immediately outside the estate. The remainder of the fund is a gift and will fall outside the estate after seven years.

A discounted gift trust can be subject to either a discretionary or an absolute (bare) trust.

A discretionary trust gives the trustees the flexibility to change the beneficiaries, but the trust is subject to a more onerous tax regime: the initial investment into the trust, less the discount, will be a CLT and there will be a 20 per cent tax charge if the NRB is exceeded. The fund will also be subject to periodic tax charges every 10 years if the value exceeds the NRB on the 10th anniversary.

A bare trust has less flexibility in that the beneficiaries are named at the outset and cannot subsequently be altered. This could be a problem if a beneficiary predeceased the settlor. It also means the right to the capital passes to the beneficiary from age 18 (unless they lack mental capacity). However, the tax regime is more favourable. The initial investment is a PET, rather than a CLT, so there is no initial tax charge even if the NRB is exceeded and the periodic charge does not apply.

A discounted gift trust is medically underwritten when it is taken out in order to provide evidence of the settlor's state of health. This is particularly important and in the event of an early death could be used to defend any challenge by HMRC that the full discount should not apply because the individual was in poor health at the time that it was taken out. If the settlor is not in perfect health, the underwriting process will take this into account and a lower initial discount will be applicable to reflect the shorter life expectancy.

19.7.2 When used

In order for a discounted gift trust to benefit from any discount at all, the settlor must take an income, therefore this type of trust is most useful when the client has an income requirement. Otherwise, they would simply be receiving income they do not need, which would accumulate in their estate, reducing the overall effectiveness of the trust.

The immediate discount can be of great value for elderly clients who may be seeking a quicker tax saving than the normal seven-year rule allows as the discounted portion is immediately outside the estate. However, a client in very poor health or over 90 will not usually benefit from a discount.

It must be appreciated that the client is not entitled to the trust capital once it has been gifted. They will receive fixed income payments, which are set at the outset, and although there are some discounted gift trusts that allow the income taken to be altered, it is fairly inflexible.

Example 19.1

To illustrate how the discounted gift trust can be used to move funds quickly outside the estate, a settlor aged 65 placing £100,000 into trust and taking an income of £5,000 per annum would benefit from a discount of approximately 66%. This would mean that £66,000 would be immediately outside the estate and the remainder (£34,000) would leave the estate after seven years (assuming the settlor survives the seven years). Furthermore, any growth achieved on the fund invested inside the trust is outside the estate immediately. If the settlor dies after seven years and investment growth of 5% per annum net of fees has been achieved, a sum of £100,000 is available to the beneficiaries.

19.8 LOAN TRUST

19.8.1 Overview

A loan trust involves a lump sum investment into an investment bond in the form of a loan to the trust. The loan is interest free and is repayable at any time. As such, the value of the loan will always form part of a client's estate and will potentially be subject to IHT. The investment bond's growth will, however, be outside the estate.

The settlor can request repayment of the loan at any time, in part or in full. If repayments are within the five per cent tax deferred allowance applicable to investment bonds, this will provide a tax-efficient income, while reducing the debt owed to the estate (and hence its taxable value).

A loan trust can be written under either a discretionary trust or a bare trust. A discretionary trust will potentially be subject to a periodic tax charge but a chargeable lifetime transfer will not occur because no initial gift is actually being made.

The loan can be waived at any time, and this would constitute a transfer of value of the outstanding loan balance to the trust, but the 'income' paid to the settlor will stop.

19.8.2 When used

Under a loan trust, the amount of the loan remains within the estate and it is only the growth that falls outside the estate. Therefore, the longer the trust is in existence, the more likely the fund is to grow and the more effective the trust will be. For elderly clients therefore there may be better options providing more immediate tax savings.

Loan trusts can be particularly useful for clients who are unsure of their future capital needs and wish to retain access to their funds, or for those clients who need a regular income and who can benefit from the five per cent tax deferred allowances. Those clients should, however, keep in mind that after 20 years of taking the five per cent withdrawals, all of the loan will have been returned and no further withdrawals can be taken. If they decide they no longer need this income, the loan can be waived at any time.

Example 19.2

Consider an example of a couple who have just retired at age 65 and have a good pension income, which is more than sufficient to meet their needs. However, they are concerned about the possibility of care costs in the future and want to retain access to further funds if needed. They put £200,000 into a loan trust and leave it to grow. In 10 years' time they do need additional income and start drawing an income from the trust of £10,000 per annum for the next 10 years. On their death, the value of the trust has grown to £400,000, £100,000 of which forms part of their estate (the £200,000 they originally loaned less the £100,000 repaid through regular withdrawals) and the remainder is paid to their beneficiaries free of IHT.

Tip

With all investment bonds that are taken out on a life assurance basis, care needs to be taken with the lives assured named, as the death of the last life assured will result in the bond being surrendered and a forced tax charge could apply. Including a number of lives assured, such as younger beneficiaries, may provide more flexibility, avoiding automatic surrender on the settlor's death. Capital redemption bonds are also available that are not linked to anyone's lifetime and could provide more flexibility where suitable.

19.9 REVERSIONARY TRUST

19.9.1 Overview

There are a number of reversionary interest trusts available and each is structured in a slightly different way. The trust structure tends to be part of the underlying insurance product for administrative simplicity. However, in most cases the settlor makes an investment into a series of individual single premium policies each of which matures on a different date, for example 100 policies maturing at the rate of 10 per year.

These policies are written in trust with the settlor being granted the right to receive the policy proceeds as they mature. There is usually also an option for the settlor to defer the maturity to a later date if the proceeds are not required. The beneficiaries have the right to benefits on the settlor's death.

Typically, the individual policies are set up such that there is a series of maturities over the course of a 10- or 20-year period. This gives the settlor the right to an 'income' stream if required, with the option to defer if not needed. The 'income' is limited to the value of each maturing policy and is taxable in the settlor's name in the tax year it is taken.

There are no immediate IHT benefits, but once the settlor has survived seven years, the value of the trust falls outside the estate.

19.9.2 When used

The reversionary interest trust tends to be most suitable for clients who do not necessarily need a regular income, but who also do not feel comfortable giving up total access to the capital. It is much more flexible than the other structures we have already covered.

It can therefore be quite useful for clients who are concerned that their income requirements may change in the future, perhaps if they needed long-term care, etc. However, it should be noted that this arrangement is considered the more aggressive form of tax planning, and should be considered with particular care and appropriate risk warnings.

Example 19.3

Consider the case of a client who has just retired and has surplus capital but is wary of gifting it because of the possibility of future care fees. If a sum, say £200,000, were placed in a reversionary trust, this could be left to grow and after seven years, the value would be outside the estate. If the client needed additional income at any time, the policies could be allowed to mature each year and the proceeds of £20,000 (plus investment growth) could be taken for up to 10 years. The less they take, the more there is available for the beneficiaries.

19.10 BUSINESS PROPERTY RELIEF SCHEMES

For elderly clients, where making gifts and relying on the seven-year rule is uncertain, investing in assets qualifying for business property relief (BPR) is attractive. These assets remain in the estate but are taxed at 0 per cent, in practice, provided they are held by the investor for at least two years and until death.

There are a number of different types of BPR schemes available in the market. Many are portfolios of AIM listed shares (most of which qualify for BPR), while others consist of bespoke companies set up with the intention of undertaking trading activities that qualify for BPR.

An investment qualifying for BPR is an attractive proposition for elderly clients who may wish to accelerate the normal seven-year time period. However, the type of assets that qualify for this relief are higher risk by nature and the client must have the risk appetite and capacity to accept this. This is not always compatible with someone in their later years. The charges for these arrangements also tend to be higher than for more mainstream investments and the IHT relief is not guaranteed as BPR is not assessed until after death.

This type of planning is perhaps most useful for clients acting under power of attorney for loved ones who have left IHT planning too late, and who did not provide any scope for gifting when the deed was drafted.

It is important to note that assets that qualify for BPR are included in the estate used to calculate the RNRB available, whereas lifetime gifts (whether or not they have passed the seven-year period) are excluded from this calculation.

19.11 LONG-TERM CARE

The number of people needing long-term care is increasing at a rapid rate and the costs of care are far outstripping inflation. Therefore the possibility of needing long-term care is almost always a part of the discussion with anyone considering IHT planning. Concerns about future care costs can lead to uncertainty about the amount of capital that a client would need to retain which can then be a barrier to making outright gifts of capital.

This is another situation where cash flow planning (see **19.3**) is invaluable because it allows for a whole range of scenarios to be modelled and stress tested such that a client can gift capital and be confident that sufficient assets have been retained to meet their future needs.

Trusts, such as those mentioned in **19.7**, **19.8** (and potentially also **19.9**), can also be an effective solution once surplus capital has been gifted.

Where clients are actually in a nursing home and are receiving care, an immediate care annuity may be worth considering. With this type of annuity, payments are made to the care home direct and are tax-free. This has the advantage of securing the care home fees and provides confidence for other capital to be given away.

Depending upon the age and state of health of the individual, the annuity rates can be quite high, and some providers offer a return of part of the capital invested in the event of early death, which can be an attractive option.

CHAPTER 20

Business planning with wills and cross-options

John Bunker

20.1 KEY POINTS

- Reliefs from inheritance tax (IHT) need to be fully utilised – it is not an element of IHT to be taken for granted, and planning between spouses is especially important. The potential to maximise business property relief (BPR) or agricultural property relief (APR) by restructuring to secure a higher rate of relief is also worth serious consideration.
- Possible tax changes need to be taken into account, not to try to avoid tax charges by crystal-ball gazing, but to make the right decisions for families enlightened by perspective.
- Two reports – one from the Office of Tax Simplification (OTS) on IHT and the other from the All-Party Parliamentary Group (APPG) on Inheritance and Intergenerational Fairness – highlight problems with the current IHT law relating to farms and businesses and suggest different ways ahead. We should learn from these reports, to advise clients in the light they shed on our current situation.
- This book is being written in part during the unprecedented crisis caused by COVID-19 and that has other specific impacts upon the context in which clients make decisions. While we cannot be blown off course by temporary events, this is such a significant time, with potentially long-lasting effects for the nation and its economy, and also for the way it might be taxed.
- Cross-option agreements are a valuable addition to the planning here and should be considered in all cases where agricultural and business holdings are held in company shares. They are also helpful to enable the full benefits of the nil rate band (NRB) discretionary trust (D/T) to be realised in an effective way. They also represent a good opportunity for the estate planning teamwork, with referrals between lawyers and financial planners (FPs), referred to in **Chapter 18**. It is important that agreements such as shareholders agreements are carefully considered when planning for clients in this way.

20.2 SECURE THE HIGHEST RATE OF BUSINESS OR AGRICULTURAL PROPERTY RELIEF POSSIBLE

20.2.1 Reminder re categories of 100 and 50 per cent relief

For any BPR, the 'relevant business property' has to be owned for at least two years.

A reminder that:

1. There are three categories of business property that can have 100 per cent relief:

   (a) a business or an interest in a business, i.e. a sole trader or partnership;
   (b) unquoted securities giving control – either on their own or with other securities/unquoted shares;
   (c) unquoted shares.

2. There are three categories of business property that give 50 per cent relief:

   (a) controlling holding of quoted shares or securities;
   (b) land or buildings, machinery or plant used in:

      (i) business by company controlled by transferor; or
      (ii) a partnership of which he/she was a partner;

   (c) land or buildings, machinery or plant used in business, where the transferor had a life interest.

In 2(c) the question would be whether the life interest trust is still appropriate, and if it is whether any other structure might secure the higher rate of relief, like a partnership with the trust.

Relief at 100 per cent is so valuable that it is crucial to see whether your client is entitled to the highest rate of relief possible. So two questions arise:

- If they are entitled to only 50 per cent relief, is it possible to increase that to 100 per cent?
- If entitled to no relief, can at least 50 per cent relief be secured, if not 100 per cent?

This is one of those 'all other things being equal' situations. They never are, equal that is, so you also need to consider:

- What is the tax cost of making such a switch, if it is possible?
- What is the business or personal perspective?

20.2.2 What is the tax cost of making such a switch, if it is possible?

The tax cost is first in any tax on any chargeable gain, then in potentially higher tax being paid to extract funds from the new structure.

Example 20.1

Brenda and Clare own a trading business in a company owned 50:50, like a partnership but in a corporate structure for limited liability, but the trading is done from premises they own in their joint names as tenants in common in equal shares. If they were partners, the land could benefit from 50% BPR on the land they own outside the partnership, or even 100% if they were able to put the land into the partnership. By contrast, a switch to a company structure for the land, transferring it into the company, would be a major step tax-wise and involve complications and extra costs if trying to extract the land at a later date.

Specific tax advice from the tax adviser/accountant for the business, or another firm if they don't have the planning expertise, is really needed. While a few solicitors might be able to give this advice, most would have to refer to another specialist.

That specialist advice might include the possibility of giving one of Brenda and Clare 'control' of the company, through, for example, the casting vote as chairman. Without either having 'control', neither of them has any relief from IHT on the land; if one had that vote and control, she would have 50% BPR but her co-owner would still have nil. There's a clear conflict of interest here so that you could not act for both, and each would need to have separate legal advice, even if there was a form of neutral tax advice from the company's accountants/tax advisers to them both.

If Brenda and Clare lived together as partners in life, as well as business, then you might want to raise the question of a civil partnership or marriage. A spouse's shares are taken into account as 'related property' for the % test, so that they would both then have 50% BPR. That step then takes us very much into the next category of question.

20.2.3 What is the business or personal perspective?

Moving assets such as land from one business structure to another is not as straightforward as it might seem at first.

For example, moving land from personal ownership to a company makes future sales, etc. more complex, and the issue of giving one party control, through a casting vote as chair, clearly has huge potential consequences. And as for civil partnership or marriage, that's whole different ball game.

20.3 EFFECTIVE USE OF BUSINESS PROPERTY RELIEF AND AGRICULTURAL PROPERTY RELIEF WITH WILLS

The value of APR and BPR at 100 per cent should never be underestimated or taken for granted. IHT planning must include making the most of the relief where it is available. We see below (**20.4**) proposals for change which make such planning all the more significant.

The key aims would be:

- Ensuring that 100 per cent relief can be claimed, if at all possible, or 50 per cent if that's an option.

- If there is any doubt about eligibility, that this is assessed even by making a gift that might be taxable, so that HM Revenue and Customs (HMRC) needs to assess eligibility.
- Where a client is married or a civil partner (using 'spouse' as shorthand for both), that the relief is secured on the first death, and not simply left until the second estate. Several good planning reasons:
  - A business or farm can often be sold between the first and second spouse's death, so securing the relief on the first death can be enhanced if the relief goes into an appropriate trust – see **20.5**.
  - If there is a risk of tax changes (see **20.4**), it can help to secure the relief before a tax change, banking the benefit while you can, especially if the potential change is due to the way the specific business operates (such as a dependence on rental income).
  - For residence nil rate band (RNRB) (see **Chapters 16** and **17**) it can help to take value out of an estate on the first death, to avoid losing RNRB by taper, remembering that APR and BPR are disregarded for the £2 million threshold calculation.
- Any structuring should enable the surviving spouse to be involved in, and take a benefit from, the farm or business where that is appropriate, as we should never lose sight of the fact that such a farm or business is not simply an asset, for tax planning, but can be a significant part of life!

20.4 PLANNING WITH A VIEW TO POTENTIAL CHANGES

Two significant reports in 2019/20 are worth noting:

- one from the OTS (**20.4.1**) as it is only semi-independent of the Treasury, and there may be a good case for some of the changes proposed, particularly in 2020;
- the other from the APPG (**20.4.2**) as it has some good analysis of the problems of IHT and, even if it is unlikely to be implemented in large part, it is a sign of a movement in thinking.

In dealing with these reports, the author is not suggesting that anyone should chase the latest report, and constantly worry clients with potential change, and there is a risk of 'crying wolf' too many times – so that clients just don't listen anymore. This is a more nuanced reflection, which it is hoped rings true as a consideration in IHT planning. Later changes in the tax will inevitably come back to prove us wrong, in some respects, but perhaps right in some others. The aim is not to be proved right, but to help clients navigate through uncertain times.

It's normal practice that governments don't accept reports in full, well thought out though they may be, no doubt much to the frustration of the writers who think through logical and coherent proposals that fit together well as a whole. Instead politicians 'cherry pick' the bits they like. Part of the process here is identifying the cherries that may be particularly attractive to government at this moment, for good and logical reasons. Taking a policy from an eminent report can give a degree of legitimacy.

20.4.1 Office of Tax Simplification review of IHT

The second OTS report, on substantive changes, in July 2019, is very relevant to businesses and farms. The OTS proposed some changes that were not simply 'simplification' but major policy change. Two of these proposals affect our planning here:

1. **Abolishing capital gains tax (CGT) uplift on death where there is a full IHT relief/exemption:** This applies to both businesses and farms, if 100 per cent APR/BPR applies, as well as to the spouse exemption. This is a double benefit that clients have relied on greatly since the rate was increased to 100% in March 1992.

   This has a distortionary effect, as it discourages business owners from making gifts of business interests to family members working in them, anticipating that by waiting until death they will have the best of both worlds – no IHT and the capital gain 'wiped out' by the CGT uplift on death.

   It is this very distortionary effect (see also **20.4.2**) that makes this a good candidate for reform at some stage, along with the seeming unfairness that no tax has to be paid.

   At the very least, we should help clients appreciate:

   - that they can't assume they will always have the best of both worlds; and
   - that the double benefit may not last for long.

2. **Increasing the 'trading threshold' for BPR from over 50 per cent to at least 80 per cent, as for CGT holdover relief:** This is the requirement (see **Chapter 15**) that a business be 'mainly trading' or, more correctly, not mainly an investment. This is a classic cliff-edge for tax: if you are just over the 50 per cent threshold you benefit from a 100 per cent tax relief, whatever the value; but if you are just below, there is no relief at all! Hence the concern that the cliff-edge is moved as proposed.

   The trading threshold is based on four factors considered 'in the round': capital value, turnover, net profit and management time.

   This follows the cases of *Brander* (*Earl of Balfour's estate*) (see **15.5.6**) and *George* (see **15.5.3**).

If it was introduced, it would have a huge impact on many businesses which depend on substantial amounts of rental income. This would include many farms, letting out cottages and other land for rental income, as many farms rely on significant BPR claims as well as APR.

It is estimated that two-thirds of all farms have diversified, in recent years, to make their farming businesses work. Land may be let out for livery stables (see the *Vigne* case at **15.5.5**), storage of equipment, clay pigeon shooting, war games, and reusing redundant barns for businesses with an office, storage or light industrial base.

If these changes were introduced, there would be a need for a lot of rethinking of business strategies, and tax planning, but in the meantime we can consider how we adapt our advice – see **20.4.3**.

20.4.2 All-Party Parliamentary Group on Inheritance and Intergenerational Fairness

The APPG reported at the end of January 2020, shortly before the economy and life of the nation was transformed by COVID-19. It thus has not perhaps had the attention it deserves, for the analysis of the issues and problems with IHT and ideas for reform that would be fairer to the different generations. It is worth noting that many of the tax breaks of the last 20–30 years have helped the 'baby boom generation' build up wealth in homes and pensions, in a way of which those under 40 can perhaps only dream. This is not to make a political comment, but an acceptance that how tax is framed does affect the development and distribution of wealth.

The APPG review was supported by STEP, as a secretariat, with a large input from the leading barrister, Emma Chamberlain, so it has some good technical input. The cross-party group of MPs recommends:

- IHT should be completely overhauled and the rate slashed to just 10 per cent in lifetime, and on death unless an estate was over £2 million when the rate would be 20 per cent;
- give everyone a tax-free limit of £30,000 each year, in place of the NRB and most reliefs;
- APR and BPR would therefore go, along with almost all exemptions – with just the one annual amount;
- spouse exemption would remain, but would be less significant as the rate is lower.

So this would be a major reform, as the APPG says it is too difficult to reform IHT any other way. The report describes IHT as 'often criticised as complex, ineffective, riddled with anomalies, distortionary and unfair. It is unpopular and ripe for reform'. In this book we have seen many examples of these problems, showing the difficulties with the tax and potential reforms. Our task here is to see what we can learn from this report, in terms of how it affects the advice we give our clients – that is what this is, after all, all about.

'Unfair' it can be, but the difficulty is that in any tax change, even if it is revenue-neutral, there are always winners and losers. So 'unfair' depends upon your personal perspective. Many have said that RNRB is very unfair, on those without descendants, or valuable homes, and even that it favours the south of England given its help to owners of valuable homes. For now, we need to focus on businesses and what we say to business clients.

'Distortionary' is a problem with IHT reliefs that applies to both farms and businesses, with two examples:

- Example: 100 per cent IHT relief (APR) even on let land distorts the value of agricultural land. The value of many farms is totally unrelated to commercial reality, the land value being enhanced by potential 100 per cent IHT relief on death.
- The income return on high capital value tied up in many cases represents a poor return on an investment, if seen in that light. Of course it is not just that. Farms are often owned in a family for many years, giving a certain quality of life, and often emotional criteria are applied to keep the farm in the family, even if it means one non-farming child loses out. Some things are more important.
- Unfairness can result in complex solutions, often involving trusts and partnerships/LLPs, to try to balance interests of two or more children.
- Example: The combined effect of both CGT uplift and 100 per cent IHT relief on death does then distort decisions about gifting business interests during a lifetime.
- Many farmers and business owners, having put their lives, hearts and souls into their venture, are reluctant to give up control – even to family members putting great effort into making it work. A parent might, for example, want to gift part of the business to a son or daughter without whom they could not manage, but the tax position then seems to work against them.
- Many, having had advice, will decide that it is better to hold on until they die when they can get both 100 per cent IHT relief and all their capital gains wiped out by the CGT uplift. While CGT is not our subject (but see **Chapter 24** on business asset disposal relief (BADR) (formerly entrepreneurs' relief (ER)) it is worth observing that BADR (and ER before it) only reduces CGT on some of the gains to 10 per cent, it doesn't give an exemption from tax. This is different from the old days of CGT retirement relief, when part of the gain was completely exempt. So the CGT uplift on death is significantly the only way to 'wipe out' the gain, and do so completely.
- The irony is that when 100 per cent relief for IHT was introduced, increased from 50 per cent, the then Chancellor told parliament that it would encourage and enable business owners to pass on shares in businesses to their family working in the business. In fact, the distortion achieves the opposite result.

- One consequence of this situation is that many promises are made, or are thought to have been made, to encourage children and family working hard in a business. This leads to many proprietary estoppel claims, when the person who says the promise was made to them, claims they are entitled to some share of the business or farm (and it does seem to apply particularly to farms, with an increasing number of such claims in recent years). It may be that some of these situations need rethinking.

20.4.3 How do we advise clients in response to these distortions?

If we accept that wholesale change of IHT, as per the APPG report, is unlikely, we must also help clients see that changes to APR and BPR are likely to come, and that we are quite likely to lose double benefit, at some time in the next few years. So don't assume that 100 per cent IHT relief and CGT uplift will stay for the medium term.

If a client is considering a gift to the next generation – consider further, but do see **Chapter 21**. It may be that there is a valuable counterweight to the distortion, that change, while not certain, is quite possible, and should be factored into the equation. Subject to the CGT position, it may be worth using holdover for the gains, if it applies, rather than put off the gift.

Furthermore, this leads us to think more about will planning for spouses, and in particular the following:

1. With the risk of the 'trading threshold' on BPR being raised to 80 per cent, it may be worth 'banking' BPR at 100 per cent on current terms, while the business still qualifies. All the more reason to ensure the business is left to a trust – see **20.5** – rather than to the surviving spouse.
2. If there is 100 per cent CGT uplift on death, make the most of it by the trust structure.
3. If putting any structures into place by will, it's more important than ever to keep them as flexible as possible, with a good letters of wishes to guide the trustees on the exercise of any discretion.
4. Be prepared that future tax changes may affect the value of farmland, and don't assume that they will always be this 'inflated' (as some say they are).
5. Appointment of trustees is as important as ever, and do include the tax strategy in the 'letters of wishes', to guide them in the tax objectives they are asked to seek to fulfil. Do also comment in the letter of wishes on the value of independent professionals acting as trustees, to explain why the client is appointing them, if they are!

20.4.4 Land and business values

Client decisions are not based solely on tax, of course, though most clients prefer to avoid tax if at all possible. One reason some don't make lifetime gifts is simply that any tax payable is then someone else's problem! Whether any tax on capital gain is payable depends of course on whether there is in fact a taxable gain. That depends upon values, and sometimes clients might say, 'chance would be a fine thing' with reference to having a choice about selling with a capital gain.

At the time of writing this chapter, there are two special factors that may affect values that may be quite short-lived or might be around for much longer. As they are both of potentially major effect they are worth mentioning, even though it would be good to know they have become dated quite quickly:

- **Post-Brexit changes** mean uncertainty for farmers, with potentially huge changes ahead, especially for those with a reliance on subsidies, for example, regarding future direct payments. This may also affect land values.
- **Disruption to businesses and values with the COVID-19 crisis**: Clearly the economic crisis caused by the shut-down of the economy, in response to the coronavirus, has been huge and unprecedented. This has affected the values of many businesses such that many are closing down, in some cases advancing retirements but in many more companies going into liquidation or entering forced sales. Many of the businesses still trading have a significantly reduced value, opening up opportunities to consider, for example gifts with reduced capital gains.

20.5 WILLS PLANNING FOR SPOUSES WITH BUSINESSES AND FARMS

20.5.1 Maximising value of APR/BPR with NRB D/Ts

A key element in IHT planning by will is to maximise the value of APR and BPR by using NRB D/T (see **Chapter 13**). This works very well for RNRB planning, as the £2 million taper threshold takes no account of APR/BPR. So to avoid tapered loss, it works to put the farm or business, etc. into the NRB D/T.

BPR at 100 per cent:

- You can put £325,000 plus all the BPR or APR assets qualifying for 100 per cent relief into the trust. Or, if the first spouse was widowed and had a transferable NRB (TNRB), this could be £650,000 (two NRBs) plus the BPR assets.
- If the business is then sold, after death, this can add good value to the trust and the IHT planning benefits. For example, a business worth £500,000, with 100 per cent relief, could be sold giving cash of £825,000 free of IHT in the trust.

BPR at 50 per cent:

- BPR assets up to £650,000 can be put into trust, with a value of £325,000.
- What qualifies for 50 per cent BPR: land, plant or machinery, occupied/used by:
  - a partnership of which the deceased was a partner; or

– a company controlled by the testator.

- This raises the question of whether it is possible or desirable to convert the land (or other asset) to a different ownership. See **20.2**.

20.5.2 What happens on the death of the second spouse?

Leaving BPR assets to a NRB D/T on the first death maximises the IHT benefit on that first death, but what happens on the death of the survivor? If it is likely the survivor will sell the business, the D/T can hold, for example the shares and then the cash proceeds when the business is sold.

However, there can be no BPR on the second death unless the widow(er) was also a partner, etc. So can we secure a second BPR claim on the second spouse's death? If the widow(er) has cash, say from life cover, could they buy the shares or business from the NRB D/T leaving cash in the trust?

This leads to the value in having a cross-option agreement in place – see **20.6**. On the second death, BPR can be secured a second time, if the widow(er) clocks up their own two-year ownership period for BPR. The rule whereby a spouse can inherit their spouse's ownership period does not apply to business assets that are bought rather than inherited.

Three drafting points:

- If you wish to put an asset with APR or BPR into a D/T, you need to leave a specific gift of the assets, such as the farm or business, or those assets qualifying for BPR or APR, to the D/T. You can't simply appropriate the business asset to the trust, to get the benefit of the relief. Wills precedent providers will give you the form of wording, but you need to look for the right thing.
- Is BPR applicable on a gift to D/T? If you are unsure whether the business will qualify for 100 per cent relief or not – for example, as to whether the business is mainly trading or mainly investment – you should consider a gift of the whole business/farm to the trust, not just any part qualifying for APR or BPR. That means that HMRC will have to assess the eligibility for relief. This clearly needs to be done in the two years post-death so that, if needed, you can vary the terms of trust – in so far as no BPR, to appoint out on, for example immediate post-death interest (IPDI) trusts for the widow(er) claiming the spouse exemption.
- One concern with D/Ts is that the trust pays the 45 per cent income tax rate on trust income. This is unless you create an income entitlement, which means the trust only needs to pay 20 per cent basic rate tax. This can be done just after the second anniversary of the death, so that it is not read back into the will, and it remains a relevant property trust for IHT purposes even if its income tax status is changed. If done before the second anniversary it would be converted to an IPDI trust under the reading back provisions of Inheritance Tax Act (IHTA) 1984, s.144.

20.6 CROSS-OPTION AGREEMENTS

20.6.1 Introduction

Cross-option (or X-option) agreements involve the two options for:

1. the executors of the deceased's estate to sell the deceased's shares or interest to the other business owners; and
2. the other business owners to buy the business interest from the executors:
   - either can exercise their option, and require the other party to comply. It doesn't invalidate BPR as there is no binding contract for sale at the date of death. It is only when the option is exercised that you have a contract;
   - it ensures that each party gets what they need:
     - the deceased's family can have the cash value for business interest; and
     - the business partners or shareholders get the deceased's business interest.

20.6.2 Funding the option: life cover to provide cash for purchase

Life insurance cover can be funded by all the partners/owner managed business (OMB) shareholders.

The life policy proceeds are written on discretionary trusts, so they can be paid to the surviving owners, outside any estate, so that they are not subject to IHT.

The amount insured should be kept under review, to ensure it continues to reflect full value, given the changing value of the business.

This presents a great opportunity to work with independent FPs:

- to refer to them to arrange the insurance, which is good business in itself and can also be an introduction to a new longer-term client; and
- for the FP to refer clients who need X-option agreements and associated IHT planning advice.

20.6.3 How this X-option agreement helps mitigate IHT

Each of partners/shareholders, if married or in a civil partnership, should write a NRB D/T will, including in the D/T the business interest.

Therefore, cash provided by the life cover helps buy the business interest from the estate and the NRB D/T of the deceased business owner receives the full cash value.

If the business interest benefits from 100 per cent BPR, this full value goes to the D/T on top of £325,000 other assets (or potentially £650,000 if the deceased was widowed and there is a TNRB included).

If only 50 per cent BPR applies, then you can put £650,000 into the D/T. (Consider further with a commercial lawyer and accountant/tax adviser if you could restructure for 100 per cent BPR.)

Therefore, you maximise the value of the NRB D/T, the maximum tax-free gift on the first death.

For the second death, it does two things:

- it reduces the taxable estate – once BPR is lost anything over, for example the NRB and RNRB, is potentially taxed at 40 per cent;
- it also takes the maximum amount out of the estate for the calculation of the RNRB £2 million threshold, reducing the risk of an unnecessary loss of RNRB by tapering away.

20.6.4 What if the spouses are partners or the surviving spouse wishes to continue the business?

You can still have a X-option agreement between the spouses, as the surviving spouse/partner may need the right/option to buy the deceased spouse's interest from the estate. It may seem a little excessive to suggest this, but the deceased's executors may have a different view and not wish to sell to the spouse. In addition, your business partner may not want to be in business with your spouse.

Life cover – to provide the cash needed to buy the business interest off the D/T – can still be provided, funded by the two spouses.

The surviving spouse can then continue the business, and clock up their own BPR ownership rights after two years, if they were not a partner. It is worth considering a two-year term assurance to cover the risk of death in the two years post the death of the spouse.

This is a way to get maximum value into the D/T, rather than leaving the business interest to the spouse outright.

CHAPTER 21

Business and lifetime planning

Helen Clarke

21.1 KEY POINTS

This chapter covers the following:

- consideration of lifetime succession planning options for businesses;
- the contrasting tax treatment of trading and investment businesses;
- tax reliefs for businesses;
- types of business structure;
- relevance of close company status for inheritance tax (IHT);
- contrasting the tax position of lifetime gifting and transfer on death;
- share transfer to family members
- the use of trusts;
- third party sale;
- management buy-out or employee ownership trust; and
- 'death-bed' planning.

21.2 INTRODUCTION

This chapter is a guide to the IHT issues that have an impact on lifetime succession planning for business owners. It is beyond the scope of this book to address in detail other taxes applicable to businesses in the context of succession planning, but they should not be overlooked in forming a strategy for handing over or selling a business. All relevant taxes must be considered when creating a strategy to meet the personal and commercial objectives of a business owner.

21.3 THE RELEVANCE OF TRADING STATUS

There is a clear distinction between the tax treatment of trading and investment businesses that affects lifetime planning and the opportunities available to business owners.

21.3.1 Trading business

The available tax reliefs for trading businesses for IHT and capital gains tax (CGT) (and see **Chapter 24** for business asset holdover relief – Taxation of Chargeable Gains Act (TCGA) 1992, s.165) make it easier to pass on a business during lifetime without any immediate tax consequences and in a controlled way, but it isn't always advisable to do so. While tax freedom affords flexibility, there may be a resulting loss of potential tax relief on death.

21.3.2 Investment business

If a business does not have trading status, it is deemed an investment business for tax purposes and then denied the benefit of BPR and TCGA 1992, s.165 business asset holdover relief for CGT.

If an investment business is retained in an estate, there will be a 40 per cent IHT charge on death on its value. Tax deferral is typically preferred, often for liquidity issues, over incurring an immediate lifetime charge to tax when undertaking succession planning. The tax outcome of proposed planning often, therefore, determines a succession planning strategy and usually involves a tax cost and tax benefit calculation.

21.4 TYPES OF BUSINESS STRUCTURE

Family and owner managed businesses are typically private limited companies and fall within the definition of a 'close' company. The owners of a limited company have less personal financial exposure and companies enjoy a favourable tax regime.

Some business owners might operate as sole traders, but they are then fully liable for all debts and typically pay more in tax. One attraction might be that there is very little financial reporting involved and full control can be retained by the owner. In reality, businesses are unlikely to operate as sole traders unless they are start-ups with little value. The personal financial risk to a sole trader is too high. A sole trader would also experience difficulties trying to borrow funds to expand a business and this highlights the limitations of the business model.

An alternative structure that limits liability is a family limited partnership (FLP). An FLP limits its partners' exposure to liabilities and it exhibits elements of partnerships and corporations. The tax status of an FLP might not be attractive due to the fact that all profit is taxed as income.

21.4.1 Close company definition

A 'close company' is defined by Corporation Tax Act (CTA) 2010, s.439 as a company which is under the control of:

- five or fewer participators; or

- participators who are directors (CTA 2010, s.439), i.e. all shareholder directors who control the business, an 'owner managed' business.

The definition is broad and captures most family and owner managed businesses for tax purposes under either or both of the above sections. The tax implications other than for IHT purposes are beyond the scope of this book.

The statutory definition of a 'participator' in a close company in CTA 2010, s.454(1) is 'a person having a share or interest in the capital or income of the company'. This extends to any 'associate' of a participator and includes shares held by close family members (CTA 2010, s.448) including children (both adult and minor), spouse or civil partner, parents and siblings. The legislation also extends to include trustees of a settlement created by a participator or an associated family member, if the participator has an interest in the settlement. It is important, therefore, to look at actual beneficial ownership including nominee arrangements.

The statutory definition of 'control' is set out in CTA 2010, s.450 which states:

> (2) A person ('P') is treated as having control of a company ('C') if P –
>
> (a) exercises,
> (b) is able to exercise, or
> (c) is entitled to acquire,
>
> direct or indirect control over C's affairs.

Different classes of shares, created for different shareholders, are commonly referred to as 'alphabet shares' as these separate share classes are identifiable by a specific letter.

21.4.2 IHT implications of close company status

A founder might want to carve out shares for the next generation as part of a succession planning exercise. This enables the founder to retain control and to enjoy the financial benefits of being a shareholder while gradually introducing the next generation to the business.

The IHT implications of a rights issue of shares in a close company can have unexpected tax consequences. Inheritance Tax Act (IHTA) 1984, s.98(3) provides that IHT value shifting is a chargeable lifetime transfer (CLT) and not a potentially exempt transfer (PET) for IHT purposes. A 20 per cent charge to lifetime IHT might be inadvertently triggered.

The rules have an impact when an alteration of share capital is necessary to enable a gift of shares to be made to the next generation.

For example, alphabet shares with no voting rights attached might be issued by the company. The use of alphabet shares enables the participator as director to control the flow of income to the alphabet shareholders and to restrict control. If the business owner then makes a gift of those shares, there will be a shift in value of the original shares held. It should also be noted that a company cannot make a PET for IHT purposes. As such, shares cannot be issued direct from the company to a non-shareholding individual other than for full consideration. If a business is an investment business, it does not qualify for BPR to reduce a transfer of value for IHT. If the close company value shifting rules apply as a result of capital restructuring, the transferor is deemed to make a CLT. The transfer must be within the NRB of the transferor so that a lifetime charge to IHT at 20 per cent does not arise.

Where a business is a mixture of trading and investment activity – for example, it has some income from renting property – it is important to be clear whether it will qualify for BPR or not. (See **Chapter 15** on BPR.)

21.5 SHARE TRANSFER TO FAMILY MEMBERS

There can be advantages and disadvantages of making a lifetime gift of a business, or an interest in it, to the next generation. It might not be a commercially viable option if none of the family members is interested in running the business or the founder needs to realise the value in the business for retirement. Any potential conflict needs to be addressed if only some family members have the commercial acumen and interest to take on the business going forward.

It should be ensured that provision is otherwise made for the non-shareholding family members who might be aggrieved to avoid a family feud. If there are insufficient assets remaining in the free estate to equalise benefit among the next generation, a life policy written in trust could be taken out. This would provide a tax-free lump sum to be paid on the death of the donor to provide for the other family members that are outside the business. This depends on the health and age of the vendor, whose life will be insured, and the affordability of premiums.

The advantages of a lifetime transfer include the following:

- Removing the value of a trading business from an estate if there are concerns over qualification for BPR or that future legislative change might restrict or reduce the availability of relief. The former is usually the motivator rather than the latter. If availability of the relief is uncertain and restructuring is not an option, it is often wise to consider lifetime succession planning to ensure a tax-efficient handover of the business to the next generation, particularly if the business is not intended to be sold as there might be liquidity issues paying the IHT. This approach also banks BPR if there are real concerns that BPR might be denied or restricted so that the whole of the business value is then chargeable to IHT on death.
- The shares are removed from the free estate of the deceased participator on death and are not then an asset of the estate for claims under the Inheritance (Provision for Family and Dependants) Act 1975.
- With lifetime succession, a business owner is able to ensure a controlled and smooth transfer of the business to the next generation in cases where family members want to be involved with the business.
- To motivate and encourage family members who work in the business. Future growth and value are then outside the estate going forward, subject to the

seven-year rule and the BPR clawback rules, if they apply. (See **Chapter 15** on BPR and clawback section.)

- In the case of an investment business, BPR will not be available on death meaning that IHT at the rate of 40 per cent will be due. While this can be paid in 10 annual instalments, the tax due might still have an adverse effect on the business and its ability to continue. The CGT implications of gifting an investment business might restrict any available planning if TCGA 1992, s.165 holdover relief is not available.
- If a gain is significant, gifting could be phased over seven-year periods to transfer to a trust to benefit from TCGA 1992, s.260 holdover relief. If this method is adopted then asset value-freezing could be considered. Otherwise, the growth of the retained shares can render any planning relatively ineffective. This can be important for investment businesses whereby the donor is limited to transferring shares in the business equal to the nil rate band (NRB) every seven years to a trust as outlined above. With a restricted long-term strategy to make gifts, the risk is that the retained shares will continue to grow significantly in value thereby increasing the IHT problem for the donor. The company can issue growth shares to be given away as part of the gifted shares. The growth shares will only have value going forward, and therefore the value at the time of the transfer is limited. There should not then be a charge to CGT.
- Where one of the partners within a partnership is considering retirement, certain planning should be undertaken in order to ensure the partnership as a whole still qualifies for BPR. By the retiring partner retaining a limited involvement in the business, the whole partnership still qualifies for BPR. If the partner retires, their interest is treated as that of a creditor of the business where their retirement payment is still due to them, therefore, BPR is not available (*Beckman* v. *IRC* [2000] STC (SCD) 59).
- For a trading business, TCGA 1992, s.165 business asset holdover relief can be elected to hold over the gain on disposal until the donees then dispose of the assets. Otherwise, business asset disposal relief (BADR; formerly entrepreneurs' relief (ER)) might be available to reduce the amount of tax on any gain to 10 per cent on up to £1 million worth of qualifying gains. Funding the tax might still present a liquidity issue. A lifetime gift means that there will then be a resulting loss of CGT base cost uplift on death.* If the availability of BADR is restricted by further legislative change, then the donees might have to pay CGT on disposal at a much higher rate. However, liquidity will be in point. Tax deferral is typically preferable.
- Benefit of minority discount for share valuation purposes of up to 50 per cent.

* The Office of Tax Simplification (OTS) has proposed (in July 2019) that estates should not benefit from CGT uplift on death as well as 100 per cent BPR. If this proposal was implemented, it would have significant effects on lifetime planning for businesses, and major strategic rethinking would be needed. (See **20.4.1**.)

The potential disadvantages might include the following:

- **Loss of CGT uplift in share value on death.** This is often in point for property investment businesses holding properties acquired several decades ago with very low base costs.
- **BPR clawback** (see **15.7**). If a donor makes a gift of a business qualifying for BPR and fails to survive seven years, the benefit of BPR might be clawed back. This happens in either of the below instances:
  - if the donor has ceased to own the gifted assets; or
  - if the assets cease to qualify for BPR in the hands of the donee. This does not apply to unquoted shares. It is targeted legislation to stop artificial tax avoidance. See **15.7** regarding the differing tax treatments of PETs and transfers of value to a relevant property trust (RPT). The whole of the PET is chargeable if death occurs within seven years. In the latter case, the cumulative total of the RPT remains unaffected. This mostly affects sole trader businesses. While it is now agreed that BPR can apply for the whole of a sole trader's business (*Revenue and Customs Commissioners* v. *The Trustees of the Nelson Dance Family Settlement* [2009] EWHC 71 (Ch), 2009 STC 802), if a transfer of some of the business assets is made and the donor dies within seven years of the gift and the donee has disposed of the assets then BPR will be clawed back. Clawback does not apply in respect of unquoted shares, it only applies in respect of business assets. If the donee has disposed of the shares therefore, clawback will not be in point.
- **Loss of BPR.** This can be insured against if one of the above instances arises. The donor or the donee can take out the cover and it can be written in trust.
- **Loss of control/asset protection.** Parents may be concerned to protect their legacy from the divorce or bankruptcy of a child. If shares are gifted then this is often on the condition that a pre-nuptial or post-nuptial agreement is entered into and that the share rights are restricted. It will be important to review and enhance the constitutional documents before any gifts are made.

21.6 SALE TO THIRD PARTY

21.6.1 Sale at arm's length

In most cases, a business owner will be looking for an exit from the business through sale to achieve financial freedom in retirement. This is particularly the case if there is no natural successor within the family. Business owners often have most of the value of their estate in their business, and it can be the only source of income. While an exit will unlock the value in the business, the resulting sacrifice is the loss of relief from IHT on the value of the business on death.

If a business qualifies for BPR, the sale proceeds will form part of the individual's chargeable estate for IHT as soon as a binding contract for sale is made (IHTA 1984, s.113). This resulting loss of 100 per cent relief is then followed by a 40 per cent tax charge on death if pre- or post-sale planning is not undertaken.

If a 'death-bed' sale is being made, then cross-option agreements should be considered rather than entering into a binding contract for sale. If a vendor died during the transaction and the business was under a binding contract for sale, then BPR would be lost to the detriment of the beneficiaries of the vendor's estate. If the sale completes pre-death, the proceeds of sale might be reinvested in other business property such as an AIM portfolio to benefit from the replacement property rules (IHTA 1984, s.107). The application of the replacement property rules overcomes the statutory two-year ownership requirement for BPR meaning that the combined period of ownership is aggregated.

The company accounts should be reviewed to ascertain the value of any credit on a director's loan account. Directors often have loan accounts and a credit balance does not attract BPR. If a balance is significant, a share issue might be considered, particularly in a death-bed case to secure BPR on that amount. IHTA 1984, s.107(4) provides that unlisted shares which are acquired under a CGT reorganisation within TCGA 1992, ss.126–136 are identified as shares which already belong to the owner. Such shares would then be deemed to satisfy the two-year test under the BPR rules. The credit on the loan account could be used to subscribe for further shares whereas otherwise it would not qualify for relief.

The case of *The Executors of Mrs Mary Dugan-Chapman and another* v. *HMRC* [2008] SpC 666 highlights 'death-bed' planning intending to rely on IHTA 1984, s.107(4). In this case there was an attempt to capitalise Mrs Chapman's loan account to secure BPR on the balance of the account. The planning would have succeeded other than for a failure to comply with the company law requirements that have to be followed on a share rights issue. The case is a helpful example, though, of how a restructure can maximise the benefit of BPR.

A sale gives financial freedom for the owner in many ways. It enables lifetime gifting to provide for the next generation. It also means that more controlled succession planning can be undertaken if the family do not want to run the family business after the death of the founder (see **Chapter 22** on alternative structuring vehicles).

21.6.2 Planning for a third party sale

If a third party sale is sought, it is important to ensure the smooth running of the business in advance of a sale. The ownership structure of the business and its balance sheet should be reviewed. If a sale is the preferred and viable option for lifetime planning, one tax consideration will be the availability of BADR for CGT purposes. While a company sale will enable lifetime gifting, the loss of BPR in an estate can have a significant impact on the IHT position.

The availability of BADR for CGT maximises the net profit on sale of a trading business if a share sale can be negotiated. If the stringent statutory requirements are met, an owner-manager is able to benefit from the reduced rate of 10 per cent tax on gains up to £1 million. In the case of a straightforward share sale, all chargeable gains on shares in a non-trading business will be taxed at 20 per cent.

If an asset sale rather than a share sale is negotiated, then the benefit of BADR is lost and the transaction will likely result in a double layer of taxation. In the case of a company, corporation tax will be due on any profit and then tax will also be due on distribution in the hands of the shareholder. A company sale is therefore typically preferable.

21.6.3 Pre-sale succession planning

If a business qualifies for BPR, a vendor has an opportunity to create a settlement to receive shares in advance of sale. If shares are transferred with the benefit of BPR at the rate of 100 per cent, there will be no entry charge to IHT irrespective of the value of the shares: the transfer should be fully relieved for IHT purposes. Shares with a value relieved by 50 per cent can be transferred up to the value of the settlor's available NRB. This presents an excellent opportunity for succession planning in a controlled way. Such planning can be enhanced through the creation of a family investment company by the vendor to afford greater asset protection. This additional planning is discussed in detail in **Chapter 22**. If shares are transferred to a family trust, this counts as a disposal for CGT purposes and holdover relief should be claimed. Holdover relief will not be available if the vendor and their spouse and any minor children are beneficiaries (TCGA 1992, s.169B).

The value of the business is relevant when deciding whether and how a trust should be structured so that the shares held by the trustees qualify for BADR on sale. If the value of the business is less than £1 million and the vendor has a full unused lifetime limit for eligible gains, it might not be advisable to make a pre-sale disposal if this means that BADR will no longer be available on those shares. Any planning needs to be undertaken before two years before an intended sale so that the trustees meet the prescribed ownership period.

In addition to satisfying the ownership period, the trust must also have a qualifying beneficiary. The qualifying beneficiary must have an interest in possession in the trust fund and this interest in possession must not be for a fixed period. The qualifying beneficiary does not have to have had their interest for a determined period of time. This can give rise to planning opportunities for pre-existing settlements. They can be rearranged in advance of a sale to ensure that there is a qualifying beneficiary. For example, if the trustees hold on discretionary trusts with a power of appointment then an interest in possession can be appointed to a qualifying beneficiary before the sale and they do not have to do so more than two years before sale.

TCGA 1992, s.165A prescribes that the company must be the personal company of the qualifying beneficiary. The same statutory tests apply that apply to an individual. The qualifying beneficiary must be an officer or employee of the company or of a company within the group and they must also hold five per cent or more of the ordinary shares of the company (TCGA 1992, ss.169J(4)(a), 169S(3); and Finance Act 2019, s.39 and Sched.16, para.2(4)).

21.7 COMPANY OWN-SHARE PURCHASE TO UNLOCK CAPITAL FOR PLANNING

A business owner might need to unlock capital in the company either to fund retirement or to enable lifetime gifts to be made to family members. One way of achieving this might be through an own-share purchase by the company. The company could purchase its own shares back from the shareholder. BADR should apply for CGT purposes if the business is a trading business and the other qualifying conditions are met. A share sale would be dependent on the ability of the company to raise liquidity. Strict statutory conditions are attached to a purchase of shares by a company which must be met to ensure that capital gains treatment is available and that the repurchase is not taxed as a distribution.

From an IHT perspective, while a share repurchase frees up capital for making PETs, the shareholder then loses the benefit of BPR to the extent that it was available and is then subject to the seven-year rule when making lifetime gifts.

21.8 EMPLOYEE OWNERSHIP TRUST

While employee ownership trusts (EOTs) are now used less frequently in planning, they can still play a useful role in genuine planning cases if an owner is seeking an exit without intending to make a third party sale. Any arrangements will need to be exempt under the disguised remuneration legislation to avoid a charge to PAYE (pay as you earn) and NICs (national insurance contributions).

EOTs were introduced by the Finance Act 2014. They offer business owners the opportunity to exit when they are not necessarily looking for third party purchasers. EOTs are useful if the circumstances fit, but in many cases they don't. As ever, every case is dependent on its individual facts and the objectives of the business owner and their personal circumstances

Shareholders considering transferring the ownership of their company into an EOT will need to consider a number of practical issues both at the time the EOT is established and the transaction undertaken, and after the transaction has completed. This is to ensure that the relevant property regime does not apply to the trust fund.

The EOT itself should be fairly inactive as a trust, as it will merely hold a certain percentage of the share capital in the company on behalf of all the employees until the end of the trust period. Nonetheless it will need to be registered as a trust with HM Revenue and Customs (HMRC) and will be required to submit an annual self-assessment tax return.

Most business owners are not in a position to be as altruistic, and often a management buy-out is a preferred route or otherwise a third party sale.

21.9 USE OF TRUSTS

If shares in a business qualify for BPR at 100 per cent, a shareholder wanting to make lifetime gifts in a controlled way using a trust can do so without incurring an entry charge to tax. This can be done if there are concerns that the company might not qualify for BPR on death or that the relief might be withdrawn or restricted.

The trust will then own shares in the company. The transfer will be chargeable to CGT unless an election is made to hold the gain over. A trust cannot be settlor interested to qualify for holdover relief. Consideration could be given to crystallising the gain and paying the lower rate of tax at 10 per cent if ER is available. Otherwise, an election under TCGA 1992, s.260 can be made to hold over the gain and the qualifying criteria must be met. Any transfer to trust should be made in advance of two years if a company sale is envisaged.

While a trust is a good vehicle to use in order to test whether BPR is available on certain business assets, there are some disadvantages to using trusts such as: ongoing administration, the specific tax rates applicable to trusts, IHT charges for RPT such as exit charges and anniversary charges if BPR ceases to be available, trusts are subject to government (HMRC) consultation and the outcome is not known, as a result, there is much uncertainty regarding the future of trusts.

21.10 PROPERTY INVESTMENT BUSINESSES

There are fundamental differences in the IHT treatment of property investment businesses and trading property businesses as outlined in **Chapter 15**. Property investment businesses only qualify for BPR if the business does not consist wholly or mainly of making or holding investments. HMRC determines each case on its facts. What is apparent from case law is that it is not the level of activity employed in a business that is the determining factor, but the nature of the business itself. For example, a business consisting of letting property will not qualify for BPR irrespective of the level of activity involved in managing the portfolio (*Martin and another (executors of Moore deceased)* v. *IRC* (1995) STC 5).

The case of *Burkinyoung* v. *IRC* (1995) STC (SCD) 29 specifically considered a company which was a property letting business, but one in which the owner was actively involved in the control and management of the let properties to a significant degree. The Special Commissioner denied relief on the basis that the level of services provided was simply what is required for a landlord and tenant relationship to exist.

The case of *DWC Piercey's Executors* v. *HMRC* [2008] SpC 687 remains authority for the proposition that development companies qualify for BPR provided that the company is actively developing land or building on it.

With the absence of BPR for property investment businesses, succession planning without prohibitive tax consequences can be limited. It is not uncommon for owners to want to retain property investment companies to provide for future generations as they have done for the current owners.

For liability purposes and for the benefit of mortgage interest relief, private limited companies are commonly the preferred vehicle to hold rental properties, particularly when considering succession planning. This enables a gift of shares to be made rather than individual properties themselves thereby enabling retention of control. Family property investment companies are a useful vehicle to enable controlled succession planning. With stamp duty land tax (SDLT) otherwise in point if there are mortgages, a gift of shares is more tax efficient. An additional attractive feature is the relatively low rate of corporation tax on profit (19 per cent for 2020/21). If profit is retained to fund additional purchases then there can be a tax saving. If profit is to be paid by way of dividend, the usual dividend tax rates apply depending on the tax status of the shareholder who receives the distribution.

As has been outlined, lifetime succession planning can be difficult due to the resulting tax implications. It is not uncommon for families to want to retain property investment companies to provide for future generations as they have done for the current owners.

If no lifetime planning is undertaken, the business will form part of the chargeable estate of the owner on death. There will be an uplift in the base value of the shares received by the beneficiaries for CGT (TCGA 1992, s.62). If the beneficiaries have capital needs or cannot otherwise fund an IHT liability they may have to sell some or all of the properties in the business. If a purchaser will buy the company then little or no CGT will be due. The purchaser's liability to SDLT will only be 0.5 per cent for a share purchase.

If individual properties are sold, if a purchaser is not willing to buy the company and inherit its history, there would be an asset sale by the company. The profits in the company on the sale of one of its assets would be taxed at corporation tax rates subject to available reliefs. The beneficiaries would need to consider how to extract the sale proceeds from the company tax efficiently after the asset sale. The most tax-efficient result would be through a winding-up of the company with the assets being distributed as capital. Otherwise, a dividend tax charge would arise.

Example 21.1

Jack is married to Jill and they both own shares in Hill Investment Company Ltd. The business is not trading and is an investment business. They have a combined holding of 52% giving them a controlling holding of the company. Their shares are caught by the 'related property' rules which treat shares as being jointly owned by married shareholders rather than their shareholdings being distinct for tax and valuation purposes (IHTA 1984, s.161(2)(a)). They want to give all of their shares to their adult children. Both of their children work in the business and the gift of shares is intended to motivate them and to manage the IHT liability that will arise on the second death as BPR is not available.

The shares do not qualify for business asset holdover relief for CGT purposes. Jack and Jill do not want to pay CGT on gifting the shares. They both decide to create a relevant property trust to elect for the contingent gains to be held over under TCGA 1992, s.260. Jack and Jill are then restricted to transferring shares valued up to their available NRBs to avoid incurring a 20% lifetime charge to IHT. They both have a full unused NRB and can also use their personal allowance.

The combined value of their shares is £450,000. This value falls within their combined NRBs. Jill's shares are worth £350,000 and Jack's shares are valued at £100,000. If they transfer their shares on the same day the related property rules for IHT will apply and the transfers will be taxed as if they held a joint shareholding. The legislation apportions the value of their combined transfers for IHT between them on a pro rata basis. This results in Jill making a chargeable transfer in excess of her NRB and triggering a 20% lifetime entry charge to IHT.

If Jack had made his gift on day 1, his transfer of value would have been £100,000 and no IHT would be due on his transfer. On day 2, the related property rules for IHT don't apply to Jill's shareholding and Jill no longer has a majority shareholding. The value of her shares will be discounted as she now has a minority shareholding, bringing the value of Jill's shares within her NRB. There is a specific valuation rule for property that would be worth more if sold with 'related property' (IHTA 1984, s.161).

There is no restriction on the discount applied where the property is not sold with related property and this is assessed on a case-by-case basis. The case law and guidance for this are set out in the HMRC *Shares and Assets Valuation Manual* (SV113130). Jill is able to transfer her shares without incurring a lifetime charge to IHT and to also benefit from a reduced value on transfer preserving some of her NRB.

The Valuation Office Agency's Inheritance Tax technical manual (**www.gov.uk/guidance/inheritance-tax-manual**) has set out a useful example at appendix 28 to illustrate this point:

> A house stands in 10 acres of parkland, which together are valued at £1,500,000. The transferor owns the house, whilst her spouse owns the surrounding parkland (the related property).
>
> A = Aggregate value of the entirety with vacant possession is £1,500,000.
>
> T = Value of transferor's interest in the house if not part of the aggregate: say £1,200,000 (i.e. what the market might pay and not the arithmetical proportion).
>
> R = Value of husband's related interest in the parkland as if not part of the aggregate: say £50,000
>
> Appropriate portion of the value of the aggregate attributable to the transferor's interest in the house:
>
> $(T \div (T + R)) \times A$
>
> £1,200,000 ÷ (£1,200,000 + £50,000) x £1,500,000 = £1,440,000

PART IV

Specialist areas

CHAPTER 22

Alternative structuring vehicles

Helen Clarke and Eleanor Black

22.1 KEY POINTS

This chapter covers the two main alternative structures for protecting family legacies for future generations:

- family investment companies (FICs);
- family limited partnerships (FLPs).

22.2 INTRODUCTION

The two most important features in lifetime wealth transfer planning are usually (a) asset protection and (b) tax mitigation for the next generation. This encompasses the desire to provide for the next generation in a timely manner while not wanting to simply hand over significant assets. Since the major overhaul to the taxation of trusts in 2006, and subsequent legislative changes since then to discourage the use of trusts for tax planning reasons, it has become harder to use a trust as a vehicle to safely transfer a legacy to the next generation in a controlled manner.

Unless the surplus wealth being given away is within the nil rate band (NRB) of the taxpayer, or the assets in question qualify for 100 per cent relief, then any planning is restricted to the NRB to avoid incurring a lifetime charge to tax at 20 per cent. While transfers can be made every seven years to a trust, this will not greatly benefit larger estates.

It is typically when asset values are significant that control becomes even more important. A donor often wants to retain control and to protect against divorce or bankruptcy in the next generation, and to enable them to be educated in managing the legacy that has been created for them. A sense of responsibility comes with wealth, and alternative structuring vehicles are often considered to protect the family legacy for future generations. The two main alternative structures that are considered are FICs and FLPs.

22.3 FAMILY INVESTMENT COMPANIES

22.3.1 Introduction

A FIC:

- is a private limited or unlimited company used for estate planning;
- enables a controlled wealth transfer;
- reduces inheritance tax (IHT);
- has no entry charge to tax or 10-year charges;
- has potential for double taxation.

A FIC has been used increasingly as part of estate planning armoury since the 2006 overhaul of the taxation of trusts. While trusts were always the vehicle of choice for controlled succession, the increased taxation and complexity in the UK has led to the use of alternative vehicles such as FICs to enable a controlled transfer of wealth. The use of FICs has increased even more in recent years due to reducing corporation tax rates. A FIC is suitable for clients who want a long-term investment structure with the flexibility to adapt to the personal and financial changes in the family. Business families transitioning to being investment families after a business sale typically feel comfortable with the familiarity of the structure.

22.3.2 Structure: the key features of a FIC

A FIC is typically a private limited company

An unlimited liability company may be appropriate in some cases and has the benefit of increased privacy and reduced reporting requirements. However, in many cases the assets and activities of the company will necessitate the use of a limited company. For example, a FIC holding a property investment portfolio would usually be a limited company to protect the position of its shareholders.

FICs commonly have two or more classes of shares

A substantial element of control can be retained by the founders of the FIC through careful drafting of the articles of association and the use of both voting and non-voting shares. A typical example would involve the principal contributors holding 'A ordinary' voting shares which give them control over the company. Non-voting 'B ordinary' preference shares are then held by other family members. However, it should be noted that HM Revenue and Customs (HMRC) can attribute up to 50 per cent of the company value to voting shares (see *Holt* v. *Holt* [1990] 3 NZLR 401) and so control is better managed through restricting share rights in the constitutional documents. Growth shares with greater rights to capital can be given to particular family members if desirable. The right to appoint directors can be retained by the founders and children can become involved in the running the FIC as and when appropriate taking all circumstances into account. Depending on asset values, a voting share might be held in a family trust.

Business property relief (BPR) and business asset disposal relief (BADR) do not apply

As the name indicates, a FIC is an investment company and it does not therefore qualify for BPR for IHT purposes, or BADR for capital gains tax (CGT). It will often be advisable to create a separate company to maintain a separation between trading and investment activities in order to preserve any reliefs.

Asset protection is often a key objective of estate planning, with a particular concern being the divorce of a family member

The articles and shareholders' agreement can be drafted to deal with these specific risks, with provision for shareholdings to be recalled in certain circumstances and generally by restricting transfer rights on death, divorce and bankruptcy. In some cases it may be appropriate to have some shares in the FIC owned by a discretionary trust for the benefit of children and/or grandchildren. A trust provides a useful solution to enabling flexibility to benefit an unborn class of beneficiaries. This is typically done by issuing a share to be held in trust. Such a share would not normally have an automatic right to income. Income can be declared at the directors' discretion when it is needed to provide for a beneficiary of the trust. The trust would exclude the founder and their spouse as potential beneficiaries.

There are disadvantages to the FIC structure

The cost of setting up and running the FIC, along with the potential for double taxation, must be weighed against the tax disadvantages of a trust structure. Using an unlimited company will give the exemption from filing accounts at Companies House, but the FICs articles and details of shareholders, directors and people with significant control will be publicly available.

22.3.3 How to fund a FIC

A FIC can be funded by a loan or share capital. Cash can be loaned to the company or used to subscribe for shares. Alternatively, other assets can be sold to the company in return for shares or with the consideration left outstanding as a debt to the shareholders.

Share capital

Cash or other assets can be transferred to the FIC in exchange for shares. It will often be preferable to subscribe for shares with cash to avoid a potential CGT charge on a sale of other assets to the FIC. Gifts to companies can trigger an immediate IHT liability, so the transfer should be for market value with consideration in the form of a loan or issue of shares to the transferor.

Funding using a loan

Typically the founders of the FIC will lend cash or sell assets to it in exchange for a loan note. The loan route is typically used as this usually enables a tax-free transfer and flexible return of capital. The loan can be interest-free and repayable on demand, or otherwise have a fixed term for repayment to avoid the risk of a chargeable transfer for IHT occurring. It is thought that by making a loan subject to a commercial rate of interest it is less open to any challenge by HMRC and therefore strengthens the planning. The founders will have the flexibility to withdraw value from the FIC in the form of loan repayments and could assign the benefit of the loan to children or other family members in the future. While the founder might not need access to capital, a loan does also enable a tax-efficient withdrawal of capital for other shareholders who otherwise would not be able to realise capital, but the loan remains a chargeable asset in the estate of the founder. If a capital need for the next generation is perceived, then usually some form of redeemable preference shares would be issued in addition to alphabet shares. (Different classes of shares, created for different shareholders, are commonly referred to as 'alphabet shares' as these separate share classes are identifiable by a specific letter.)

22.3.4 Inheritance tax

There will not usually be any IHT implications at the funding stage as there will be no initial loss to the estate of the founder. It should be noted that if redeemable preference shares are being created then the intended donee (or their bare trustee) should subscribe direct for them to prevent a base cost valuation issue arising for CGT.

The IHT benefit is gained through making a gift of shares when the company has been formed. A gift of shares will be a potentially exempt transfer (PET) for IHT purposes, as an outright gift, so the founder can potentially transfer value substantially higher than the NRB without an immediate charge to IHT. Taper relief will give an incremental reduction to the IHT payable if the donor dies within 3–7 years of the transfer. The absence of an immediate IHT charge on a significant transfer of value is one of the key benefits of using a FIC rather than a trust structure. The capital value of the FIC can then continue to grow in the hands of the children rather than the founders. If the shares in the FIC are held by more than one child, the value of each holding is likely to be discounted for IHT purposes.

If a trust is used to hold some or all of the FIC shares, it will be subject to the relevant property regime for IHT, discussed in detail at **Chapter 7**.

22.3.5 Other taxes

A gift or issue of FIC shares by the founders could give rise to a chargeable gain in certain circumstances. Transfers of assets other than cash to the FIC may attract CGT and stamp duty or stamp duty land tax (SDLT).

The FIC's liability to SDLT will need to be considered if property is being transferred to the FIC. Transfers of additional residential property attract the additional three per cent charge (Finance Act (FA) 2003, s.53) and property valued over £500,000 will attract SDLT of 15 per cent on the entire value unless it falls within one of the reliefs (FA 2003, Sched.4ZA).

Although there can be significant IHT benefits to the FIC structure, there is potential for double taxation on profits at company and shareholder level. Income and gains in the FIC will generally be taxed at 19 per cent corporation tax, although most dividends received are exempt from corporation tax (Corporation Tax Act (CTA) 2009, s.931A).

Any dividends paid to shareholders will be taxed at their marginal rate above the first £1,000 (for 2020/21) each year. On liquidation, the gains on the share disposals would be taxable to CGT at either 10 or 20 per cent.

22.3.6 Use of a discretionary trust

A trust can be used to hold some or all of the shares in a FIC to give further flexibility and asset protection. Parents may not want shares in the names of their children and/or may want the flexibility to benefit future generations. A discretionary trust can have a class of potential beneficiaries that includes children and grandchildren, with the power to add further beneficiaries if desirable.

A gift of shares to a trust would be a chargeable lifetime transfer for IHT, so the founders could transfer assets up to their available NRB to the trust, but anything over that would give an immediate 20 per cent IHT charge. There would be the option of holdover relief for assets attracting CGT. The trust can then subscribe for shares at par value and loan funds to the FIC. Alternatively, the founders can transfer shares in the FIC to the trust before it has any assets and then loan funds to the FIC, with the trust enjoying the growth in value going forward.

Typical planning involves holding one share with limited value in a trust, for example a 'G' share, to provide for future grandchildren. If a voting share is to be held in trust, the implications for the charges in the relevant property regime must be considered. A balanced decision will need to be taken on the facts contrasting the perceived control aspect against a likely tax cost.

22.3.7 Anti-avoidance and potential risks

The IHT reservation of benefit rules may need to be considered if the founders continue to receive remuneration for services from the FIC. Where loans are used, the settlements income tax anti-avoidance legislation may need to be considered

(Income Tax Act (ITA) 2007, s.701 and HMRC's TSEM4015). The FIC structure will be most beneficial from an IHT planning perspective if it is created from surplus assets which the donor wants to pass on as soon as appropriate.

Anti-avoidance legislation will need careful consideration in certain circumstances – particularly in the context of loans to the FIC. The transactions in securities rules (ITA 2007, ss.682–713)) will re-designate capital distributions as income distributions in a wide range of circumstances and could affect the treatment of loan repayments from the FIC. HMRC has indicated that loans could be caught by the settlements legislation for income tax (Income Tax (Trading and Other Income) Act (ITTOIA) 2005, ss.619–648), resulting in income from the FIC being taxable on the lender.

The winding-up of the FIC will require consideration of the targeted anti-avoidance rule (TAAR) (introduced in FA 2016), which applies to distributions on the winding-up of a close company where at least five per cent of the ordinary share capital and voting rights are held by the taxpayer. Under the TAAR, a distribution is treated as an income distribution instead of a capital distribution if at any time in the two years following the distribution, the recipient is involved with a trade or activity similar to the one carried on by the company wound up and the reduction of income tax is one of the main motives (ITTOIA 2005, s.369B). The general anti-abuse rule (GAAR) and disclosure of tax avoidance schemes (DOTAS) (see **4.7**) provisions may also need consideration, particularly for more complex arrangements.

The potential for future changes to the treatment of close company distributions should be borne in mind when considering a FIC structure. HMRC has previously indicated a dislike of 'money-boxing' whereby surplus undistributed profits are retained within a company until capital tax treatment on liquidation, rather than being distributed to shareholders as dividends. HMRC's consultation in 2015 discussed the possibility of amending the existing legislation and re-introducing some form of the close company apportionment rule, where undistributed profits would be apportioned to shareholders as a deemed distribution (see **www.gov.uk/government/consultations/company-distributions**).

Further to a public access information request made in early 2020, it was publicised in the *Financial Times* that HMRC had set up a special taskforce to review the use of FICs. It is understood that structures with a value in excess of £20 million and involving family offices are being scrutinised due to a perceived lack of accurate tax reporting.

22.4 FAMILY LIMITED PARTNERSHIPS

22.4.1 Introduction

An FLP:

- is a limited partnership – not a separate legal entity;
- is used to manage wealth across multiple generations;

- requires active management of assets;
- has no IHT relevant property charges;
- has regulation and cost implications.

FLPs are used less frequently for estate planning other than in estates of considerable size, for example over £10 million. This is largely due to the cost implications of managing family wealth in an FLP. FLPs are usually used to manage and transfer multi-generational wealth. Unlike a FIC, the FLP is not a separate legal entity distinct from the individual partners.

22.4.2 Structure and funding

An FLP is established under the Limited Partnerships Act 1907. The structure must include a general partner who manages the business of the partnership and at least one limited partner. The limited partners are not liable for debts or obligations of the FLP beyond what they have contributed. The limited partners are not allowed to take part in the management of the business. Usually a parent will be the general partner and then other family members can invest as limited partners. If the family transfers assets other than cash then CGT will need to be considered.

The FLP will usually be funded by parents or grandparents who may not be limited partners themselves. The gift of funds to the FLP on behalf of a child or grandchild will be a PET for IHT purposes.

22.4.3 Running the FLP

Generally the business of an FLP will be holding and managing the underlying partnership assets. The business must be carried on with a view to making a profit in accordance with normal partnership principles, so simply holding assets as investments without any active management will not be sufficient. The partnership agreement will require careful drafting, particularly when it comes to transfers of partnership interests and capital withdrawal.

The general partner can be an individual or a corporate entity. Consideration of the reservation of benefit rules is necessary where an individual will be paid for their services as general partner or benefit from the FLP via a corporate general partner.

22.4.4 Practical considerations

FLPs can be an attractive long-term planning option for families with significant surplus wealth. The structure enables the founders to retain a significant degree of control of the family wealth while potentially transferring larger amounts more tax efficiently than via a trust structure. As with a FIC structure, an FLP will not attract a 20 per cent IHT charge or ongoing relevant property charges in the same way as trusts. The tax transparency of the structure may also be attractive.

There are complicated tax and non-tax issues to consider before using an FLP structure. FLPs are likely to be classified as a collective investment scheme, which will mean additional regulation and cost implications, although this may be offset to some extent by the saving of IHT relevant property charges for trusts. The terms of the partnership agreement and the role and structure of the general partner will need careful consideration.

CHAPTER 23

Grossing up, etc. on death

Anthony Nixon

23.1 KEY POINTS

This chapter covers the following:

- **Simple grossing up:** This is the classic form of grossing up.
- **Charity gifts and 36 per cent inheritance tax (IHT):** A different grossing up calculation applies where at least 10 per cent of the 'baseline amount' is given to charity.
- **Double (or 'four-stage') grossing up**.
- **Abatement:** A grossed up legacy for IHT can never exceed the value of the taxable estate and so abates to that value.
- **Inheritance Tax Act (IHTA) 1984, s.39A:** This section comes into play in estates which are partly exempt and partly taxable, and which include assets that qualify for business property relief (BPR) and/or agricultural property relief (APR). However, for some assets s.39A does not apply and can be ignored.

23.2 INTRODUCTION

Where part of an estate on death is exempt from IHT and another part is not, it is often necessary to carry out a grossing up, or other, calculation, in order to work out how much IHT must be paid.

The way the rules work means that, often, a variation within IHTA 1984, s.142 can change the tax calculation. If the change results in less IHT to pay, it may be advantageous for beneficiaries to join in a variation together and share the IHT saving.

The rules are set out in IHTA 1984, ss.36–42, which make up Chapter III of Part II of IHTA 1984, and, as is demonstrated by the extracts quoted in this chapter, are one of the most difficult parts of the IHT legislation to understand.

In theory, the rules can apply to lifetime transfers of value, but they are most commonly encountered when there is an IHT charge on death. This chapter deals only with the rules on death.

It is usually the exemptions for gifts to spouses and to charities, in IHTA 1984, ss.19 and 23, that are relevant, but the rules can also apply to the IHT exemptions in:

- s.24 – certain political parties;
- s.24A – housing associations;
- ss.25 and 26A – national purposes (national museums, art galleries, libraries, etc.);
- s.30 – heritage property.

It is not helpful that this part of IHTA 1984 describes all non-residuary gifts in a will as specific gifts. This expression covers not only what lawyers know as specific legacies (gifts of particular assets) but also what are called general legacies and demonstrative legacies, including gifts of cash, forgiving loans, paying IHT that would otherwise be payable by the recipients of lifetime gifts, and the spouse's statutory legacy on intestacy.

In this chapter we use the word 'legacy' for what the legislation calls specific gifts. The term 'residuary gifts' has its normal meaning.

Two general points on these rules:

1. The rules are applied separately to separate 'titles' of assets passing on a death. For example, the following are all separate titles and must be looked at independently:

   - the free estate;
   - assets in which the deceased had a qualifying interest in possession;
   - joint assets passing by survivorship; and
   - assets in which the deceased reserved a benefit.

   In practice, the rules usually only apply to the free estate.
2. The figures used in calculating the amount of any exemptions will not necessarily reflect the actual values on which IHT is payable. Some of the calculations use notional IHT figures. If there is aggregated property, such as a qualifying interest in possession (QIIP), the actual IHT will always be different from the notional figures.

For more information see HMRC's *Inheritance Tax Manual* IHTM26001–26214. However, take great care in applying these paragraphs, because many of the examples have clearly not been updated for some years, and some use an out-of-date nil rate band (NRB).

23.3 SIMPLE GROSSING UP

23.3.1 Overview

The classic, and simplest, form of grossing up is needed when a will leaves:

- one or more substantial legacies to taxable beneficiaries, which are free of IHT; and
- residue to one or more exempt beneficiaries.

If the legacies to taxable beneficiaries are over the available IHT threshold, one must calculate the corresponding 'gross' gift: this is the amount that would have to have been given, if the legacy had been subject to its own IHT, in order to end up with the same net value.

The arithmetic is relatively straightforward, at least when compared with calculations later in this chapter – the steps are as follows:

- Work out the available NRB (allowing for gifts in the seven years before death, transferable NRB, etc.) and deduct it from the net of IHT total of the legacies to taxable beneficiaries. (At this stage ignore assets aggregable on death, such as interests in possession – in this part of the calculation the NRB does not have to be shared.)
- If the result is nil or negative, no grossing up is needed.
- If the result is positive, calculate 100/60ths of that result and add back to it the available NRB.
- That total is the amount of the grossed up legacy.

The 100/60ths fraction follows from the fact that, after taking 40 per cent IHT from the amount of the legacy which exceeds the NRB, 60 per cent is left. More simply, 100/60ths can be expressed as 5/3rds.

Any aggregable gifts are now brought back into the overall IHT calculation, using the grossed up legacy, calculated as above.

Example 23.1

Trevor died on 1 November 2019 leaving a free estate of £1,000,000 and with an aggregable interest in possession in a trust worth £350,000, whose assets pass direct to his children. He made no gifts in the seven years before his death and none of his assets qualify for special reliefs.

Trevor's will gives:

- £200,000 free of IHT to each of his two children;
- residue to Trevor's (first and only) wife Tilly absolutely.

All of the aggregable trust is liable to IHT but, as outlined above, only the taxable legacies in the free estate have to be grossed up.

The legacies total £400,000. The grossing up calculation is:

- Deduct £325,000 NRB from the total gifts of £400,000: this leaves £75,000.
- Gross up by 5/3: this is £125,000.
- Add back the NRB of £325,000; the gross taxable gift is £450,000.
- The remaining £550,000 of the free estate is the spouse-exempt gift of residue to Tilly.

Doing the calculation backwards confirms that the grossing up is correct. If Trevor had given £450,000 to his children, subject to those legacies bearing their own IHT, IHT would have been £50,000 (40% of (£450,000 – £325,000) or 40% of £125,000), leaving £400,000.

Because of the aggregable settled property, this is not the end of calculating IHT on Trevor's estate. The taxable £450,000 in the free estate now has to be added to the £350,000 trust, to give a total taxable value of £800,000. The actual IHT is £190,000 (40% of (£800,000 – £325,000) or 40% of £475,000). This has to be apportioned 450:350 between free estate and trust, so that £106,875 (and not £50,000) is payable from the free estate and £83,125 from the trust.

Each of the children receives:

- £200,000 free of IHT; and
- half of the £350,000 trust assets less £83,125 IHT payable from the trust.

Tilly receives residue which is £1,000,000 less:

- £400,000 legacies to children;
- £106,875 IHT payable from the free estate.
- All other testamentary expenses.

23.3.2 Planning point 1

If Trevor's aggregable interest in possession was one in existence on 22 March 2006, the aggregation with Trevor's free estate could have been avoided if, during Trevor's lifetime, the trustees had arranged for Tilly to have an interest in possession on Trevor's death. Tilly's interest would be a transitional serial interest and the ending of Trevor's interest on his death would obtain the spouse exemption. Ending Tilly's interest some months afterwards would be a potentially exempt transfer (PET).

In the author's view this could be done even if Tilly was not a beneficiary of the trust, provided the trustees had a power of advancement, either under Trustee Act 1925, s.32 or otherwise, which could be exercised over the whole of Trevor's interest. Creating a transitional serial interest for Tilly in these circumstances would clearly be for the benefit of the remainder beneficiaries since it would, at least, defer and, if Tilly lived long enough, eliminate the IHT that would otherwise be payable on the trust on Trevor's death.

Unfortunately it is too late to do anything about this after Trevor's death.

23.3.3 Planning point 2

IHT on the gifts to Trevor's children might be saved, even after Trevor's death, if, by IHTA 1984, s.142 variation, those gifts were redirected to Tilly, either absolutely, or on immediate post-death interest (IPDI) trusts, and she subsequently made the gifts.

Beware the case of *Lau* v. *HMRC* [2009] STC (SCD) 352 where it was decided that an understanding that the spouse would make gifts back was held to be consideration under IHTA 1984, s.142(3), so that the variation (or, in that case, disclaimer) did not meet the conditions of s.142.

A better plan is for the s.142 variation to put in place an interest in possession for the spouse, which is deemed to start from death and so treated as a spouse-exempt IPDI, and for the trustees to have the power to end it. There is then no consideration outside the variation, so s.142(3) ceases to be a problem.

While it is not absolutely clear, it is best for the spouse's interest not to end in the two years after death, when it is arguable that it falls foul of s.142(4).

23.4 CHARITY GIFTS AND 36 PER CENT INHERITANCE TAX

23.4.1 Overview

The grossing up fraction is different if IHTA 1984, Sched.1A applies, so that the estate qualifies for the reduced 36 per cent IHT rate. This depends on at least 10 per cent of the 'baseline amount' being given to charity.

Broadly, the baseline amount is the taxable value of the estate, after deducting both available NRB and all exemptions and reliefs, other than charity relief under IHTA 1984, s.23.

Example 23.2

Peter, who was divorced from his wife many years ago, died on 1 November 2019. His estate was worth £1,100,000. He had made gifts in the seven years before his death using all of his £325,000 NRB. There are no other assets to be aggregated for IHT on Peter's death and none of his assets qualify for special reliefs.

Peter's will gives:

- £300,000 free of IHT to each of his two children;
- residue to Cancer Research UK.

On the face of it, the gift to Cancer Research qualifies the estate for the 36% IHT rate.

But does it? Grossing up the £600,000 legacies by 5/3 makes the taxable value £1,000,000, and reduces the charitable residue to £100,000 (the 'donated amount'), which is less than 10% of the baseline amount (in this case, the total £1,100,000 value of the estate).

Fortunately, IHTA 1984, Sched.1A, para.6 tells us that, in order to check whether the donated amount is 10% or more of the baseline amount, we gross up using 36%. The grossing up fraction is then 100/64 (as opposed to 100/60 or 5/3 for 40%).

Grossing up £600,000 at 100/64 gives £937,500. This leaves a residue of £162,500, which is clearly more than 10% of £1,100,000.

Again, we can check back and see that 36% IHT on £937,500 would be £337,500, leaving a net £600,000.

23.4.2 Planning point 3

Qualifying for the 10 per cent charity exemption is another area where IHTA 1984, s.142 variations can increase the sum of human happiness.

Suppose Peter's estate were worth only £1,025,000. Grossing up the £600,000 legacies at 100/64 would be £937,500, leaving Cancer Research with a notional £87,500, about 8.5 per cent of the £1,025,000 baseline amount. So the 36 per cent rate is not available and we must gross up the non-charity legacies at 40 per cent. As above, this makes the taxable amount of the legacies £1,000,000, IHT £400,000 and the charity now gets only £25,000 (if that is not all consumed in administration expenses!).

If Peter's children were prepared to forgo just £5,000 each of the legacies to them, grossing up those legacies of £590,000 at 100/64 would make them £921,875. This would leave a notional residuary charity gift of £103,125 (£1,025,000 – £921,875) which is more than 10 per cent of the baseline amount of £1,025,000.

23.5 DOUBLE (OR 'FOUR STAGE') GROSSING UP

23.5.1 Overview

This more intricate procedure is needed if either:

- some taxable legacies are free of IHT and others bear their own IHT; or
- only part of residue is exempt;

or:

- both of the above.

Now we are within IHTA 1984, ss.38(4) and (5), which read:

> (4) Where the specific gifts not bearing their own tax are not the only gifts with respect to which the transfer is or might be chargeable, the amount referred to in subsection (1) above [the grossed up value of the net of IHT legacies] is such amount as, after deduction of tax at the assumed rate specified in subsection (5) below, would be equal to the sum of the value of those gifts.
>
> (5) For the purposes of subsection (4) above –
>
> (a) the assumed rate is the rate found by dividing the assumed amount of tax by that part of the value transferred with respect to which the transfer would be chargeable on the hypothesis that–
>
> (i) the amount corresponding to the value of specific gifts not bearing their own tax is equal to the aggregate referred to in subsection (3) above, and
>
> (ii) the parts of the value transferred attributable to specific gifts and to gifts of residue or shares in residue are determined accordingly; and
>
> (b) the assumed amount of tax is the amount that would be charged on the value transferred on the hypothesis mentioned in paragraph (a) above.

HMRC describes this as 'four-stage grossing up' and, usefully, sets out the process in IHTM26152. The four stages are:

1. Gross up legacies to taxable beneficiaries that are free of IHT, as described under simple grossing up (**23.3**).
2. Add that grossed up amount to:

   – any legacies to taxable beneficiaries that are subject to their own IHT; and
   – any legacies to exempt beneficiaries;

   and deduct the total from the value of the net estate to find an initial, notional, value for residue. Then, if necessary, divide that notional residue into taxable and exempt parts, as provided for in the will, and find the 'initial determination of the chargeable estate', made up of the total of:

   – grossed up value of free of IHT legacies to taxable beneficiaries;
   – legacies to taxable beneficiaries which bear their own IHT; and
   – non-exempt part of initial residue value.

3. Re-gross up free of IHT legacies to taxable beneficiaries, now using the estate rate that would apply to the notional initial value for the chargeable estate determined at stage 2.
4. Repeat stage 2, with the revised grossed up figure from stage 3, to arrive at the actual values of the taxable and exempt parts of the estate.

Example 23.3

June died on 15 November 2019 leaving a free estate of £2,500,000. No assets qualify for special reliefs, there is no lifetime cumulation and there are no aggregable assets.

June's will gives:

- house and chattels (total value £625,000) to her husband Jerry;
- a legacy of £475,000 free of IHT to her daughter (from her first marriage, which ended in divorce) Denise;
- half the residue to Jerry;
- the other half of residue to Denise.

Stage 1

Gross up the legacy of £475,000 to Denise – following simple procedure outlined above:

£325,000 + 5/3 of (£475,000 – 325,000) = £575,000

Stage 2

Initial determination of the chargeable part of the estate:

Adding gross legacy to Denise (£575,000) to exempt legacy to Jerry (£625,000) – total £1,200,000 leaves an initial value for residue of £1,300,000.

Exempt half given to Jerry and taxable half given to Denise are both £650,000.

Initial chargeable estate is gross legacy to Denise (£575,000) plus taxable half of residue (£650,000) = £1,225,000.

Stage 3

Re-gross free of IHT legacy at the estate rate that would apply if the chargeable estate was £1,225,000:

IHT on £1,225,000 would be 40% of (£1,225,000 – £325,000) or £360,000, an estate rate of £360,000/£1,225,000 or 29.38775%.

The technical way to gross Denise's IHT-free £475,000 is to multiply by 100/(100 – 29.38775); this is 100/70.61225.

A simpler method is to calculate the post-IHT value of the chargeable estate of £1,225,000 (£1,225,000 – £360,000 = £865,000) and multiply Denise's IHT-free £475,000 by £1,225,000/£865,000.

By either method, the grossed legacy is now £672,687.

Stage 4

Final calculation of the chargeable part of the estate:

Adding regrossed legacy to Denise (£672,687) to exempt legacy to Jerry (£625,000) (which totals £1,297,687) leaves a residue of £1,202,313.

Exempt half given to Jerry and taxable half given to Denise are both £601,156.50.

Value of the part of June's estate liable to IHT is regrossed legacy to Denise (£672,687) plus taxable half of residue (£601,156.50) = £1,273,843.50.

Actual IHT is 40% of (£1,273,843.50 – £325,000) or £379,537.40. Note that this is not the same as the notional IHT at Stage 3.

Nor, of course, would the actual IHT be the same if there were aggregable assets, as in **Example 23.1**.

23.5.2 Planning point

Just as under **Example 23.1** an IHTA 1984, s.142 variation could save IHT. There are a number of possibilities, but, as in **23.3.2**, the best option might be an interest in possession for Jerry in the whole estate, to be ended by a PET to Denise at a later time.

23.6 ABATEMENT

Abatement for the purposes of calculating IHT is not the same as abatement of legacies in administration, although both will often arise in the same estate and may have the same, or a similar, practical result.

A grossed up legacy for IHT can never exceed the value of the taxable estate and so abates to that value.

Example 23.4

Dave inherits an investment property worth £1.3 million from his uncle William, who left the residue of his £1.6 million net estate to charity.

Simple grossing up of £1,300,000 ((5/3 x (£1,300,000 – £325,000)) + £325,000) would be £1,950,000. However, this does not mean that IHT is payable on £1,950,000. It cannot be payable on more than the actual net estate of £1.6 million.

The IHT exhausts the residuary estate, so that the charities receive nothing and Dave has to pay some of the IHT out of his legacy.

23.7 IHTA 1984, S.39A ('INTERACTION' IS HMRC'S NAME)

23.7.1 Overview

IHTA 1984, s.39A comes into play only in estates which are partly exempt and partly taxable, and which include assets that qualify for BPR under IHTA 1984, s.106 and/or APR under s.116. However, s.39A does not apply, and can be ignored, if all assets that qualify for BPR and/or APR are the subject of legacies to taxable beneficiaries:

> (1) Where any part of the value transferred by a transfer of value is attributable to –
>
> (a) the value of relevant business property, or
> (b) the agricultural value of agricultural property,
>
> then, for the purpose of attributing the value transferred (as reduced in accordance with section 104 or 116 below), to specific gifts and gifts of residue or shares of residue, sections 38 and 39 above shall have effect subject to the following provisions of this section.
>
> (2) The value of any specific gifts of relevant business property or agricultural property shall be taken to be their value as reduced in accordance with section 104 or 116 below.
>
> (3) The value of any specific gifts not falling within subsection (2) above shall be taken to be the appropriate fraction of their value.
>
> (4) In subsection (3) above 'the appropriate fraction' means a fraction of which –
>
> (a) the numerator is the difference between the value transferred and the value, reduced as mentioned in subsection (2) above, of any gifts falling within that subsection, and
> (b) the denominator is the difference between the unreduced value transferred and the value, before the reduction mentioned in subsection (2) above, of any gifts falling within that subsection;

and in paragraph (b) above 'the unreduced value transferred' means the amount which would be the value transferred by the transfer but for the reduction required by sections 104 and 116 below.

(5) If or to the extent that specific gifts fall within paragraphs (a) and (b) of subsection (1) of section 38 above, the amount corresponding to the value of the gifts shall be arrived at in accordance with subsections (3) to (5) of that section by reference to their value reduced as mentioned in subsection (2) or, as the case may be, subsection (3) of this section.

(6) For the purposes of this section the value of a specific gift of relevant business property or agricultural property does not include the value of any other gift payable out of that property; and that other gift shall not itself be treated as a specific gift of relevant business property or agricultural property.

The object of the rules is to prevent a double discount, by claiming both spouse/charity exemption and BPR/APR on the same value. This is done by reducing the value of non-residuary legacies in line with the proportion the taxable value of the estate (i.e. the value after any BPR and APR) bears to its total value. That proportion is called, in s.39A, 'the appropriate fraction' (IHTM calls it the 's.39A fraction').

As with everything else in this part of IHTA 1984, the reduction is made only in order to calculate how much of the estate liable to IHT qualifies for exemption.

Example 23.5

Harry's estate consists of assets qualifying for 100% BPR worth £800,000 and non-relievable property worth £600,000 (total value £1,400,000).

Harry's will includes a cash legacy of £550,000 to his widow Doris and gives the rest of his estate to his children.

The IHTA 1984, s.39A rules prevent the whole £550,000 spouse legacy being deducted from the taxable value of the estate, to leave only £50,000 taxable.

This is done by reducing the legacy to Doris (the only non-residuary legacy in this case) by the appropriate fraction. The appropriate fraction is £600,000/£1,400,000 so that spouse exemption is available for only 6/14ths of the gift to Doris, or £235,714. IHT is therefore payable on £364,286 (£600,000 – £235,714).

23.7.2 Planning point 5

Again, if Doris and the children agree, they could rewrite the will to include legacies of the farm business plus cash of £50,000 to the children and to give residue to Doris. This would not be affected by IHTA 1984, s.39A, so that only the £50,000 legacy would be liable to IHT. If the farm business is to be sold, the practical result, apart from this tax saving, is the same.

The same rules give a measure of relief to taxable gifts by restricting the amount of any grossing up, because legacies left free of IHT are grossed up only after they have been reduced to the appropriate fraction.

Where an asset qualifying for BPR or APR is specifically given, its value is ignored in arriving at the s.39A appropriate fraction. This is why the rules have no application (see **6.2** above) where the only gifts with BPR/APR are the subject of non-residuary legacies.

HMRC's manual IHTM26129 outlines a six-step process for applying the s.39A rules.

1. Apply BPR and/or APR to the net value of the free estate without, at this stage, allowing any spouse or charity, etc. relief. In technical IHT terms this is 'the value transferred by the transfer of value' (the value for IHT of the property devolving under the deceased's will or intestacy). (As with the grossing up rules, ignore property devolving under any other title such as aggregated IIP trusts, joint assets passing by survivorship or assets in which benefit has been reserved.)
2. Identify the value, before and after relief, of any non-residuary legacy of assets qualifying for BPR and/or APR.
3. If any assets qualifying for BPR and/or APR pass other than by non-residuary legacies, reduce any other non-residuary legacies (whether or not they qualify for spouse, charity, etc. relief) by the appropriate fraction. Their values for the purposes of allocating exemptions are their reduced values.
4. Where grossing up is necessary, gross up the reduced value of taxable legacies.
5. Calculate the value of residue using the reduced values, with grossing up where it applies.
6. The value of the free estate liable to IHT is now:

   – the value transferred (as Step 1); minus
   – the total of the reduced values of any exempt specific and residuary gifts.

CHAPTER 24

Introduction to business asset disposal relief (formerly Entrepreneurs' Relief)

Liz Beadsley

24.1 KEY POINTS

- Business asset disposal relief (BADR) reduces the effective rate of capital gains tax (CGT) to 10 per cent on a material disposal of business assets by individuals up to a lifetime limit of £1 million of gains.
- What qualifies as a material disposal of business assets depends on whether the individual is in business on their own as a sole trader, a partner in a partnership, or a shareholder in their personal company. Trustees can also benefit from this lower rate of CGT in certain circumstances.
- The legislation for BADR is to be found in Taxation of Chargeable Gains Act (TCGA) 1992, ss.169H–169V.
- This chapter addresses a number of concepts, which determine whether this relief applies and how it works, including:
  - what are qualifying disposals by individuals;
  - the disposal of part of a business;
  - what is a personal company, a trading company, an associated disposal of an asset;
  - what is the qualifying period of ownership; and
  - qualifying disposals by trustees;

  as well as the amount of relief (substantially reduced in 2020); the interaction with other reliefs; and investors' relief.

24.2 BUSINESS ASSET DISPOSAL RELIEF AND IHT PLANNING

BADR (formerly entrepreneurs' relief (ER)) is a business relief from CGT, but it is relevant to inheritance tax (IHT) planning in three respects:

1. **A gift of business assets:** It is important to note the consequences for CGT/BADR: how will any gift of a business, interest in a business or a

business asset be treated for CGT; will any gain be taxable; and what will happen to any rights to BADR that have built up?

2. **The long-term treatment of CGT may affect IHT planning:** In considering the right structures of ownership and benefit, including arrangements between spouses, the potential shape of BADR may affect investment in businesses and choices as to when (if at all) to make lifetime gifts of any business assets.
3. **Interaction with CGT holdover relief on gifts of assets:** While any gift of assets needs to take account of the capital gain, business assets can benefit from 'holdover' relief so that the gain is passed on to the new owner, and how IHT and CGT interact is important.

24.3 QUALIFYING DISPOSALS BY INDIVIDUALS

A material disposal of business assets is:

- for a sole trader or partner in a partnership, the disposal of the whole or part of the business;
- for a partner, the disposal of the whole or part of their interest in a partnership.

Where an asset has previously been used in the business it can also qualify if disposed of within three years after the business has ceased.

24.4 DISPOSAL OF PART OF A BUSINESS

When only some of the assets of the business are sold, the important question for BADR is whether a part of a business has been disposed of. A disposal of a business asset or assets is not necessarily a disposal of the whole or part of a business and the outcome will depend on the facts of each case.

This is a similar provision to one that concerned a predecessor to BADR, retirement relief, and there are a number of decided cases concerning retirement relief, mostly concerning farming businesses, that can help.

The main cases, including *McGregor* v. *Adcock* (51TC692); *Atkinson* v. *Dancer* (61TC598); and *Mannion* v. *Johnston* (61TC598) are detailed in HMRC's *Capital Gains Manual* at CG64020 and CG64021, and discussed at CG64030.

The activities included in the disposal need to be capable of being carried on independently as a business for relief to be due. If an asset or assets have been sold but no particular activity or set of activities went with the asset disposal, that would not be a disposal of part of the business and relief would not be due.

For example, in *McGregor* v. *Adcock* a distinction was drawn between the sale of part of a business and the sale of individual business assets. In this case, farmland of 4.8 acres was sold – substantially the same business continued after the sale as had been carried on before and therefore relief was not due as there was no disposal of any part of that business.

24.5 PERSONAL COMPANY

A disposal of shares or securities in a trading company or holding company of a trading group that is also the individual's *personal company* will qualify as a material disposal.

For a company to be the individual's 'personal company', the individual has to:

- be an officer or employee of the company or of one or more companies in the group;

and either:

- hold at least five per cent of the *ordinary share capital* of the company and be able to exercise at least five per cent of voting rights in the company, and either or both (the 'economic interest' test applying to disposals after 28 October 2018):
  - by virtue of that holding, the individual is beneficially entitled to at least five per cent of the profits available for distribution to equity holders and, on a winding up, would be beneficially entitled to at least five per cent of the assets; or
  - in the event of a disposal of the whole of the ordinary share capital of the company, the individual would be beneficially entitled to at least five per cent of the proceeds; or
- for disposals on or after 6 April 2013, the shares were acquired by the individual on or after 6 April 2012 on the exercise of an option under the Enterprise Management Initiative (EMI) scheme.

24.6 ORDINARY SHARE CAPITAL

Ordinary share capital means all of a company's issued share capital (however described) other than capital the holders of which have a right to a dividend at a fixed rate but have no other right to share in the company's profits. It is the nominal value of the ordinary shares that has to be taken into account rather than the number of shares or amount subscribed.

24.7 TRADING COMPANY

The legislation defines a 'trading company' as a company which carries on trading activities and does not carry on other activities to a substantial extent.

A 'trading group' is defined as a group of companies, one or more of which carries on trading activities, and whose members' activities taken together do not include activities other than trading activities to a substantial extent.

HMRC's views on what is considered substantial are contained in CG64090 and define it as more than 20 per cent.

This is the 'trading threshold' to which the Office of Tax Simplification (OTS) compared the IHT trading threshold for BPR in its report on IHT in July 2019 (*Inheritance Tax Review – second report: Simplifying the design of Inheritance Tax*). The logic of the OTS was to bring the two thresholds into line, which would mean increasing the BPR threshold from at least 50 per cent to 80 per cent, even though they operate rather differently.

> **Tip**
>
> In any planning with business clients, it is worth advising them that this threshold may change, so that any decisions on the balance between trading and investment activity (such as letting out premises for rental income) can factor in possible change.

There are a number of factors that can be taken into account when reviewing the status of a company, and the following are set out in CG64090:

- income from non-trading activities;
- the asset base of the company;
- expenses incurred, or time spent, by officers and employees of the company in undertaking its activities;
- the company's history;
- balance of indicators – some indicators may point one way whilst the rest point the other way and therefore the relevance of each will need to be weighed up in the context of the particular case and looked at in the round.

24.8 ASSOCIATED DISPOSAL OF AN ASSET

A disposal of an asset that has been held by a partner or employee personally and used in the business of the partnership or company (or group) employing the individual, and where the disposal is associated with a material disposal by the partner or employee under one of the circumstances already outlined, can also qualify for BADR.

Broadly, for it to be a *material disposal* for the purposes of an associated disposal of an asset, an individual must dispose of:

- at least a five per cent interest in the assets of a partnership; or
- if the partnership interest is less than five per cent, all of that interest; or
- five per cent of the ordinary shares in, or securities of a company (or interests in such shares or securities) that is the individual's personal company, or the shares or securities disposed of are at least five per cent of the value of the securities of the company.

There must be a link between the 'material disposal of business assets' and the 'associated disposal' for BADR to be due in respect of the associated disposal. The condition is satisfied when both disposals together constitute part of the process of 'withdrawal from participation in the business'.

Relief will not be due unless the disposal of the asset owned by the individual (rather than the partnership or company) is related to the individual's reduction of their interest in the assets of the partnership, or holding in the company, as the case may be.

While goodwill is included in the definition of a business asset, where the disposal is made to a close company where the person owns five per cent of the ordinary share capital or five per cent voting rights of the purchasing company any gain will not qualify for relief. What this means is that relief will not be available on incorporation of a sole trader or partnership.

24.9 QUALIFYING PERIOD

The individual has to meet all the qualifying conditions throughout a period of two years (one year prior to 6 April 2019) ending with:

- the disposal of the whole or part of a business, or shares in their personal company; or
- for a disposal following the cessation of business or of shares in a company that has ceased to be a trading company or member of a trading group, the date the business ceased.

For shares acquired under an EMI scheme, the period from grant of the option to exercise counts towards the two-year period.

24.10 QUALIFYING DISPOSALS BY TRUSTEES

The disposal of an asset, which includes company shares and securities by certain trustees where there is a qualifying beneficiary may qualify for BADR.

The legislation contained in TCGA 1992, s.169J provides that there is a disposal of trust business assets where the following conditions are met:

- trustees of a settlement dispose of 'settlement business assets', defined as assets which are part of the settled property of the settlement and are shares in or securities of a company (or interests in such shares or securities) or assets (or interests in such assets) that have been used for the purposes of a business;
- an individual is a 'qualifying beneficiary' of the settlement, that is an individual who throughout the relevant two-year period has an interest in possession* (other than an interest in possession which has a fixed term) in the whole of the settled property of the settlement, or in a part of the settled property that contains the settlement business assets disposed of (*any interest in possession (IIP) not a qualifying interest in possession (QIIP) for IHT purposes); and
- one or other of two 'relevant conditions' is satisfied:

- where the settlement business assets disposed of are shares in or securities of a company, throughout a period of two years ending within the three years up to the date of the disposal the company is the qualifying beneficiary's personal company and is either a trading company or the holding company of a trading group, and the qualifying beneficiary is an officer or employee of the company, or of one or more companies which are members of the trading group;
- where the settlement business assets are assets or interests in assets that have been used for the purposes of a business, they have been used for the purposes of the business carried on by the qualifying beneficiary throughout the period of two years ending within the three years up to the date of the disposal, and the qualifying beneficiary ceases to carry on the business on the date of the disposal or within the period of three years before that date. A business carried on by the qualifying beneficiary includes a business carried on by a partnership of which the qualifying beneficiary is a member, and ceasing to carry on the business includes the qualifying beneficiary ceasing to be a member of the partnership or the partnership ceasing to carry on the business.

The period of two years applies to disposals after 5 April 2019. Prior to that date, the period was one year. If the date of disposal is on or after 6 April 2019 and the business ceased to be carried on before 29 October 2018, then the relevant period continues to be one year.

Although the legislation indicates that only the qualifying beneficiary has to hold shares for a period of two years to the date of disposal, HMRC has taken the view that the trustees should also own their shares throughout the two-year period to qualify for the relief. HMRC has lost a case, *Skinner* [2019] UKFTT 0516 (TC), at the First-tier Tribunal on this point but is challenging the decision.

24.11 CLAIMS

As set out in TCGA 1992, s.169M, an individual must claim BADR in their self-assessment tax return if one has been issued.

For a trust disposal, the claim must be made jointly by the trustees and the qualifying beneficiary, so cannot be made in a return.

The claim must be made on or before the first anniversary of 31 January following the tax year in which the qualifying disposal is made. The claim may be amended or revoked within the time limit.

24.12 AMOUNT OF RELIEF

There is an overriding limit on the amount of BADR that can be claimed during an individual's lifetime. The limit is now £1 million for disposals on or after 11 March

2020. Previously the limit was £10 million, having been increased to that for disposals on or after 6 April 2011.

It should be noted that the reduction in the lifetime limit from 11 March 2020 carries with it three anti-forestalling measures to counteract possible attempts to bank the previous limit of £10 million before the change.

These measures are set out in Finance Act 2020, Sched.3 and cover situations where a contract was made before 11 March 2020 but completed on or after that date subject to certain conditions; or there was a reorganisation of share capital or share for share exchange on or after 6 April 2019 but before 11 March 2020 and an election is made on or after 11 March 2020 to disapply the share for share rules so that CGT is paid at the date of the reorganisation or share exchange. Where an election is made, the election date is treated as the date of disposal and the lower limit will apply.

Trustees do not have their own lifetime allowance. Where a claim is made by trustees, the BADR claimed by the trustees reduces the beneficiary's lifetime allowance.

Where both the beneficiary and the trust make a qualifying disposal on the same day, the disposal by the individual who is the qualifying beneficiary is treated as having taken place before the disposal of trust business assets.

Where there is a disposal of trust business assets and there is at least one other beneficiary apart from the qualifying beneficiary only part of the gain may be eligible for relief. The amount of the gain that qualifies for BADR is calculated by reference to the proportional entitlement to the income of the relevant settled property where the other beneficiary(ies) has an interest in the settled property of the settlement, or in that part of the settled property that includes the business assets that are the subject of the disposal of trust business assets.

If the qualifying beneficiary is entitled to the whole of the income no adjustment is necessary. However, if the qualifying beneficiary is entitled to say one-half of that income the relevant proportion of the gain qualifying for BADR would be one-half of the amount of the gain.

24.13 INTERACTION WITH OTHER RELIEFS

24.13.1 Gifts of business assets

It is possible that the material disposal for BADR purposes is actually a gift and could qualify under TCGA 1992, s.165. If a claim is made under s.165, no chargeable gain will arise and therefore there will be no gain on which to claim BADR. Should the transferee later make a material disposal, whether they qualify for BADR will depend on their own circumstances.

If only part of the assets in the material disposal for BADR are subject to a s.165 claim, a gain will remain and a claim for BADR can be made on any gain that remains chargeable.

The reduction in the lifetime limit to £1 million will result in a greater focus on family tax planning for companies qualifying for BADR. Any tax planning involving transfers of shares will need to ensure that the relief for gifts of business assets will apply to the full disposal, and that the recipient will qualify for BADR in the future.

24.13.2 Business property relief (BPR)

Both business property relief (BPR) and BADR are available for shares in trading companies and individuals may at some stage want to rely on either one or both reliefs. It is worth noting that there are a number of differences between BPR and BADR, and planning for both will require detailed consideration of the requirements for each. One major difference is the requirement for BADR that the company be trading, whereas for BPR it has to be carrying on a business. (See also the comments on the trading threshold at **24.7**.)

24.13.3 Gifts to spouses

While gifts to spouses can be attractive from a tax planning perspective, you should not lose sight of the impact on BADR. Will the spouse qualify for BADR in their own right, for example by holding at least five per cent of the shares and voting rights and being an employee or officer of the company? Also will they have held the shares for the two-year qualifying period if a sale is likely in the short term?

24.13.4 Interaction with the Enterprise Investment Scheme (EIS)

Where a gain that would have qualified for BADR has been deferred using EIS relief, legislation was included in the Finance Act 2015 to enable a claim for BADR on a subsequent chargeable event.

24.13.5 Share for share exchanges

Where shares or securities in one company are exchanged for shares or securities in another company and TCGA 1992, s.127 applies such that the new shares stand in the shoes of the old shares, it may be that the old shares would have qualified for BADR but the new shares do not. In those circumstances, it is possible to elect to disapply s.127 so that a gain accrues at the time of the reorganisation. That election has to be made within one year of 31 January following the tax year in which the qualifying disposal has been made. Any such election for a trustee disposal must be made jointly with the qualifying beneficiary.

24.13.6 Dilution of shares

With effect from April 2019, legislation was introduced to enable investors to retain some BADR when a share issue to other investors causes their own shareholding to fall below the five per cent minimum holding.

The investor is allowed to treat the gain arising immediately before the share issue as qualifying for BADR. That gain is calculated by reference to the market value at that date. This gain is treated as arising at the date of the dilution, although it is possible to defer that gain until a later disposal. The gain from the date on which the shareholding is diluted to the disposal of the shares will be chargeable at normal capital gains tax rates without the benefit of BADR.

24.14 INVESTORS' RELIEF (IR)

24.14.1 Overview

Investors' relief (IR) was introduced in the Finance Act 2016 and aims to encourage external investors to invest in unlimited companies. Crucially most employees or officers of companies are not eligible for this relief, unlike BADR.

There are, however, similarities to BADR in that it reduces the rate of CGT to 10 per cent (TCGA 1992, s.169VC(2)) and has a lifetime limit of £10 million (TCGA 1992, s.169VK). It is available to both individuals and trustees. Unlike BADR, there is no minimum shareholding requirement.

Shares must be:

- new ordinary shares acquired by subscription;
- subscribed for wholly in cash and fully paid up at the time of issue;
- issued by the company on or after 17 March 2016;
- held continuously for a period of at least three years. The three-year period is counted from 6 April 2016 for shares issued before then (therefore the first claim for IR will not be possible until 2019/20); and
- at the time of issue the company must be unlisted.

The trading company definition for BADR also applies to IR. The investment must be at arm's length, for genuine commercial reasons and not as part of an arrangement where one of the main purposes is to secure a tax advantage.

The individual must not be a 'relevant employee', so must not be a director or employee of the company, except in limited circumstances. Relief is still available if the individual becomes an unremunerated director following the purchase, or an employee of the company 180 days after the share issue provided that there was no reasonable prospect that they would be an employee at the time of issue.

The investor (or associate of the investor) must not receive value from the company (or a person connected with company) at any point in the period beginning one year before the date the shares were issued and ending immediately before the anniversary of the issue date.

There are identification rules for disposals, distinguishing between 'qualifying shares' 'potentially qualifying shares' and 'excluded shares' (TCGA 1992, s.169VB(1)), which enable the maximum potential IR to be preserved. Qualifying shares and excluded shares are disposed of in priority to potentially qualifying shares.

Where the share for share exchange rules under TCGA 1992, s.126 apply to a reorganisation, the investor can elect to disapply the rules if they want to crystallise the tax relief. The election must be made on or before first anniversary of 31 January following the tax year in which the reorganisation takes place.

24.14.2 Application of investors' relief to disposals by trustees

TCGA 1992, s.169VH enables some gains by trustees to qualify for relief under IR, for shares they have subscribed for on or after 17 March 2016. The subscription must have been made wholly in cash.

In a similar way to BADR, the relief for trustees works by enabling the trustees to utilise some of the qualifying beneficiary's lifetime allowance, and a joint election by both the trustees and the qualifying beneficiary has to be made.

To be a qualifying beneficiary they must:

- have held an interest in possession in the settled property (comprising the shares) throughout the three years ending on the date of the share disposal; and
- not be a relevant employee at any time in that three-year period (ending on the date of the share disposal). As for individuals, the beneficiary will not be regarded as a relevant employee even if they are a director provided they are not remunerated throughout this three-year period. The difference between the unlimited period for individuals and the three-year period for a qualifying beneficiary should be noted.

CHAPTER 25

Stamp duty land tax (SDLT) issues in estate planning

John Bunker and Sarah Cardew

25.1 KEY POINTS

- In two of the three elements of estate planning – legal and tax planning – it is always valuable to consider whether there might be potential tax consequences, including stamp duty land tax (SDLT), that need further consideration.
- SDLT only applies in England and Northern Ireland, as land and buildings transaction tax (LBTT) applies in Scotland (from 1 April 2015); and land transaction tax (LTT) applies in Wales (from 1 April 2018).
- Inheritance tax (IHT) mitigation can interact with SDLT measures in three important areas for planning:
  - **Estates:** How beneficiaries are treated, and whether we can adapt our estate administration or structure inheritances better in wills or post-death variations.
  - **Trusts:** What interests are held in any trust and, if that trust may affect SDLT on a property purchase, whether the trust might be restructured before the transaction is completed or the purchase needs to be made differently.
  - **Lifetime gifts:** Before we advise on gifts, or even simply assist with the legal documentation, can we ensure that no SDLT issue arises that may need review?
- Two big SDLT developments are key for beneficiaries of estates, trusts or lifetime gifts:
  - **Three per cent higher rate additional dwellings (HRAD) charge, from 1 April 2016:**
    - where you buy a property but already have an interest in another;
    - many beneficiaries first buy a property after inheriting money, etc.;
    - so if a residential property in an estate or trust:

    - when are they treated as owning, for SDLT purposes?
    - and can we help avoid an HRAD charge?
  - **First time buyers' relief (FTBR) from 22 November 2017:**
    - this reduced the SDLT charge on buying a first home;
    - which may be lost if one had previously owned a residential property interest;
    - so we need to consider how inheritances might affect this, and whether we can structure any gifts differently to avoid beneficiaries losing FTBR.

NB: FTBR is not applicable in practice from 8 July 2020 to 31 March 2021, with the temporary increase to the SDLT nil rate band for residential house sales from £125,000 to £500,000, although HRAD still applies.

- Two alternative ways of proactively helping clients could both be extremely worthwhile:
  - **flagging up a potential issue**, to allow time to avoid the trap, so clients can either proceed knowing the potential consequences or seek more detailed advice; or
  - **offering detailed advice**, if your firm is able to provide that, with a view to finding the right solution, by flagging up the issue and the cost of reviewing it.

  In each case, be mindful of the planning practice points made with reference to residence nil rate band (RNRB), in **17.2**, as some points arise that are similar to those in that other major area of tax change. You should get credit from clients for picking up, and bringing to their attention the point(s), even if they do not instruct you to do any extra work.

  When you are providing any tax advice to clients, the tax avoidance legislation must always be borne in mind. Broadly, you must be able to demonstrate to HM Revenue and Customs (HMRC) that the transaction was not artificially structured for the avoidance of tax.

25.2 HIGHER RATE ADDITIONAL DWELLINGS (HRAD) CHARGE – THE EXTRA THREE PER CENT

Can we help beneficiaries avoid being hit by an HRAD charge? There is a specific provision for estates (see **25.2.5**) of which we need to help clients make best use; and it is now good practice to ask all beneficiaries of estates whether they are planning to buy a residential property. If they are, there may be better ways to administer the estate; and there may be proactive advice to offer on planning – for example, a variation. It is worth noting that HRAD still applies under £500,000, even though no normal SDLT is payable up to that level, in the temporary period to 31 March 2021.

25.2.1 HRAD basics

If a purchaser, or any of a number of purchasers,

(a) owns any share in another residential property;
(b) at midnight on the day of completion; and
(c) it's a 'major interest' – i.e. a freehold or lease with at least seven years to run, and not subject to a lease with at least 21 years to run; and
(d) the value of the interest or consideration is £40,000 or more,

then an extra three per cent above the standard rates of SDLT is charged on the whole purchase price, not simply that interest.

For example (using the temporary rates which apply until 31 March 2021):

- £250,000 = £7,500;
- £300,000 = £9,000;
- £500,000 = £15,000.

The legislation is in Finance Act (FA) 2016, s.128, with a new Sched.4ZA in Finance Act (FA) 2003.

A dwelling anywhere in the world counts, not just in England, etc.

Married couples and civil partners ('spouses') are treated as one for this SDLT charge:

(a) So a spouse cannot buy one property in one name, and a second in the name of the other spouse!
(b) It's an objective question of fact as to which is the main home, with no choice.
(c) Compare this with unmarried partners, who can each have their 'own home' without HRAD.

25.2.2 No exemption for a first home, only for replacements of a main home

If someone has any interest in another property worth £40,000 or more, and then buys their own first home, they will pay the HRAD charge on their purchase.

The three per cent charge will not apply if the purchase is a replacement of their main home, i.e. they already have a main home and sell and replace it. This assumes they are buying their second, third, fourth, etc. main home, but not their first home.

This seems strangely contrary to the public policy of encouraging first time buyers.

It therefore becomes critical to know at what point one is treated as 'owning' a home within an estate or trust.

25.2.3 Replacement of your main home

The relief for a replacement main home can apply in two situations:

(a) buying simultaneously with a sale, or within three years of selling a main home; or
(b) buying a new home before selling, paying the HRAD charge upfront but reclaiming that charge on a sale of the previous main home within three years,

provided in (a) in the three-year period prior to the purchase, the period in which they disposed of their home, that the property sold was their only or main residence; and during that three years they had not acquired another property with the intention of it being a main home.

It is in either case an objective test of what is their main home – and one lesson learned in the first four years of the HRAD is that the HMRC assessment of what is objectively a person's main home often does not agree with the client's understanding. Many have found themselves feeling that the wrong property was treated as their main home.

There is no equivalent of the CGT election for the principal private residence (PPR).

Be clear of the precise wording of the replacement provision, in Condition D (FA 2003, Sched.4ZA, para.3(5)), as you have to satisfy the very specific requirements. For example, to replace a main residence, you must have a sale and purchase – you don't satisfy the exemption if you leave a rented home to a new bought home.

Example 25.1

Tom and Kirsty have been married for three years, and prior to that they each had their own home. When they moved into Tom's house in 2018 they let out Kirsty's flat. They have now decided to sell the flat, and buy a new house in a better position, with the idea of letting out Tom's house. They never had the titles transferred into their joint names, but understand they have only one main residence between them so it is Tom's house for now. They plan to buy for £600,000 so the HRAD charge, if they don't qualify for the replacement exemption, would be £18,000.

Compare this with if they sold Tom's house, which has been their main residence for the last two years. In this case as they would be replacing their main residence they would not be liable for HRAD on their new purchase.

25.2.4 Trusts

What trust interests amount to 'owning' a residential property for the purpose of HRAD? 'Owns' includes being entitled under bare trusts and interest in possession (IIP) trusts; and 'IIP' here means any income entitlements, not just a qualifying interest in possession (QIIP) for IHT purposes. So, for example, if an income entitlement was created out of a discretionary will trust, but more than two years after death (so that it was not read back to the date of death), it will be an IIP (while remaining a relevant property trust (RPT) for IHT purposes) but not a QIIP trust (as it would have been if the appointment on the life interest had been within two years of death).

Trustees will pay the three per cent extra on all purchases except:

- a purchase by a bare trust or an IIP trust;
- a purchase for a beneficiary's main home;

and:

- where that beneficiary and the trust have no other residential property interest; *or*
- the purchase is replacing that beneficiary's previous main home.

Compare this with an IIP trust that buys a first main home for a beneficiary, and the trust holds another property interest, where they would pay the three per cent HRAD.

Therefore, encourage any trust beneficiary planning to buy a new property, to take advice as soon as possible, so that the structure and tax charges can be changed, if possible and appropriate.

In some cases one may want to avoid an IIP, to avoid the three per cent charge, so they buy untainted by the trust; in other cases they will want to ensure it is an IIP or a bare trust if it is the beneficiary's main home (as above).

25.2.5 Estates

When do beneficiaries 'own' a residential property in an estate?

- Not from the date of death, but:
  - from when the property is assented or appropriated to the beneficiary; or
  - possibly from when the estate is ready to be wound up, if in practice there is nothing more to be done, and to not wind up would be unnaturally prolonged.
- However, a beneficiary will not be treated as owning, for three years, if:
  - in the three years from when they inherit, they have no more than 50 per cent; and
  - their spouse (including a civil partner) doesn't own the other half; and
  - they don't acquire the other half during that three-year period.

NB: This is a special rule for HRAD, and is very helpful in practice, but it does not apply to FTBR.

25.2.6 Planning points for estates

In administering estates, these points are worth considering, to add value for your clients:

1. Always check with residuary beneficiaries (or anyone left any share of a residential property) whether they have any plans to buy a new residential property, and if they do, then tread carefully and offer the proactive, additional advice referred to in **25.1**.
2. If anyone has up to 50 per cent of a share of an estate, or property, and is planning to buy a share of the property of another beneficiary, which would take their beneficial interest over the 50 per cent level, you should flag up the third limb of the condition on the three-year rule above, as this would be a big potential loss if the condition were breached.
3. A beneficiary may wish to delay appropriation/assent so that the beneficiary is not entitled, or the three-year period does not start running, if it is both relevant and possible.
4. If a beneficiary is buying a first home with part of their inheritance, consider also the effect on FTBR (see **25.3**), where the rules are very different, but it may be possible to plan to avoid HRAD and also benefit from FTBR.
5. If a beneficiary is buying a home of sufficient value, it may even be worth doing a deed of variation to create a discretionary trust, so that any property in the estate will not be treated as 'owned' by the beneficiary for SDLT purposes. Clearly a cost/benefit analysis will need to be carefully done here, but the amount of SDLT saved can be significant and so justify a fair amount of cost before the saving is lost. One could set up a trust, including the client as a beneficiary, and the trust could be wound up later, if the costs of creating/running the discretionary trust would be significantly less than the SDLT HRAD charge!

In these cases, it is important to be clear who is benefiting from the work, whether a separate letter of engagement is needed, and to issue a new fee estimate in any event, etc.

Example 25.2

Jane and Linda are civil partners, who have moved into Jane's rented flat in a London suburb and you are acting for Linda in her late father's estate. She and her brother Robert have half each of the residuary estate but Robert wants to get rid of their father's house, currently valued at £400,000, fast, whereas Linda wants to keep it for now as an investment, as she feels the value is too low and will recover in the medium term. Neither Jane nor Linda have owned a home before and wish to buy a new home with some of the money Linda has inherited.

You advise that as she and Jane are civil partners they only have one main residence between them, that her half share of a house in the estate is disregarded for three years after it is appropriated or assented to her, but neither she nor Jane can buy the second half off Robert as that will lose her the three-year exemption. As they are looking to buy their first home, with no general exemption for that, if they bought the second half in either name they would have a potential liability for HRAD on the new home they buy, as they will be treated as owning another property interest of at least £40,000.

They plan to buy their new flat for £500,000, the potential HRAD @ 3% being £15,000 (ignoring for this purpose the normal SDLT rates), but also tell you that they have two children of Linda's and one of Jane's from previous relationships.

One option would be to do a deed of variation of part of Linda's inheritance, if sufficient besides her half of the house, to an IPDI trust of which the three children could be income beneficiaries. Linda and Jane could be potential beneficiaries under a power of appointment. There would be costs of setting up and running the trust but these could be significantly less than £15,000. You could then aim to have that trust buy the second half of the house off Robert. However, timing is all important here. (See also **Example 25.4** re FTBR.)

The second half of the house will be owned in due course by the trust, of which Jane and Linda are not income beneficiaries, so they are not treated as 'owning' an interest. They could then potentially buy the second half off Robert, paying SDLT on the consideration there, and even HRAD if the children were not occupying the property as their home (but with 3% x 1/2 £400,000 far better than 3% x £500,000). They may be able to avoid that HRAD charge if it were their main home as income beneficiaries of the trust.

Linda and Jane could proceed with their purchase first, so that the three-year rule should apply to the first half of the property Linda inherited and protect them from the HRAD charge on their new home.

25.2.7 Granny annexes

A big issue when the legislation went through parliament was the granny annexe that was treated as a separate property, as for council tax, where it worked for the council tax deduction but not if a HRAD charge would be due. If one member of the family bought the main property, and at the same time a separate one for 'granny', in which they also had an interest, it would potentially have meant a higher charge. If any one person has an interest in both, three per cent extra tax could be charged.

So if a client were gifting for IHT, as part of a new 'granny annexe' arrangement, or you were simply advising on the structuring of ownership for tax, you need to watch the terms of the exemption in the SDLT provisions, to try to avoid a HRAD charge.

There is a specific exemption in Condition C in FA 2003, Sched.4ZA, para.5, which requires:

- the two or more dwellings are to be bought as part of the same chargeable transaction (so it doesn't help a buyer if they acquire the granny annexe in a later purchase);
- if one purchased dwelling (dwelling A) is subsidiary to dwelling B,
  - if A is situated within the grounds of, or within same building as, B; and
  - the chargeable consideration, attributable on a 'just and reasonable basis' to B, is equal to or greater than two-thirds of total of dwellings A, B and

each of the other purchased dwellings situated within the grounds of, or within the same building as, dwelling B;

– i.e. valuation is crucial and a good chartered surveyor may be needed.

Example 25.3

Bodhi and Mary are buying a house in the adapted outbuildings of a country house, and they have two other dwellings in the same converted development. One is a flat being bought by their daughter, Jo, and her partner Noah, in their names, the other a cottage for Bodhi's mum, Naomi. They are going to share ownership of Naomi's adjoining cottage, but its value is £250,000 and their own house is £600,000, so the cottage is less than a third of the total value of both.

They are providing some money to Jo and Noah for their flat purchase and had thought of taking an equitable interest in that property which has a value of £150,000. However, if they did that, the total value would be £1 million and the main house (B in the bullets in **25.2.7**) would be only 60% of the total of the purchased dwellings, not at least 2/3. So you advise them to lend the money, with an equitable charge on Jo and Noah's flat, so that it is excluded from the equation. (See also **Example 25.5** re FTBR.)

25.3 FIRST TIME BUYERS' RELIEF (FTBR)

If beneficiaries are planning to buy a first home, can we make them aware of FTBR and any effect of their inheritance? Can we help them improve a claim for FTBR – by the manner of estate administration or by proactive advice?

25.3.1 FTBR basics

FTBR was introduced by the Budget on 22 November 2017, with effect from that date, about 20 months after the HRAD. If you are liable for HRAD, then you are not able to claim FTBR, which is clear – but there are some cases not within the HRAD provisions that fail for FTBR, i.e. there is a gap in the middle and it doesn't join up! For example:

- FTBR has no equivalent of the £40,000 de minimis that applies to HRAD, which means that any beneficial share of a residential property could stop a claim for FTBR.
- Also, the test is whether you have owned any interest in any residential property at any time – not just what you own at midnight on the day you complete the purchase!
- So you need to watch gifts of small shares of a beneficial interest in property inadvertently denying relief.

- How are inheritances – if of a share of the estate – treated? Not as owned from the date of death, but it appears to be from the date the property was appropriated or assented, as for HRAD, but without the special three-year rule. The alternative, of when the estate is ready to distribute, also applies.
- What about a specific gift of property? There is some uncertainty, but it appears the estate still needs to be ready to distribute, with tax and liabilities paid, etc., so that until that point, the ownership does not run.

25.3.2 FTBR planning

Some points worth considering, to add value for your clients:

- **Bare trusts** owning property can claim FTBR but not IIP trusts – a big difference from HRAD, so if there were a life interest in an IIP trust it would need to be converted to a bare trust to enable a claim for FTBR. Do take care that it qualifies as a bare trust for SDLT legislation, which is rather different from IHT legislation.
- **Where a property interest is being gifted**, consider whether it will affect the donee's ability to claim FTBR in future. It's always good to check whether any proposed donee has not yet owned a home, so that they might wish to claim FTBR if buying a new property.
  - Are there any alternative gifts that can be made?
  - Is a gift of cash or investments possible/better?
  - Could a property interest be held in a discretionary trust?
  - Or a life interest trust – if set up in a lifetime it would be an RPT (for IHT) but then also an IIP for SDLT purposes. If only a life interest – and not a bare trust – a FTBR claim could be saved.
  - At least bring the risk to the client's attention, so that they can weigh up the pros and cons.
- If drafting a will or an inheritance post-death, consider whether there are any other options.
- Would a deed of variation post-death save FTBR if redirected? There is no 'reading back' provision for SDLT, as there is for IHT and CGT, but the test for FTBR is to consider whether at the relevant time the client has ever owned an interest. If the property was not appropriated or assented then they have not yet owned, so that, in practice, they never inherited in the first place. An alternative to consider is disclaiming an inheritance.

Example 25.4: Jane and Linda (continued from Example 25.2)

Neither of Jane and Linda has owned a property before, so they can potentially claim FTBR, which would not be possible if either of them had owned a property interest before. If Linda does inherit her half share, once it is appropriated or assented to her she will lose FTBR as the three-year rule does not apply as it does for HRAD. Whatever its value, they will have another interest in a residential property and will not qualify for FTBR on the purchase of their flat for £500,000.

If there is the option to postpone the assent or appropriation of the half share of the house from the estate until after they buy their flat, they might preserve the FTBR. They are buying after 1 April 2021, when the temporary SDLT rates no longer apply, but need to watch that £500,000 is the limit for FTBR. If the price were to increase they would be over the FTBR limit.

Example 25.5: Jo and Noah (continued from Example 25.3)

Jo and Noah are buying their first home, but they will not qualify for FTBR if Jo's parents have an interest in the property. If any person buying has previously owned a residential property interest FTBR would be lost. So this also supports the proposal that they take a loan from Jo's parents.

CHAPTER 26

Tax planning and mental incapacity

Kelly Greig

26.1 KEY POINTS

It is sometimes thought that all is lost if an individual loses mental capacity in terms of the ability to carry out effective tax planning. However, this is not necessarily the case. Of course, it also depends on the nature of the act that is intended. It may be possible, for example, for someone who has lost the necessary mental capacity to still utilise their ISA allowance each year and make use of their annual capital gains tax (CGT) exemption but much more difficult to undertake effective inheritance tax (IHT) planning.

While inter vivos tax planning for someone who lacks the necessary mental capacity is a very broad area, this chapter will focus on IHT planning, covering the following areas:

- Mental Capacity Act (MCA) 2005;
- mental capacity to gift;
- what if the donor lacks the necessary mental capacity?
- what constitutes a gift?
- what if a Court of Protection (COP) application is necessary?
- what is in P's 'best interests'?
- business property relief (BPR);
- statutory wills;
- disclosure of P's will; and
- post-death tax planning.

26.2 MENTAL CAPACITY ACT 2005

MCA 2005 provides a legislative framework for those that lack capacity and states (s.1 'The principles'):

(1) The following principles apply for the purposes of this Act.

(2) A person must be assumed to have capacity unless it is established that he lacks capacity.

(3) A person is not to be treated as unable to make a decision unless all practicable steps to help him to do so have been taken without success.

(4) A person is not to be treated as unable to make a decision merely because he makes an unwise decision.
(5) An act done, or decision made, under this Act for or on behalf of a person who lacks capacity must be done, or made, in his best interests.
(6) Before the act is done, or the decision is made, regard must be had to whether the purpose for which it is needed can be as effectively achieved in a way that is less restrictive of the person's rights and freedom of action.

26.3 MENTAL CAPACITY TO GIFT

For the most part when people talk about IHT planning, they are usually talking about gifting assets in some way. There are of course other usual tools available in terms of making use of exemptions, and these are discussed later.

MCA 2005 directs a two-stage test for determining mental capacity:

- **Stage 1 – Diagnostic test:** Is there an impairment or disturbance in the functioning of the person's mind or brain?
- **Stage 2 – Functional test:** Is the impairment or disturbance sufficient that the person lacks the capacity to make that particular decision?

Does P (the person being assessed for capacity) satisfy the requirements of MCA 2005, s.3:

- understand the information relevant to the decision;
- retain that information;
- use or weigh that information as part of the process of making the decision;
- communicate their decision (whether by talking, using sign language or any other means).

The relevant test for the requisite mental capacity to gift is the common law test set out in the case of *Re Beaney (deceased)* [1978] 1 WLR 770. (For discussion on whether it is MCA 2005 or the common law (*Re Beaney*) that should be followed to assess capacity to gift, see the case of *Kicks* v. *Leigh* [2014] EWHC 3926 (Ch).) From *Re Beaney*:

> the question in each case is whether the person concerned is capable of understanding what he does by executing the deed in question when its general purport had been fully explained to him.

It is the case that the larger the gift that is to be made in relation to the size of the donor's estate, the more the test is to veer towards the test of testamentary capacity. It is therefore important to consider the test set out in *Banks* v. *Goodfellow* [1870] LR 5 QB 549 which states:

> It is essential to the exercise of such a power that a testator [1] shall understand the nature of the act and its effects; [2] shall understand the extent of the property of which he is disposing; [3] shall be able to comprehend and appreciate the claims to which he ought to give effect and, with a view to the latter object, [4] that no disorder of the mind shall poison

> his affections, pervert his sense of right, or prevent the exercise of his natural faculties; [5] that no insane delusion shall influence his will in disposing of his property and bring about a disposal of it which, if his mind had been sound, would not have been made. [Numbers added for convenience.]

Despite the introduction of MCA 2005, which should nonetheless still be borne in mind, it has been determined that the common law test in *Banks* v. *Goodfellow* (above) is still the correct test for determining testamentary capacity (*Walker* v. *Badmin* [2015] EWHC 71 (Ch)).

The Law Society practice note 'Making gifts of assets' (December 2019) provides some guidance on the things to consider when acting for a client who wishes to gift (see: **www.lawsociety.org.uk/support-services/advice/practice-notes/making-gifts-of-assets/**).

It is important to consider whether your client has the necessary mental capacity to make any gift that is proposed.

The STEP Mental Capacity Special Interest Group has produced handy assessment tools for determining capacity for a person (P) to make various decisions including the *Mental capacity assessment tool for the decision of capacity to make a lifetime gift*. This sets out the relevant test.

If there is doubt as to whether your client has the capacity to gift, then it is important to obtain a medical report on capacity. Remembering that capacity is decision-specific, it is important that the medical practitioner is directed to the correct test. It is therefore helpful to provide the STEP tool to the medical practitioner prior to them undertaking any assessment of capacity.

When the capacity assessment is returned, it is suggested that this is reviewed to ensure that the medical practitioner has understood and applied the correct test of mental capacity and has not just made a blanket statement as to capacity. It is helpful to ensure that they have gone into sufficient detail in their report for you to satisfy yourself that P is capable or incapable as it is likely to be relied upon later. It is also important to note that capacity is decision- and time-specific: the report will be valid for that particular decision. It may therefore be the case that P has capacity to gift £3,000 annually, but not to make a large one-off gift of, say, £500,000.

26.4 IF THE DONOR LACKS THE NECESSARY MENTAL CAPACITY

It may be possible for an attorney or a deputy (or perhaps some other interested person) to make the gift on the donor's behalf.

The power to gift on behalf of someone who lacks capacity is set out in MCA 2005, s.18(1)(b). However, this is subject to 'the principles' as set out above. MCA 2005, s.12 provides specific restrictions in respect of attorneys making gifts. The court has power pursuant to MCA 2005, s.23 to authorise the making of gifts which do not fall within the scope of s.12.

The question, however, is, when can the gift be made by the attorney or deputy and when is the approval of the Court of Protection (COP) required?

The COP case of *MJ and JM* v. *The Public Guardian* [2013] EWHC 2966 (COP) set out some helpful guidance.

This case was an application to the COP for retrospective approval of gifts, made by P's deputies, as well as ratification of expenses incurred. The deputies had made various gifts to charities as well as to themselves and other relatives on the basis that this is what P would have wanted.

The court pointed out to the deputies that they had no authority to make these gifts without the proper approval of the court. Although there is standard wording in an unrestricted order appointing the deputy to make gifts, the authority is narrow in nature and is restricted to the making of gifts to charities that P supported or does support and gifts on customary occasions to persons who are related or connected to P. Such gifts must not be unreasonable having regard to all the circumstances. There is a similar provision in MCA 2005, s.12(2) for attorneys acting under a lasting power of attorney (LPA).

The court went on to provide guidance on gifting for deputies and attorneys going forward including setting out some de minimis exceptions that do not require the authority of the court. Although the court did not want to be too prescriptive of the amounts that could be gifted without further authority as each case will vary, Senior Judge Lush suggested that gifts up to the annual exemption for IHT purposes (£3,000) or small gifts (£250 per person) for up to 10 people should be acceptable in the following circumstances:

1. P has a life expectancy of less than five years;
2. the estate exceeds the nil rate band (NRB) for tax purposes.

NB: This case was decided prior to the introduction of the residence NRB (RNRB) but it is thought that P would need to have a potential IHT liability to qualify and so it can be assumed that the reference to the NRB includes the RNRB for these purposes.

The gifts are affordable having regard to P's care costs and will not adversely affect P's standard of care and quality of life.

There is no evidence to suggest that P would be opposed to gifts of this magnitude being made on their behalf.

Any gifts that are likely to exceed this amount or do not fit the criteria above are likely to need the approval of the COP.

Since *Re GM*, the Office of the Public Guardian (OPG) has published a practice note dealing with attorneys and deputies making gifts on behalf of P. (See 'Public Guardian practice note (PN7) giving gifts': **www.gov.uk/government/publications/public-guardian-practice-note-gifts/public-guardian-practice-note-pn7-giving-gifts-web-version**.) This provides helpful guidance to attorneys and deputies on the extent of their duties and powers and such gifts which may require the further sanction of the court.

Consider the following example:

Example 26.1

Mary lacks mental capacity to gift and is aged 96. She has an estate that far exceeds the NRB for IHT purposes.

Prior to losing mental capacity Mary was regularly making use of her annual gift exemption (£3,000) and would also gift the grandchildren money at Christmas.

Mary is entitled to NHS continuing healthcare and so her care is fully funded by the NHS.

Her expenditure is minimal.

Mary's attorneys could continue to gift the annual £3,000 (perhaps £1,000 to each of the three children) and continue to pay gifts to the grandchildren at Christmas as part of the small gifts exemption. This would not require the permission of the court, as it meets the test set out by the court.

The fact that Mary was gifting prior to her loss of capacity is helpful evidence that she is likely to have not opposed the gifts being made on her behalf.

However, if the attorneys wished to gift £100,000 of Mary's assets, even though she has no real need for these monies, authority from the COP will still be required.

26.5 WHAT CONSTITUTES A GIFT?

An attorney or a deputy is permitted to provide for someone other than P, using P's assets to the extent that P would be expected to meet those needs (MCA 2005, Sched.4, para.3(2)). However, an attorney or a deputy needs to be mindful of any potential conflict of interests. Should they be the person to benefit from the financial provision, then an application to the COP for approval will usually be required (*In Re Buckley* [2013] COPLR 35). The OPG's Mental Capacity Act Code of Practice states (at para.7.60):

> A fiduciary duty means attorneys must not take advantage of their position. Nor should they put themselves in a position where their personal interests conflict with their duties. They also must not allow any other influences to affect the way in which they act as an attorney. Decisions should always benefit the donor, and not the attorney. Attorneys must not profit or get any personal benefit from their position, apart from receiving gifts where the Act allows it, whether or not it is at the donor's expense.

However, see *Re Various Lasting Powers of Attorney* [2019] EWCOP 40 (para.68):

> A proportionate approach has to be taken to considerations of conflict of interest, balancing the risk of abuse against the objective of facilitating autonomous decision making. In my judgment, where the donor whilst he had capacity used his own funds to benefit another (including the attorney) in the way contemplated, or where there is an express statement in the instrument of the donor's wish that his funds be used in the way

> contemplated, there should be no requirement for the attorney to seek prior authority from the Court to use the donor's funds to benefit another, even if the attorney is in a position of conflict of interest.

This case was in relation to various mandatory statements set out in various LPAs to provide for certain individuals in the event that the donor lost capacity. The court held that, as MCA 2005, s.4 (best interests) cannot be overridden and decisions must all be made taking into account s.4, a preference to benefit would be valid, however a mandatory instruction would not be.

Some examples of gifts that are likely to require court approval:

- interest-free loans;
- payment of adaptations to a property that another person may benefit from or if the property is held in another person's name and with P not gaining any interest in the property;
- a relative living in P's property rent-free, where P is deriving no benefit.

However, see *Re Various Lasting Powers of Attorney* (para.54):

> . . . an attorney's use of his donor's funds to benefit someone else is not a 'gift', when it is not linked to a 'customary occasion' as defined by s12(3) of the [MCA 2005], and the attorney is under a degree of obligation in respect of it.

26.6 WHAT IF A COURT OF PROTECTION APPLICATION IS NECESSARY?

If P lacks the necessary capacity to gift assets and the gifting does not fall within the de minimis exceptions, then an application to the COP will be necessary for authorisation.

Practitioners should consider the Court of Protection Rules 2017, SI 2017/1035, Part 9 and the accompanying practice direction 9E ('Applications relating to statutory wills, codicils, settlements and other dealings with P's property') before making an application to the court.

The following will be required for the application:

1. COP1 – Court of Protection application form.
2. COP1A – Supporting information for 'property and affairs' applications.
3. COP1C – Supporting information for statutory will, codicil, gift(s), deed of variation or settlement of property.
4. COP3 – Assessment of capacity.
5. COP24 – Witness statement.
6. A draft of any trust deed if the assets are to be transferred into trust.

With regard to the assessment of capacity, it is important that you ensure that the medical practitioner addresses the correct test of mental capacity in relation to the application that is to be made. It will be necessary to provide them with a clear letter setting out what you are trying to achieve and the relevant test of capacity. It is useful to give the medical practitioner details of P's assets and the amount being given away and to whom. This can then be discussed with P when undertaking the assessment. If the medical practitioner is of the view that P lacks capacity, it is helpful to ask them to produce a report showing that they have used the correct test and then ask them to complete the COP3.

If there is any urgency in the application, this should be brought to the attention of the court at the outset. If the matter becomes urgent during proceedings, then a COP9 application together with accompanying witness statement should be sent to the court, highlighting the new urgency.

You will need to serve copies of the application on all persons who are materially affected by the application. This includes those that you wish to benefit, but also those who are due to lose out, i.e. anyone who would benefit from P's will (or intestacy if relevant). They will then have a chance to put forward their views and potentially object to the application.

It is helpful, for those who are served with copies of the applications and who have no objections, to notify the court of such. Also, if they are in agreement, for them to notify the court by filing a COP5. This will enable matters to move far more quickly.

It is likely that the official solicitor will be invited to act for P to advocate for what is in their best interests.

If the official solicitor accepts the appointment, they will consider the papers and consider what further information (if any) they require in order to make a decision as to their position. They may also decide to visit P, especially if P's capacity is borderline and/or they have very express current views.

It is important in your application to show:

1. What the IHT (or other tax) consequences are, based on the current circumstances and what would happen with the proposed gift. If P is required to survive for a certain period for the savings to take effect this should be noted.
2. That P is unlikely to ever need the assets that are the proposal of the gift. A well-executed cash flow analysis, from a financial planner, should be able to assist with this. It would need to show that P's current and future needs could be met from other funds – see *Re G (TJ)* [2010] EWHC 3005 (COP) (para.23):

   > . . . it is appropriate in this case to be cautious in making assessments . . . as to what the future might bring . . . I am satisfied that the payments which I am asked to direct in favour of C will come out of funds which are surplus to Mrs G's own proper requirements for the remainder of her days.

   See also *PBC* v. *JMA and others* [2018] EWCOP 19 (para.64):

   > . . . where the court is considering the authorisation of gifts, affordability is a 'necessary but not sufficient' consideration. The future needs of the protected person must be considered on a cautious basis, and the level of gifting not such as may put in doubt the donor's ability to meet those needs.

3. The cash flow analysis should show all income and expenditure, including

provision for increased care needs or any other anticipated needs. In addition, provision should be made for an increase in such costs. The analysis should be crash-tested to account for any movements in the market.

4. Why the proposed gift is in P's 'best interests' (see below as to best interests).
5. If P had a history of undertaking tax planning activity, especially IHT planning, then it is helpful to illustrate this in your application. This is more likely to succeed than in a case where perhaps P considered it their civic duty to pay tax. See, however, the submissions made by David Rees acting for the applicant in *PBC* v. *JMA* where he said (para.54; emphasis in original):

   > in the absence of evidence that P is going to act in a manner which does *not* mitigate tax, the default position should be that most people are motivated by a desire to save tax if that benefits their relatives.

   However also see the judgment in that same case (para.66):

   > Mitigation of tax, particularly taxes of inter-generational effect and even by completely lawful 'vanilla' means, is a matter on which there may be a range of views. The Mental Capacity Act does not permit the Court to rely on default positions, assumptions or generalisations in making a decision about whether gifts to effect tax mitigation are in the best interests of a particular protected person. The Court must decide the application on nothing more and nothing less than a case-specific application of [MCA 2005] section 4.

6. If P had provided any written statements stating their intent to maintain an individual or to provide gifts, it is helpful if this is included in the application.

26.7 WHAT IS IN P'S BEST INTERESTS?

26.7.1 Meaning of 'best interests'

All actions taken, including gifting or inheritance tax planning generally must be shown to be in P's 'best interests'. MCA 2005, s.4 covers best interests and includes the following factors to be taken into account:

1. the past and present wishes and feelings of P, including any written statement prepared by him when he had capacity (it is therefore the case that, for example, if P had made a will leaving all to son A but the proposed gift was large and to son B, you would need to show reason to override P's capacitous decision);
2. the beliefs and values likely to influence P's decision if P had capacity; and
3. any other factors that P would be likely to consider if P had capacity to do so.

ADS v. *DSM* [2017] EWCOP 8 supports the proposition that P's wishes and feelings should be taken into account.

In addition, there have also been a line of cases suggesting that the best interests of P include being remembered for having done the right thing.

Re P [2009] EWCOP 163 established that while P's wishes should be taken into account overriding this is the primary rule that decisions must be made in P's best interests (para.41):

> First, . . . [t]he only imperative is that the decision must be made in P's best interests. Second, although P's wishes must be given weight, if as I think, Parliament has endorsed the 'balance sheet' approach, they are only one part of the balance. I agree that those wishes are to be given great weight . . . Third, any attempt to test a decision by reference to what P would hypothetically have done or wanted runs the risk of amounting to a 'substituted judgement' rather than a decision of what would be in P's best interests.

The judge went on to say (para.44) that being remembered for having done the right thing was important:

> [F]or many people it is in their best interests that they are remembered with affection by their family and as having done 'the right thing' by their will.

'Best interests' is not a 'substituted judgement' test (*Briggs* v. *Briggs and others* [2016] EWCOP 53):

> 56. In my view, the factors that will give indications as to what the individual P wants include the interests of other people who P would have been likely to take into account and so, for example, many if not most Ps when they had capacity would have taken into account their relationship with others (e.g. spouse and children), how they think their children should be parented and the impact on those closest to them of what they decide to do.
>
> 57. Pausing there, it is clear and important to stress that a conclusion on what P would have done is not determinative of the MCA best interests test and so, by stating that the MCA enables the Court to do for the patient what he could do for himself if of full capacity, the Supreme Court is not saying that a conclusion on what the patient would have done is decisive. The test is not a 'what would P have done test', it is a best interests test and so a test that requires the decision maker to perform a weighing or balancing exercise between a range of divergent and competing factors.

In addition, the MCA Code of Practice states (para.5.38):

> In setting out the requirements for working out a person's 'best interests', section 4 of the Act puts the person who lacks capacity at the centre of the decision to be made. Even if they cannot make the decision, their wishes and feelings, beliefs and values should be taken fully into account – whether expressed in the past or now. But their wishes and feelings, beliefs and values will not necessarily be the deciding factor in working out their best interests. Any such assessment must consider past and current wishes and feelings, beliefs and values alongside all other factors, but the final decision must be based entirely on what is in the person's best interests.

It is also important to note that 'best interests' does not necessary mean self-interest. From *Re G (TJ)* (above), per Morgan J (at para 35):

> . . . the word 'interests' in the phrase 'best interests' is not confined to matters of self interest or, putting it another way, a court could conclude in an appropriate case that it is in the interests of P for P to act altruistically.

And from *Re A* [2015] EWCOP 46 (para.35):

> In considering A's best interests at a particular time, the decision-maker must take a holistic approach and consider her welfare in the widest sense, not just financial, but social and emotional.

Consider the views of Senior Judge Lush in *Re KGS* [2012] EWCOP 302 (at para.39), in which it was decided that it was not in the best interests of P to make the proposed gifts to mitigate a potential inheritance tax liability:

> . . . it is not the function of the court to anticipate, ring-fence or maximise any potential inheritance for the benefit of family members on the death of a protected party, because this is not the purpose for which the compensation for personal injury was intended. The position would be different, of course, if the individual concerned had substantial funds surplus to his requirements that were derived from another source, such as an inheritance or a lottery win.

However it is unlikely that tax mitigation as a sole benefit is likely to be enough (*PBC* v. *JMA and others* [2018] EWCOP 19 (para.68)):

> I have not entered the tax mitigating effect of the proposed gifts as an independent factor on either side of the balance sheet. Payment of tax from her estate after her death will have no direct impact on JMA either way and it is no part of the Court of Protection's function to protect either an inheritance or a revenue stream. Inheritance tax mitigating effect can in my view only meaningfully be considered in the best interests balancing exercise as a mechanism which either supports or goes against the particular individual's wishes and feelings, values and beliefs about gifting and tax planning. In the circumstances of this case, I am satisfied that it is subsumed in the positive factor of enhancing benefit to those whom JMA wished to benefit.

26.7.2 The process

The Official Solicitor will contact all persons materially affected to understand their views. They will then present their position. It is possible to reach an agreement between all of the parties and present this to the court. Ultimately it is the court who has the final say as to whether the application is successful or not.

If all parties agree, an oral hearing may not be necessary; however, if the matter is contested then an oral hearing may be required.

You may find it helpful to contact those persons materially affected by the proposals prior to submitting the application to gauge their views. If in agreement, it can be helpful to set this out in the application.

26.8 BUSINESS PROPERTY RELIEF

26.8.1 Overview

A popular form of inheritance tax planning for those who lack mental capacity is utilising the BPR exemption from IHT (IHTA 1984, s.104).

The benefits of this type of tax planning are as follows:

1. The product or asset is only required to be held for two years for the exemption to be available, rather than the donor having to wait for seven years for an asset to be outside their estate for inheritance tax planning centred around gifting.
2. The donor still holds the asset, and therefore if they are in need of the funds, they can get access to them.
3. If the donor lacks capacity, in some circumstances it is not necessary for an application to be made to the COP for authority to invest in the same way that it would be necessary for a gift to be made.

When utilising the BPR exemption, attorneys and deputies need to be mindful, as with gifting, that any form of IHT planning is in the best interests of P.

26.8.2 *Re PP* [2016] EWCOP 65

Re PP [2016] EWCOP 65 involved an application to the COP for ratification of gifts and subsequent removal of the attorneys acting for P due to their conduct. Additionally P's son-in-law, acting as P's attorney, had invested a large proportion of P's assets in investments that were high-risk and produced a low return. As these investments qualified for BPR, the sole reason for the investment was to benefit from this relief.

The judge considered the potential conflict of interests when making decisions as an attorney or a deputy where P will never see a benefit (because the benefit occurs after their death) especially if the attorney or deputy is set to benefit or is connected to someone who would benefit (in this case, the attorney's wife was due to benefit from the estate) (*Re PP* (September 2016), District Judge Batten at para.62, on the rest of the taxable estate):

> I also consider that BB did not act in PP's best interest in instructing an IFA to make investments whose primary purpose was for the saving of IHT. I consider that BB has a conflict of interest in carrying out a review of the IHT saving Octopus investments and deciding whether they are in PP's best interests and in making future decisions about investments solely in PP's best interests without regard to whether JB, he and their family will benefit.

Following this case, it is considered best practice to apply to the COP for approval for investment of P's assets into solutions that would qualify for BPR if the attorney or deputy (i.e. the person making the decisions about investment) is likely to benefit from P's will or intestacy or, if they are connected to someone who will benefit. This is especially the case if (as will commonly be the case) the only or major reason for investment is for the saving of IHT.

Such an application would be made in a similar manner to the gifting applications mentioned above with supporting information:

1. A recommendation from a financial adviser suggesting a suitable BPR effective product. The report should also address issues of liquidity of the asset including how long it would take to receive funds should P need access to those assets and the level of risk P would be taking.
2. It is helpful if you are able to show the court that P has sufficient other assets not to be invested in such a product to rely on to meet their needs for the long term.
3. Confirmation as to why it is in P's best interests to make the investment.
4. If P had a history of undertaking IHT planning, it is helpful to bring this to the attention of the court.
5. It is also helpful to notify the court if P has previously held assets that qualified for this relief and the circumstances surrounding that holding.

26.9 STATUTORY WILLS

The tax planning required P's estate may not be the gifting of assets during P's lifetime or the investment in exempt assets, but rather the restructuring of P's existing will or putting in place a will for the first time if P is currently intestate.

If P lacks the necessary testamentary capacity (see *Banks* v. *Goodfellow*, above) then the COP has jurisdiction to authorise the execution of a will for P (MCA 2005, ss.16, 18 and Sched.2, para.2).

Again, reference should be made to the relevant COP practice direction 9E ('Applications relating to statutory wills, codicils, settlements and other dealings with P's property').

Changes proposed may include ensuring that gifts of the main residence are left to lineal descendants in order to be able to claim the residence nil rate band, incorporating a NRB discretionary trust if P is married with a combined estate of over £2 million in an attempt to reduce the estate on second death to below the £2 million threshold in order to claim the residence nil rate band (RNRB), and gifts to charity to claim charity exemption but also the reduced tax rate of 36 per cent.

The application requires much the same forms as an application for authorisation of gifts.

The COP3 'Assessment of capacity' form should specifically refer to the relevant test of testamentary capacity.

A draft of the proposed will should be provided, together with copies of any current will.

If there is an IHT saving then it is helpful to include in your application computations showing the tax payable on the basis of no application being made, and then again with the proposed will in place.

Again if P had a history of undertaking tax planning, or there is some evidence showing that they were particularly opposed to paying IHT, it is helpful to include this in your application.

Finally and most importantly, as with all applications, it is necessary to show how the proposed change is in P's best interests.

26.10 DISCLOSURE OF P'S WILL

If acting as a deputy or an attorney for P, it will be necessary to obtain a copy of their current will to assess whether it is suitable and in cases where P lacks the necessary testamentary capacity to change their will, whether any changes need to be made. The joint Solicitors Regulation Authority (SRA), COP, Law Society, Legal Ombudsman, OPG and STEP practice note: *Access to and disclosure of an incapacitated person's will* (March 2017) contains useful guidance regarding disclosure of a client's will in circumstances where they cannot provide instructions. The will forms part of P's property and financial affairs and therefore unless contrary instructions have been provided an attorney or a deputy appointed to deal with property and financial affairs is entitled to a copy.

26.11 POST-DEATH TAX PLANNING

It may be the case that the IHT planning required is in relation to a post-death variation where P is a beneficiary.

It is possible to change the will or intestacy of an individual after death, even where the beneficiary lacks the necessary capacity to action this themselves.

IHTA 1984, s.142 provides that if within two years of death any dispositions are varied or benefits disclaimed, such variation or disclaimer is not a transfer of value and IHT is charged as if the variation had been made by the deceased or the disclaimed benefit had never been. Such variation or disclaimer has similar reading back provisions for CGT (Taxation of Chargeable Gains Act 1992, s.62).

Consider the following example.

Example 26.2

Jane and Jack are married. Jane has advanced dementia and is living in a nursing home. Jack is a farmer and continues to farm until his death. His entire estate passes to Jane and so benefits from spouse exemption, but his farm and farmhouse would have qualified for agricultural property relief (APR) if it did not.

Jack's son Robert has been working on the farm, but had no legal interest in it.

Robert is the beneficiary of Jane's will and also would have benefited from Jack's will if Jane had predeceased Jack.

Jane lacks testamentary capacity and capacity to gift.

Jane is in no need of the farm assets as she has sufficient assets of her own to fund her care and other needs.

Robert knows that the farm needs to diversify in order to make money and be sustainable. He is also slightly reluctant to continue to farm without having any interest in the asset. The farm may need to be sold. It is likely that valuable reliefs will now be lost, increasing the IHT bill on Jane's death.

An application could be made to the COP for either a disclaimer of the gift, provided Jane has received no benefit from it or a deed of variation to be executed on behalf of Jane to ensure that the farm passes to Robert now and securing the relief.

The application could be shown to be in Jane's best interests if you consider the following:

1. Perhaps Jane, while lacking the necessary capacity to gift, is keen to see Robert carry on the family business.
2. Perhaps there were promises as to intention (promissory estoppel) and the move would prevent litigation and family dispute.
3. The tax saving will benefit the family generally.
4. If the farm is sold, will Robert move away – and potentially see his mother less.
5. Jane would be remembered for having done the right thing.

26.12 CONCLUSION

It is entirely possible to consider IHT planning for those who have borderline capacity or those who are incapable. However, care must be taken.

The key is a good report on mental capacity addressing the correct legal test and if any application is to be made a well-researched, well-evidenced application is likely to take you a long way. However, the fundamental point is demonstrating that any action is in the best interests of P. That obligation is paramount and cannot be excluded.

CHAPTER 27

Domicile and deemed domicile

Eleanor Black, Ashley Hill and Alex Ruffel

27.1 KEY POINTS

This chapter covers:

- common law domicile;
- deemed domicile;
- domicile election.

27.2 COMMON LAW DOMICILE

27.2.1 Introduction

The English common law concept of 'domicile' affects a number of areas of UK law, taxation and international law. There are particular rules in relation to inheritance tax (IHT), which have undergone significant change in the last few years.

As a general rule, a person with a UK domicile is subject to IHT on their worldwide assets. A person who is domiciled outside the UK is only subject to IHT on assets situated in the UK. Foreign assets held by a non-UK domiciled individual are categorised as 'excluded property' for IHT purposes and trusts created by a non-UK domiciled individual that hold non-UK assets can have 'excluded property trust' status and escape relevant property 10-year and exit charges.

Central to the concept of domicile is that at any point each individual has a natural or permanent 'home'. The process for establishing a person's domicile is largely subjective and turns on their circumstances and intentions (and in some cases those of their family). Under UK law, every individual will always have one, but only one, common law domicile at any time. The three types of common law domicile are (discussed below):

- domicile of origin;
- domicile of dependence;
- domicile of choice.

Strictly speaking, a UK domiciliary will actually be domiciled in England and Wales; Scotland; or Northern Ireland, as each is governed by a separate legal system. In a federal country, such as the US, an individual will be domiciled in a particular state or province.

Establishing a person's domicile may be relevant for reasons other than tax treatment. For example, a person cannot bring a claim on a deceased's estate under the Inheritance (Provision for Family and Dependants) Act 1975 unless the deceased was domiciled in the UK at their date of death.

27.2.2 Domicile of origin

Under UK law, all individuals are born with a 'domicile of origin' (*Henderson* v. *Henderson* [1967] P 77, [1965] 1 All ER 179). Where an individual's parents are married at the date of the individual's birth, that individual's domicile of origin will be the same as their father's domicile at that date. If an individual's parents are not married at the date of birth or the father has died prior to the birth, their domicile of origin will be the domicile of their mother at the date of birth.

In the case of adoption, the child will take the domicile held by the adoptive father at the date of adoption, or, if there is no adoptive father, their adoptive mother.

A person's domicile of origin can be displaced in two ways. The first is by the individual acquiring a 'domicile of dependence'. The second is by the individual acquiring a 'domicile of choice'. Both are discussed in the following paragraphs. Once displaced, the domicile of origin sits 'dormant' and may be revived if the individual's new domicile is abandoned.

A domicile of origin is difficult to displace. There are many individuals with a non-UK domicile of origin who have been living permanently in the UK for a long time but have not done enough to acquire a UK domicile under common law.

27.2.3 Domicile of dependence

Until an individual reaches the age of 16 (or marries), their domicile will change along with that of their parent (father or mother as applicable) or any other person on whom, for the purposes of establishing domicile, they are dependent. If the parent acquires a new domicile, then it will also become their child's 'domicile of dependence'.

If a child has a domicile of dependence at the point when they reach the age of 16 (before 1974, the age was 18 or 21, depending upon the law as to majority applying at the time), that domicile will usually become their domicile of choice. From that point onwards, they will also have the ability to abandon that domicile and either revert to their domicile of origin or acquire a new domicile of choice.

Case law suggests that it will be easier to demonstrate that a domicile of choice has been abandoned where it was originally acquired as a domicile of dependence (*Henderson* v. *Henderson* [1967] P 77, 82–83). In the case of *Harrison* v. *Harrison* [1953] WLR 865, Harrison was born with an English domicile of origin in 1930 and acquired a domicile of dependence in South Australia when he moved there with his parents as a minor. Before Harrison reached the age of majority (at the time this was

21) he moved to New Zealand with the intention of settling there permanently. Prior to his 21st birthday Harrison moved back to England temporarily, still maintaining his intention to settle permanently in New Zealand. It was held that Harrison had abandoned his domicile of choice (acquired as a dependant) and his domicile of origin in England had revived on the date he reached the age of 21. He had not acquired a domicile of choice in New Zealand as he had not been resident there since reaching 21.

Women married before 1974 automatically took their husband's domicile as a domicile of dependence. (The US/UK Double Taxation Agreement contains an exception to this rule. Where a marriage takes place before 1 January 1974 between a woman who is a US national and a UK domiciled man, it will be deemed to take place on 1 January 1974 for the purposes of determining the US woman's domicile.) Women who marry on or after 1 January 1974 are not subject to this rule (Domicile and Matrimonial Proceedings Act 1973). Since 1 January 1974, the only people who are legally dependent for domicile purposes are those who are under 16, unmarried or lack the mental capacity to make decisions concerning future residence. The Act does not apply in Scotland so different rules apply there. Where a woman has married before 1 January 1974 and had her husband's domicile as a domicile of dependence, from 1 January 1974 she will retain that domicile as a domicile of choice. That domicile of choice will continue until it is lost under the usual rules.

27.2.4 Domicile of choice

Acquiring a domicile of choice

Once an individual reaches 16, it is possible for them to establish a domicile of choice. Generally, for an individual to have acquired a domicile of choice in a jurisdiction, two elements must be present; they must: (a) physically reside in that jurisdiction and (b) have formed the intention to make that jurisdiction their permanent and indefinite home (*Udny* v. *Udny* (1869) LR 1 Sc&Div 441, 458). 'Permanent' in this context generally means for an indefinite period. The intention must be in respect of a particular territory – it is not enough to intend to settle permanently in one of several countries (*Henwood* v. *Barlow Clowes International Ltd* [2008] EWCA Civ 577).

In some cases, detailed evidence from family and friends will be required to determine whether someone has formed the necessary intention to reside somewhere permanently or indefinitely.

Abandoning a domicile of choice

An individual may abandon their domicile of choice. In those circumstances either the domicile of choice will be replaced with a new domicile of choice or the individual's domicile of origin will revive.

To abandon a domicile of choice a person must *both*:

(a) cease to reside in the territory in question; and
(b) give up the intention to reside there indefinitely.

Whether or not a person has successfully abandoned a domicile of choice can be particularly difficult to ascertain. It has been held that leaving the jurisdiction but remaining undecided as to whether the move is permanent will not necessarily amount to abandonment. Equally, it should not be assumed that a domicile of choice will be retained until a permanent intention to reside elsewhere develops (*Henwood* v. *Barlow Clowes International Ltd* above).

Example 27.1

Lucia is born in England with a Spanish domicile of origin. In 2005 she moves to France and acquires a domicile of choice in France. Lucia moves to Australia to do some travelling in 2010 but still plans to return and settle permanently in France. In 2012, while still in Australia, Lucia meets and marries someone from England. Shortly after that she forms the intention to settle permanently and indefinitely in England with her new partner, but does not actually move to England until 2016.

What is Lucia's likely domicile position? Her Spanish domicile of origin would have revived in 2012 on the abandonment of her French domicile of choice. The Spanish domicile is likely to have been replaced with an English domicile of choice when Lucia arrived in England in 2016.

A child who has acquired a domicile of dependence will revert to their domicile of origin if the relevant parent or guardian abandons their domicile of choice without displacing it with a new domicile of choice.

Factors to consider – change of common law domicile

A person may have to sever all ties with a country on a long-term basis in order to demonstrate a subjective intention to settle permanently elsewhere. When considering a possible change in domicile status, HM Revenue and Customs (HMRC) and the courts will look at a wide range of factors, such as:

- the location of real estate, investments or business interests held by the individual;
- the individual's residence, citizenship or nationality status;
- the amount of time spent in different countries and the length of residence in the new country;
- the laws under which the individual's will is made and the residence of executors; and
- involvement in social and community activities.

Establishing a person's domicile can be a complicated and uncertain process, potentially requiring a meticulous examination of a person's background, lifestyle and plans throughout their life. Each case will be determined on its particular facts and no single factor will be conclusive.

27.3 DEEMED DOMICILE

27.3.1 Introduction

For UK tax purposes, a person is domiciled in the jurisdiction of their common law domicile unless and until they fulfil the requirements to become 'deemed domiciled' in the UK. The deeming rules apply for UK tax purposes only. For example, an individual may be simultaneously 'deemed domiciled' in the UK for UK tax purposes but 'domiciled' elsewhere for succession law purposes.

The Finance (No.2) Act 2017 introduced significant changes, which took effect from the 2017/18 tax year, to the UK's deemed domicile rules. Prior to this, the concept of 'deemed domicile' had only been relevant for IHT purposes, but the recent changes also apply to income tax and capital gains tax (CGT). The three taxes are now largely aligned for deemed domicile purposes, but there are some differences in the IHT rules that should be noted.

There are four ways that a person can be deemed UK domiciled for IHT purposes when they are non-UK domiciled under general law:

1. They have been tax resident in the UK in at least 15 of the preceding 20 tax years and for at least one of the last four tax years (including the tax year in which the event occurs to which their domicile is relevant) – see **27.3.2**.
2. They were born in the UK with a UK domicile of origin and have become UK resident and are therefore a 'formerly domiciled resident' (FDR) – see **27.3.3**.
3. They have been UK domiciled at common law in the last three calendar years – see **27.3.4**.
4. They have made an election to be deemed UK domiciled under the special rules for spouses – see **27.4**.

27.3.2 Long-term residents (LTRs)

Prior to 6 April 2017, an individual became deemed domiciled in the UK for IHT purposes once they had been resident in the UK in at least 17 of the 20 tax years ending with the year of the relevant transfer. They did not have to be resident for the entirety of the tax years in question, so it was possible for an individual to arrive in the UK towards the end of tax year 1, leave just after the start of tax year 17 and be deemed domiciled for IHT in tax year 17, despite having only been in the UK for just over 15 years. This old deemed domicile rule did not apply to income tax or CGT.

With effect from 6 April 2017, an individual will be deemed domiciled in the UK for IHT purposes if they meet two conditions:

1. Condition 1 is that they are resident in the UK in 15 or more of the previous 20 tax years (Inheritance Tax Act (IHTA) 1984, s.267(1)(b)).
2. Condition 2 is that they are either UK resident in the tax year in question or were UK resident in one of the three prior tax years (s.267(1)(b)(ii)). Note that this condition does not apply for income tax and CGT.

An individual's tax residence is determined by the UK's statutory residence test for tax years 2013/14 onwards. For tax years prior to 2013/14, residence is determined by a combination of statutory rules and case law principles.

Sometimes a tax year of UK residence will be a 'split year'. This will often be the case where an individual either starts to live or work abroad or starts to live or work in the UK. In these circumstances, the year can be split into a 'UK part' where income and gains are subject to UK tax and a 'non-UK part' where UK tax is not charged. Split years will count as full years of UK residence when applying the 15/20 year rule.

Example 27.2

Bejal, who is non-UK domiciled, becomes resident in the UK for the first time in January 2006. 2005/06 is Bejal's first tax year of residence and 2019/20 is her 15th tax year of residence. Bejal will become deemed UK domiciled as an LTR from 6 April 2020.

Bejal leaves the UK in February 2023 and does not return. Her last UK-resident year was 2022/23. She will retain her deemed domiciled status until the start of her fourth consecutive year of non-UK residence, at which point she will no longer meet Condition 2 above. Bejal will therefore lose her deemed UK domiciled status from 6 April 2026, despite still meeting Condition 1 (of the 20 previous tax years (2006/07 to 2025/26) she was UK resident for 17).

27.3.3 Formerly domiciled residents (FDRs)

The concept of the FDR was introduced with the other changes in 2017. The IHT rules (IHTA 1984, ss.267(1)(aa), 272) for FDRs are very similar to the rules for income tax and CGT.

To be an FDR for IHT purposes in a particular tax year, an individual must:

1. have been born in the UK with a UK domicile of origin;
2. be UK tax resident in that tax year; and
3. have been UK resident in one of the two preceding tax years.

Condition 3 above means there is a grace period of one tax year when a person who will qualify as an FDR returns to the UK. This grace period does not apply for income tax and CGT.

If an individual born in the UK with a UK domicile of origin returned to the UK and took up UK tax residence before 6 April 2017, then they will become deemed UK domiciled as an FDR from that date.

Significantly, trusts settled by an FDR prior to becoming deemed domiciled are not given excluded property status while the individual qualifies as an FDR (IHTA 1984s.48(3E)). This is not the case for excluded property trusts settled by a person before they acquired deemed domicile status as an LTR under the 15/20 year rule.

An individual will cease to be an FDR from the beginning of the tax year following their year of departure from the UK (although they may still be treated as deemed domiciled under the 15/20 year rule). So an FDR who leaves the UK in the 2019/20 tax year will lose their deemed domiciled status from 6 April 2020.

Example 27.3

Tam was born in the UK in 1960 with a UK domicile of origin. At the age of 20, Tam moved to Austria to work and decided to settle there permanently. Tam acquired a domicile of choice in Austria. In November 2010 he transferred non-UK assets into a trust.

In May 2019 Tam returned to the UK to spend some time with family and became UK resident in the tax year 2019/20 onwards. He retained the Austrian domicile of choice as he maintained his intention to settle in Austria permanently. Tam's non-UK assets will remain outside the scope of IHT for the tax year 2019/20. If Tam dies on or after 6 April 2020 while UK resident, his worldwide assets will be subject to IHT.

The 2010 trust has a 10-year anniversary in November 2020. Tam is UK tax resident in 2020/21 and was UK resident in 2019/20 (i.e. one of the two prior tax years). Although the trust property was excluded property on creation, as Tam meets the FDR conditions on the 10-year anniversary, the trust property will not be treated as excluded property and a 10-year charge will arise (subject to the availability of exemptions and reliefs). However, relief will be available for the part of the 10-year period that he was not an FDR.

27.3.4 UK common law domicile in the last three years

As discussed at **27.2.4**, a person can lose a common law domicile by acquiring a domicile of choice elsewhere or reverting to their domicile of origin. Where an individual successfully loses a common law UK domicile, they will remain deemed UK domiciled for IHT purposes for three calendar years from the point at which they lost their UK domicile (IHTA 1984, s.267(1)(a)).

This 'three calendar year' tail after being common law domiciled should not be confused with the 'three tax year' tail when someone who has become deemed UK domiciled as an LTR subsequently leaves the UK (see **27.3.2**). If an LTR with a UK domicile of choice emigrates from the UK and immediately abandons their UK common law domicile, the 'three calendar year' tail is irrelevant as the LTR 'three tax year' tail will always be longer. However, the 'three calendar year' tail will be relevant in cases where the common law domicile is not immediately displaced.

Example 27.4

Alejandra has a Peruvian domicile of origin. She arrives in the UK in the 2004/05 tax year and becomes deemed UK domiciled as an LTR on 6 April 2019. By 2024 Alejandra has formed the intention to remain in the UK permanently and indefinitely and has therefore acquired a UK domicile under common law.

She leaves the UK in January 2028 for a temporary work placement in Hong Kong and becomes non-UK resident from the 2028/29 tax year onwards. Under the LTR rules, Alejandra will remain deemed domiciled until 6 April 2033. However, she had initially intended to return to the UK and it is not until October 2030 that she abandons her common law UK domicile. Alejandra will be deemed domiciled under the 'three calendar year' rule until October 2033.

27.4 DOMICILE ELECTION

27.4.1 Property passing to a non-UK domiciled spouse

In most cases, transfers between married couples and civil partners during lifetime and on death are exempt for IHT purposes (IHTA 1984, s.18). There is an exception to this rule where a transfer is made from a UK domiciled (or deemed UK domiciled) spouse to a non-UK domiciled spouse. In that instance, only £325,000 will be exempt in addition to any available nil rate band (NRB) (IHTA 1984, s.18(2)). Prior to 6 April 2013, this limited spouse exemption was £55,000. Thus if there is a full NRB available, a total of £650,000 can now be left to a non-domiciled spouse, whereas it would only have been £380,000 until 5 April 2013.

This limited spouse exemption was introduced to address the issue of chargeable assets in the hands of a UK domiciliary passing free of IHT to a non-UK domiciled spouse who could then hold them offshore as excluded property.

Non-UK domiciled spouses can make an election to be treated as UK domiciled for IHT purposes (a further type of deemed domicile status exclusively for IHT) (IHTA 1984, s.267ZA). This will mean that their worldwide assets will be subject to IHT, but they will benefit from the unlimited IHT exemption when they receive assets from their spouse.

27.4.2 Making an election

The key conditions for and implications of a domicile election are set out below:

- The election only applies to lifetime and death transfers occurring after 5 April 2013.
- A 'lifetime election' can be made by the non-UK domiciled spouse while both spouses are still alive.

- A 'death election' can be made within two years of the UK domiciled spouse's death by either the non-UK domiciled spouse or their personal representatives if they have also died.
- The election can be backdated, but only for up to seven years before the election takes effect. As only transfers from 6 April 2013 onwards are affected, this seven-year period can only be fully utilised by elections dated 6 April 2020 onwards (IHTA 1984, s.267ZA(2)). Backdating in this way will effectively turn any potentially exempt transfers (PETs) to the non-UK domiciled spouse in that period into spouse-exempt transfers for IHT.
- The election is irrevocable and must be made in writing to HMRC.
- An election will automatically cease to have effect once the non-UK domiciled spouse has been non-UK resident for four consecutive tax years after making the election.
- There is no prescribed form of election, but HMRC guidance suggests that the following details are included (*Inheritance Tax Manual*, IHTM13043, HMRC):
  - full name and address, date of birth and (if appropriate) date of death of the person making the election;
  - full name of their UK domiciled spouse or civil partner; and
  - date the election is to take effect from.

27.4.3 Planning considerations

In the right circumstances, a domicile election can avoid a significant IHT charge on the first death and increase the assets passing to beneficiaries on the second death. However, an election will not always be appropriate and there are a number of factors to consider, such as the life expectancy of the surviving spouse, whether or not they will remain in the UK and whether or not the assets are likely to significantly increase in value before the death of the survivor. If the non-UK domiciled spouse is likely to settle abroad after the UK domiciled spouse dies it may be worth making an election on the expectation that the majority of the estate will eventually revert to excluded property status.

Backdating an election can be an effective way to deal with lifetime transfers to the non-UK domiciled spouse that may otherwise become chargeable transfers on the death of the UK domiciled spouse. It is important to review this period carefully and also consider any transfers made by the non-UK domiciled spouse. If the non-UK domiciled spouse has made transfers to trust which are excluded property for IHT purposes, a backdated UK domicile election could result in an unexpected 20 per cent IHT charge. Furthermore, the settlement would be permanently within the relevant property regime.

An election will often be preferable where the UK domiciled spouse holds the majority of the assets as the whole estate can be IHT exempt on an outright gift or interest in possession (IIP) on the first death. In any case, the implications of a lifetime or death election should be reviewed carefully, taking into consideration previous transfers, relevant personal circumstances and future plans. (For some of the circumstances in which a lifetime election may be particularly useful, see *Clarke's Offshore Tax Planning 2018–19*, para.[38.12].)

CHAPTER 28

Excluded property and double taxation

Eleanor Black, Ashley Hill and Alex Ruffel

28.1 KEY POINTS

This chapter covers the following:

- establishing the location of an asset for inheritance tax (IHT) purposes;
- understanding key categories of 'excluded property'; and
- an overview of unilateral and bilateral relief for double taxation.

28.2 LOCATION OF ASSETS FOR INHERITANCE TAX PURPOSES

In many cases, foreign assets owned or settled by non-UK domiciled individuals will be 'excluded property' and not subject to IHT charges. It is therefore often important to establish whether a particular asset is situated outside the UK for IHT purposes. The 'situs' rules for IHT are generally found in common law, although in some cases it will be necessary to consider statutory provisions or the impact of a double tax treaty.

Some of the key rules are as follows (see the *Inheritance Tax Manual* IHTM27021–IHTM27151 where other assets are discussed):

- Immoveable property is situated where it is physically located. The position can become more complicated where the laws of two jurisdictions are relevant and their definitions of 'immoveable property' differ.
- Chattels are situated for IHT purposes where they are physically located at the relevant time. There are special rules for works of art, which will not be subject to IHT if they are normally kept outside the UK but were brought into the UK solely for public exhibition, cleaning or restoration (IHTA 1984, ss.5(1)(b), 64(2)). There are special rules for ships and aircraft.
- Registered shares and securities are located where they are registered (the tax residence of the company is irrelevant).
- Debts are usually located where the debtor resides. There are special rules for certain kinds of debt. Judgment debts are located where the relevant judgment is issued.
- A specialty debt is generally a debt created by deed or instrument under seal and can be secured or unsecured. There has been uncertainty around HM

Revenue and Customs' (HMRC's) position on specialty debts since 2013. Prior to this, HMRC's view was that both secured and unsecured specialty debts were situated where the document evidencing the debt was physically located. (In January 2013, HMRC updated its guidance, stating it now believes that 'these debts are situated where the debtor resides'. In 2014, HMRC commented further that 'many' specialty debts 'are likely to be located where the debtor resides, or where property taken as security for the debts is situated'.) HMRC's most recent guidance states:

- Where a specialty debt is secured solely on UK land, or other tangible UK property, the debt will have a UK situs for IHT purposes.
- Where a specialty debt is unsecured, the situs is usually where the relevant deed or document evidencing the debt is physically located. (See IHTM27079 for further detail. The guidance also states that where both the debtor and creditor are resident in the UK and the deed has been removed from the UK, HMRC may argue that the debt is nevertheless situated in the UK for IHT purposes.)

- Cash held in bank accounts is located for IHT purposes where the bank is physically located – usually the branch where the account is managed. The bank account is effectively a debt owed by the bank.
- Life policies will usually be located where the proceeds are stipulated to be payable under the terms of the policy. Where the policy does not specify where proceeds are payable, it will usually be located where the life assurance company is resident. This will usually be where the company has its head office (for further information see IHTM27101–IHTM27104).

28.3 INTRODUCTION TO EXCLUDED PROPERTY

A number of Inheritance Tax Act (IHTA) 1984 provisions that give effect to an occasion of charge also provide that the charge does not apply in respect of 'excluded property'. When determining whether a particular asset is excluded property for IHT, one or more of the following will be relevant:

(a) the nature of the asset;
(b) its location for IHT purposes; and
(c) the domicile or residence of a relevant individual.

Non-UK situate property will generally be excluded property if a non-UK domiciled individual is beneficially entitled to it (IHTA 1984, s.6(1)). Similarly, non-UK situate trust property settled by an individual when they are non-UK domiciled will often be excluded property (IHTA 1984, s.48(3)). Section **28.4** discusses the exception for indirectly held UK residential property; **28.5** describes categories of UK property that qualify as excluded property in certain circumstances; **28.6** discusses settled property; and **28.7** covers reversionary interests, which are usually excluded property (IHTA 1984, s.48(1)).

28.4 UK RESIDENTIAL PROPERTY

28.4.1 Overview

Non-UK domiciled individuals and trusts settled by non-UK domiciled individuals can effectively turn the value of UK property into excluded property by holding it via offshore structures such as non-UK holding companies: the non-UK domiciled individual or trust will directly hold a non-UK asset (e.g. the foreign company shares) and not the underlying UK asset.

The ability to do this in respect of 'UK residential property interests' (UKRPIs) was severely limited by legislation introduced in the Finance (No.2) Act 2017. This change followed several other measures which were introduced to make the 'enveloping' of UK residential property (i.e. holding it via an 'opaque' entity rather than directly) less tax-advantageous. The relevant provisions are contained in IHTA 1984, Sched.A1.

From 6 April 2017, interests in non-UK close companies or partnerships (or their disposal proceeds) and the value of certain loans or non-UK assets used as security for loans will not be excluded property to the extent that their value is derived from or related to a UKRPI (IHTA 1984, Sched.A1).

The most common example of a UKRPI is an interest in a dwelling (IHTA 1984, Sched.A1, para.8(1)(a)). The definition also covers certain other types of land which include a dwelling, as well as contracts for off-plan purchase.

Example 28.1

Karam is non-UK domiciled. In 2003 he transferred a British Virgin Islands (BVI) company valued at £5 million to a discretionary trust for the benefit of him and his family. The company's only asset was a UK residential property. As Karam is non-UK domiciled and the shares were a non-UK asset, the gift to trust had no IHT implications: there was no chargeable lifetime transfer as the shares were excluded property.

Karam is also the sole shareholder of a Jersey company, which owns a UK residential property. The company has no other assets. The shares are valued at £10 million. Prior to 6 April 2017 these shares would not have been chargeable to IHT on Karam's death, nor would there have been any IHT consequences of him making a gift of those shares to an individual or trust.

Since 6 April 2017, the shares in both companies are no longer treated as excluded property as their value is fully attributable to UKRPIs. The shares in the BVI company are subject to anniversary and exit charges. The shares in the Jersey company will be subject to 40% IHT on Karam's death. Any gift of the shares to an individual will be a potentially exempt transfer (PET) and any gift to a trust will be a chargeable lifetime transfer.

Where the directly held 'envelope' asset is an offshore company, these rules will only apply where:

- the company would qualify as a close company if it were UK resident; and
- the relevant individual has at least a five per cent interest in the company (IHTA 1984, Sched.A1, para.2(3)).

A close company is a company that is resident in the UK and controlled by either five or fewer shareholders or any number of directors who are also shareholders (Corporation Tax Act (CTA) 2010, s.439; and see **21.4.1**). The legislation states that when applying the five per cent interest condition, the value of the person's interest is to be treated as increased by the value of any 'connected person's' interest (IHTA 1984, Sched.A1, para.2(4)). HMRC guidance states 'if the combined stake is 5% or more in value then the de minimis exclusion does not apply'. (See IHTM04312, example 5. See also Questions and Answers produced by ICAEW, STEP, CIOT and the Law Society dated 16 July 2018, Question 4 regarding the difference between valuing the aggregate of the interests and increasing the value by the value of connected party interests.)

Structures with an offshore parent company and one or more subsidiaries are also caught by the rules.

Offshore structures caught by these UKRPI rules are potentially subject to an IHT charge on any transfers which occur on or after 6 April 2017. If a person makes a transfer of property that would fall within these rules before 6 April 2017 but dies on or within seven years after 6 April 2017 there will not be an IHT charge.

The rules apply to all UK dwellings, regardless of whether or not they are occupied or let. They also apply to UK land under contract for an off-plan purchase. There are exceptions for certain dwellings such as hospitals and schools. Where a property is used for both residential and commercial purposes, the residential element will be subject to IHT.

28.4.2 UKRPIs and relevant loans

The Finance (No.2) Act 2017 also introduced rules governing loans that are used, directly or indirectly, by individuals, trustees or partnerships to finance the acquisition of UK residential property. These rules are also found in IHTA 1984, Sched.A1. Such loans will be 'relevant loans' and will not be excluded property (Sched.A1, para.3).

Loans made to close companies are not relevant loans but are still caught by the rules because the loan creditor will be a participator in the company and have an interest in the company. This interest in the company will not be excluded property to the extent that it is attributable to a UKRPI or a relevant loan.

A loan is a relevant loan if it is used for:

- the acquisition of a UKRPI (Sched.A1, para.4(1)(a)(i));
- the maintenance or enhancement of a UKRPI (Sched.A1, para.4(3)); or

- the acquisition of participation rights in a close company or a partnership interest whose value is attributable to a UKRPI (Sched.A1, para.4(1)(a)(ii)).

The loan can be used directly or, for example, it can be traced through the purchase and sale of other assets or loans made to another borrower to finance a UKRPI.

Example 28.2

Cuiying, a non-UK domiciled individual, makes a loan of £1 million to an offshore trust. As the debtor (the trust) is non-UK resident, Cuiying has a foreign-situs loan. The trust uses the loan to subscribe for shares in a BVI company. The company uses the subscription funds to purchase a UK residential property. Prior to 6 April 2017 the loan would have been excluded property as it is non-UK property owned by a non-UK domiciliary. Since 6 April 2017 the loan is a relevant loan and no longer excluded property.

If Cuiying had made the loan directly to the BVI company, the loan would not have been a relevant loan. Instead he, as the loan creditor, has participation rights in the company which will be denied excluded property status to the extent that their value is attributed to a UKRPI. A 'participator' in a company for the purposes of IHTA 1984, Sched.A1 can be a shareholder or a loan creditor.

The loan would also have been a relevant loan if the borrower had been an individual or partnership rather than a trust, or if the borrower had purchased the UK residential property directly.

Money or money's worth held or otherwise made available as security, collateral or guarantee for relevant loans will not qualify as excluded property to the extent that its value does not exceed the value of the relevant loan (IHTA 1984, Sched.A1, paras.2(2)(b)(iii) and 3(b)).

Example 28.3

Hiromu is resident and domiciled in Japan. He borrows £4 million from a Japanese bank and uses the funds to purchase a UK residential property worth £6 million. The loan from the Japanese bank is formally secured over X's investment portfolio of non-UK shares worth £8 million.

The loan from the bank to X is a relevant loan. Under IHTA 1984, Sched.A1, para.3(b), the value of the collateral up to the value of the loan is potentially chargeable to IHT. Hiromu's taxable estate for IHT will be £6 million (the value of the collateral capped at the loan value (£4 million) plus the value of the property less the value of the loan (£6 million – £4 million = £2 million)).

Questions and suggested answers produced in July 2018 by ICAEW, STEP, CIOT and the Law Society highlight various areas of uncertainty in relation to the new rules, including some issues in relation to collateral and double charges. (See Q&As

produced by ICAEW, STEP, CIOT and the Law Society dated 16 July 2018, Question 11 regarding collateral and the potential for double charges.) In the example above, there is no potential double charge as the creditor of the relevant loan (the bank) is not within the charge to IHT.

The loan ceases to be a relevant loan on the disposal of the UKRPI (IHTA 1984, Sched.A1, para.4(4)). On the sale of the property by the borrower the relevant loan will immediately revert to excluded property in the hands of the lender.

The position is different where the disposal is of participation rights or a partnership interest rather than the UKRPI itself. Where an individual or a trustee:

- disposes of their partnership interest or participator rights/shares or loans; or
- receives repayment of a relevant loan,

the value of the disposal or repayment will remain chargeable to IHT for two years from the date of the disposal (IHTA 1984, Sched.A1, para.5). If a replacement asset is purchased with the sales proceeds, then any increase in value will not be charged to IHT. This is an anti-avoidance measure designed to stop people selling their interests just before death to take them outside the IHT charge.

Where the offshore entity disposes of its interest in the residential property this two-year extension of the rules will not apply and the share of the offshore entity owned by the individual will immediately revert to excluded property status.

Example 28.4

Oriana is the non-UK domiciled settlor of an offshore trust. She makes a loan of £1 million to the trust which purchases a UK property via an offshore company. Oriana has made a relevant loan which would be subject to IHT if outstanding on her death.

The trustees repay the loan in February 2019. £1 million will still be chargeable to IHT if Oriana dies before 2021 and she will make a PET of any amount up to £1 million that is gifted before 2021.

If instead the offshore company had sold the UK property while Oriana's loan to the trust was still outstanding, the loan would immediately become excluded property.

28.5 UK ASSETS WITH EXCLUDED PROPERTY STATUS

In certain circumstances, UK property will be excluded property:

- UK government stocks and securities will be excluded property if the donor is non-UK resident at the date of transfer (IHTA 1984, s.6(2)).
- UK government investments (premium bonds, national savings certificates, etc.) will be excluded property where held by an individual domiciled in the Isle of Man or the Channel Islands (IHTA 1984, s.6(3)).

- Authorised unit trusts and open-ended investment company (OEIC) holdings will be excluded property if the person beneficially entitled is non-UK domiciled at the date of the transfer (IHTA 1984, s.6(1A)).
- Certain 'relevant decorations or awards', such as decorations awarded for valour, are excluded property provided they have not been sold (IHTA 1984, s.6(1B)).
- Certain property paid to or owned by an individual in a visiting force is excluded (IHTA 1984, ss.3(1), (2), 4(1), 5(1) and 155(1)(b)).

In addition, foreign currency accounts held in a UK situs bank account will left out of account on the death of the owner, if the owner is neither UK resident nor UK domiciled (IHTA 1984, s.157).

28.6 EXCLUDED PROPERTY SETTLEMENTS

28.6.1 Introduction

The key provision governing the excluded property status of trust property is set out in IHTA 1984, s.48(3). This section was recently amended by the Finance Act (FA) 2020 and now states that that settled foreign property (but not a reversionary interest) is excluded property if the settlor was non-UK domiciled (and non-UK deemed domiciled) at the 'time the property became comprised in the settlement'.

The residence of the settlor and the trustees is irrelevant. This general position is subject to the rules in relation to formerly domiciled residents (FDRs) (discussed at **27.3.3**) and indirectly held UK residential property (discussed at **28.4**). The position may also be affected by the provisions of a double tax treaty.

Foreign assets held in an excluded property trust will not be subject to an immediate IHT charge on entry or 10-year anniversary and exit charges. It is important to remember that the initial transfer of assets to the trust can still result in a capital gains tax (CGT) charge and there will be no holdover relief if the settlor retains an interest in the settlement. If, however, the settlor is a remittance basis user and the gain is on foreign assets, a UK charge can usually be prevented.

Where a trust has a non-UK domiciled settlor, it is generally best to ensure that its directly held assets are non-UK situated for IHT purposes. If it is beneficial to hold UK assets for a limited time, the trustees should ensure that assets are removed from the UK on chargeable occasions. For example, cash held in a UK bank could be moved to an offshore account before a 10-year anniversary.

Settlement of UK assets by a non-UK domiciled individual will result in an immediate IHT charge on assets above the value of the nil rate band (NRB) (and any annual exemptions) in the same way as for a UK domiciled individual. UK situated assets held directly by trustees may also give rise to an IHT charge on a 10-year anniversary. A charge could also arise on UK property on the death of the settlor where they have a qualifying interest in possession or a reservation of benefit.

28.6.2 Excluded property settlements and deemed domicile

Settled excluded property will remain excluded property if the settlor becomes a long-term resident (LTR) or becomes UK domiciled under common law, even if the settlor is a beneficiary of the trust. This is not the case for settlements created by non-UK domiciled individuals who subsequently become FDRs. For any tax year that a person is an FDR, the settlement will cease to comprise excluded property.

Example 28.5

George is UK resident and non-UK domiciled. In 2001 he transfers cash in a French bank account to a discretionary trust (Trust 1) and shares in a Jersey company to a qualifying interest in possession trust (Trust 2) for his nephew. The beneficiaries of Trusts 1 and 2 are UK domiciled.

The cash in Trust 1 and shares in Trust 2 are both excluded property as George was non-UK domiciled when that property became comprised in the settlement. Therefore Trust 1 is not subject to 10-year and exit charges under the relevant property regime and in the same way there is no IHT charge on the termination of the nephew's life interest in Trust 2. However if, for example, the trustees had used the cash in Trust 1 to purchase a UK property it would no longer be excluded property and would be subject to relevant property charges from that date.

George becomes deemed UK domiciled as an LTR on 6 April 2017. This does not affect the excluded property status of the property already in the trusts but any property George adds to the trusts in the future would not be excluded property.

28.6.3 Treatment of additions and transfers between settlements

Before FA 2020 was passed, IHTA 1984, s.48(3) required a trust's settlor to be non-UK domiciled at the 'time the settlement was made' in order to benefit from excluded property status. IHTA 1984, s.82 deals with assets transferred from one settlement to another and must be read in conjunction with IHTA 1984, s.81, which provides that where property is transferred between settlements, it is treated for the purposes of the relevant property regime as remaining comprised in the first settlement (IHTA 1984, s.81). Ten-year and exit charges are therefore computed by reference to the commencement date of the first settlement. Determining whether the transferred settlement property remains excluded property on leaving the transferor trust is more complicated. Prior to the FA 2020 changes, IHTA 1984, s.82 provided that where property was excluded property by virtue of IHTA 1984, s.48(3) and moved between two settlements, it only continued to be excluded property if the settlor of the transferee trust was non-UK domiciled when they made the transferee trust.

The application of this rule was analysed in *Barclays Wealth and Michael Dreelan* v. *HMRC* [2015] EWHC 2878 (Ch). In that case, the settlor (S) had set up one trust (T1) when he was non-UK domiciled. S became deemed domiciled and then set up another trust (T2) and shares from T1 were appointed to T2 and then sold. Just before the 10-year anniversary of T1, the cash proceeds were appointed back to T1 and held in non-UK accounts.

The taxpayer argued that T1 was 'made' when the settlor was non-UK domiciled and that the property should be treated as having never left T1 when applying the excluded property rules. HMRC argued that the cash lost its status as excluded property when appointed to T2 and that an occasion of 'settlement' covers not just the original settlement but subsequent appointments. Therefore the domicile at the date of transfer to each trust was relevant for determining excluded property status.

The Court of Appeal found in favour of the taxpayer, and held that under the deeming provisions in IHTA 1984, s.81(1), and on the particular facts of the *Barclays Wealth* case, the property could be treated as never having left T1. This meant that non-UK property could be transferred between settlements and retain its excluded property status even if the settlor had become UK domiciled. The court did not give a view on whether any additions to an excluded property settlement after the settlor had become deemed UK domiciled could be construed as forming part of the original excluded property settlement as a result of the similar wording in IHTA 1984, s.48(3).

FA 2020 made changes to the IHT legislation to address the uncertainty following the *Barclays Wealth* decision. The new IHTA 1984, s.48(3) confirms that where property is added to an excluded property settlement, it is the domicile of the settlor at the time of the addition that will be relevant rather than the domicile of the settlor at the time that the settlement was originally created. This change takes effect retrospectively in that it applies to all IHT occasions from 22 July 2020 onwards even if the relevant addition was made before that date.

There are also new provisions in IHTA 1984, s.82 to determine the status of property that is transferred between settlements. The new rules contain different tests for establishing excluded property status depending on whether the transfer was made before or after the date that FA 2020 was passed. Where property is transferred from one settlement to another after 22 July 2020 it will only be excluded property if the settlor of the transferor settlement is non-domiciled immediately before the transfer or has died (IHTA 1984, s.82A).

28.6.4 UK residential property

UK residential property held by a trust via an offshore company or partnership would have been excluded property in the hands of the trustees prior to 6 April 2017. Since that date, such property is subject to anniversary and exit charges under the relevant property regime. Relief is available for the period that property was excluded property under the old rules. For example, for a 10-year charge occurring in April 2022 the rate of charge would not exceed approximately five per cent (5/10 multiplied by six per cent) to account for the five years from 2012 to 2017 that the property was excluded property.

28.7 REVERSIONARY INTERESTS

The general rule is that any reversionary interest is excluded property, wherever it is situated (IHTA 1984, s.48(1)). A reversionary interest is defined as any 'future interest under a settlement, whether it is vested or contingent' (IHTA 1984, s.47). For example, where property is left to A for life with the reminder to B for life, remainder to C, B and C both have reversionary interests.

There are various anti-avoidance exceptions to the above rule. These include the following:

- Where the reversionary interest is purchased for consideration (IHTA 1984, s.48(1)). For example, if person A owns a reversionary interest and person B purchases it and then makes a gift of it to their child, without the consideration exception person B would not have made a transfer of value as the reversionary interest is excluded property. The anti-avoidance rules provide that B has made a potentially exempt transfer as they acquired the reversionary interest for consideration.
- Where a lease is created otherwise than for full consideration for life or lives, it is treated as a settlement for IHT (IHTA 1984, s.48(1)(c)). For example, person A grants a lease of property to person B for life for consideration of £25,000 when the full value is actually £100,000. A is treated as having the reversionary interest which is not excluded property.
- Where the settlor or their spouse is beneficially entitled to the interest. For example, if person A creates an interest in possession of their property for their child for full consideration, without anti-avoidance legislation A would have the reversionary interest which would be excluded property and could be given away without a transfer of value.

HMRC's view is that the situs of a reversionary interest will usually be determined by the residence of the trustees of the property to which the interest relates (IHTM04286). If a reversionary interest falls within one of the exceptions above, it will still be excluded property if the reversionary interest is situated outside the UK and the beneficial owner is non-UK domiciled (IHTA 1984, ss.6(1) and 48(3)(b)).

28.8 RELIEF FROM DOUBLE TAXATION

28.8.1 Background

Many other countries have a tax that operates in a similar way to IHT. The estates of international individuals can therefore be subject to double taxation, particularly where, as in the UK, estate tax can apply on a worldwide basis. Different jurisdictions use different 'connecting factors' when making an assessment to tax, which means there is a greater chance of overlapping tax. For example, an individual can be liable to estate tax on a particular asset in one country on the basis of 'domicile' (as defined by that jurisdiction), and in another on the basis of residence, nationality or its situs rules. This is further complicated by each jurisdiction having its own definitions of these concepts, so that a person may be 'domiciled' or an asset 'situated' in more than one jurisdiction.

The two main types of relief from double taxation are (discussed below):

(a) 'unilateral relief,' where foreign tax paid is given as a credit against the UK IHT (IHTA 1984, s.159); unilateral relief can apply to both lifetime and death charges; or
(b) 'bilateral relief' given under one of the 10 IHT tax treaties the UK has with other countries; double tax treaties can also provide relief in the form of a tax credit but may give other types of relief, such as removing one country's ability to tax a particular asset altogether; bilateral relief is only available on death transfers.

Where both treaty relief and unilateral relief are available, the relief that gives the greatest benefit to the taxpayer will be given (IHTA 1984, s.159(7)). (See also *McCutcheon on Inheritance Tax*, 7th edn, Sweet & Maxwell, 2018, chapter 33 for detailed discussion of unilateral and bilateral relief.)

28.8.2 Unilateral relief

Unilateral relief will only be available where the foreign tax:

- is of a sufficiently similar character to UK IHT or is chargeable on or by reference to death or lifetime gifts;
- is chargeable on the same disposition and property as the UK tax; and
- has already been paid by the person with the relevant liability (IHTA 1984, s.159(6)).

The particular rules for calculating the amount of relief depend on where the property is situated. Where the property is situated in the same overseas country that is taxing the asset and not in the UK, the relief will be the lower of the foreign tax paid and the UK IHT charged (IHTA 1984, s.159(2)).

Where the property is situated in:

- a third jurisdiction; or
- both the UK and the overseas territory/territories,

the amount of foreign tax to be relieved is determined by a formula in the legislation (IHTA 1984, s.159(3)). There is no provision for a tax credit where the relevant asset is situated in the UK only.

The rate of UK IHT attributable to the value of the property is calculated by looking at the average rate of UK tax charged on the total estate (rather than the IHT in relation to that particular asset).

28.8.3 Bilateral relief

The IHT treaties with the UK can be split into two groups. First, there are four surviving treaties which were made under the old estate duty regime. These are with France, India, Pakistan and Italy. Second, there are six treaties which have been entered into since capital transfer tax/IHT was introduced. These treaties are with South Africa, the Netherlands, the US, Ireland, Sweden and Switzerland.

Estate duty treaties – France, Italy, Pakistan and India

These treaties only apply to IHT charges on death (France – Double Taxation Relief (Estate Duty) (France) Order 1963; India – Double Taxation Relief (Estate Duty) (India) Order 1956; Italy – Double Taxation Relief (Estate Duty) (Italy) Order 1968; Pakistan – Double Taxation Relief (Estate Duty) (Pakistan) Order 1957). This includes charges on the death estate, gifts with reservation of benefit (GROBs) and property in which the deceased had a qualifying interest in possession (QIIP) (IHTA 1984, s.158(6) and s.4). It is generally considered that the treaties do not apply to charges as a result of failed PETs. (The treaties apply to IHT chargeable by virtue of IHTA 1984, s.4. Failed PETs do not fall within s.4.)

Each treaty provides that a person with a non-UK domicile will only be charged to IHT on their UK assets provided certain conditions are met. Significantly, the estate duty treaties can override the UK deemed domicile rules so that an individual will prevent an IHT charge on their foreign-situated assets despite being deemed UK domiciled. This is because the IHT legislation states that the deemed domicile rules are ignored for the purpose of interpreting the treaties. (IHTA 1984, s.267(2) disapplies the deemed domicile rules in s.267(1) when it comes to interpreting the treaty. Section 267(1) contains the LTR, FDR and three-year deemed domicile rules discussed in **Chapter 27**. Section 267ZA(6)(a) disapplies the spouse election deemed domicile rule for the purpose of interpreting the treaties.)

Under the treaties with India and Pakistan, the individual must be non-UK domiciled under UK common law and domiciled in India or Pakistan (as appropriate) under that country's domestic law for the above rule to apply. The French and Italian treaties can still restrict UK IHT to UK assets where a person is UK domiciled under UK domestic law provided they are French/Italian domiciled under both local law and the relevant treaty tie-breaker clause.

As stated above, a key condition for this deemed domicile override is that the individual is domiciled in the non-UK country under that country's local laws. The Indian and Pakistani concepts of domicile are similar to the UK concept but the French and Italian concepts are akin to residence. Therefore, it is generally more likely that an individual will find themselves both deemed UK domiciled and also Indian or Pakistani domiciled (under the relevant local law) rather than French or Italian.

The treaties with Pakistan, France and India all state that for an IHT exemption to apply to foreign assets, those assets must not pass under a 'disposition or devolution' governed by Great Britain (England, Wales and Scotland) (the treaties refer to 'Great Britain' rather than the UK as Northern Ireland had a different estate tax regime prior to the introduction of capital transfer tax in 1975). Therefore, where one of these treaties is in point, it will often be appropriate for the individual to have a non-UK law will. The Italian treaty only restricts the IHT exemption in respect of property passing under a 'settlement' regulated by UK law, rather than any 'disposition or devolution'. (See *Clarke's Offshore Tax Planning 2018–19*, para.[105.7] for further discussion.)

Only non-UK situs property can be exempt from IHT under the treaties. As a starting point, the UK common law rules are applied to determine whether an asset is situated in the UK. If there is a conflict with the situs rules of the contracting state where an asset could be subject to tax in both states, the treaties contain their own situs rules to resolve the position.

Along with chargeable PETs, the estate duty treaties do not apply to the charge on lifetime transfers to trust or any further charge as a result of death within seven years. However, if a person has a qualifying interest in possession in a foreign law trust which aggregates with their estate on death or alternatively has reserved a benefit in a trust they settled, the treaties could prevent an IHT charge on death.

Example 28.6

Rabeal is domiciled in Pakistan under both UK law and Pakistani law. She became deemed UK domiciled for IHT purposes (under the old 17 out of 20-year rule) in March 2005. In 2008, Rabeal created a discretionary trust under Guernsey law and settled £300,000 held in an offshore bank account. The transfer is a chargeable transfer for IHT purposes (although it was covered by Rabeal's NRB allowance) and the trust will be subject to the relevant property regime's anniversary and exit charges.

Rabeal is a discretionary beneficiary of the trust so has made a GROB. On her death in 2020 she is still deemed UK domiciled but domiciled in Pakistan under both UK and Pakistani law. Usually the value of the trust would be included in her estate for IHT purposes but under the UK/Pakistan treaty there is no IHT charge as the assets are non-UK and pass under foreign law (Guernsey law). If Rabeal has made a foreign law will, only the UK property in her estate will be charged to IHT.

IHT treaties – USA, Switzerland, Sweden, South Africa, the Netherlands and Ireland

The other six IHT treaties entered into by the UK were all concluded after the introduction of capital transfer tax/IHT.

Many countries' concept of domicile is much more strongly related to residence than the UK concept of domicile, which means that individuals may find themselves domiciled both in their country of residence and in the UK.

The treaties aim to limit double taxation by (in most cases) giving the contracting state of 'treaty domicile' sole taxing rights which are then subject to exceptions (most commonly the other contracting state has a right to tax immoveable property and certain business assets). (The Republic of Ireland has a different approach – providing primary taxing rights to the country where the asset is situated, with a credit available in the other country.) For each treaty there is a tie-breaker clause to determine where a person is 'treaty-domiciled' where they are domiciled in both the UK under UK domestic law and in the other contracting state under that state's domestic law.

In circumstances where both states can tax an asset, the treaties provide credit relief.

The treaties with the Netherlands, the US, Switzerland and Sweden override some of the UK deemed domicile provisions in certain circumstances. These treaties also include provisions which increase the amount of the limited spouse exemption available under IHTA 1984, s.18(2A) where certain conditions are met. Some treaties have specific clauses to regulate IHT charges on settlements.

Domicile tie-breaker

Most treaties follow the Organisation for Economic Co-operation and Development (OECD) Model in the case of both domicile and residence tie-breaker provisions. The IHT treaties' tie-breaker clauses for dual domicile follow the OECD Model Double Taxation Convention on Estates and Inheritances and Gifts, as follows:

1. The first tie-breaker test under the OECD Model looks at where the person has a 'permanent home' available to them.
2. If they have a permanent home in both states or neither state, the individual will be treaty domiciled where they have their 'centre of vital interests', which means where their personal and economic relations are closer.
3. If this cannot be determined, the next test looks at where the individual has their habitual abode.
4. Where the individual habitually lives in both countries or neither country, the final tie-breaker looks at nationality.
5. If the person is dual national or a national of neither state, then treaty domicile must be determined by agreement.

It may be necessary to look at how the provisions of a particular treaty interact with the new rules in relation to UK residential property interests discussed at **28.4**. IHTA 1984, Sched.A1, para.7(1) states that no double taxation arrangements will prevent an IHT charge under that section if either: there is no foreign tax of a similar character on the chargeable transfer; or there is but that tax is charged at an effective rate of 0 per cent (unless this is due to a relief or exemption). The wording of this treaty override is ambiguous and will need to be considered carefully alongside the foreign state's tax position.

Index